Dedicated to Jeff Sutherland, Kent Beck, and my family, without whom this book would have been impossible

Ken Schwaber

Dedicated to Laura, David, Daniel and Sara for their love, patience, and inspiration

Mike Beedle

Agile Software Development with Scrum

Ken Schwaber and Mike Beedle

SERIES IN AGILE SOFTWARE DEVELOPMENT

Robert C. Martin, Series Editor

Pearson Education International

VP and Editorial Director, ECS: *Marcia J. Horton*
Publisher: *Alan R. Apt*
Associate Editor: *Toni D. Holm*
Editorial Assistant: *Patrick Lindner*
VP and Director of Production and Manufacturing, ESM: *David W. Riccardi*
Executive Managing Editor: *Vince O'Brien*
Managing Editor: *David A. George*
Production Editor: *Sarah E. Parker*
Composition: *PreTeX, Inc.*
Director of Creative Services: *Paul Belfanti*
Creative Director: *Carole Anson*
Art Director: *Heather Scott*
Art Editor: *Greg Dulles*
Manufacturing Manager: *Trudy Pisciotti*
Manufacturing Buyer: *Lisa McDowell*
Senoir Marketing Manager: *Jennie Burger*

© 2002 by Prentice Hall
Prentice-Hall, Inc.
Upper Saddle River, NJ 07458

Printed in the United States of America

10 9 8 7 6 5 4 3 2 1

ISBN 0-13-207489-3

Pearson Education LTD., London
Pearson Education Australia PTY, Limited
Pearson Education Singapore, Pte. Ltd
Pearson Education North Asia Ltd
Pearson Education Canada, Ltd.
Pearson Educación de Mexico, S.A. de C.V.
Pearson Education -- Japan
Pearson Education Malaysia, Pte. Ltd
Pearson Education, Upper Saddle River, New Jersey

Foreword

"Work can and should be an ennobling experience." So begins *Scrum – Agile Software Development*, one of the sanest and most practical books on agile software processes.

Software process is one of the hot topics of this decade. We've seen processes like XP, Adaptive, Crystal Clear, RUP, etc. We've seen the formation of the Agile Alliance; a group of experts dedicated to the promotion of people-oriented software processes that work without getting in the way. We've seen the creation of a commercial product based upon nothing but process. And we've seen dozens, if not hundreds, of books, lectures, classes, and articles extolling the virtues of one process or another.

In the midst of this hubbub, Ken Schwaber and Mike Beedle bring us Scrum. Scrum is an agile software development method with a proven track record. In this book you will read how the method was created, and some stories of the projects that made use of it. You'll read about how the authors battled to create a method that helped them get projects done in the presence of rapidly changing requirements. You'll read about what worked and what didn't, the problems they had, and the way they solved them. You'll read about how you can adapt their work to your particular needs.

Mike and Ken are uniquely qualified to author this book. Both have been active in the software industry for decades. Mike has been a manager of many software projects, and runs a successful software consultancy. Mike has fought the process battles many times. He knows what works and what doesn't. Ken has been involved with software process for a large portion of his career. He defined and built a software product that automated heavyweight software processes and created the methodology automation industry. From this experience he learned that such processes were not amenable to creating software in real market environments. But that's a story you can read in the book. Ken is a well-known management consultant who has helped dozens of project teams reach their goals.

This is a book for executives, software managers, project leaders, and programmers. It describes, in no uncertain terms, how each of these roles can apply the simple but effective principles and techniques of Scrum.

If you have to get a project done, and you want to use a process that helps you when you need help, and gets out of the way when you don't, then you should read this book. It is liable to be the catalyst of an ennobling experience.

Robert C. Martin

Foreword

When I finished at my grammar school at 18 I spent a year working in industry before going to University. My career direction at the time was electrical engineering, and in my year I learned a great deal about the engineering approach to building things. When I left university and entered the world of software development I was attracted to graphical modeling methodologies, because they helped put engineering discipline into software development.

At the heart of the engineering approach is a separation of design and construction, where construction is the larger part of the job and is a predictable process. Over time I began to find that this separation wasn't really useful for my software work. Doing the separation required too many tasks that didn't seem to really contribute to producing software. Furthermore, the construction part of the task wasn't really that predictable, and the design portion was much longer than the engineering approach assumed.

In Chapter 2 Ken describes a particular moment that brought this question home for him, when he spend time with DuPont's process engineering experts. There he learned the difference between defined and empirical processes, and realized that his software development needed to be controlled using an empirical approach.

We aren't the only ones who've been asking these questions about the nature of software development. Over the last few years there's been increasing activity in the area of what is now called Agile Methodologies, a new breed of software processes which are based on an empirical approach to controlling a project.

And software projects do need to be controlled. For many people, moving away from defined processes means descending into chaos. What Ken learned at DuPont was that a process can still be controlled even if it can't be defined. What Ken and Mike have written here is a book that shows you one way of doing that. Practices such as sprints, scrum meetings, and backlogs are techniques that many people using Scrum have used to control projects in chaotic circumstances.

In the future, we'll see more need for Scrum and the future developments built upon it. Software development has always been difficult to control. Recent studies indicate that the average project takes twice as long to do as its initial plans. At the heart of Scrum is the notion that if you try to control an empirical process with a system designed for defined processes, you are doomed to fail. It's becoming increasingly apparent that a large proportion of software projects are empirical in nature and thus need a process like Scrum. If you're running a project, or buying software, with difficult and uncertain requirements in a changing business world, these are the kinds of techniques you need.

Martin Fowler

Preface

This book was written for several audiences. Our first audience is application development managers that need to deliver software to production in short development cycles while mitigating the inherent risks of software development. Our second audience is the software development community at large. To them, this book sends a profound message: *Scrum represents a new, more accurate way of doing software development that is based on the assumption that software is a new product every time that it is written or composed.* Once this assumption is understood and accepted, it is easy to arrive at the conclusion that software requires a great deal of research and creativity, and that therefore it is better served by a new set of practices that generate a self-organizing structure while simultaneously reducing risk and uncertainty.

Finally, we have also written this book for a general audience that includes everyone involved in a project where there is constant change and unpredictable events. For this audience Scrum provides a general-purpose project management system that delivers, while it thrives on change and adapts to unpredictable events.

Software as "new product" as presented in this book, is radically different from software as "manufactured product", the standard model made for software development throughout the last 20 years. Manufacture-like software methods assume that predictability comes from defined and repeatable processes, organizations, and development roles; while Scrum assumes the process, the organization, and the development roles are emergent but statistically predictable, and that they arise from applying simple practices, patterns, and rules. Scrum is in fact much more predictable and effective than manufacturing-like processes, because when the Scrum practices, patterns and rules are applied diligently, the outcome is always: 1) higher productivity, 2) higher adaptability, 3) less risk and uncertainty, and 4) greater human comfort.

The case studies we provide in this book will show that Scrum doesn't provide marginal productivity gains like process improvements that yield 5-25% efficiencies. When we say Scrum provides higher productivity, we often mean several orders of magnitude higher i.e. several 100 percents higher. When we say higher adaptability we mean coping with radical change. In some case studies, we present cases where software projects morphed from simple applications in a single domain to complex applications across multiple domains: Scrum still managed while providing greater human comfort to everyone involved. Finally, we show through case studies that Scrum reduces risk and uncertainty by making everything visible *early and often* to all the people involved and by allowing adjustments to be made *as early as possible.*

Throughout this book we provide 3 basic things: 1) an understanding of why this new thinking of software as new product development is necessary, 2) a thorough description of the Scrum practices that match this new way of thinking with plenty of examples, and 3) a large amount of end-to-end case studies that show how a wide range of people and projects have been successful using Scrum for the last 6 years.

This last point is our most compelling argument: The success of Scrum is overwhelming. Scrum has produced by now billions of dollars in operating software in domains as varied as finance, trading, banking, telecommunications, benefits management, healthcare, insurance, e-commerce, manufacturing and even scientific environments.

It is our hope that you, the reader of this book, will also enjoy the benefits of Scrum, whether as a development staff member wishing to work in a more predictable, more comforting, and higher producing environment, or as a manager desiring to finally bring certainty to software development in your organization.

Thanks to our reviewers: Martin Fowler, Jim Highsmith, Kent Beck, Grant Heck, Jeff Sutherland, Alan Buffington, Brian Marick, Gary Pollice, and Tony D'Andrea. Ken would like to thank Chris, Carey, and Valerie. Mike would like to thank Laura, David, Daniel, and Sara. Together, we would like to thank our editors at Prentice Hall, Alan Apt and Robert Martin, as well as Jeff Sutherland for his many contributions to Scrum, and Kent Beck for demanding that we write this book.

Mike Beedle, Chicago
Ken Schwaber, Boston

Contents

List of Tables

List of Figures

CHAPTER 1

Introduction

> "In today's fast-paced, fiercely competitive world of commercial new product development, speed and flexibility are essential. Companies are increasingly realizing that the old, sequential approach to developing new products simply won't get the job done. Instead, companies in Japan and the United States are using a holistic method; as in rugby, the ball gets passed within the team as it moves as a unit up the field." (Reprinted by permission of *Harvard Business Review* From: "The New New Product Development Game" by Hirotaka Takeuchi and Ikujiro Nonaka, January, 1986. Copyright 1986 by the Harvard Business School Publishing Corporation, all rights reserved.) —

This book presents a radically different approach to managing the systems development process. Scrum implements an empirical approach based in process control theory. The empirical approach reintroduces flexibility, adaptability, and productivity into systems development. We say "reintroduces" because much has been lost over the past twenty years.

This is a practical book that describes the experience we have had using Scrum to build systems. In this book, we use case studies to give you a feel for Scrum-based projects and management. We then lay out the underlying practices for your use in projects.

Chapters 5 and 6 of this book tell why Scrum works. The purpose of these chapters is to put an end to the ungrounded and contentious discussion regarding how best to build systems. Industrial process control theory is a proven body of knowledge that describes why Scrum works and other approaches are difficult and finally untenable. These chapters describe what process control theory has to say about systems development, and how Scrum arose from this discipline and theory. These chapters also lay out a terminology and framework from which empirical and adaptive approaches to systems development can ascend and flourish.

Scrum [Takeuchi and Nonaka], is a term that describes a type of product development process initially used in Japan. First used to describe hyper-productive development in 1987 by Ikujiro Nonaka and Hirotaka Takeuchi, Scrum refers to the strategy used in rugby for getting an out-of-play ball back into play. The name Scrum stuck because of the similarities between the game of rugby and the type of product development proscribed by Scrum. Both are adaptive, quick, self-organizing, and have few rests.

Building systems is hard and getting harder. Many projects are cancelled and more fail to deliver expected business value. Statistically, the information technology industry hasn't improved much despite efforts to make it more reliable and predictable. Several studies have found that about two-thirds of all projects substantially overrun their estimates [McConnell].

We find the complexity and urgency of requirements coupled with the rawness and instability of technology to be daunting. Highly motivated teams of highly skilled developers sometimes succeed, but where do you find them? If you are looking for a quick, direct way to resuscitate a troubled project, or if you are looking for a cost-effective way to succeed with new projects, try Scrum. Scrum can be started on just one project and will dramatically improve the project's probability of success.

Scrum is a management and control process that cuts through complexity to focus on building software that meets business needs. Scrum is superimposed on top of and wraps existing engineering practices, development methodologies, or standards. Scrum has been used to wrap Extreme Programming. Management and teams are able to get their hands around the requirements and technologies, never let go, and deliver working software. Scrum starts producing working functionality within one month.

Scrum deals primarily at the level of the team. It enables people to work together effectively, and by doing so, it enables them to produce complex, sophisticated products. Scrum is a kind of social engineering aiming to achieve the fulfillment of all involved by fostering cooperation. Cooperation emerges as teams self-organize in incubators nurtured by management. Using Scrum, teams develop products incrementally and empirically. Teams are guided by their knowledge and experience, rather than by formally defined project plans. In almost every instance in which Scrum has been applied, exponential productivity gains have been realized.

As authors of Scrum, we have evolved and used Scrum as an effective alternative to traditional methodologies and processes. We've written this book to help you understand our thinking, share our experiences, and repeat the success within their own organizations.

In this book, we'll be using the word "I" from now on rather than "we", "Mike", or "Ken". Unless otherwise identified, "I" will hereafter refer to Mike Beedle in chapters 6 and 7, and to Ken Schwaber elsewhere.

1.1 Scrum At Work

The best way to begin to understand Scrum is to see it at work. After using Scrum to build commercial software products, I used Scrum to help other organizations build systems. The first organization where Scrum was tested and refined was Individual, Inc. in 1996.

Individual, Inc. was in trouble and its leaders hoped that Scrum could help them out. Individual, Inc. published an online news service called NewsPage. NewsPage was initially built using proprietary technology and was subsequently licensed to companies. With the advent of the Internet, Individual, Inc. began publishing Personal NewsPage as a website for individuals.

Eight highly skilled engineers constituted the Personal NewsPage (PNP) product development team. Though the team was among the best I've worked with, it suffered from a poor reputation within Individual, Inc. It was said the PNP team couldn't produce anything, that it was a "total disaster." This belief stemmed from the fact that there hadn't been a new PNP release in nearly nine months. This was in 1996, when Internet time hadn't yet taken hold of the industry, but nine months was already far too long. When I discussed this situation with marketing, product management, and sales, they said they couldn't understand the problem. They would tell the PNP team what they wanted in no uncertain terms, but the functionality and features they requested never were delivered. When I discussed the situation with the disgruntled PNP team, it felt that it was never left alone to develop code. The engineers used the phrase "fire drill." The team would think about how to deliver a required piece of functionality, start working on it, and it would suddenly be yanked off onto the next hot idea. Whenever the PNP team committed to a project, it didn't have enough time to focus its attention before product management changed its mind, marketing told it to do something else, or sales got a great idea that had to be implemented immediately.

The situation was intolerable. Everyone was frustrated and at odds with each other. Competition was appearing on the horizon. I asked Rusty, the head of product management, to come up with a list of everything that people thought should be in PNP. He already had a list of his own and was reluctant to go to everyone and ask for his or her input. As he said, "If the PNP team can't even build what we're asking it to do now, why should we waste the effort to go through list building again?" However, Rusty did as I asked and compiled a comprehensive list. He also met with the PNP team to see if it knew of technology changes that needed to be made to implement the requirements. These were added to the list. He then prioritized the list. The PNP team gave development time estimates. Rusty sometimes changed priorities when it became apparent that items with major market impact didn't take much effort, or when it became apparent that items with minor market impact would take much more effort than they were worth.

I asked Rusty to change the product requirements process. People currently went straight to the PNP team to ask for new product features and functionality. I thought it could be more productive if it only had one source of work and wasn't interrupted. To implement this, Rusty suggested that people take their requests only to him. He added their requests to his list. He then reprioritized the list based on their presentation of the feature's importance, his estimate (after talking to someone on the PNP team) of how long it would take to implement, and the other work on the list. I advised Rusty to put every suggestion on the list. He never had to say "no." Instead, he only had to prioritize. There were no "bad" ideas, just ideas that probably would never get implemented. Rusty advised everyone at Individual, Inc. that the PNP team would only schedule work for PNP based on his prioritized list of work. He started calling his list the Product Backlog list.

Rusty liked the Product Backlog list. He never had to finalize requirements for a product release. Instead, he just maintained a list of what was needed in the product, based on the best information available to him at the time. The list was always current and always visible. He kept the Product Backlog list on a spreadsheet on a public server, so everyone knew what was going into the product next. Another benefit was that the PNP team wasn't interrupted as much. Individual, Inc. was a small company, where everyone knew each other. It had previously been hard to keep people from going straight to the PNP team with requests. Sometimes they would try approaching an engineering friend and asking for a favor: "Could you just sneak this one feature in, this once?" But Rusty insisted that all the engineers on the team stand firm. He became the keeper of the requirements, all listed by priority on the Product Backlog list.

I suggested that the company adopt a practice I had used previously: iterative, incremental development. I called each iteration a Sprint, and the results of the iteration were called a Product Increment. I suggested using Sprints so the PNP team would be left alone to focus on its task of building product functionality. It wouldn't be asked over and over again, "How's it going, are you ready to build the next thing? Have you implemented the last thing?" Sprints were intended to give the team control of its time and destiny. I also suggested a fixed duration for every Sprint. The PNP team asked for thirty days, which it felt would be enough time to build and test an increment of functionality. The team suggested putting each Product Increment into production on the web server at the end of every Sprint. The team was suggesting monthly Internet releases! All of my experience had been with shrink-wrapped software, where a new release had to be distributed to all customers who then had to schedule its implementation. Since PNP was an Internet product, it only needed to be updated in one place for all users to realize the benefits. Of course, if the team put up something that didn't work, all users would be immediately affected, so testing took on a new importance.

The PNP team met with Rusty to determine what to develop in the first Sprint. There was a lot of negotiation at this meeting, with much discussion about the details of the requirements and how to implement them. Some of the estimates changed as the implementation details were thought through. Some lower priority Product Backlog was included because it was essentially "free" once an area of code was opened for a higher priority backlog item. The meeting lasted all day. At the end of the meeting, the team had committed to implement a certain amount of the Product Backlog during the Sprint, and it had worked out a rough idea of the design and implementation details. Everyone knew what the PNP team was going to do for the next thirty days.

Of course, the PNP team was still approached innumerable times (even by Rusty) with requests to develop functionality that was not on the Product Backlog for the current Sprint. People who made these requests were asked to wait and to put these items in the Product Backlog. If their requests became top priority, they would be implemented in the next Sprint. Because the Sprint was only for thirty days, everyone could accept waiting until the end of the Sprint.

The PNP team worked without interruption during the Sprint, other than for product support and maintenance needs. PNP was still a little shaky because of the old quick and dirty process used to respond to "emergency" functionality requests. The existing policy was for the more junior engineers in technical support to make the fixes. However, these engineers were not familiar enough with the code to fix it. In order to solve this problem, I instituted the following policy: whoever writes code owns it forever. Although this detracted from the PNP team's ability to fully focus on the Sprint work, it quickly improved the quality of the code.

During the Sprint, the PNP team questioned me about what engineering techniques had to be used, what type of documentation was required, and what design artifacts had to be created. Eventually, after consulting technical support, we all agreed that how the team did its work was up to them. This was especially the case since each team member owned the code that he or she wrote in perpetuity. However, I did stipulate the PNP team had to produce an updated product technical illustration with each Sprint (and release) that could be used to understand the product design and code.

At the end of the Sprint, the PNP team had implemented the functionality it had committed to – and more. Since it had an opportunity to focus on its work for the first time, it had accomplished more than expected. The team was ready to present the Sprint Product Increment, the new release. Rusty had the team demonstrate it to management and some of the customers. The audience was delighted, and immediately authorized the team to put the new functionality up on the production web server. After a drought of nine months, the PNP team had produced a new release within one month. The team went on to repeat this performance again and again. Before I left, it had generated another five releases.

While the PNP team was working on its first Sprint, the rest of the organization was still asking it to do "favors." The team had a hard time turning down the requests, especially in a small company in which people were all friends. I decided to be the bad guy for the team. I instituted a quick, daily meeting where the team would report what it was doing. If I spotted anything that wasn't in the Product Backlog for that Sprint, I would talk to the team member who reported it after the meeting. I'd ask him or her who had asked them to do this additional work. I'd instruct him or her not to do the work. I'd go to the requestor and explain why their request wasn't being worked on, and then I'd go to Rusty to let him know of the violation. I ensured that the team was able to work on what had been agreed to and nothing else. I became the buffer between the team and the chaos of changing requirements and competitive pressures. I helped to protect the team so it could focus on its Sprint commitments. The role I assumed became known as the Scrum Master.

I had a hard time arranging the daily meeting because of the limited availability of conference rooms. When I found a room, I'd have to let everyone know which room and when we could use it. Inevitably, the word wouldn't get to someone, so not everyone would be present. New requests could slip through the cracks. I went to management and requested an office be set aside for the PNP team. I equipped this office for the team's design meetings and daily status meeting. These meetings became known as Daily Scrums, and they were held at the same time and place every day.

Everyone on the PNP team showed up for these meetings because they were helpful. The meetings were primarily to provide assistance to the PNP team. If it brought up anything it needed or anything that was getting in its way, I'd do whatever I could to remove the impediments. Once everyone on the PNP team realized this, they started to bring up other things that were getting in their way that they thought I might be able to help them with. Suddenly, a management representative was available at least once a day to help the team.

The PNP team and I got together every day for our Daily Scrum. I had scheduled 15 minutes for the meeting, but I had a hard time at first meeting the deadline. When someone reported what he or she had done, others would ask about the design. The whole team would then discuss the design, helping optimize it. Philosophical debates about best engineering practices broke out. When a decision had to be made, the whole team would try to help make it. When everyone else at Individual, Inc. found out about these meetings, they started to come. They would ask questions, offer suggestions, and generally slow everything down. Even though these visitors were well intentioned, the focus of the team was being diffused by comments and suggestions. The meeting was turning into a chaotic free-for-all, and its benefits were decreasing by the day.

Because of everything that happened during the meeting, I was unable to estimate the duration of the Daily Scrum ahead of time. Worse, the whole team had to stay through the duration of the Daily Scrum to listen. Scrum had been brought in to increase the team's productivity, but the Daily Scrum was starting to turn into a massive waste of the team's time. I instituted some very simple practices to solve this problem and return the Daily Scrum to its initial intent. First, only the team members were allowed to talk. No one else could talk. If you weren't on the team and you wanted to attend, you had to stay quiet. Second, the team was only allowed to talk about three things – what it had done since the last meeting, what it was planning on doing before the next meeting, and what was impeding its work. I called on the team members to report by going clockwise around the circle until everyone had reported.

As I ran the daily Scrums for the PNP team, it became apparent that I was fulfilling a management job. I blocked interference, allowed the team to keep focused, removed impediments and helped the team reach decisions quickly. This was a radical change, a flip, to what management had previously done. The team figured out how to do what it had committed to do. Management's new and primary job was to maximize the team's productivity, to be there to help it do the best that it could.

When I left Individual Inc., Scrum had been implemented in all three major product lines. At that time, Individual, Inc. went through a complete change in management, removing the founder and bringing in new people. Because of Scrum, though, the teams stayed focused and continued to regularly crank out new releases.

1.2   Quick Tour of Scrum

After Individual, Inc. I had a set of nomenclature and practices for Scrum. Let's take a quick tour of this Scrum. Figure 1.1 shows the overview of the Scrum process.

Scrum is often used when a systems development project is being initiated. List all of the things that the system should include and address, including functionality, features, and technology. This list is called the **Product Backlog.** The Product Backlog is a prioritized list of all product requirements. Product backlog is never finalized. Rather, it emerges and evolves along with the product. Items that have high priority on the Product Backlog are the ones that are the most desired. Product backlog content can come from anywhere: users, customers, sales, marketing, customer service, and engineering can all submit items to the backlog. However, only the **Product Owner** can prioritize the backlog. The Product Owner effectively decides the order in which things are built.

Small, cross-functional teams perform all development (**Scrum Teams**). These teams take on as much Product Backlog as they think they can turn into an increment of product functionality within a thirty-day iteration, or **Sprint**. Every Sprint must finish by delivering new executable

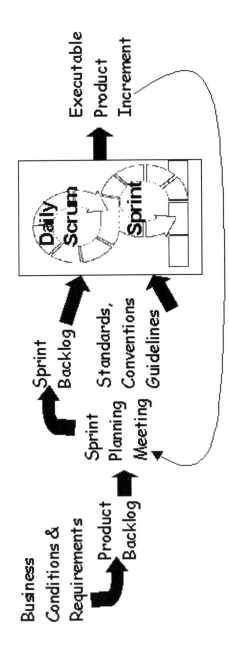

FIGURE 1.1: Scrum Summary

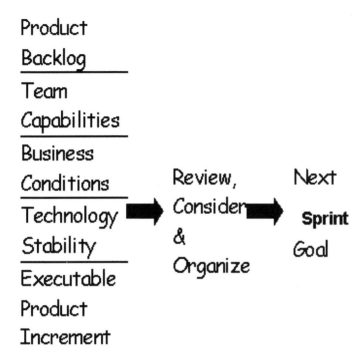

FIGURE 1.2: Input for new Sprint

product functionality. Architecture and design emerge across multiple Sprints, rather than being developed completely during the first Sprints. See Figure 1.2 Input for new Sprint for an overview of how a new Sprint is formed.

Multiple teams can develop product increments in parallel, all teams working from the same Product Backlog. The Scrum Teams are self-organizing and fully autonomous. They are constrained only by the organization's standards and conventions, and by the Product Backlog that they have selected. How the Product Backlog will be turned into a product increment is up to the team to decide. The team maintains a list of tasks to perform during each Sprint that is called a **Sprint Backlog**.

Scrum relies on team initiative and integrity. During the Sprint, a management representative (**Scrum Master)** enforces Scrum practices and helps the team to make decisions or acquire resources as needed. The team must not be disturbed or given direction by anyone outside of it while it is in a Sprint.

The Scrum Team meets daily for a short status meeting, called the **Daily Scrum**. At the Daily Scrum, progress is reviewed and impediments identified for removal by management. The Daily Scrum is an excellent place to observe how much progress a team is making.

At the end of the Sprint, the team gets together with management at a **Sprint Review Meeting** to inspect the product increment the team has built. They either build on what was developed, scavenge it, or throw it away. However, the pressure to build on what's been developed is high. The thirty day Sprint duration ensures that the worst that happens is that thirty days are lost should the team prove unable to develop any useful product functionality.

After the product increment is inspected, management often rearranges the Product Backlog to take advantage of what the team has accomplished. The Product Backlog has more meaning when viewed in light of the partially developed product. Sometimes so much product is built that management selects an earlier release schedule. In this case, the next Sprint can be used to release the product.

Once the Product Backlog has been stabilized, the team again selects top priority Product Backlog for the next Sprint. The team then goes through another iteration of work, pushing through another Sprint. This cycle continues until the product – based on **Empirically Managing** cost, time, functionality, and quality – is deemed potentially releasable. Release Sprints are then devised to bring the product to release-readiness.

Scrum is straightforward. By stripping away inappropriate and cumbersome management practices, Scrum leaves only the essence of work. Scrum leaves a team free to go to it, to work its heart out and build the best products possible. Although the Scrum process seems simple and skeletal, it provides all the necessary management and controls to focus developers and quickly build quality products.

1.3   Statements About Scrum

"The problem for engineers is that change translates into chaos, especially when a single error can potentially bring down an entire system. But, change also translates into opportunity. It's as simple as this: if there is time to put a certain amount of functionality into the product easily, then there is time to put in more functionality at the price of a certain amount of disruption and risk. Thus does madness creep into our projects - we will tend to take on as much risk as we possibly can."

> *James Bach. (Courtesy of Cutter Information Corp.)*

1.3.1   From Jeff Sutherland

Jeff invented many of the initial thoughts and practices for Scrum prior to formalizing and commercializing Scrum with Ken Schwaber. This is a retrospective on Scrum and its implementation in five companies.   —

Scrum was started for software teams at Easel Corporation in 1994 where I was VP of Object Technology. We built the first object-oriented design and analysis tool that incorporated round-trip engineering in the initial Scrum-based project. A second Scrum-based project implemented the first product to completely automate object-relational mapping in an enterprise development environment. I was assisted by two world-class developers, Jeff McKenna, now an Extreme Programming (XP) consultant, and John Scumniotales, now a development leader for object-oriented design tools at Rational Corporation.

In 1995, Easel was acquired by VMARK, and Scrum continued there until I joined Individual in 1996 as VP of Engineering. I asked Ken Schwaber to help me incorporate Scrum into Individual's development process. In the same year I took Scrum to IDX when I assumed the positions of Senior VP of Engineering and Product Development and CTO. IDX, one of the largest healthcare software companies, was the proving ground for multiple-team Scrum implementations. At one point, I had over 600 developers workings on dozens of products. In 2000, I introduced Scrum to PatientKeeper, a mobile/wireless healthcare platform company where I became CTO. So I have experienced Scrum in five companies, with consulting assistance from Ken Schwaber in three of those companies. These companies varied widely in size and were proving grounds for Scrum in all phases of company growth: from startup, to initial IPO, to mid-size, and then to large company with a 30-year track record.

There were some key factors that influenced the introduction of Scrum at Easel Corporation. The book *Wicked Problems, Righteous Solutions* [DeGrace] reviewed the reasons why the waterfall approach to software development does not work today. Requirements are not fully understood before the project begins. The user knows what they want only after they see an initial version of the software. Requirements change during the software construction process. New tools and technologies make implementation strategies unpredictable. DeGrace and Stahl reviewed "All-at-Once" models of software development that uniquely fit object-oriented implementation of software.

The team–based "All-at-Once" model was based on the Japanese approach to new product development, Sashimi and Scrum. We were already using production prototyping to build software. It was implemented in slices (Sashimi) where an entire piece of fully integrated functionality worked at the end of an iteration. What intrigued us was Takeuchi and Nonaka's description of the team building process in setting up and managing a Scrum [Takeuchi and Nonaka]. The idea of building a self-empowered team where everyone had the global view of the product being built seemed like the right idea. The approach to managing the team that had been so successful at Honda, Canon, and Fujitsu resonated with the systems thinking approach being promoted by Senge at MIT [Senge].

We were also impacted by recent publications in computer science. Peter Wegner at Brown University demonstrated that it was impossible to fully specify or test an interactive system designed to respond to external inputs, i.e. Wegner's Lemma [Wegner]. Here was mathematical proof that any process that assumed known inputs, like the waterfall method, was doomed to failure when building an object-oriented system. We were prodded into setting up the first Scrum meeting after reading Coplien's paper on Borland's development of Quattro Pro for Windows. The Quattro team delivered one million lines of C++ code in 31 months with a 4 person staff growing to 8 people later in the project. This was about 1000 lines of deliverable code per person per week, probably the most productive project ever documented. The team attained this level of productivity by intensive interaction in daily meetings with project management, product management, developers, documenters, and quality assurance staff.

Our daily meetings which we started at Easel were disciplined in the way we now understand as the Scrum pattern [ScrumPattern]. The most interesting effect in a Smalltalk development environment was "punctuated equilibrium". A fully integrated component design environment leads to rapid evolution of a software system with emergent, adaptive properties resembling the process of punctuated equilibrium observed in biological species.

It is well understood in biological evolution that change occurs sharply at intervals separated by long periods of apparent stagnation, leading to the concept of punctuated equilibrium [Dennett]. Computer simulations of this phenomenon suggest that periods of equilibrium are actually periods of ongoing genetic change of an organism. The effects of that change are not apparent until several subsystems evolve in parallel to the point where they can work together to produce a dramatic external effect [Levy]. This punctuated equilibrium effect has been observed by teams working in a component based environment with adequate business process engineering tools, and the Scrum development process accentuates the effect.

By having every member of the team see every day what every other team member was doing, we began to get comments from one developer that if he changed a few lines of code, he could eliminate days of work for another developer. This effect was so dramatic that the project accelerated to the point where **it had to be slowed down.** This hyper productive state was seen in several subsequent Scrums but never so dramatically as the one at Easel. It was a combination of the skill of the team, the flexibility of Smalltalk, and way we approached production prototypes that evolved into deliverable product.

A project domain can be viewed as a set of packages that will form a release. Packages are what the user perceives as pieces of functionality and they evolve out of work on topic areas. Topic areas are business object

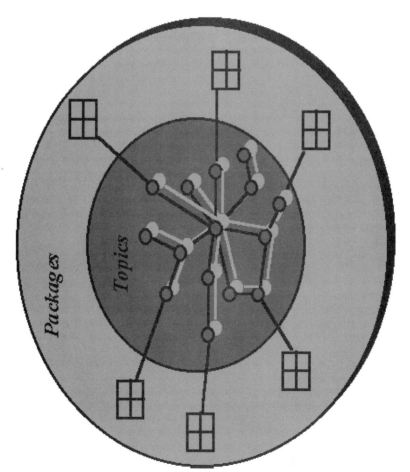

FIGURE 1.3: Initial Scrum View of a Software System

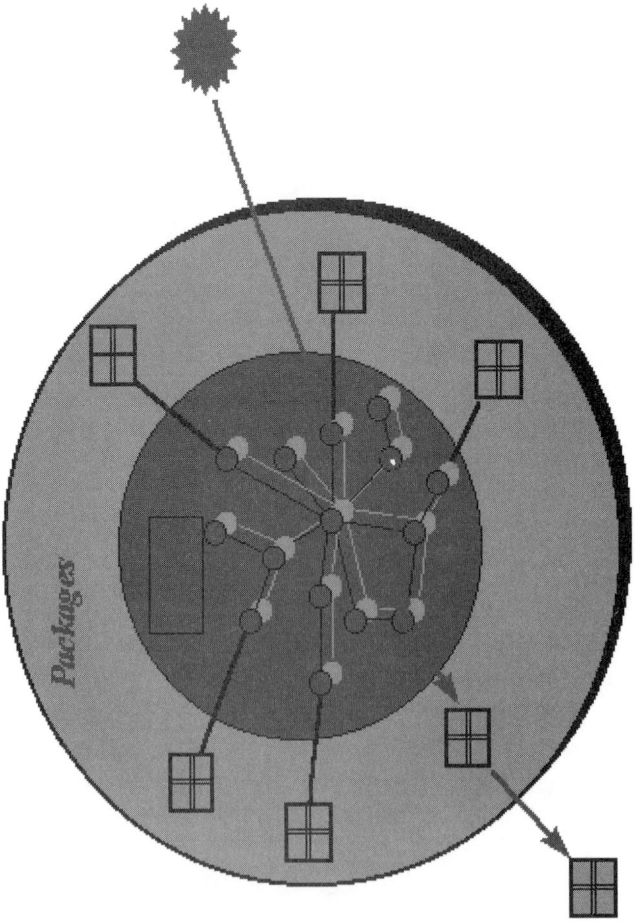

FIGURE 1.4: Firing a Synchstep

components. Changes are introduced into the system by introducing a unit of work that alters a component. The unit of work in the initial Scrum was called a Synchstep.

System evolution proceeds in Synchsteps. After one or more Synchsteps have gone to completion and forced some refactoring throughout the system, or often simply provided new functionality to existing components, a new package of functionality emerges that is observable to the user. These Synchsteps are similar to genetic mutations. Typically, several interrelated components must mutate in concert to produce a significant new piece of functionality. And this new functionality appears as a "punctuated equilibrium" effect to builders of the system. For a period of time the system is stable with no new behavior. Then when a certain (somewhat unpredictable) Synchstep completes, the whole system pops up to a new level of functionality, often surprising the development team.

The key to entering a hyper productive state was not just the Scrum organizational pattern. We did constant component testing of topic areas, integration of packages, and refactoring of selected parts of the system. These activities have become key features of XP [Fowler].

Furthermore, in the hyper productive state, the initial Scrum entered the "zone". No matter what happened or what problems arose, the response of the team always was far better than the response of any individual. It reminded me of the stories about the Celtics basketball team at their peak, where they could do no wrong. The impact of entering the "zone" was not just hyper productivity. The personal lives of the people were changed. People said they would never forget working on such a project and they would always be looking for another experience like it. It induced open, team-oriented, fun–loving behavior in unexpected persons and eliminated those who were not productive from the team through peer embarrassment.

When Easel Corporation was acquired by VMARK (now Informix), the original Scrum team continued their work on the same product. The VMARK senior management team was intrigued by Scrum and asked me to run a senior management team Scrum once a week to drive all the companies' products to the Internet. These meetings started in 1995 and within a few months, the team had caused the introduction of two new Internet products and repositioned leading current products as Internet applications. Some members of this team left VMARK to become innovators in emerging Internet companies. So Scrum had an early impact on the Internet.

In the spring of 1996, I returned to a company I cofounded as VP of Engineering. Ken Schwaber has documented much of the Scrum experience at Individual. The most impressive thing to me about Scrum at Individual was not that the team delivered two new Internet products in a single quarter, and multiple releases of one of the products. It was the fact that Scrum eliminated about 8 hours a week of senior management meeting time starting the day the Scrum began. Because the company had just gone public at the beginning of the Internet explosion, there were multiple competing priorities and constant revision of market strategy. As a result, the development team was constantly changing priorities and unable to deliver product. And the management team was meeting almost daily to determine status of implementation of priorities that were viewed differently by every manager.

The solution was to force all decisions to occur in the daily Scrum meeting. If anyone wanted any status or wanted to influence any priority, they could only do it in the Scrum. I remember in the early phase, the SVP of Marketing sat in on every meeting for a couple of weeks sharing her desperate concern about meeting Internet deliverables and timetables. The effect on the team was not to immediate respond to her despair. Over a period of two weeks, the team self-organized around a plan to meet her priorities with achievable technical delivery dates. When she agreed to the plan, she no longer had to attend any Scrum or status meetings. The Scrum reported status on the web with green lights, yellow lights, and red lights for pieces of functionality. In this way the entire company knew status in real time, all the time.

During the summer of 1996, IDX Systems hired me away from Individual to be their SVP of Engineering and Product Development. I replaced the technical founder of the company who had led development for almost 30 years. IDX had over 4000 customers and was one of the largest healthcare software companies with hundreds of developers working on dozens of products. Here was an opportunity to extend Scrum to large-scale development.

The approach at IDX was to turn the entire development organization into an interlocking set of Scrums. Every part of the organization was team based, including the management team that included two vice presidents, a senior architect, and several directors. Front line Scrums met daily. A Scrum of Scrums that included the team leaders of each Scrum in a product line met weekly. The management Scrum met monthly.

The key learning at IDX was Scrum scales to any size. With dozens of teams in operation, the most difficult problem is ensuring the quality of the Scrum process in each team, particularly when the entire organization has to learn Scrum all at once. IDX was large enough to bring in leading productivity experts to monitor productivity on every project. While most teams were only able to meet the industry average in function points per month delivered, several teams moved into a hyper productive state producing deliverable functionality at 4-5 times the industry average. These teams became shining stars in the organization and examples for the rest of the organization to follow.

In early 2000, I joined PatientKeeper, Inc. as Chief Technology Officer and began introducing Scrum into a startup company. I was the 21st employee and we grew the development team from a dozen people to 45 people in six months. PatientKeeper deploys mobile devices in healthcare institutions to capture and process financial and clinical data. Server technology synchronizes the mobile devices and moves data to and from multiple backend legacy systems. A complex technical architecture provides enterprise application integration to hospital and clinical systems. Data is forward deployed from these systems in a PatientKeeper clinical repository. Server technologies migrate changes from our clinical repository to a cache and then to data storage on the mobile device. Scrum works equally well across technology implementations. The key learning at PatientKeeper has been around introduction of Extreme Programming (XP) techniques as a way to implement code delivered by a Scrum organization. While all teams seem to find it easy to implement a Scrum organizational process, they do not always find it easy to introduce new XP programming. We have been able to do some team programming and constant testing and refactoring, particularly as we have migrated all development to Java and XML. It has been more difficult to introduce these ideas when developers are working in C and C++, our legacy technology.

After introducing Scrum into five different companies with different sizes and different technologies, I can confidently say that Scrum works in any environment and can scale into programming in the large. In all cases, it will radically improve communication and delivery of working code. The next challenge for Scrum, in my view, is to provide a tight integration of the Scrum organization pattern and XP programming techniques. I believe this integration can generate more hyper productive Scrums on a predictable basis. The first Scrum did this intuitively before XP was born and that was its key to extreme performance and life changing experience. In addition, the participation of Scrum leaders in the Agile Alliance [Agile], which has absorbed all leaders of well-known lightweight development processes, will facilitate wider use of Scrum and its integration with extreme programming.

1.3.2   From Ken Schwaber

Ken developed and formalized the Scrum process for systems development.   —

My company, Advanced Development Methods (ADM), built and sold process management software in the early 1990's. Many IT organizations used ADM's product, MATE (Methods and Tool Expert), to automate their methodologies. For example, Coopers & Lybrand used MATE to automate SUMMIT D^{TM}, their systems development methodology, for both internal use and use by their customers. IBM also used MATE, automating its outsourcing, software development, and change management methodologies with it. The methodologies that MATE automated for these companies were the traditional "heavy" methodologies.

In MATE's heyday, the backlog of development work was daunting. Coopers & Lybrand and IBM were using MATE extensively, as were many of their customers. The number of requests for new functionality, new interfaces, and "nice-to-haves" was quite large. It was chaos! To help make sense of everything, I built a Product Backlog list; here I listed all requested functionality, planned technology, planned enhancements, and major bugs. I worked with our customers, including Coopers & Lybrand and IBM, to prioritize the list. However, the priorities never stayed still. They were always changing based on the most recent input from a customer or potential customer.

When I looked at everything ADM had to do, I was overwhelmed. I figured the next release was probably a year away. I realized that even if ADM achieved everything on Product Backlog, no one would be satisfied since requirements would have changed by the release date. In desperation, I started identifying product functionality that could be built in monthly cycles. At the end of the month, I'd review what had been built with the customers to see if I was on track. To my surprise, the customers were delighted with this approach. When they saw what ADM had built, they often changed their minds regarding their priorities. They often wanted to take immediate advantage of what was at hand, maybe with a few more tweaks.

I changed ADM's development process to use two sequential cycles of one month each. In the first cycle, ADM would build functionality. In the second cycle, ADM would prepare it for release. If any engineers had extra time during the release cycle, they'd work on adding more to the next release cycle. The two-cycle approach seemed simple enough, but it had ramifications on the development and release environments. ADM really had to have the code management and release management systems and procedures thoroughly in place for this to work. Daily builds became a necessity. The rapid release cycle forced me to significantly upgrade all of the engineering practices. As a result, ADM became very efficient.

ADM built MATE using object-oriented technology (OO). In 1993, Jeff Sutherland, an active member in the Object Management Group (OMG) and the various OOPSLA SIG's (and a good friend) asked what methodology was used by ADM. Jeff was sure that ADM was using one of its client's methodologies. I still remember the look on Jeff's face when I told him, "None – if ADM used any of them, it would be out of business."

Jeff wanted to know what methodology ADM used because he was impressed by the short duration of ADM's development cycles and the frequent releases of MATE. He wanted to understand so he could make OO similarly productive. At that time, OO wasn't delivering the productivity that its proponents had initially promised and criticism was mounting.

Jeff had been head of engineering and development at Easel and then VMARK (both major software product vendors) and had long used and advocated OO. Jeff had also read about a new product development philosophy called Scrum. Jeff had implemented his interpretation of it at both Easel and VMARK. He hoped that my experience with the major methodologies would help him further formulate Scrum.

That conversation with Jeff was the beginning of a joint effort to formalize Scrum. We read everything that we could get our hands on, sometimes surprising ourselves when other fields such as complexity theory added to our understanding. We saw corollaries in chaos and complexity theory, recognized the beauty of emergent processes, and gained a better understanding of self-organization. We were profoundly influenced by research regarding software development practices at Borland and Microsoft. Of particular influence was their fierce focus on code. The final research occurred at DuPont's Experimental Station in Wilmington, Delaware, where experts in process control theory reviewed our work and provided the theoretical foundations for Scrum.

Jeff and I worked together to create a formal description of the Scrum process. Scrum went from being a collection of thoughts that Jeff and I posted on our websites to a development methodology that I presented at OOPSLA'96. Since then, Scrum has become a major alternative to classic product development approaches. It has been adopted both by managers who wanted to ensure they got the best product they could, and by engineers who wanted to ensure they would be able to do their best work. Since its introduction, Scrum has been used in thousands of projects worldwide. Mike, Jeff and I have personally implemented Scrum in hundreds of projects, and we've worked with and advised others in the United States, Europe, Australia, New Zealand, Singapore, the Philippines, Hong Kong, Ethiopia, and Indonesia. Scrum has been implemented for single projects as well as an organizational product development process. Scrum has been used for such diverse, complex efforts as readying a product and customer base for a new Y2K compliant release, preparing a tunable laser subsystem for fiber optic networks for a trade show, and rapidly creating advanced teleradiology systems.

1.3.3   From Mike Beedle

Mike has long been a Scrum innovator and practitioner. Mike recently has wrapped Extreme Programming engineering practices with Scrum.   —

I am the president and founder of e-Architects Inc., a software development consulting company in Chicago specializing in distributed objects and Internet technologies.

I started practicing Scrum *explicitly* in the fall of 1995, when I saved a company's division from going bankrupt. I had the good fortune to read a message from Jeff Sutherland and to recognize that this was in fact *very* important information. He announced that he and Ken Schwaber were working on a method called Scrum that basically documented what people *really* did to deliver systems. I was fascinated with the information provided at their websites and I immediately adopted the practices in a project I was running in Chicago. The project was successful and the rest is history: I became a Scrum convert and Scrum practitioner for life. To read the whole story please see Chapter 7: Advanced Scrum Applications, Case Study of Large Project: An Outsourcing Company.

Since then, however, I have used Scrum in almost every project I have been involved with for the last 6 years and I have introduced Scrum to many companies: William M. Mercer, Nike Securities, Motorola, Northwest Bank, Lincoln Reinsurance, AllState Insurance, and Caremark. With Scrum, e-Architects has developed many applications in a wide-range of domains and environments, and it has always contributed significantly to simplify and accelerate software development. For the last year, we have also wrapped XP with Scrum with superb results: XP enhances the quality of the software developed and Scrum enhances the day-to-day management of the projects. I call this union of Scrum and XP XBreed, which stands for "crossbreed". Find more information on this at: www.xbreed.net.

I have been involved in professional software development for the last 23 years. And since then, I have seen many kinds of software development: 1) big five methods like Andersen's Method/1, 2) varied software vendors' methods like IBM's and Microsoft's software development methods, 3) mission-critical methods like Texas Instruments, MCI, Sprint, Goldman Sachs, 4) CMM government contractors like Motorola, General Dynamics, 5) methods given by methodologists like De Marco's, Yourdon's, Booch's, Rumbaugh's, Schlaer-Mellor's, Jacobson's, including the later unified process frameworks like RUP© (Rational Unified Process^{TM}); and even several kinds of 6) hacking, *a la* novice programmer and *a la* MIT's 60's style.

I definitely haven't seen all styles of software development, but I have seen enough to say – though this may sound strange – that *despite the method used, most everyone that delivers software to production eventually starts doing something very similar to Scrum.* In other words, the Scrum practices are hidden but simple universal *patterns* that have been forgotten by most of us. In fact, another way we have looked at Scrum in the last few years is just as collection of organizational patterns [ScrumPattern].

As an experiment, do this: take three programmers and give them a project and a room. To begin the project, they will talk to the customer and find out what the customer wants and what is important to him or her. Together with the customer they will create a prioritized "feature list" – in Scrum we call this a Product Backlog. To actually implement something, they will meet with the customer and choose some features to implement first based on the priority of the features – in Scrum we call the meeting a Sprint Planning Meeting and the list of items to be implemented the Sprint Backlog. As they develop the software, they will run into issues and add them to their iteration "to do" list (i.e. their Sprint Backlog). To see where everyone is, they will have informal meetings to tell each other what they are working on, what issues they have and what they will be working on next – in Scrum we call these meetings Daily Scrums. As they implement features they will show their management and their customer how things look – in Scrum we call this Sprint Review Meeting.

However, if managing a software project is so simple, why do we have thousands of volumes of project management without this information? If these activities are so natural and common sense, why is this knowledge not explicit? If these activities are taking place despite the method used when deliveries to production take place, why are they not documented? If these are the steps that really drive a project, why do we waste our time with other things?

This is why I am writing this book. This information is first and foremost, important, but it is also the most *natural, simple, and common sense* way to manage a software project. Somewhere along the line, we forgot this basic and instinctive way of managing software projects, but unfortunately, we pay a very high price for this memory loss.

I cordially invite you to try Scrum. You won't regret it.

1.4   How the Book Is Organized

Chapters 2, 3, and 4 are for the reader that wants to understand Scrum and apply it to a project or organization.

Chapter 2 (*Get Ready for Scrum!*) provides an overview of how Scrum is different, why it works, and what it feels like in a Scrum project.

Chapter 3 (*Scrum Practices*) is a step-by-step description of how Scrum works. Follow the instructions in this chapter and you'll be using Scrum.

Chapter 4 (*Applying Scrum*) defines management principles and practices for building products and systems with Scrum. Iterative, incremental systems development requires empirical management practices. This chapter shows how to use these practices.

Chapters 5 and 6 provide the theoretical underpinnings for Scrum and other similar system and product development practices. These chapters are for the advanced reader.

Chapter 5 (Why Scrum?) lays the theoretical foundations for Scrum as an empirical process control mechanism for systems and product development. Described within the context of universal "noise", this chapter lays out why, in theory and practice, the empirical approach works and the defined approach doesn't work. This chapter provides the basis for overturning inappropriate application of defined processes to systems development projects.

Chapter 6 (*Why Does Scrum Work?*) includes some interesting ways to look at Scrum. These perspectives can help you understand how and why Scrum works. These perspectives offer us, the authors, points for more research and definition into the Scrum process.

Chapters 7, 8, and 9 provide additional information that is useful for the readers that have proceeded past the initial Scrum project.

Chapter 7 (*Advanced Scrum Applications*) provides some guidance for those who want to apply Scrum in different kinds of circumstances. Particular attention is paid to reuse and large projects.

Chapter 8 (*Scrum and the Organization*) discusses the impact that Scrum can have on an organization as impediments are removed and the organization adjusts itself to high productivity development.

Chapter 9 (*Scrum Values*) describes the values that emerge when an organization uses Scrum.

CHAPTER 2

Get Ready For Scrum!

Scrum is different. Work feels different. Management feels different. Under Scrum, work becomes straightforward, relevant, and productive. —

2.1 Scrum Is Different

I've spent a good part of my professional life building technology products and systems. I've had successes, and I've certainly had failures. I think I'm not alone when I say that most systems development projects are difficult. I suspect also that they are harder than they need to be. I remember a project when I worked with a plant manager at a pharmaceutical company. Together, he and I implemented a complicated material requirements planning system. As we were about to successfully complete the project, I congratulated him and told him that he could make a lot of money helping other companies implement similar systems. He looked at me aghast, and said, "I'll never go through something this gruesome again. I can't wait to go back to just managing the business!" His observation was one of many that led me to think that something was wrong; there must be a more straightforward way to build and implement systems.

Every project is different. The technology, the requirements, and the people are different every time. I've studied a variety of approaches to project management in an effort to make my life easier and the teams more productive despite their differences. I've tried new development environments, modeling tools, technologies, methodologies, people approaches, everything and anything to improve the process of building a system. I've found some things that improved my life, like always using the best engineers, forming cross-functional teams, and facilitating design sessions around white boards. These tactics all help, but without Scrum these projects were all eventually overwhelmed by the complexity inherent in systems development projects.

I once placed my hopes on commercially available methodologies. They contain templates of work that have previously been used to build systems. They therefore contain tried and true processes that other professionals have successfully used. Companies that build software for a living usually sell methodologies. I always assumed that for this very reason, the methodologies must be really good.

Methodologies are like cookbooks: follow their recipes and a successful system will result. Some methodologies are modest in scope and depth, while others contain literally thousands of pieces of work, or tasks, tied together into templates. Each template is appropriate for a specific type of development project.

Over the years I used commercial methodologies, they added definition to my projects. I knew what to do, when to do it, and I could assign people to the work. I felt like I was more in control and each project had a lot to show for it. Unfortunately, my success rate did not increase. One company that I worked at cancelled a major project after two years. I toured the project space not long after its cancellation and found a ghost town. There were hundreds of cubicles full of workstations and books of standards, training materials, requirements manuals, and design documents. Unfortunately, this project hadn't been successful. The project never even reached the software construction phase of the project, so no functionality was ever delivered.

As I mentioned earlier, I ran a software company in the early 1990's that developed and licensed a process management product called MATE. Our largest customers were Coopers & Lybrand and IBM, and they wanted us to employ their methodologies to build MATE. I attempted it and was thoroughly displeased with the results. At the time, my company's requirements were always changing and we were working with new technologies. It looked like the methodologies should help, but instead they just got in our way, decreased our flexibility, and generally slowed us down.

I wanted to understand the reason why my customers' methodologies didn't work for my company, so I brought several systems development methodologies to process theory experts at the DuPont Experimental Station in 1995. These experts, led by Babatunde "Tunde" Ogannaike, are the most highly respected theorists in industrial process control. They know process control inside and out. Some of them even taught the subject at major universities. They had all been brought in by DuPont to automate the entire product flow, from forecasts and orders to product delivery.

They inspected the systems development processes that I brought them. I have rarely provided a group with so much laughter. They were amazed and appalled that my industry, systems development, was trying to do its work using a completely inappropriate process control model. They said systems development had so much complexity and unpredictability that it had to be managed by a process control model they referred to as "empirical." They said this was nothing new, and all complex processes that weren't completely understood required the empirical model. They helped me go through a book that is the Bible of industrial process control theory, *Process Dynamics, Modeling and Control* [Tunde] to understand why I was off track.

In a nutshell, there are two major approaches to controlling any process. The "defined" process control model requires that every piece of work be completely understood. Given a well-defined set of inputs, the same outputs are generated every time. A defined process can be started and allowed to run until completion, with the same results every time. Tunde said the methodologies that I showed him attempted to use the defined model, but none of the processes or tasks were defined in enough detail to provide repeatability and predictability. Tunde said my business was an intellectually intensive business that required too much thinking and creativity to be a good candidate for the defined approach. He theorized that my industry's application of the defined methodologies must have resulted in a lot of surprises, loss of control, and incomplete or just wrong products. He was particularly amused that the tasks were linked together with dependencies, as though they could predictably start and finish just like a well defined industrial process.

Tunde told me the empirical model of process control, on the other hand, expects the unexpected. It provides and exercises control through frequent inspection and adaptation for processes that are imperfectly defined and generate unpredictable and unrepeatable outputs. He recommended I study this model and consider its application to the process of building systems.

During my visit to DuPont, I experienced a true epiphany. Suddenly, something in me clicked and I realized why everyone in my industry had such problems building systems. I realized why the industry was in such trouble and had such a poor reputation. We were wasting our time trying to control our work by thinking we had an assembly line when the only proper control was frequent and first-hand inspection, followed by immediate adjustments.

Based on this insight, I have since formulated with others the Scrum process for developing complex products, particularly software systems. Scrum is based on the empirical process control model. For those interested, more details on why Scrum works are presented in Chapter 5: *Why Scrum?* and Chapter 6: *Why Does Scrum Work?*

Scrum is a way of doing things that is completely different from what most people in the software and product development industry are used to. All of the assumptions, mechanisms, and ways of looking at things are so different that a new way of thinking evolves as you begin to use Scrum. Scrum feels and looks different because it is based on the empiricism. Less time is spent trying to plan and define tasks, and less time is spent creating and reading management reports. More time is spent with the project team understanding what is happening and empirically responding. Most people really understand Scrum only when they begin to use it. A light bulb goes off when they experience its simplicity and productivity. They realize how inappropriate more traditional models of development process are for our industry.

The following case study covers an implementation of Scrum and the application of empiricism. In it, I describe working closely with a team to build a product while using the Scrum process. In this example, I made decisions and encouraged the team to act differently than they were used to acting. I taught them by example to approach their work in an entirely different way. By the time we had completed the first Sprint, the team was already behaving differently. They had seen Scrum work, and now they were Scrum users. They had come to embody the values integral to Scrum, such as empiricism, self-organization, and action.

As you read the case study, think about what is missing from it. There is no formal project planning phase. There aren't any Pert charts. There are no roles and individual assignments. Notice how the team is able to get on with its work and build valuable product increments anyway. Notice the team self-organize from a dispirited group of individuals waiting for instructions into a team that takes the initiative and acts. By the end of the first Sprint, the team had adopted a completely new set of values and begun to act unlike any other team at the organization.

2.2   A Noisy Project

The project was to build a middleware business object server and its accompanying business objects. A large financial institution wanted to develop the product to connect its online transactions to its legacy databases. The institution needed to handle increasing transaction volumes, to standardize database access, and to carry out the implementation of new technologies such as telephone, wireless, and handheld input devices. This technology was all devastatingly complicated, including choices and learning curves for object technology, transaction management, hardware, operating systems, and development environments. To complicate matters, this was a technically sophisticated company, so proponents for various alternatives to each technology choice were numerous and vociferous. Furthermore, team members were working at multiple locations, and the team therefore needed to use a multi-site development environment technology. It had chosen to use an enterprise-wide code management software, but had not yet begun to do so.

The project was truly hellish. A development team had been chartered and charged. When I first began working with the team, it had been in existence for four months, but had not built any product. It was waiting for a budget. It was waiting for funding for new servers, for the last team members to be assigned, for the code management software to be licensed, and for someone who knew how to administer the code management software to be hired.

To begin implementing Scrum, I started holding Daily Scrum meetings. These meetings are supposed to be quick status updates. This was not the case at the first Daily Scrums. The first meeting took three hours, rather than the customary fifteen minutes. Everyone was completely dispirited and demoralized. Team members talked not about what they were doing, but about what was preventing them from doing anything. Many people complained that management didn't support the project, and everyone was upset the budget hadn't been formalized. Without a budget, the team couldn't order servers or license the code management software. For that matter, the team couldn't attract new team members, since it looked as though it was going nowhere fast. The team was without funding, without a sponsor, and without the tools that it needed.

2.3   Cut Through the Noise By Taking Action

One of the fundamental principles of Scrum is "the art of the possible." That is, Scrum instructs teams not to dwell on what can't be done, but to think about what can be done. Teams are put in a time box and told to create product. It is important to focus on what can be done and how the problem can be solved with the available resources. This team had a name, a scope, and definition, and it was staffed with some really solid engineers, all of whom had workstations and access to a lot of software. I asked the team what it could do with the available resources. I also asked the team whether it believed that the problem it was trying to solve was important to the organization.

The team confirmed that the problem was real and it was eager to tackle it. Some team members were aware that a customer service project was being held up by the very problem they were supposed to solve. The customer service project was supposed to implement access to the legacy databases, but was unable to proceed because this team had not yet built the middleware server that would handle legacy database access. Clearly, this team had been chartered because of a critical organizational need, and it had an important mission to accomplish. Until the team could get moving, other projects would continue to be held up.

The team quickly identified a core set of transactions that the customer service project needed it to enable. The team members felt that they had enough skills to build a middleware object server to implement these transactions, so long as someone from the customer service team worked with them as a domain expert. They felt they knew AIX, Tuxedo, and CORBA well enough to use that technology to implement the solution. They "borrowed" an RS6000 server from the server room to develop and prototype their work. The project manager, Herb, presented this plan of attack to his management. Since this effort required no additional funding and no administrative action, Herb was authorized to proceed. I got together with the team and devised a goal for the first Sprint. The Sprint goal was:

Sprint Goal: to provide a standardized middleware mechanism for the identified customer service transactions to access backend databases.

The team figured out the work they would have to do to meet the Sprint goal. The following tasks came up:

Map the transaction elements to backend database tables.

Write a business object in C++ to handle transactions via defined methods and interfaces.

Wrap the C++ in a CORBA wrapper.

Use Tuxedo for all queuing, messaging, and transaction management.

Measure the transaction performance to determine whether scalability requirements can be met.

2.4   Self-Organization

After identifying these objectives, the team began the Sprint. Since the team was using familiar technology, there were no major technological problems. However, two team members were at a remote site. Because the team didn't have an enterprise-wide code management system, it couldn't readily do multi-site code management. This problem was resolved by partitioning responsibilities between the two sites, and verbally coordinating whenever either site had to use code under the other's control.

The team met and decided who would do what work. When one team member wanted to work with the Tuxedo expert to learn the product, the team figured out how the rest of the team could pick up the slack. As the team started doing the work, it would meet frequently on its own to design the product and further identify and parse the work. The team did this on its own. It knew the Sprint Goal and its commitment. The team was figuring out how to live up to its commitment.

2.5   Respond Empirically

After ten days, the team started to feel like it was going to fail. The technology was up and working, it had figured out the CORBA wrapper, and it had accessed the appropriate databases. However, the team felt that it couldn't get the entire selected customer service transaction set mapped and linked to the database within the Sprint. The transaction data was too complicated and involved too many tables and indices for the mapping to be completed in thirty days.

The team had incorrectly anticipated the complexity and the scope of the work it had assigned to itself. But had it failed? Not in the eyes of Scrum. Working with a host of difficult technologies and unknown transactions, the team had built the development environment, put up a middleware server using Tuxedo, and had started implementing the customer service transactions. It was doing great. The team had done the best that it could rather than sitting around and doing nothing.

Again, I focused the team on the art of the possible. What could it do within the Sprint and still meet the goal? The goal wasn't to complete the entire transaction set, even though that was what the team had expected to be able to do. The goal was to prove the viability of a middleware object server providing database access to the customer service transaction set. No one even knew whether management would approve and fund this approach. The team quickly identified that they could address a reduced scope of transaction data elements involving fewer tables and indices, and then proceeded to automate this.

2.6   Daily Visibility Into the Project

On the fourteenth day of the Sprint I held our Daily Scrum. When it came to Tom's turn to report, he indicated that a Senior-Vice President, Lou, had instructed him to build something that was not within the scope of work for the Sprint. Consequently, he had been unable to do the work that the rest of the team had expected of him, though he would try to catch up. I immediately went to Lou's office and asked what was up. Lou had been offsite and had learned that a potential customer was interested in additional functionality. He had decided to help the team out by instructing one of its members to start developing that functionality.

Lou hadn't been at all of the Scrum training, so he didn't know that interrupting a Sprint is almost always more counterproductive than it is helpful. Lou didn't know that the team was protected during the Sprint from external chaos, complexity, and uncertainty. Lou said that if he saw a $100 bill on the ground on the way to the train, he would bend over and pick it up, and that he didn't see how this situation was any different. I told Lou that, in the greater scheme of things, his family would probably appreciate his getting home on time more than the $100. I explained to Lou the importance of not disrupting a Sprint, and he agreed to refrain from doing so in the future. By the end of the Sprint, the feature that Lou had wanted to be demonstrated was no longer on the radar of this potential customer anyway. Apparently, it had only been of interest to the customer as a conversation topic with Lou at the offsite.

2.7   Incremental Product Delivery

At the end-of-Sprint demonstration, the team really impressed management with its pragmatism and empiricism. With only the resources it had on hand, it had proven that its approach was technically feasible. In fact, it had put the technology to use for customer service functionality. Although a thorough requirements study might eventually have uncovered better technical approaches, the team had used available resources to solve the problem both for the customer service team and for the company as a whole. The team had been productive with what was on hand.

The team had run performance measures on its solution and proven that the approach could handle the expected transaction volumes. In an online session, it showed management part of the transaction going through the middleware to the databases, retrieving and displaying selected data, and doing so with performance and scalability that could be sustained.

The team presented an increment of product that was successful, could be discussed, and could be built upon. If the team had not gotten its act together, the organization as a whole would have been thirty days closer to a transaction volume meltdown. Instead, because of their empiricism, effort and initiative, the organization had something that worked and that could be modified and built upon. Incremental product delivery can be very powerful, providing an organization with real progress in a short period of time. Previously, the organization was wrapped around its spokes discussing how to proceed.

The team had provided a starting point, a prototype that validated the approach and could be built upon. The team quickly gained formal status and funding, and eventually came up with a solution for legacy database access.

By using Scrum, the team was able to cut through the noise and start delivering valuable product. Time that would have otherwise been wasted was spent working. The team was able to focus itself and deliver product. Management was able to help the team stay focused. The team continued for another year, building a general-purpose middleware business object server with access to specific databases. The team members became consultants to other organizations that used the middleware. As they consulted, they spread Scrum.

In the next sections, I'll describe the details of the Scrum practices I implemented in this case study so that you, also, can implement Scrum and manage Scrum projects.

CHAPTER 3

Scrum Practices

A set of Scrum practices and rules establishes an environment within which products can be rapidly and incrementally built in complex environments. These practices have been established experientially through thousands of Scrum projects. —

In this chapter, I'll describe how to make Scrum work. I'll start by introducing the Scrum Master, the person that manages the Scrum process in an organization. Then I'll discuss setting up a project by defining the Scrum Teams and building the list of work that drives the Sprint iterations. The Daily Scrum and the End-Of-Sprint review are looked at next, and I'll describe how to inspect and respond to the unexpected. Lastly, I'll talk about the combustion chamber, the Sprint iteration, where teams grapple with complex requirements and technology to build product increments.

Scrum practices have evolved during its application to thousands of development projects. I strongly recommend these practices be strictly adhered to until you understand why and how Scrum works from experience, not just reading this book. Once Scrum is working well in your organization, once people have adopted the values that make Scrum work, then you can make adjustments. Before you start tinkering, make sure you've learned from experience. Think of Scrum like skiing. Until you've been up on skis and experienced the sensation of skiing, you can't adequately understand the impact of changes. Learn first, then make changes.

3.1 The Scrum Master

The Scrum Master is responsible for the success of Scrum. —

The Scrum Master is a new management role introduced by Scrum. The Scrum Master is responsible for ensuring that Scrum values, practices, and rules are enacted and enforced. The Scrum Master is the driving force behind all of the Scrum practices in this chapter; he or she sets them up them up and makes them happen.

The Scrum Master represents management and the team to each other. At the Daily Scrum, the Scrum Master listens closely to what each team member reports. He or she compares what progress has been made to what progress was expected, based on Sprint goals and predictions made during the previous Daily Scrum. For example, if someone has been working on a trivial task for three days, he or she probably needs help. The Scrum Master tries to gauge the velocity of the team: is it stuck, is it floundering, is it making progress? If the team needs assistance, the Scrum Master meets with it to see what he or she can do to help.

The Scrum Master works with the customers and management to identify and institute a Product Owner. The Scrum Master works with management to form Scrum teams. The Scrum Master then works with the Product Owner and the Scrum teams to create Product Backlog for a Sprint. The Scrum Master works with the Scrum teams to plan and initiate the Sprint. During the Sprint, the Scrum Master conducts all Daily Scrums, and is responsible for ensuring that impediments are promptly removed and decisions are promptly made. The Scrum Master is also responsible for working with management to gauge progress and reduce backlog.

The Team Leader, Project Leader, or Project Manager often assume the Scrum Master role. Scrum provides this person with the structure to effectively carry out Scrum's new way of building systems. If it's likely that many impediments will have to be initially removed, this position may need to be filled by a senior manager or a Scrum consultant.

How does the Scrum Master keep the team working at the highest possible level of productivity? The Scrum Master does so primarily by making decisions and removing impediments. When decisions need to be made in the Daily Scrum, the Scrum Master is responsible for making the decisions immediately, even with incomplete information. I've found that it's usually better to proceed with some decision than no decision. The decision can always be reversed later, but in the meantime, the team can continue working. As for impediments, the Scrum Master either personally removes them or causes them to be removed as soon as possible. When the Scrum Master does the latter, he or she makes visible to the organization a policy, procedure, structure, or facility that is hurting productivity.

A Scrum Master has certain personality traits. He or she is usually focused and determined to do whatever is necessary for their Scrum teams. Some people aren't appropriate as Scrum Masters. They aren't comfortable being that visible and taking that much initiative. Removing impediments requires determination and stubbornness.

3.2   Product Backlog

Product Backlog is an evolving, prioritized queue of business and technical functionality that needs to be developed into a system.
—

The Scrum Master is responsible for employing the Scrum process to build a system or product. The requirements are listed in the Product Backlog. The Product Backlog represents everything that anyone interested in the product or process has thought is needed or would be a good idea in the product. It is a list of all features, functions, technologies, enhancements, and bug fixes that constitute the changes that will be made to the product for future releases. Anything that represents work to be done on the product is included in Product Backlog. These are examples of items that would go on the Product Backlog:

Allow users to access and view account balances for last six months.

Improve scalability of product.

Simplify installation process when multiple databases are used.

Determine how workflow can be added to product.

Product Backlog is initially incomplete, just an initial list of things that the product or system needs. The first Product Backlog may be a list of requirements that is gleaned from a vision document, garnered from a brainstorming session, or derived from a marketing requirements document. Sources of Product Backlog are as formal or informal as the hosting organization. To get the first Sprint going, Product Backlog only needs to contain enough requirements to drive a thirty-day Sprint. A Sprint can start from only concepts and a wish list.

The Product Backlog emerges from this initial list as the product and the customer's understanding of their needs emerge and evolve. Backlog is dynamic. Management repeatedly changes it to identify what the product requires to be appropriate, competitive, and useful. As long as a product exists, Product Backlog also exists.

Backlog originates from many sources. Product marketing generates features and functions. Sales generates backlog that will cause the product to be more competitive or please a particular customer. Engineering generates backlog that builds technology that holds the whole product together. Customer Support generates backlog to fix major product flaws.

Product Backlog is sorted in order of priority. Top priority Product Backlog drives immediate development activities. The higher a backlog item's priority, the more urgent it is, the more it has been thought about, and the more consensus there is regarding its value. Higher priority backlog is clearer and has more detailed specification than lower priority backlog. Better estimates are made based on the greater clarity and increased detail. The lower the priority, the less the detail, until you can barely make out the backlog item.

In addition to product features and technology, backlog items include issues. Issues require resolution before one or more backlog items can be worked on. For example, if response time is erratic and becoming a hot topic in the industry press, then this might be included as an issue in the Backlog. This issue is not ready to be defined as something to develop. However, it needs to be dealt with and perhaps turned into Product Backlog in the form of features or technology to be developed. Issues are prioritized, just like regular Product Backlog. The Product Owner is responsible for turning issues into work that the Scrum Team selects for a Sprint. Until he or she converts the issue to regular Product Backlog, it remains as "unworkable" Product Backlog. This ensures that the team isn't swamped by having to think about outstanding issues while it works.

As a product is used, as its value increases, and as the marketplace provides feedback, the product's backlog emerges into a larger and more comprehensive list. Requirements never stop changing. It makes little sense to pretend that this is not the case and attempt to set requirements in stone before beginning design and construction.

All you need is a product vision and enough top priority items on the backlog to begin one iteration, or Sprint, of incremental development on the product.

3.2.1   Product Owner Solely Controls the Product Backlog

Only one person is responsible for managing and controlling the Product Backlog. This person is referred to as the Product Owner. For commercial development, the Product Owner may be the product manager. For in-house development efforts, the Product Owner could be the project manager or the user department manager. This is the person who is officially responsible for the project. This person maintains the Product Backlog and ensures that it is visible to everyone. Everyone knows what items have the highest priority, so everyone knows what will be worked on.

The Product Owner is one person, not a committee. Committees may exist that advise or influence this person, but any person or body of people wanting an item's priority changed has to convince the Product Owner to make the change. Organizations have many ways of setting priorities and requirements. These practices will be influenced by Scrum across time, particularly through the meeting that reviews product increments (Sprint Review). The practice Scrum adds is that only one person is responsible for maintaining and sustaining the content and priority of a single Product Backlog. Otherwise, multiple conflicting lists flourish and the Scrum teams don't know which list to listen to. Without a single Product Owner, floundering, spin, contention, and frustration result.

For the Product Owner to succeed, everyone in the organization has to respect his or her decisions. No one is allowed to tell the Scrum Teams to work from a different set of priorities, and Scrum Teams aren't allowed to listen to anyone who says otherwise. All of the decisions that the Product Owner makes are highly visible, as they are reflected in the prioritization of the Product Backlog. This visibility requires the Product Owner to do his or her best, and makes the role of Product Owner both a demanding and a rewarding one.

3.2.2 Estimating Backlog Effort

As backlog is created, the Product Owner works with others to estimate how long it will take to develop. To reach the estimate, he or she talks to the developers, technical writers, quality control staff, and other people who understand the product and technology. This estimate includes the time it takes to perform all of the requisite architecture, design, construction and testing. The estimate will be as accurate as the Product Owner and team are at estimating; this means that the accuracy may vary wildly until the team becomes experienced at estimating. Since the team will build the backlog into code, their estimate is the best available.

Estimating is an iterative process. Estimates change as more information emerges about the backlog item and the item becomes better understood. Because higher priority backlog is better understood, the time estimates for these items are usually more accurate. If the Product Owner can't get a clear, believable estimate for a top priority backlog, he or she should consider redefining the backlog item, lowering its priority, or making it an issue instead of work.

The Product Backlog estimate is not binding on the Scrum team. The estimate does not mean, "this is how much time there is to build this functionality, and no more." The estimate is a starting point, a best guess, from which the Sprint can be empirically constructed and managed. The Scrum team selects the amount of Product Backlog that it believes it can handle in a Sprint based on these estimates. If the Product Owner hasn't worked with the team to create realistic estimates, the amount of Product Backlog selected may differ significantly from expectations.

Starting with the top priority backlog, the Product Owner develops estimates for each item. As the project gets underway, more will be known about available components, the utility of development tools, and the capability of the team. The estimates can then be revised.

3.3 Scrum Teams

> A team commits to achieving a Sprint goal. The team is accorded full authority to do whatever it decides is necessary to achieve the goal.   —

The Scrum Master meets with the Scrum Team and reviews the Product Backlog. The Scrum Team commits to turn a selected set of Product Backlog into a working product. The Scrum team makes this commitment every Sprint. The team has full authority to do whatever is necessary to do so. It is only constrained by organizational standards and conventions. Show it what to do, and it will figure out how to do it. Over time, teams get used to Scrum and begin committing to more and more work.

3.3.1 Team Dynamics

Every individual has their own strengths and weaknesses, comes from a unique background, and is trained and gains skills through a unique education and job history. Mix these individuals into a small team and you gain the strengths of team dynamics. You also can anticipate prejudice, resentments, petty squabbles, and all of the other negative attributes of human relationships. The team's commitment to produce a product increment each Sprint leads it to solve differences and draw on strengths.

A team member once came to see me to complain about a fellow team member who was encountering family problems. He was very upset and wanted the person removed from the team. I asked him if the team was better off with or without the person, if the person was contributing anything of value. He conceded that there were valuable contributions, but it was unfair that the other team member was distracted. I asked if he thought this other team member could do better, given the circumstances. He agreed that if he were in a similar situation, he would have a similar problem focusing. He also granted that he had worked with the fellow team member before and found him worthwhile. Our discussion led him to understand that this person was doing the level best he could, everything taken into consideration.

Scrum is structured to provide teams an environment within which they can do their best. Since the team commits to goals, the team members are often frustrated when things happen that undercut their commitments and anticipations. However, Scrum is empirical, and the team can reduce functionality and still meet goals, and management can adjust based on the product increment delivered at the end of the Sprint. In my experience, a team self-organizes to draw on its strengths rather than succumb to its problems. Each team member's best changes day by day, but the team's best tends to be rather predictable.

As a Scrum Master, I'm often tempted to help a team resolve its internal problems. Experience has taught me not to. The team has committed to a goal. When I help them resolve differences, I'm taking some of their responsibility away. The team committed to the goal; the team gets to figure out how to meet the goal, as best they can.

3.3.2 Team Size

The size of the team should be seven people, plus or minus two [Miller]. Teams as small as three can benefit, but the small size limits the amount of interaction that can occur and reduces productivity gains. Teams larger than eight don't work out well. Team productivity decreases and the Scrum's control mechanisms become cumbersome. Leading Daily Scrum meeting may become too difficult for the Scrum Master if the team is too large. Most importantly, large teams generate too much complexity for an empirical process.

If more than eight people are available, I strongly recommend breaking them into multiple teams. Identify one team. Let it select backlog and make a commitment for a Sprint. Then form another team. Let it select from the remaining backlog, commit, and proceed to Sprint. Based on each team's expertise, it will select the priority Product Backlog that it can best handle. Minimize the interaction and dependencies between the teams and maximize the cohesion of the work within each team. Make sure that the members of each team are working on things related to what their fellow team members are working on. I have managed product development with up to ten teams, coordinating their work with a daily "Scrum of Scrums." Scrum Masters from each team meet after the Daily Scrums for their own Daily Scrum.

3.3.3   Team Composition

Teams are cross functional. A Scrum Team should include people with all of the skills necessary to meet the Sprint goal. Scrum eschews vertical teams of analysts, designers, quality control, and coding engineers. A Scrum Team self-organizes so that everyone contributes to the outcome. Each team member applies his or her expertise to all of the problems. The resultant synergy from a tester helping a designer construct code improves code quality and raises productivity.

A team selects the amount of Product Backlog and establishes the Sprint goal. In most development processes, a manager tells each team member what to do and how long to take to do it. How can managers make this commitment for teams? In Scrum, no third party can commit a person or team to do work.

Who should be on a Scrum Team? I prefer to have at least one very experienced engineer as part of the team. They mentor junior engineers. During each Sprint, a team is required to test what it builds. Some teams include quality assurance testers to do testing. Other teams make the regular engineers test their own code. A technical writer is often included on a team. When no writer is assigned, engineers write rough user documentation themselves. Regardless of the team composition, it is responsible for doing all of the analysis, design, coding, testing, and user documentation.

Most team members are assigned full time to the team. Other team members are part time. Someone with particular domain or technical knowledge may not be available full time. Some team members aren't needed full time, such as a systems administrator or database administrator. When a team member commits to work on a Sprint, he or she commits based on what work can be done given the hours he or she is assigned to the team. Each team member knows his or her availability when making commitments. The team is interested in results and increments of product, not in time management. With time and experience, a team's skills in accurately estimating what it can do in a Sprint improves. The skill improves as the team learns the domain and the technology. The accuracy improves as the team realizes that Scrum does protect it from interference and interruptions.

There are no titles on teams. Teams self-organize to turn the requirements and technology into product functionality. This type of stateless, ego-less, development team is flexible to address any work that arises. Scrum avoids people who refuse to code because they are systems architects, or designers. Everyone chips in and does his or her best, doing or learning how to do what is needed. Scrum Team members don't have job descriptions other than doing the best possible. No titles, no exceptions.

Team composition may change at the end of a Sprint. The Scrum Master or Project Manager may choose to bring some new team members with more specific expertise or advanced capabilities. Management can also trade out under-performers and problem employees. Every time team membership is changed, the productivity gained from self-organization is diminished. I recommend that care be taken when changing team composition.

3.3.4   Team Responsibilities and Authority

The team is responsible for meeting the goal to which it commits at a Sprint planning meeting. The amount of backlog it will address is solely up to the team. Only the team can assess what it can accomplish over the next thirty days. The team has the authority to make any decisions, do whatever it needs to do, and ask for any impediments to be removed. Most organizations have no trouble holding people responsible. Management is sometimes surprised when a team assumes the authority necessary to meet their commitments. During a Scrum, only the team can define its work. The team may turn to others for advice and counseling, but it can take or reject whatever advice is offered. A team often goes through a short period during which it doesn't understand that it has full authority. It too is shocked and incredulous to find out that nobody else is going to tell it what to do. This surprise quickly disappears and the productivity of self-organization takes hold.

Although a team has the authority to decide how to do its work, the team is responsible for using and conforming to any existing charters, standards, conventions, architectures, and technology. These ensure that the products of the project and the Scrum Team fit in with other organizational products and can be understood by others. These charters, standards and conventions must be in place prior to the start of a Sprint.

If the team ever feels that it doesn't have the authority to meet the goals to which it committed, the team can call for an abnormal Sprint termination. The team calls for another Sprint Planning meeting. This is quite dramatic! The team found that assumptions it made during the Sprint planning meeting were incorrect and that it can't proceed.

3.3.5 Working Environment

It is important to equip a team with the best possible tools. It's incredibly shortsighted to take expensive engineers performing important work and to hobble them with inadequate tools and infrastructure. One team I worked with needed workstations for the contractors. I requisitioned them. The workstations arrived with 15-inch monitors, the organizational standard. The team was doing multiple-window development and 15-inch monitors would require constant task switching to keep the most current work on top. A larger monitor would be better. The distributor returned within two hours with the larger monitors. I then worked with management to change the workstation standard.

Use open working environments. Such environments allow people to communicate more easily, make it easier to get together, and facilitate self-organization. When I walk into open team areas, I can immediately tell how the team is doing. Silence is always a bad sign. I know that people are collaborating if I can hear conversations. When I enter a cubicle environment, there is often silence, indicating an absence of interaction. Cubicles are truly the bane of the modern workplace. They quite literally keep people apart and break teams up.

If I were starting another software company, I'd gut whatever space I had, put in wood or concrete floors, cover the walls with whiteboards, and scatter telephone and network connections throughout. Then I'd issue everyone a rolling desk, a rolling file cabinet, and a cart with a computer and monitor. I'd let people form their own work groups, clusters of furniture formed on the basis of who was working with whom at the time. I've been in facilities like these, and they're fantastic. You can hear the hum of activity and feel the energy in the air. It is always obvious that good things are happening at these places. Of course, not every company is able, or even willing, to make this kind of renovation. There are other ways to facilitate teamwork by changing layout, though. At a company without enough conference rooms, I turned several offices into one team room. Once the team moved into its new room, productivity skyrocketed.

A Scrum Team sets its own working hours, though it is subject to some constraints. Teams are responsible for not disrupting the organizational environment (such as working from 10pm to 6am daily). However, the organization owes it to the team to let it figure out when it can work best. Also, team members need to work when the rest of the team is present.

3.4 Daily Scrum Meetings

> Software development is a complex process that requires lots of communications. The Daily Scrum meeting is where the team comes to communicate.   —

Each Scrum Team meets daily for a 15-minute status meeting called the Daily Scrum. During the meeting, the team explains what it has accomplished since the last meeting, what it is going to do before the next meeting, and what obstacles are in its way. The Daily Scrum meeting gets people used to team-based, rapid, intense, co-operative, courteous development. Daily Scrums improve communications, eliminate other meetings, identify and remove impediments to development, highlight and promote quick decision-making, and improve everyone's level of project knowledge. That's a lot of benefit from just 15 minutes a day! An impediment I hear over and over is that team members have to attend status meetings. I tell the team not to go to these other status meetings. Anyone who needs to know what's going on with the project can come to the Daily Scrum and listen.

The Scrum Master is responsible for successfully conducting the Daily Scrum. The Scrum Master keeps the Daily Scrum short by enforcing the rules and making sure that people speak briefly. This requires a fair amount of courage since the rules apply equally to everyone. It's difficult to tell a Senior Vice President not to interrupt.

By listening carefully during a Daily Scrum meeting, managers can get a sense of what the team is doing and how likely it is to succeed. Attending a Daily Scrum is easier and more informative than reading a report, and Daily Scrums have the additional benefit of being a boon for the team as well as for its managers. Scrum is direct and open. Because the reporting interval is only 24 hours, it's easy to continuously monitor a team. A Scrum Master can quickly see if a team member is up to his or her ears trying to get a piece of technology to work. Has a team member lost interest in the project? Is someone not working because of family problems? Is the team quarreling over something? What attitudes are demonstrated during the meeting?

I was once given a very tasteful conference room to use as a Scrum Room. I knew it was tasteful because it had paintings on the walls but no whiteboards. I requested whiteboards for a whole month, but my requests were ignored. Finally, I improvised: I started using sticky flip chart paper. This is a fantastic product: you write on a flip chart pad, tear off the pages you want to keep, and stick them to the wall with adhesive on the back of each page. One day I ran out of paper on the pad. I looked around, but couldn't find anything else to use. Finally, I took down a picture and started writing on the walls with magic marker. Pretty soon the walls were covered with writing. Everyone came to see, aghast that this social taboo had been violated. The Facilities Department heard about this, of course, and responded by repainting the walls and (finally!) installing whiteboards. The moral of this story is that you should use your facilities as best you can to keep your productivity high.

3.4.1   Establishing a Meeting Room

The Scrum Master should establish a meeting place and time for the Daily Scrum. The room in which the Daily Scrum is held is called the Scrum Room. The team holds its Daily Scrum in this room every working day at the same place and same time. The room should be readily accessible from the team's primary working location. It should be equipped with a door (to close during the meeting), a speakerphone (for team members who will attend by calling-in), a table, at least enough chairs for each team member to sit around the table, and white boards (for recording notes, issues, and impediments and for general brainstorming after the Daily Scrum). Of course, Scrum has been successfully implemented in environments that did not have well appointed Scrum Rooms. The most important thing is that the time and location of the Daily Scrum be constant. I've started out by holding Daily Scrums in the corner of a cafeteria, on a lawn, and even in a neighboring coffee shop. It is only a matter of time before management sees the value of the Daily Scrum and rushes to provide a Scrum Room, or if management has already provided one, to improve the facilities in the Scrum Room.

> A chicken and a pig are together when the
> chicken says, "Let's start a restaurant!"
> The pig thinks it over and says, "What
> would we call this restaurant?" The chicken
> says, "Ham n' Eggs!"
> The pig says, "No, thanks. I'd be commit-
> ted, but you'd only be involved!"

3.4.2   Chickens and Pigs

Team members commit to a goal and do the work that is required to meet it.
They are called pigs because they, like the pigs in the joke, are committed
to the project. Everyone else is a chicken. Chickens can attend Daily
Scrums, but they have to stand on the periphery. Chickens are not allowed
to interfere with the meeting in any way, such as talking, gesticulating, or
making noise. Chickens are present as guests and must follow Scrum rules.

I once implemented Scrum at an organization that published trade
journals on the Web, starting with just one team for one magazine. Everyone else wanted to find out how Scrum worked, though, so I invited them
to the Daily Scrum. Soon over thirty chickens were in the room. Any room
with that many people has too much movement and too many distractions.
There are many chickens that need to be present at the Daily Scrums, including those who need to keep track of the Sprint - such as users, product
managers, and management. But the Daily Scrum is not a spectacle. Keep
attendance to a minimum. I suggest you not use a team's Daily Scrum as
a sort of training program for others teams.

3.4.3   Starting the Meeting

The Scrum Master is responsible for ensuring that the Daily Scrum goes
well. Scrum Masters ensure that the room is setup for the meeting. They
get any team members working from remote locations set up on a conference phone before the meeting starts[1]. Also, they work to minimize the
distractions that occur during the meeting so everyone can stay focused
and the meeting can be kept short. For example, a good Scrum Master
might even set the chairs up around the table before the meeting begins so
that people don't get caught up in side conversations as they move chairs
around. The Scrum Master's job is to increase the productivity of the
team in any way possible. Arranging chairs is one small demonstration of
commitment.

---

[1] "Paul Martin had a daily Scrum in his office which was so small everyone had to
stand up. A third of the team was in his office, a third in Burlington, and a third in
Seattle. This was one of the best running Scrums I have seen. It produced the web
framework for all of IDX's products." Jeff Sutherland, 2001. (Private Correspondance.)

The team should arrange themselves in a circle, generally around a focus such as a table. Some Scrum Teams sit, while others have found that standing encourages brevity. Team members seat themselves in any order as they arrive. People not on the team sit or stand around the periphery, outside of the team circle. When guests sit around the table, or interject themselves into the team circle, they feel free to interject comments and to have side conversations. This makes it hard to control the meeting duration. If chickens are placed outside the circle, they are physically reminded that they are observers, and not participants.

Every team member must arrive on time for each Daily Scrum. The meeting starts promptly at the designated time, regardless of who is or is not present. Many Scrum Masters highlight the importance of promptness by imposing a small fine for tardiness. Any team member who doesn't attend or doesn't show up on time is fined $1, which is collected immediately by the Scrum Master. This money is periodically given to a charity.

3.4.4   Format of the Daily Scrum

During the Daily Scrum, only one person – from the pigs – talks at a time. That person is the one who is reporting his or her status. Everyone else listens. There are no side conversations. Starting to his or her immediate left, the Scrum Master goes around the room and asks team members to answer three questions.

What have you done since last Scrum? This question addresses only the last 24 hours, unless a weekend or holiday has occurred in the interim. Team members only mention the things they have done that relate to this team and this Sprint. For example, the team isn't interested in other work that part-timers might be doing unless it relates directly to their own work. If team members are doing work other than what they had planned to be doing for this Sprint, that other work should be identified as an impediment. Anything not related to the team's work is probably an impediment.

What will you do between now and the next Scrum? This question relates only to this Sprint and this team. What is each team member planning to work on? The work a team member expects to do should match the work that has been planned by the team. If team members state they are going to be doing other work, they should be asked why. The team might need to meet after the Daily Scrum to talk about the new work. Other team members have to adjust their work based on the new work. Getting answers to these questions can help the team and management assess whether the work is proceeding regularly and as expected, or if adjustments are needed.

What got in your way of doing work? If a team member was unable to work or anticipates being unable to work on what he or she planned, what got in his or her way? That is to say, what is getting in the way of the team? Each team member has planned and committed to a goal and is empirically figuring out the work to meet the goal. What is slowing down individual team members, and therefore the team as a whole? Although team members have worked within the organization and are used to its culture and style, the Scrum Master should encourage them to think "outside of the box." If this were the perfect work environment, what else would it have? More specifically, what could help the team be more productive, both as a group of individuals and as a cohesive team?

Team members should keep their responses to these questions brief and to the point. They shouldn't elaborate or describe how the work was done or will be done unless they want to highlight help they may need. For instance, a team member may report that he or she intends to complete implementing a feature in a module, but he or she is having difficulty understanding how a specific algorithm works. Or the team member may report that he or she is going to check in some code but can't get the source code management system to work without crashing.

The Daily Scrum is not a design session and should not turn into a working session. Don't discuss design or start to solve a problem. There isn't enough time or flexibility in the Daily Scrum to begin working through issues of this magnitude. By limiting the meeting's scope, the Scrum Master can keep the duration in check and constant. If the scope of the Daily Scrum expands, no one will know how much time to allocate to the meeting.

3.4.5   Identifying Impediments

If a team member identifies something that is stopping him or her from working effectively, the Scrum Master is responsible for recording and removing that impediment. Impediments should be written down on the white board on the wall. If the Scrum Master doesn't fully understand the impediment, he or she should meet with whoever mentioned it after the Scrum Meeting to learn about it. The following are common impediments:

Workstation, network, and/or server are down

Network or server are slow

Required to attend human resource training session

Required to attend status meeting with management

Asked by management to do something else

Asked to do something other than what this team member committed to for this Sprint.

Unsure about how to proceed

Unsure of design decision

Unsure how to use technology

The Scrum Master's top priority is removing impediments. If team members inform the Scrum Master that he or she can do something to make them more productive, the Scrum Master should do it. The Daily Scrum gives the Scrum Master direct information on what he or she can do to improve the productivity of the team.

If the impediments aren't promptly resolved, the team will report the next day that it is still impeded. It is a bad sign if the team members stop reporting impediments even though they haven't been resolved. This usually means that the team members have lost their confidence that the Scrum Master can and will resolve their impediments. If, for some good reason, an impediment cannot be removed, the Scrum Master should report on this at the next Daily Scrum.

If the open impediments on the white board get to be lengthy, this may indicate that the larger organization isn't supporting the team. In this case, the Scrum Master may have to cancel the Sprint. This is a very powerful card to play. It should be played only when the Scrum Master is very concerned that the organization's support for the project is so low as to render the team ineffective. Low support could be because this is an unimportant project or because the organization is unable to effectively support any projects. The reason doesn't matter to this project. The Scrum Master has observed that there are many impediments and management is unwilling or unable to remove them. The Scrum Master should very carefully and intensely discuss these observations and the consequences of the lack of support with management before canceling the Sprint. Once the decision has been made to cancel the Sprint, the Scrum Master is effectively stating that there isn't enough management support or organizational effectiveness for the project to succeed. See the later section on "*Abnormal Termination of Sprints*" for more details.

3.4.6   Making Decisions

A Scrum team has full authority to make all of the decisions necessary to turn the Product Backlog into a Product Increment to meet the Sprint Goal. The team is free to do whatever is necessary to make the best decision possible and do the best work. The team members can interview others, bring in consultants, read books, browse the web, or whatever they need (within budgetary constraints). A team member may identify indecision as an impediment (e.g. "I don't know if I should do this or that."). The Scrum Master is then responsible for making a decision, preferably then and there. When first implementing Scrum for a team, the Scrum Master should be careful not to make too many decisions for the team. Delegated decision-making is new in most organizations. The Scrum Master helps the team learn to make its own decisions to fulfill its commitments. The more the team relies on outsiders to make its decisions, the less control it has over its commitments.

When the team is uncertain, it should acquire whatever information is necessary to become more certain. Sometimes a team asks for someone else to make a decision because it feels that the decision is risky, or sensitive. In this case, the Scrum Master should meet with the team after the Daily Scrum and work through to a decision. A team should make a decision by acting on the best information that it has and by relying on its instincts. Most snap decisions are more acceptable than holding up work to wait for someone else to decide. The team usually has a far better handle on the alternatives than anyone else. Also, completed work has momentum and usually will be "good enough," or at the very least, it will be far better than nothing.

Most of the time the decision will be acceptable. Sometimes, though, a decision results in unacceptable product functionality or application of technology. This becomes apparent when the product increment is reviewed at the end of the Sprint. If an incorrect decision isn't visible at this review, it is probably irrelevant. Otherwise work can be redone to correct the bad decision. Because Sprints are so short, bad decisions rarely impact more than thirty days worth of work.

If the Scrum Master can't make a decision during the meeting, he or she is responsible for making a decision and communicating it to the whole team within one hour after the end of the Scrum.

3.4.7   Establishing Follow-Up Meetings

If any discussion is needed other than the status provided by answering the three questions, a follow-up meeting may be requested. After a team member gives his or her status, another team member can interject, "I'd like to address this more after the Scrum. Anyone who's interested should hang around afterward." More than one team member may want to address the topic in more depth. This conversation may get into discussing design or requirements alternatives or interpretations. A team member may be working on the same thing and wants to share information. This sharing will be of indeterminate length and may lead to design discussions. A team member may have done something like this before or may know an easier way to do the work. This may lead to another team member suggesting another approach, resulting in a design discussion. A working meeting is needed to reach a decision or to discuss design or standards. In each of these cases, the conversation that starts is open-ended. Other team members may join in and more time will go by. All of these discussions are worthwhile and should happen. They should happen after the Daily Scrum, though. Keep all working sessions outside of the Daily Scrum, or else the distinction between a status session and a working session will become blurred and the time for the Scrum won't remain short and fixed.

3.5   Sprint Planning Meeting

> Customers, users, management, the Product Owner and the Scrum
> Team determine the next Sprint goal and functionality at the
> Sprint Planning meeting. The team then devises the individual
> tasks that must be performed to build the product increment.
> —

3.5.1   Sprint Planning Meeting Overview

Scrum Teams meet with the Scrum Master and others to plan each Sprint.
The Sprint planning meeting actually consists of two consecutive meetings.
At the first meeting, the team meets with the Product Owner, management, and users to figure out what functionality to build during the next
Sprint. At the second meeting, the team works by itself to figure out how
it is going to build this functionality into a product increment during the
Sprint. Input to this meeting is the Product Backlog, the latest increment
of product, and the capabilities and past performance of the team. See
figure 3.1 for an overview of planning a new Sprint.

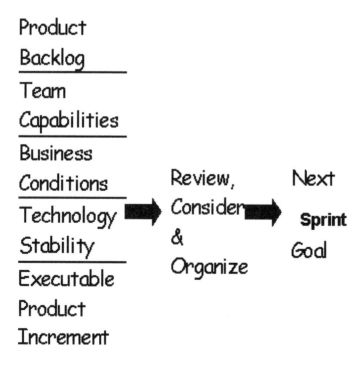

FIGURE 3.1: Input for new Sprint

3.5.2   Identify Product Backlog and Goal for Next Sprint

To start the meeting, the Product Owner presents the top priority Product Backlog. He or she leads a discussion about what changes to the backlog are appropriate, given what was demonstrated at the end of the previous Sprint (see *Sprint Review*). What does everyone want the team to work on next? Working with the Product Owner, management, and customers, the team identifies the Product Backlog that it believes it can develop during the next Sprint (30 calendar days).

These are examples of top priority Product Backlog:

Implement a middleware alternative for providing secure, recoverable access by applications to legacy databases

The client account modification functionality in the account management system loses transactions when it or the databases crash. Secure these transactions.

The client account modification functionality has to identify "high value" accounts in real-time

The Product Backlog is a mix of functionality and technology. The first backlog item could have been more precise if the technology already had been decided upon. For example, it could have read:

"Implement an object-oriented middleware connection between applications and legacy databases that is secure and recoverable using Tuxedo from BEA systems and using CORBA-compliant wrappers."

In the absence of directions to the contrary, the team is free to choose how it implements the functionality. In this example, the team only selected the first, highest priority, Product Backlog. The team has committed to attempt to implement this functionality on some new technology. The team, of course, doesn't know exactly what can be done, how amenable the technology will be, or how difficult or simple the functionality will be.

Having selected the Product Backlog, a Sprint Goal is crafted. The Sprint Goal is an objective that will be met through the implementation of the Product Backlog. For instance, this Sprint Goal could be:

Sprint Goal: to provide a standardized middleware mechanism for the identified customer service transactions to access backend databases.

The reason for having a Sprint Goal is to give the team some wiggle room regarding the functionality. For example, the goal for the above Sprint could also be: "Automate the client account modification functionality through a secure, recoverable transaction middleware capability." As the team works, it keeps this goal in mind. In order to satisfy the goal, it implements the functionality and technology. If the work turns out to be harder than the team had expected, then the team might only partially implement the functionality. At the Sprint Review meeting, management, customers, and the Product Owner review how and to what degree the functionality has been implemented. They review how the Sprint Goal has been met. If they are dissatisfied, they can then make decisions about requirements, technology or team composition. During the Sprint, though, the team alone determines how to meet the Sprint Goal. At the end of the Sprint, any incomplete work returns to the Product Backlog.

3.5.3   Define Sprint Backlog to Meet Sprint Goal

After establishing the Sprint goal, the team determines what work will have to be performed in order to reach the goal. All team members are required to be present when this is determined. The team may also invite other people to attend in order to provide technical or domain advice. The Product Owner often attends. A new team often first realizes that it will either sink or swim as a team, not individually, in this meeting. The team realizes that it must rely on its own ingenuity, creativity, cooperation, collaboration, and effort. As it realizes this, it starts to self-organize to take on the characteristics and behavior of a real team. During this meeting, management and the user should not do or say anything that takes the team off the hook or makes its decisions for it.

The team compiles a list of tasks it has to complete to meet the Sprint goal. These tasks are the detailed pieces of work needed to convert the Product Backlog into working software. Tasks should have enough detail so that each task takes roughly four to sixteen hours to finish. This task list is called the Sprint Backlog. The team self-organizes to assign and undertake the work in the Sprint Backlog. Sometimes only a partial Sprint Backlog can be created. The team may have to define an initial architecture or create designs before it can fully delineate the rest of the tasks. In such a case, the team should define the initial investigation, design, and architecture work in as much detail as possible, and leave reminders for work that will probably have to be done once the investigation or design has been completed. At that time, the work will be more fully understood and another team meeting can be convened to detail it.

To meet the above Sprint Goal, some of the Sprint Backlog that the team might devise is:

Map the transaction elements to back-end database tables.

Write a business object in C++ to handle transactions via defined methods and interfaces.

Wrap the C++ in a CORBA wrapper.

Use Tuxedo for all queuing, messaging, and transaction management.

Measure the transaction performance to determine whether scalability requirements can be met.

The team modifies Sprint Backlog throughout the Sprint. As it gets into individual tasks, it may find out that more or fewer tasks are needed, or that a given task will take more or less time than had been expected. As new work is required, the team adds it to the Sprint Backlog. As tasks are worked on or completed, the hours of estimated remaining work for each task is updated. When tasks are deemed unnecessary, they are removed. Only the team can change its Sprint Backlog during a Sprint. Only the team can change the contents or the estimates. The Sprint Backlog is a highly visible, real time picture of the work that the team plans to accomplish during the Sprint, and it belongs solely to the team.

Sometimes the Scrum Team discovers that it has selected too much Product Backlog to complete in a single Sprint. If this happens, the Scrum Master immediately meets with the Product Owner and the Scrum team. They collectively identify Product Backlog that can be removed while still meeting the Sprint Goal. If no backlog can be removed, they work together to identify functionality with scope or depth that can be lessened.

Teams become better at Sprint planning after the third or fourth Sprint. At first, a team tends to be nervous about taking on responsibility and it under-commits. As it becomes more familiar with Scrum processes, as it starts to understand the functionality and technology, and as it gels into a team, it commits to more work.

3.6   Sprint

The team works for a fixed period of time called a Sprint.   —

The Scrum Team has decided what it will accomplish during the upcoming Sprint. It now sprints to accomplish the Sprint Goal. The team is free to accomplish this goal as it sees fit, adapting to the circumstances, technology, and organizational terrain as best it can.

During conflicts, the military will put teams of soldiers into insertion points in areas of operations. Each team is assigned a mission to accomplish and self-organizes to accomplish it. The team has all the supplies and training that it is expected to need. Since the insertion point is usually in the middle of a complex, even chaotic, situation, the team's knowledge of the situation or what to do to reach the goal is limited to a game plan. The team is intended to improvise in order to accomplish its mission. At some predetermined time, the mission ends and the team is picked up.

Scrum was first described in similar terms [Takeuchi and Nonaka]: "Typically, the process starts with management giving the project team a broad goal. Rarely do they hand out a clear-cut new product concept or a specific work plan. Thus, while the project team has extreme freedom, it is also faced with extreme challenges embodied within the goal. The project team is typically driven to a state of 'zero information' as the extent of the challenge essentially makes prior knowledge inapplicable. Thus the team must fend for itself and find a way to coalesce into a dynamic group."

"According to several of the companies surveyed, the process tends to produce significant quantities of mistakes. However, these are viewed invariably from the plus side as being valuable learning experiences. In the end, the bottom line is that the chaotic process tends to produce more revolutionary products faster than the old sequential development process. It also tends to develop the project team members into 'triple threat' players as each person's knowledge base is broadly expanded through their interaction."

3.6.1   Product Increments Are Mined from Chaos

After the overall goals and objectives are established at the Sprint planning meeting, the Scrum Team is dropped into the insertion point for a Sprint. The team is asked to do its best to turn the complex requirements and unpredictable technology into a product increment. It is asked to tame chaos, to turn complexity into predictable product. What a job!

Scrum asks people to try to wrest a predictable product from unpredictable complexity. Some people can't handle this type of assignment. During the Sprint, they may decide that they want out. Other people relish the chance to build something that requires their best effort. Those who succeed at Scrum are the individuals that will form the core of an organization. Scrum helps identify these people.

Management has invested thirty days of a team in the Sprint. Regardless of what the team accomplishes, it has acquired valuable working knowledge of the requirements and technology. Even when the team produces nothing tangible, it has nonetheless gone through a very useful learning process. The team has trained itself to take another crack at a reconstituted Sprint goal. It has a deeper understanding of the terrain and complexity, and is better equipped for success.

3.6.2   No Interference, No Intruders, No Peddlers

A team is let loose for the thirty day Sprint. The team has committed to the goal and accepted the responsibility of building a product increment that meets the goal. It has the authority to act as it sees fit. No person outside the team can change the scope or nature of the work the team is doing during a Sprint. No one is allowed to add more functionality or technology to the Sprint. No one can tell the team how to proceed in its work. This really is like the military insertion point.

Many organizations are initially uncomfortable with the idea of letting a team loose for a Sprint. It just doesn't feel right. It feels too risky. But, is it really so strange for management to trust a team of its own employees to figure out the best and most appropriate things to do? How much of a risk is this really? Management has assigned the best people available to the team. What the team will do is defined in the Sprint Goals and Product Backlog. The risk is limited to thirty calendar days of the team's Sprint. Management can see how the team's doing by attending Daily Scrums and, failing that, can always inspect the most recently updated version of the Sprint Backlog. At the end of the thirty days, management meets with the team. At the very worst, the team has built nothing but has learned much. More often, the team has built something that reflects its best efforts. The team often exceeds expectations. Once the creative juices get flowing, teams become hotbeds of creativity and productivity. A Sprint is management's bet that employees are capable and know what they are doing.

3.6.3   Sprint Mechanics

Sprints last for thirty calendar days. A team takes this long to get its arms around a problem and to produce a product increment. Management usually can't refrain from interfering if more than thirty days goes by, so the Sprint is limited to thirty days. First-time Scrum users usually want to change the length of the Sprint to, say, sixty days, two weeks, or one week. It is worth resisting this temptation. Thirty days is an excellent compromise between many competing pressures. Adjustments can be made to the duration after everyone has more experience with Scrum.

The team has complete authority during the Sprint. It can work as many hours or as few hours as it wants. It can hold meetings whenever it wants. It can hold design sessions from 6am to 10pm. It can spend days interviewing vendors and consultants, or surfing the web for information. The team has absolute authority, because management has given the team free reign for thirty days.

Every product development project is constrained by four variables, (1) time available, (2) cost, in people and resources, (3) delivered quality, and (4) delivered functionality. A Sprint greatly fixes the first three variables. The Sprint will always be thirty days long. The cost is pretty well fixed to the salaries of the team members and the development environment. This is usually in place before a Sprint starts. However, teams can add the cost of consultants or tools during Sprints to remove impediments if the budget is adhered to. Quality is usually an organizational standard. If it isn't, the team needs to devise quality targets prior to Sprinting.

The team has the authority to change the functionality of the Sprint so long as it meets its Sprint Goal. The team does this is by decreasing or increasing the scope or depth of the functionality delivered. For example, the team can change the depth of functionality to "check account balance." The team can implement this functionality by checking all possible accounts, or only one account. The design and code to perform each implementation is significantly different. At the Sprint Review meeting, the depth to which the functionality is implemented is demonstrated and discussed. Any remaining, unimplemented functionality is re-entered onto the Product Backlog and reprioritized.

The team has two mandatory accountabilities during the Sprint: (1) Daily Scrum meetings and (2) the Sprint Backlog. These are working tools for the team. Daily Scrum meetings must be promptly attended by all team members, whether in person or via telephone. Team members cannot just send in a passive status report, such as by email or fax. The Sprint Backlog must be kept up-to-date and as accurate as the team's activities, so that it constitutes an accurate and evolving picture of the team and the work that it is doing. As team members work on Sprint backlog, they adjust the estimates.

During the Sprint, all work that is performed is measured and empirically controlled. More or less work may end up being accomplished depending on how things proceed. Factors influencing the amount of work accomplished include the team's ability to work together, the skills of team members, the details of the work to be performed, and the capability of the tools and standards with which the team has been provided. Because Scrum allows the team to change the amount of work it performs during the Sprint, the team has some flexibility, and is able to do more or less so long as it meets its Sprint Goals.

The team is required to deliver a product increment at the end of the Sprint. Daily product builds are an excellent way for the team to measure its progress. Prior to the build, the team should update the test suite and follow each product build with a smoke, or regression, test. Performing code check-ins for the builds is also a good idea, as it improves team communication and coordination.

3.6.4   Abnormal termination of Sprints

Sprints can be cancelled before the allotted thirty days are over. Under what kind of circumstances might a Sprint need to be cancelled? Management may need to cancel a Sprint if the Sprint Goal becomes obsolete. A company as a whole may change direction. Market conditions or technological requirements might change. Management can simply change its mind. In general, a Sprint should be cancelled if it no longer makes sense given the circumstances. However, because of the short duration of Sprints, it rarely makes sense for management to cancel a Sprint.

Sometimes the team itself may decide that a Sprint should be cancelled. A team comes to better understand its abilities and the project's requirements during a Sprint. The team may realize mid-way through the Sprint that it cannot achieve its Sprint Goal. Even if the team's knowledge of its work has not changed, the Sprint could still need to be cancelled. For example, the team might run into a major roadblock. Sometimes, the team feels that it has met its Sprint goal, and decides to cancel the Sprint because it wants more direction from management before proceeding to implement more functionality.

That the team has the power to cancel its own Sprint is very important. The team is able to stay focused because it can terminate the Sprint if someone tries to change the nature or scope of its work. Everyone knows this, and is consequently reluctant to make any such changes. Sprint terminations consume resources, since everyone has to regroup in another Sprint planning meeting to start another Sprint. Usually, the first question that is asked when a Sprint is terminated is: "Who is responsible for this meeting occurring early?" Because people don't want to be named as the answer to this question, very few Sprints end up being terminated.

3.7   Sprint Review

> The Sprint Review meeting is a four-hour informational meeting. During this meeting, the team presents to management, customers, users, and the Product Owner the product increment that it has built during the Sprint.   —

Before the days of satellites and global positioning systems, ocean-going ships attempted to "fix" their position every morning and evening. The navigation officer measured the angle of three or more stars relative to the horizon, plotted the ship's position relative to each star, and found the intersection of the lines plotting the ship's relative positions to these stars. This was called the "fix." It determined a ship's true position, and "fixed" errors in previous estimations of the ship's location. Currents, wind, faulty steering mechanisms, and poor previous fixes might result in miles of difference between the ship's estimated and real position. During bad weather, fixes often couldn't be made for days at a time because of poor visibility, and the estimated position of the ship became progressively more wrong. As ships approached shore, they would often stay away from the coastline until a good fix could be obtained. The last fix was the best information possible, though, and the ship's officer would set the course based on it.

The Sprint Review provides a similar fix on a project. The team has estimated where it will be at the end of the Sprint and set its course accordingly. At the end of the Sprint, the team presents the product increment that it has been able to build. Management, customers, users, and the Product Owner assess the product increment. They listen to the tales the team has to tell about its journey during the Sprint. They hear what went wrong and what went right. They take a fix on where they really are on their voyage of building the product and system. After all of this, they are able to make an informed decision about what to do next. In other words, they determine the best course to take in order to reach their intended destination. Just like "shooting the stars" provides regularity to shipboard life, the thirty-day Sprint cycle provides a meaningful rhythm in the team's life and even in the company's life. The Sprint Review meeting happens every thirtieth day, and the team builds product during the other twenty-nine days.

Management comes to the Sprint Review to see what the team has been able to build with the resources that it has been given. Customers come to the Sprint Review to see if they like what the team has built. The Product Owner comes to the Sprint Review to see how much functionality has been built. Other engineers and developers come to the meeting to see what the team was able to do with the technology. Everyone wants to see what the team has built, what the Sprint was like, how the technology worked, what shortcuts had to be taken, what things it was able to add, and its ideas as to what can be done next.

The Scrum Master is responsible for coordinating and conducting the Sprint Review meeting. The Scrum Master meets with the team to establish the agenda and discuss how the Sprint results will be presented and by whom. The Scrum Master sends all attendants a reminder a week before the meeting, confirming the time, date, location, attendees, and agenda.

To prepare for the meeting, the team considers what attendees need to see in order to understand what has been developed during the Sprint. The team wants everyone to understand as many dimensions of the product increment as possible. What should attendants learn from this meeting? They should gain an understanding of the system and technical architecture and design that hold the product together, as well as the functionality that has been built onto the architecture. They should be familiarized with the strength and weaknesses of the design and technology so they will know what limitations to be taken into account, and what advantages to leverage when planning the next Sprint.

The best presentations usually start with the Scrum Master giving a concise overview of the Sprint. The Sprint goal and Product Backlog are compared to the actual results of the Sprint, and reasons for any discrepancies are discussed. A team member can display and review a simple product architecture diagram. The most effective architecture diagrams display both the technical and functional architecture. Previously completed technology and functions are highlighted on the diagram. Technology and functionality produced during the past Sprint are then added onto the diagram, and team members demonstrate the functionality as it is added to the diagram. For the most part, the Sprint Review meeting is held in just one place, but during the demonstration of product functionality, the meeting will often move from one workstation and office to another.

During the meeting, everyone visualizes the demonstrated product functionality working in the customer or user environment. As this is visualized, consider what functionality might be added in the next Sprint. The product increment is the focal point for brainstorming. For example, someone could suggest the following after seeing the product increment demonstrated: "If we did "controlled patient costs" manually, we could use this right now in registration!" or "This would solve the problems that we're having tracking inventory in the districts. What would we have to do to make this work off the inventory database?" As the team demonstrates the product increment, it helps the attendees understand the weaknesses and strengths of the product increments, and the difficulties and successes it experienced pulling it together.

No one should prepare extensively for the meeting. In order to enforce this rule, PowerPoint presentations and their ilk are forbidden. If the team feels that it has to spend more than two hours preparing for the meeting, then it usually has less to show for the Sprint than it had hoped, and it is trying to obscure this fact with a fancy presentation. Sprint Review Meetings are very informal. What matters is the product the team has been able to create. The Sprint Review is a working meeting. Questions, observations, discussions and suggestions are allowed and encouraged. If a lot of give and take is needed, it should happen. Remember, though, that the meeting is informational, not critical or action-oriented. Everyone should get an understanding of the product increment, as this is the knowledge they will need for the Sprint Planning meeting.

We have discussed the practices of Scrum. You should now have a good sense of what you need to do to run a Sprint with a Scrum team from the Product Backlog. In the next chapter, I'll discuss how to implement Scrum in your organization and manage a Scrum project.

CHAPTER 4

Applying Scrum

This section presents how to implement and manage Scrum within an organization. —

4.1 Implementing Scrum

If engineering practices are candy bars, then Scrum is a candy bar wrapper. That is to say that Scrum is superimposed on and encapsulates whatever engineering practices already exist. The ease of implementing Scrum often comes as a surprise. Implementing new practices, cultures, and methodologies is usually difficult, and can even be painful, but implementing Scrum is not. Scrum simplifies existing work by allowing a team and management to focus on just the next thirty days. Management practices such as pert charts, time reporting, and lengthy status meetings to control a project can be discarded.

Scrum changes how people think of work. As an organization uses Scrum, the roles that managers and workers within that organization play evolve. Managers begin to expedite more and do less paperwork. Workers become empowered and begin to focus more on their work. Scrum challenges practices and structures that get in the way of focused work. How organizations respond to the challenge of Scrum varies widely from organization to organization. But while an organization formulates its response, Scrum is letting it get the product out the door.

Managers are sometimes caught flat-footed by the changes that Scrum effects. When the Sprint starts, they feel like they have nothing to do: the team has taken over responsibility for figuring out what to do and is organizing itself to accomplish its goals. Then the manager's day starts filling up as the manager begins working the organization to remove impediments to the team's progress. The manager makes decisions during the daily Scrum, and then validates these decisions within the larger organization. The manager blocks interference and helps the team focus. The manager becomes a coach and a good friend to the team.

4.1.1 Implementing Scrum for New Projects

When I implement Scrum, I'm sometimes asked to start with a new project. I work with the team and customer for several days to devise a "starter" Product Backlog. The starter backlog consists of some business functionality and the technology requirements. To implement this functionality, the team designs and builds an initial system framework with the selected technology. The team implements user functionality into this framework. The team may have to connect the functionality to a preliminary or existing database. Under these circumstances, the goal for the first Sprint is:

"Demonstrate a key piece of user functionality on the selected technology."

When the team defines the Sprint Backlog to meet this goal, it includes tasks necessary to build the development environment, set up the team, employ code management and build management practices, implement the target system technology on a test platform, and build the functionality. This constitutes a pretty full Sprint.

This initial Sprint has two purposes. First, the team needs to settle into a development environment in which it can construct functionality. Second, the team builds a working part of the system to demonstrate to the customer within thirty days. Demonstrating functionality this quickly invigorates customer involvement and thinking. The customer realizes the system is for real, right now, and thinks, "Now that the system is really being built, I'd better decide what I want from it. I'd better get involved!" The first Sprint gets the team and customer into a regular thirty-day rhythm of defining and delivering, defining and delivering.

While the team is working on the first Sprint, the Product Owner and customers build more Product Backlog. The Product Backlog doesn't have to be complete; it only needs to include enough top priority items to drive the next few Sprints. As the Product Owner and customers get a feel for Scrum, they start taking a longer view of Product Backlog. If a system or product vision isn't available, the Product Owner and customer will forge one. They will then construct Product Backlog on the basis of this vision.

4.1.2 Implementing Scrum for Ongoing Projects

I'm often called upon to use Scrum to get an existing project or product development effort focused, productive, and generating code. A team is often struggling with changing requirements and difficult technology. The team may not have built any functionality yet, but instead has tried to deliver requirements documents or business models. A development environment already exists and the team is familiar with the targeted technology.

In this case, I start by conducting Daily Scrums as the Scrum Master. I want to find out what is impeding the team. I may let these initial Daily Scrum meetings go on for hours. The team talks out its problems, including why it can't build software and how frustrated it is. I then challenge the team: "What can you build in the next thirty days?" I want to see the team work together to build something, to prove that it can develop software. I try to get the team to focus on functionality that is important to the customer. What really impresses the customer, though, is that the team can build something at all within thirty days. In many instances, the team has gone for months without producing any functionality and the customer has given up. My most immediate goal is to get the team to believe in itself, and to get the customer to believe in the team. The Sprint Goal is:

"Demonstrate any piece of user functionality on the selected technology."

At the Daily Scrums, I identify other impediments to the team's progress and help to remove them. If the team is able to build functionality during the first Sprint, the customer and team collaboratively determine what to do next at the Sprint Review and Sprint Planning meeting. I have never had a team fail to meet this challenge.

4.1.3 Improving Engineering Practices

As I implement Scrum, I evaluate the engineering practices that the team employs. Sometimes they are fine, sometimes they hinder the team, and sometimes they are missing. I use the Daily Scrum to identify any deficiencies. I then work with the team and management to improve them.

If an engineer reports in a Daily Scrum that he or she is working on a model, I might meet with the entire team after the meeting to discuss modeling practices. Is the team building models to guide its thinking about how to structure the code? Or is the team building models because it's been told that it has to build models before coding? If modeling is an existing practice, I might then discuss with engineering management whether the team can make modeling optional for this project. We'll have a discussion about the value of models as documentation, particularly since models go out of date as the system evolves. Keeping models synchronized with code is a maintenance burden on any organization. I usually recommend that management adopt a more "agile" practice, such as the one recommended by Scott Ambler (http://www.extreme-modeling.com/). I advocate an empirical approach in my discussions with management. Does the team become more productive if models are optional? If yes, then the team only uses models to guide their thinking. Does the code quality suffer if models are only used to guide thinking? If yes, then modeling is required where more rigor is needed.

If the team doesn't report any problems with the daily build at the Daily Scrum, I inquire why not. Daily builds always have problems. I sometimes find out that there is no daily build process. I view the absence of a daily build as dangerous. Without it, the team isn't required to synchronize its code. Without the daily build, the team might not know that the code doesn't compile cleanly. Without the daily build, there is no way to test the product daily. The team doesn't even know if the code holds together. If the team doesn't perform daily builds and tests, the team may have made less progress than it thinks. The daily build ensures that the team moves forward from a sound base every day.

As Scrum Master, I make judgments on a team's engineering practices (or lack of practices). The best Scrum Masters are also good engineers. The Scrum Master helps the team improve its engineering practices, just as a coach teaches a team to play better. He or she causes the team to reevaluate and discard wasteful practices, and to assess, design and adopt new practices. For instance, Mike Beedle likes many Extreme Programming practices. He has helped Scrum teams implement them within their projects.

4.2   Business Value through Collaboration

In this section, the term "management" refers interchangeably to the users, customers, or investors who fund the development projects.   —

Some people read about Scrum and think that it's a cop out. They think:

"Since everything is empirical, teams can reduce functionality or increase costs in order to meet goals! The system isn't even a fixed thing since the Product Backlog keeps emerging and evolving. How do I know what to expect, how do I stop the project from slipping and going out of control? How do I stop the team from slacking off, from letting the organization and the customer down? I want to be able to set a date and a cost. Then I'll hold the team responsible for delivering. If the team can't deliver, I'll contract to someone who can! This Scrum stuff doesn't provide me with adequate controls!"

These fears arise when someone doesn't know Scrum controls a project through active management involvement. The traditional approach to systems development begins by defining the system vision and overall requirements. The development organization (or external contractor) estimates the cost, and the expense of the system is budgeted. The system is developed and implemented. The customer expects the system to deliver the business value he or she envisioned, but often this expectation can't be verified for months after implementation. This is the "over the wall" approach to system development because there is little interaction between customer and development team.

Scrum requires much more collaboration between management, the customer, and the development team. The customer, aided by the team, still builds a vision and system requirements (Product Backlog). The myth that requirements can be definitively stated at the beginning of a project is dropped, however. A small set of high-priority requirements is stated initially, usually enough for three months of Sprints; the rest of the requirements emerge as the product emerges. The team prepares estimates and the customer allocates a budget for the initially foreseeable Product Backlog.

The team then develops new business functionality in thirty-day increments, or Sprints. At the end of each Sprint, management and the team review the functionality and consider its value. Is the cost of the functionality justified? Is development progressing as predicted? Are costs spiraling, and, if so, what can be done about it? Will the organization attain business value from the functionality that was demonstrated? Given what functionality has been developed so far, what should be developed next? Scrum provides management with direct control of the project at least every thirty days.

At the end of the first three Sprints, management is usually so pleased with the progress and the functionality already delivered that they budget for more functionality. Management looks at the Product Backlog and determines what they want to budget. If they want to budget for six months of functionality, they simply project the cost of the last Sprint over the next six months. The team(s) will continue to deliver functionality as long as the customer funds the development.

In my experience, Scrum teams deliver. I've mentioned that a Scrum team can reduce functionality to meet a Sprint Goal. However, I should note that the opposite is usually the case. Scrum lets the team find creative ways to meet their commitments. Teams usually rise to the occasion, take their commitments to heart, and surprise management at the Sprint Review by demonstrating more than they initially committed. Teams excel in the environment that Scrum provides. They usually do better than even they had estimated.

Management sometimes struggles with letting go of the planned, defined approach. Managers are used to defining everything at the beginning of a project and contracting a fixed price, fixed date with a team. This illusion of predictability is very reassuring and not easily cast aside. This illusion removes flexibility from the equation, though. Scrum asks management and customers to work with the Scrum team to create business value. Often, managers are only willing to give up their old bad habits when they experience the increased productivity and flexibility of Scrum. To others, the current situation is so bad they are willing to try anything that makes sense.

In the next section, I discuss how to manage empirically, using Scrum to maximize business value. I show how to measure the work planned for a release, to determine how quickly the work is being completed, and to estimate when the work will be done. More importantly, I show how to adapt to the realities of the work, adjusting costs, functionality, dates, and quality to meet an organization's requirements and maximize business value.

Projects are complex, unpredictable affairs, and management should always expect the unexpected. I'll discuss how to collaborate and make tradeoffs as a project proceeds. I'll show how to manage such questions as, "If I want more functionality in the release, what is the new probable release date given the team's productivity?" and "If I want an earlier release date, what functionality can I exclude given the team's productivity?"

Before we dive into the details of how to empirically manage a project, let's see what the experience feels like. Let's look at a project that lasts months rather than years and can be completed with one team. Let's see what it feels like for a first-time Scrum manager to manage empirically in a classic business environment.

4.2.1   Example of Scrum Management

Say you are the project manager for a rewrite of a system to implement new security and privacy capabilities. You are scheduled to appear before the Executive Committee to present the project and secure adequate funding and quality staff for it. The Executive Committee has never heard of Scrum before and is probably expecting that you have everything planned out on a pert chart. In preparation for the project, you draft a Product Backlog, tentatively select a team, prepare a budget, and identify a probable completion date.

Your **Product Backlog** lists the major pieces of work and requirements for the project. The team will have to identify security and privacy requirements, select appropriate products, open up and implement the products within the system, and test the system to ensure that it meets the security and privacy standards. You've detailed what has to be done and solicited the potential team's opinion in order to get accurate estimates of how much work each item entails. The estimates are the number of days that you think that the team you've selected will take to address and turn each backlog item into an updated system. You've brought in a security consultant from one of the vendors to review and revise your estimates. In short, you feel confident that you know what you're talking about.

The **Scrum Team** that you've selected consists of engineers who are familiar with the system and the best testers that you can find. You've also identified a consultant who knows the security and privacy regulations completely and has implemented several solutions previously. You've spoken with management and with other project managers to get the people on your team freed of other assignments if you get the go-ahead. All of your Product Backlog estimates are based on having this team assigned to the project.

The **project budget** consists of the costs for the team, consultant costs, travel costs, overhead, the cost of some new servers for development and testing, vendor software costs, and the cost of converting space into a Scrum Team room.

The **completion date** has been determined by adding up the work in the Product Backlog and dividing it by the amount of work that the team can accomplish every Sprint. You've assumed that everyone on the team is available eighteen days per month, having assessed everyone's vacation schedules and made some reasonable assumptions about sick time.

It's time to present to the Executive Committee. You discuss the project requirements and show how they are formatted in a prioritized Product Backlog. You discuss that this is a pretty complex project since it implements some not-yet-selected security and privacy software into existing systems. More complexity may occur as your team opens up the code because the code quality and clarity is suspect. A team has been identified with domain knowledge and you've added a consultant with specific security skills. You indicate to the Executive Committee that this project has enough complexity that you will be using a new development process called Scrum. You don't elaborate or make a big deal of Scrum, simply indicating that it will give you and the team the flexibility needed to handle the project's complexity. Scrum will let you and management collaborate monthly to keep on top of things and respond to unexpected problems promptly. You request that the Executive Committee appoint a Steering Committee for this monthly collaboration and for ongoing guidance.

You then present your project plan using a graph (see Figure 4.1, Project Plan). The graph indicates that the project will be complete within eight months. The Y-axis shows the estimated hours of Product Backlog work. The X-axis shows the number of months the project continues. The line shows a regular decrease in the estimated remaining work over the project's lifetime. In the eighth month, no work remains and the project is complete.

You intend to be done in eight months. Nonetheless, you warn the Executive Committee that estimating the duration of a project can be pretty complicated, and you promise to keep them apprised of your progress at each monthly meeting with the Steering Committee. There's some grumbling: some members of the Executive Committee want to know why you can't tell them precisely when you'll be done, just like the other project managers have. You discuss with them the complexity of the technology and requirements. You indicate that there's going to be a lot of learning on this project, that it contains a lot of research as well as development. You indicate that you can't guarantee an exact completion date because of these uncertainties and complexities, but that you will collaborate with the Steering Committee on a monthly basis. You, the team, and they will

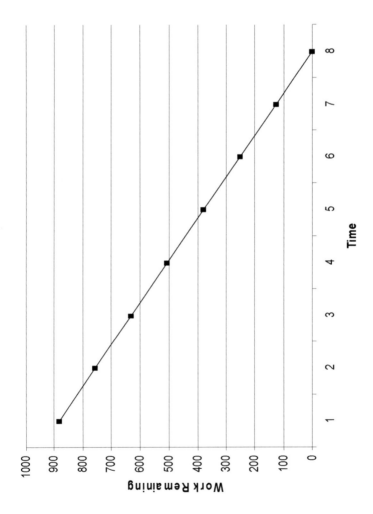

FIGURE 4.1: Project Plan

empirically determine the next best steps every thirty days to ensure that business value is maximized.

During the first Sprint, the team has to spend more time setting up the project environment than anticipated. The servers arrive late, and the development software has to be upgraded to work on the new operating system release. As a result, the team was able to complete less of the Product Backlog than planned. At the Sprint Review, the team demonstrates some initial security capabilities built into an existing business function. The functionality is a little less than the team had hoped to have completed, but it still demonstrates how the security functionality will work. You then review a revised project plan with the Steering Committee (see Figure 4.2, Project Plan with first correction).

This plan shows that the team was unable to complete as much Product Backlog as it had anticipated during the first month. Unless the Steering Committee wants to change the degree of security to be implemented or the scope of functionality to be addressed, the project right now looks like it will be complete approximately two weeks later than anticipated. The project looks like it will have two more weeks of cost. You are collaborating with the Steering Committee about what to do based on what you've found to date.

What you've presented to the Steering Committee is often called a "slip." Slip is a negative word, reflecting that the team didn't know what it was doing. Exactly right! The team was unable to estimate and predict everything that happened during the Sprint. An unexpected thing happened! This unexpected thing caused a two-week "slip." In complex technology projects with emerging requirements, you should expect the unexpected. Scrum provides you with direct, immediate visibility into the slip at least every thirty days. At that time, management and the team can collaborate on what should be done next, given the new reality. Every thirty days corrective action can be taken, rather than waiting for milestones or the end of the project. In this case, the Steering Committee directs you to continue as projected. They want to see what will happen during the next thirty days.

During the second Sprint, the team was able to accomplish more than anticipated. A vendor was selected and its security product was implemented into some of the system. The product simplifies the work that you had anticipated, so the team was able to easily replace and extend the security it built into the system during the last Sprint. The team has worked with you to re-estimate the product backlog. The new project plan that you present to the Steering Committee at the Sprint Review is shown in Figure 4.3, Project Plan with second correction.

Figure 4.3, Project Plan, shows that the team was able to find a solution that reduces the overall work estimated for the project. As a result,

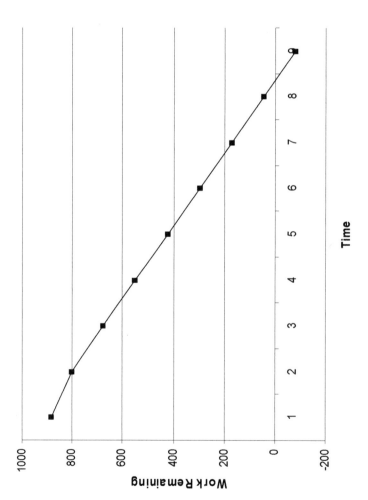

FIGURE 4.2: Project Plan with first correction

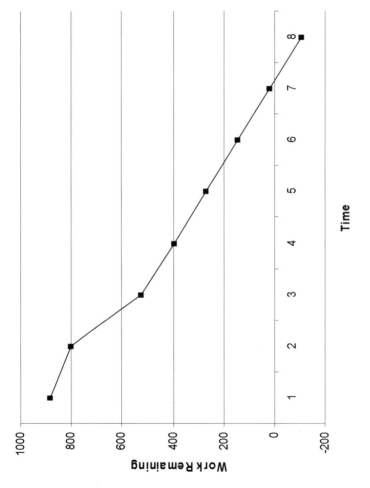

FIGURE 4.3: Project Plan with second correction

you now estimate that the project will be complete three weeks earlier than anticipated[1]. The Steering Committee is now starting to understand empirical management. It is seeing what is really happening every month and making appropriate decisions. The Steering Committee is able to guide the project month-by-month based on results, not promises. Consequently, it is glad that it didn't change anything the prior month.

The members of the Steering Committee were pleased to get to hear from the Scrum team directly and see some of the new product implemented. One Scrum team member demonstrated an attempted security breach and how the new software responded. This led to a discussion about the types of breaches that the project anticipates. The Steering Committee again directs you to proceed, and also asks you where the Daily Scrum meeting is held. They want to look in and see what's happening.

4.3   Empirical Management

Throw out the pert charts, because Scrum requires much less tedious but much more involved management action.

Management that employs Scrum is like a coach at the rugby or soccer game. It does everything possible to help the team play its best. It watches the team, makes substitutions, gets water, shouts advice, and cares passionately about the team and the game. The project is constantly changing. The activities within the project are constantly changing. Management watches while the game evolves and tries to help, but the game is in the team's hands (or feet).

As management watches a Sprint evolve, it is assessing progress and making decisions about how to help the team be more productive and how to help the team cope with what it is encountering. If a team is struggling with technology far more complicated than initially envisioned, management thinks about what would help. Is training helpful? Would a consultant be useful? Should the technology be replaced? Management studies the team during the Sprint. Between Sprints, management works with the team to make adjustments that make the next Sprint better. All of the changes result from direct observation.

Scrum demands the liberal application of common sense. If the date can't be met, reduce the functionality that will be delivered. If the functionality can't be reduced, reduce some of the capabilities within the functionality. Increase the cost by adding another team that Sprints in parallel, or bring in experts. Scrum will put all of the information that is needed to make these decisions at management's fingertips. Management then has to decide how to maximize business value from the project.

---

[1]The security product is so powerful and easy to use that you suspect all the remaining work will be easier than anticipated. However, you want to get another Sprint of experience before changing the estimates.

FIGURE 4.4: Observations

Management is primarily responsible for doing anything possible to increase team productivity and then adapting to the results. Management should live and breathe to help the teams. Nothing is more important. If the team needs meeting rooms, executives can do nothing better than move out of their corner offices to make sure the team keeps charging ahead.

Scrum provides two types of information to management: **first-hand observations** (see Figure 4.4, Observations), and **backlog graphs** charts. Management must actively, intelligently use these to stay on top of the project and make decisions. There is no place for hands-off management with Scrum.

4.3.1   Use Frequent, First-Hand Observations

Scrum provides direct visibility into the progress of the project.

Daily Scrums provide a direct view into each team's progress. Management attends and observes team spirit, each member's participation, team member interaction, work that is being completed, decisions that need to be made, and impediments that need to be removed.

Listen closely at the Daily Scrum to what is being said as well as how it is being said. If a team member is discouraged, find out why. How can he or she rearrange the work or get help to make more progress? If most of the team seems to be floundering, what are they having trouble with?

What expertise can be brought to bear? Meet with the team afterwards and talk through its problems. If you hear conflicting approaches to a design, gather the individuals afterwards and talk through the design. If a team member hasn't been to a Scrum for several days, where is he or she? How can you bring him or her back to work? Is he or she at an unnecessary organizational meeting? Listen closely and see what you can do to help the team. The team will do the best it can do. You monitor what is happening and see how you can help it communicate better, organize better, go around obstacles, and be more productive.

At Sprint Reviews, the Scrum Team demonstrates to management what it has been able to produce. The team demonstrates the real, executable product functionality that it has built. Maybe the team has also developed models, designs, architectures, and use cases. These artifacts are only useful to the degree that they've guided team thinking. What really matters is the product functionality delivered. You can't ship a design. You can ship working code.

During the Sprint Review, the team discusses what happened during the Sprint. What problems did it encounter with the technology? What alternate approaches and designs did it use? What contradictions did it find in the requirements? To what degree was it able to meet the Sprint goal? To what depth is the product functionality implemented? How well tested is the code? How stable of a base does the product increment represent for the future? How well is the team working together? What other expertise could it use?

These questions are fodder for management action. Carefully listening to the team helps you formulate better decisions. How should you change the team composition, if at all? Does the team need to do more technology, infrastructure, environment, or design work in the next Sprint? Does the next Sprint need to deepen already implemented functionality, or start adding new functionality? At the end of the Sprint, you are provided the best available information to make these decisions. You can now effectively help the team prepare for the next Sprint.

4.3.2 Backlog, Assessing Progress and Predicting the Future

Management sets objectives. Management then reports progress towards meeting these objectives. We had planned for this release by the end of the third quarter; will it be ready? Management needs to be able to answer questions about:

Sprint progress – how is the team progressing toward its Sprint goal?

Release progress – when will the release be ready with the quality and functionality desired? Do changes need to be made to the release to get it by a certain date? Do additional resources need to be added to get the release on time with the needed functionality?

Product progress – how is the product filling out compared to what's needed in the marketplace?

First hand observations provide part of the answer to these questions. The work backlog provides the rest of the answer. Work backlog is the amount of work remaining to be done at any point in time. Backlog trends can be derived by plotting estimated work remaining in backlog across time. The backlog trend indicates the team's ability to decrease its backlog. Backlog trends will vary by team and will vary across time. Variables such as team skills, backlog estimate accuracy, and unexpected complexities affect the trend line.

Work backlog and backlog trends can be assessed for a Sprint and for a product release. Less reliably, backlog and trends can be assessed for a product or an entire system, delivered in multiple releases.

Sprint Backlog consists of the tasks that the Scrum Team has devised for a Sprint. These tasks are work to transform the selected Product Backlog into the Sprint goal. They are estimated in hours, usually ranging from four to sixteen hours of work each. At the Sprint Planning meeting, the team constructs this backlog and estimates the amount of time to complete each backlog item. The team might use dependency diagrams to ensure that they've figured out all of the work. As a team member works on a Sprint backlog item, he or she is responsible for updating the estimate of the remaining hours to complete that work. This estimate may go up if the work is more complicated than initially estimated. The estimate may have been too high, so less work is required than anticipated. Regardless, once a task is started, the team members doing the work update this estimate daily until the backlog item is completed and work remaining is zero.

Unanticipated work is often discovered and uncovered by the team as it builds the product increment. The team is responsible for creating new backlog items for this work and estimating the work to complete each of them.

Release Backlog is that subset of Product Backlog that is selected for a release. The Product Backlog list is all work that is known for a product. Starting at the highest priority work, the Product Owner segments this work into probable releases. The first seventy-two Product Backlog items are targeted for a Release 11.2 due in the third quarter of 2001. The seventy-third to one hundred sixtieth Product Backlog items are targeted for a Release 11.3 due in the first quarter of 2002. As the Scrum teams build product during each Sprint, the Product Owner may empirically adjust the Product Backlog planned for each release. If more work is getting done than expected, the Product Owner may opt for an earlier release date, or a release with some of the functionality initially planned for Release 11.3.

Each Product Backlog item has an estimate that was entered by the Product Owner. Release backlog is estimated in days. The Product Owner is responsible for describing the Product Backlog items and working with the team to reach the best possible estimates. The Product Owner revises these estimates when more details regarding each item become available.

Product Backlog consists of all work that can be foreseen for a product. Backlog consists of product features, functionality, infrastructure, architecture, and technology work. The Product Owner estimates the amount of work in days to implement each item. Product backlog that is not included in the next product release tends to be of less interest to management and the Product Owner. This Product Backlog usually is less precisely described and estimated than the backlog for the next release. Predictions based on the estimates for these backlog items tend to be less reliable than release estimates because the Product Backlog contains many lower priority items that would be nice to have but may never be implemented. The owner of the Product Backlog is responsible for keeping these estimates up-to-date as best as possible.

4.4   Managing a Sprint

Managing a Sprint means helping the team to meet its Sprint goal. The team has selected the Product Backlog and established a Sprint goal. You help the team by removing impediments and making decisions. You can also help the team by monitoring its work and progress toward completion. If the team doesn't appear able to complete all of its work, you can help it reassess how it can reduce the work and still meet the Sprint goal. If this is impossible, you can work with it to consider canceling and reformulating the Sprint. As you and the team work together, you will get better at establishing and meeting Sprint goals.

The team constructed the Sprint Backlog and keeps it updated. The Sprint Backlog is all of the work that the team identifies as necessary to meet the Sprint goal. You can help the team track the progress through the Sprint Backlog graph.

To create this graph, determine how much work remains by summing the backlog estimates every day of the Sprint. The amount of work remaining for a Sprint is the sum of the work remaining for all of the Sprint Backlog. Keep track of these sums by day and use them to create a graph that shows the work remaining over time. By drawing a line through the points on the graph, you can identify a team's progress in completing a Sprint's work.

A friend of mine asked, "The estimates are of effort, the mapping is against time. How do you determine duration from effort if the tasks have no preordained sequence?" This question indicates the difficulty shifting from a pert chart-based, time reporting structure to an empirical approach. Duration is not considered in Scrum. Work remaining and date are the only variables of interest, with work remaining managed to reach zero by the end of the Sprint.

Figure 4.5, Perfect Backlog Graph, is an example of a suspiciously perfect Sprint's backlog graph.

Figure 4.5 shows a Sprint finishing with zero work remaining. The work remaining line descends linearly from 1680 hours to zero hours over the thirty day Sprint, declining by 56 hours of work per day. All the tasks were completed according to initial estimate, the team worked regularly the same amount each day with everyone at work, and no new work or shortcuts were uncovered.

If you ever see a Sprint Backlog trend graph like the above, be wary. For a graph like this to reflect reality, the team had to prepare a perfect Sprint Backlog during the Sprint Planning meeting. No additional work was required, and no work had to be removed. The team also updated the Sprint Backlog estimates every day, reducing the estimates on all tasks by 56 hours. The likelihood of this happening approaches zero. Compare the graph to what you've been hearing in the Daily Scrums. No team can ever be this good and this methodical. For instance, this graph shows that the team is reducing the amount of work 56 hours per day, every day. Does this mean that the team works Saturday and Sunday as well as work days? That's what the graph says!

Figure 4.6, More Likely Backlog Graph, is a much more likely backlog chart for a Sprint.

In Figure 4.6, the diamonds represent the sum of estimated work remaining for all Sprint Backlog for each day. A line connecting the diamonds tracks estimated work remaining across a Sprint. As you manage Sprints, you will learn to interpret these graphs. There are general interpretations, and specific patterns that you will find for your teams.

In the Sprint graphed above, what actually happened is described in Table 1, Sprint Signature Description.

The team was in a time-box, a Sprint of thirty days. On day 18, the team had too much functionality to complete by the end of the Sprint. The team met with the Product Owner and Scrum Master to assess if it could still meet the Sprint Goal with some work removed or some functionality implemented with less detail. Some work was removed and the team proceeded to meet the Sprint Goal within thirty days.

Work remaining reporting updates the estimated number of hours required to complete a task. **This should not be confused with time reporting, which is not part of Scrum. There are no mechanisms in Scrum for tracking the amount of time that a team works. Teams are measured by meeting goals, not by how many hours they take to meet the goal. Scrum is result oriented, not process oriented.**

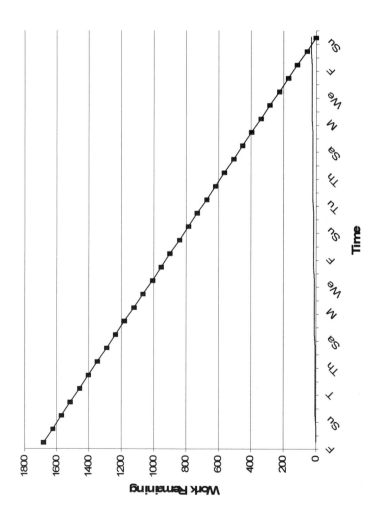

FIGURE 4.5: Perfect Backlog Graph

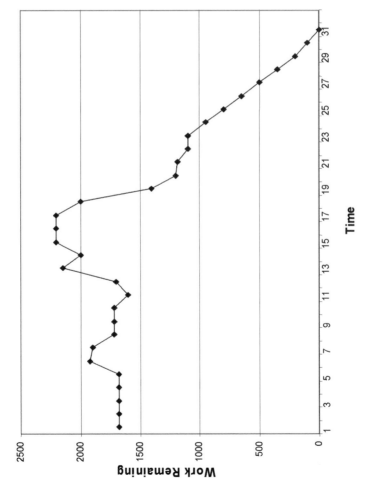

FIGURE 4.6: More Likely Backlog Graph

4.4.1   Sprint Signatures

As a team works together, it develops its own style of creating and maintaining the Sprint Backlog. It also demonstrates unique work patterns; some teams working consistently, some in bursts, some at the end of a Sprint. Some teams seek pressure, while others seek regularity. Across time, the backlog charts of each team develop predictable patterns. They stabilize as the team learns the technology, the business or product domain, and each other. These chart patterns are called Sprint signatures. When you graph how a team works, you see its signature. The signature should be a reflection – another validation – of what you hear in the daily Scum meeting. Once a team settles into a signature, watch for changes. Just like a person changes their signature when stressed, so does a team. Signature changes are another source of information to help manage a team.

For instance, some teams always have Sprint Backlog that keeps going up during the first part of the Sprint, and then descends dramatically. Assess the measurements and determine whether this is because of inadequate Sprint planning, overwork during the last ten days (which usually causes poor quality), or infrequent estimation of work remaining. Let's look at some signatures and interpret what they might mean.

Whenever the estimated hours remain the same from day to day, the team isn't updating its estimates as it works (or, less likely, no one worked). Figure 4.7, Sprint signature, shows this happening. You will see this type of signature from newer Scrum teams. During the first ten days, the team apparently forgot to update the Sprint Backlog with new estimates. On the eleventh day, it was reminded of this responsibility. It updated the estimates, which on the twelfth day reflected 1100 estimated hours of work remaining. The team had similar problems estimating the Sprint Backlog from the 15th to 25th day. Management and the Scrum Master can't use this graph to help them understand what's going on in the Sprint, or what they can do to help. Until the Scrum Master gets the team to update the Sprint Backlog as it works, management will have to rely on observations during the Daily Scrum to get information.

Figure 4.8, Sprint signature for underestimating, is classic for a new Scrum team. The team is learning to work together as well as learning the technology, the development environment, and/or the domain. Its estimating skills aren't that good yet. The team has their Sprint Planning meeting on the first day and estimates 1680 hours of work in the Sprint Backlog. The team then goes home for the weekend. On the first week of work, the team re-estimates Sprint Backlog as it works on it. Each day, the estimated remaining hours increase as the team discovers new work and revises estimates upward for existing work. The team again goes home for the weekend on the 9th and 10th days. During the next week, including the weekend, the team makes a concerted effort and gets a lot of work done.

Period	Event
Day 1	Sprint planning meeting, Sprint Backlog established with a 1680 estimated hours of work.
Days 2-3	Weekend days, no work done and no changes in estimated work remaining.
Days 4-5	The team worked but didn't adjust the estimated work remaining figures on their tasks. The estimated work remaining didn't show a drop because of this neglect.
Days 6-8	The team started adjusting estimated work remaining figures on tasks. On day 6, the estimates showed more work. Then work remaining declined.
Days 9-10	Weekend days, no work done and no changes in estimated work remaining.
Day 11	Some work done by the team and the estimated work remaining declined.
Days 12-15	The team discovered that some more tasks were required and that some of the tasks it was working on would take more time than first estimated. Estimated time remaining jumps to 2150 hours.
Days 16-17	The team is discouraged by all of the work remaining and didn't work during the weekend. No changes in estimated time remaining.
Day 18	The team works more and its remaining work declined. The team then met with the Product Owner and the Scrum Master to determine what tasks could be reduced or removed while still meeting the goals of the Sprint. Some Sprint Backlog was dropped; other estimates were lowered because not as much functionality had to be supported. Overall estimated work remaining reduced to 1400 hours. If all of this work is completed, the team will still meet the Sprint Goal, although with functionality implemented less completely.
Day 19	The team continues work toward the Sprint Goal using new Sprint Backlog. Estimated work remaining declines.
Days 20-30	Team is motivated because it can still meet the Sprint Goal if it works hard. The team works regularly including during the weekends. Estimated work remaining declines to zero as the team meets its Sprint Goal by the 31st day.

TABLE 4.1: Sprint signature description

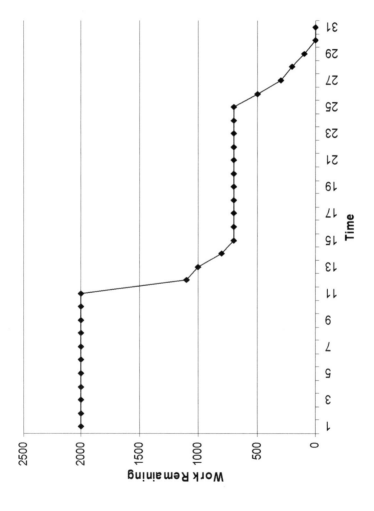

FIGURE 4.7: Sprint signature

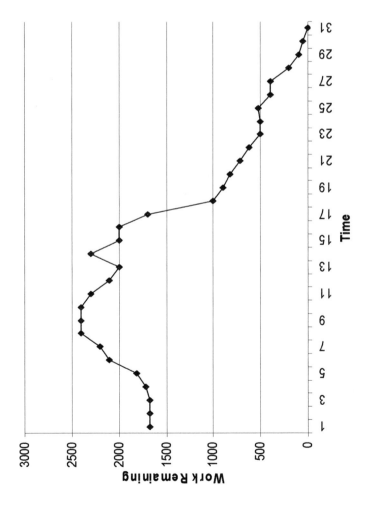

FIGURE 4.8: Sprint signature for underestimating

The estimated remaining work is down to 1700 hours by the end of the 17th day, Sunday. On the 18th day, the team is discouraged that it will not get all of the work done by the end of the Sprint, so the team meets with the Scrum Master, project manager, and Product Owner. Collectively, they figure out how they can lessen the depth of the functionality and still meet the Sprint goals. They remove about 700 hours of work from the Sprint Backlog, reducing the estimated remaining work to 1000 hours. The team then works steadily to complete the Sprint. This team will be more careful in its estimates for the next Sprint, which should be easier since it is more experienced in the domain, technology, and collaboration using Scrum.

In Figure 4.9, Sprint signature for overestimating, a Scrum team makes its initial estimate and begins working after the weekend. At the end of every day, the work remaining is far less than it had expected. The team was unsure of the technology and the domain. As a result, it consistently overestimated the work. By the 11th day, the Scrum team realizes that it is going to be done well before the end of the Sprint on the 30th day. On the 12th, the team meets with the Scrum Master, project manager and Product Owner. The team could complete the product increment and close out the Sprint early (the trend line indicates zero work remaining on about the 17th day). Or, the team can deepen the degree to which it is implementing the functionality, building in more design and architecture. The team has its teeth into the work and recommends that it be allowed to take on more work. Everyone concurs. The team continues and successfully closes out the Sprint with more and deeper functionality than it had initially estimated.

As I've monitored backlog trends, I've found that teams tend to go from one signature type to another as they learn the domain, tools, Scrum, and as they self-organize. After three or four Sprints, however, a team tends to stabilize around a signature that characterizes its collective personality: risk takers, cautious, methodical, or over timers. Once the team starts updating the work remaining figures regularly, I've found that the signature reflects what I see daily in the Scrum meetings.

4.5   Managing a Release

The product is released to meet customer or marketplace obligations. The release balances functionality, cost, and quality requirements against date commitments.

I first presented Scrum at OOPSLA'96. The presentation was followed by some heated discussion. I had emphasized the empirical nature of Scrum, where management trades off cost, functionality, time, and quality as work progresses and more is known about requirements and the technology. The most heated criticism was, "I have to tell my management exactly what it's going to get, what the budget is, and when I'll deliver.

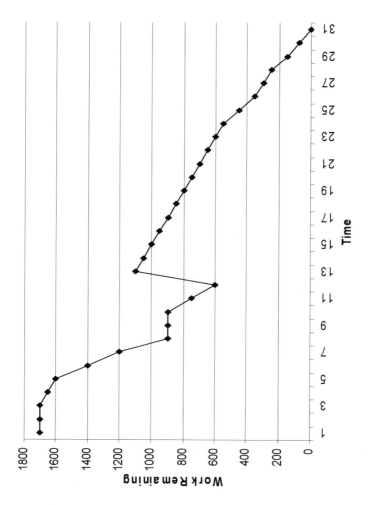

FIGURE 4.9: Sprint signature for overestimating

My management expects that from me." Another attendee was the product manager at a large software company. He had to annually present the release plan to the board, and he didn't want to tell them that cost, functionality, time and quality would have to be varied empirically as the release was worked on. He said, "My board would fire me if I presented that to them."

Scrum provides an alternate way to work with the management and board of directors. For example, Jeff Sutherland, VP of Engineering, went to the President of Easel Corporation, and asked him, "Have you ever seen a development team meet a traditional project plan." He said, "No." Jeff said, "I think the only thing you can trust is working software that the team can demo. If you give the team complete freedom for 30 day Sprints, at the end of the Sprint you will see exactly where the product is, for better or worse." He said, "Fine, for the first time I will know where product development really stands and can make the appropriate decisions. I'm willing to take the risk of giving the team autonomy for defined periods."

These comments reflect a dilemma in the software industry. We systems professionals know that tradeoffs have to be made, that everything can't be known in advance. Our management wants predictability. We usually wind up telling our management what they want to hear. Is that so bad? Management doesn't know, and it pretty much gets what we said, unless a real catastrophe occurs. What we lose is our management's participation, knowledge, guidance, and wisdom. If management understood that we were making tradeoffs, it could participate and collaborate. There would be no surprises. By telling management that we can deliver exactly what we say, we're setting management up for the big surprise.

4.5.1 Manage Cost, Date, Quality and Functionality

The customer is paying for the product. The product isn't a fixed entity. It's a tradeoff between the money the customer wants to spend, the business value that they want to get for the money, the date on which they feel they need the product, and the expected quality. Anyone who has had a house built for them knows this type of negotiation. They know that the negotiation doesn't just happen at the start of the job, it happens throughout the job. Building software is a lot more unpredictable than building a house.

Management's job is to manage the four variables of cost, date, functionality, and quality as development proceeds. Management helps the customer tradeoff one variable against another, while still meeting their objectives. Sometimes management and the team can deliver on all four variables. More often, management has to intelligently and openly negotiate and make tradeoffs between the four variables with the customers.

While discussing the four variables with customers, don't hide anything. I've seen products promised for a date when the project manager already knew he or she would have to deliver shallower functionality or provide a product that wasn't stable. But the project manager didn't want to disappoint the customer, so he or she agreed to the date without disclosing the reduced functionality and quality. Excruciating honesty, sharing what we know and believe, is best. Then we can work closely with the customer during development based on what's really happening, not spend time trying to cover up. **Establishing an open, honest relationship with the customer is the most important aspect of Scrum; Scrum makes everything visible; it's real hard to cover up incorrect expectations that you established with the customer.**

4.5.2   Basis for Tradeoffs

The product backlog graph is the quantitative tool for making tradeoffs between cost, time, functionality and quality for a release. This graph tracks the estimated days of work remaining through a release. Each product backlog item contains its amount of estimated work remaining. The Product Owner updates these values weekly. The graph uses the y-axis for the estimated work remaining, and the x-axis for the project or release time scale. Plot the sum of estimated days remaining on that date. Keep track of these plots across time. Even though you might think that backlog should always go down, new work is always being discovered as the product is being built. Expect the backlog to go up and down.

A release that is going just the way you expected, with a release in week 20, is shown in Figure 4.10, Excellent Release Control.

There is too much complexity and too many variables in even the simplest project for Figure 4.10 to ever occur. Figure 4.10 implies that the Product Owner was able to predict everything the product would require prior to the project beginning. No additional functionality was added during the release, or if functionality was added an exact amount of other functionality was removed. The graph also implies that the Sprint team was able to regularly and systematically proceed with development on this system without any surprises or unexpected complexities.

More likely you will graph a backlog chart over the course of a project that looks like Figure 4.11, Release with reduced functionality.

The Product Owner initially estimated 5400 hours of work for the system to be completed and released on the 20th month. Two Scrum Teams were established and assigned to the project. This graph looks like the Product Owner started getting worried about the seventh month. The Product Backlog was not being reduced quickly enough for the release to occur on the 20th month. Perhaps coordinating the number of Scrum teams was harder than anticipated. Perhaps the domain was hard for the

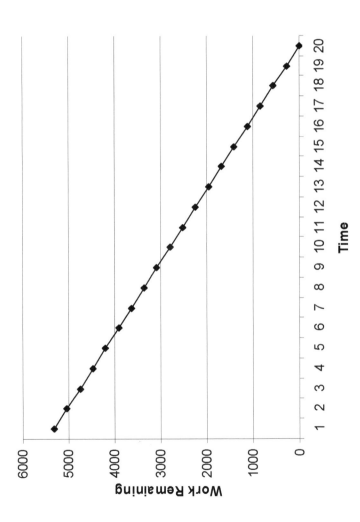

FIGURE 4.10: Excellent Release Control

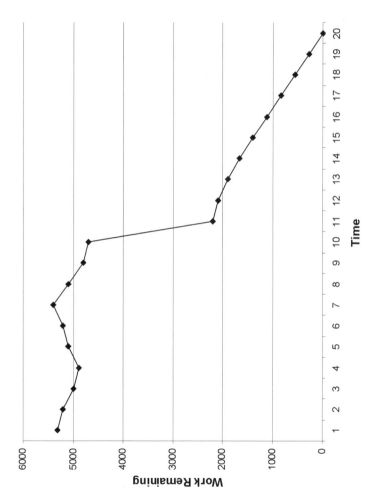

FIGURE 4.11: Release with reduced functionality

developers to understand, the technology was difficult to get to work, or the functionality was underestimated. The backlog work was not decreasing on a slope that would meet the release date during the 20th month. To determine the work slope, or trend, draw a line representing average slope over a period of time. Project it to determine when no work is likely to be left. In Figure 4.11, the Product Owner and users needed the release by the 20th month. When they drew trend lines during months 8 and 9, their suspicion that there was too much work were confirmed. They met with the team and reassessed what functionality could be delivered to meet release objectives by the 20th month. As a result of the meeting, a number of functions were dropped from this release and others made shallower. Remaining Product Backlog dropped from 4800 to 2200 days. The project proceeded and the teams were able to meet the release date with the new functionality.

On some projects, management is able to increase the costs without changing the release date or functionality. One way to increase costs is to add teams to the project. The multiple teams work together in parallel on the same Product Backlog.

In Figure 4.12, Release with second team added, the Product Owner and management monitored the work trend for the first five months. They assessed that they were not going to meet the scheduled release date unless they changed something. They were proactive, and created and added a second team to the project. Since members of the second team were already familiar with the domain and technology, the second team was immediately productive. The result of adding the second team was more work done per month than initially planned. This was the selected alternative when more work than originally expected was discovered.

Figure 4.13, Release date slipped, shows another project where the Product Owner and management again assessed that the backlog wasn't dropping as quickly as had been expected. However, the product wasn't top priority, so they chose to let the release date slip. They plotted the trend line around the ninth month (when the team had stabilized) and projected a four-week slip. The customer agreed to the slip and the release date was changed.

Adjusting cost, time, quality, and functionality may have to be done more than once during a release if trends are not going as expected.

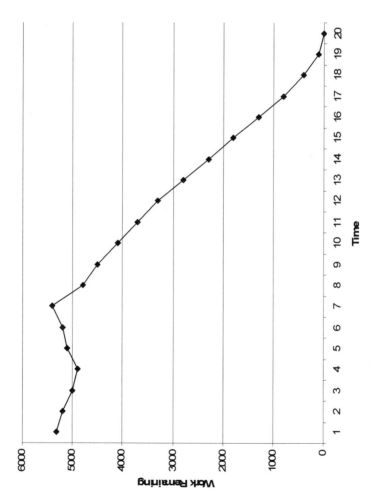

FIGURE 4.12: Release with second team added

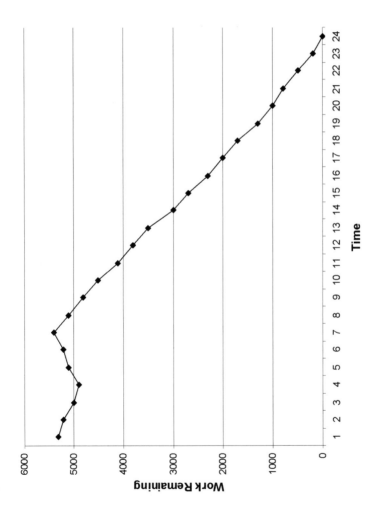

FIGURE 4.13: Release date slipped

CHAPTER 5

Why Scrum?

Scrum is built on an empirical process control model which is radically different from the defined model that most processes and methodologies use. This section provides the framework for Scrum. ——

Why Scrum? presents the heart and soul of Scrum. Scrum is based on completely different assumptions and foundations than the current systems development methodologies. Scrum is based on an empirical process control model rather than the traditional defined process control model. This section shows why the empirical model is appropriate for systems development projects and the current defined model is not. Once you understand Scrum's empirical roots, you will be able to understand why Scrum looks and feels different, why it works, and how it is a true paradigm shift.

I introduced Individual, Inc. in Chapter 1, Introduction. The PNP team was unsuccessfully trying to develop a product in a very noisy, conflicting, complicated, frustrating environment. Everyone had the top priority feature to be built and needed it to be built now. Scrum allowed the team to cut through the noise and complexity. The team was able to focus for thirty day Sprints and build the product one increment at a time. In this section, I'll discuss the noise that teams such as the PNP team tried to work within. I'll discuss how this is common to all systems development projects, and I'll describe how Scrum solves the problem.

5.1 Noisy Life

In this context, the term "noise" refers not to a sonic phenomenon, but to the unpredictable, irregular, nonlinear parts of system development. Noise is the unanticipated part of any activity that disrupts the habits of a lifetime. Noise is what causes that unexpected glitch that requires my full attention. Noise is everywhere. Noise agitates the signals on my mobile phone so I have trouble understanding the other person. Noise distorts electricity traveling across power lines and causes my PC to shut down. My kids make noise and keep me from hearing my wife. When noise-to-signal ratio is too high, the sound of what I want to hear is obscured by the sound of what I don't want to hear, or the noise.

Even a really solid number like "0.00" starts displaying its noise when I look out past those first two decimal points. I can take a measure of the kitchen counter: it's 12 feet 4 inches. But I'd better be more precise, like 12.38 feet, because I need a fit without any gaps. But my measurement has noise from rounding. The space for the counter is really 12.374452 feet. And when I cut the counter, there will be more noise from the width of the saw blade. Noise, imprecision, uncertainty, unpredictability are everywhere.

Complexity theory can be seen as a whole new way of understanding the causes and patterns of noise. Noise, it turns out, is an inherent part of everything. It has always existed; rounding is a mechanism for ignoring it. Perfect, precise numbers are illusions that allow me to believe in predictability. If I assume that the length of my kitchen counter is 12.38 inches, and all the other noise being made is compatible with the noise of this length; I'll get away with glossing over the noise behind this number, and the counter will fit.

A great example of interference can be found on the American Psychological Association web site. You can find it on the cover of this book as Figure 5.1, Color Test. Don't read the words in the Color Test. Just say what color they're printed in out loud, as fast as you can. You're in for a surprise!

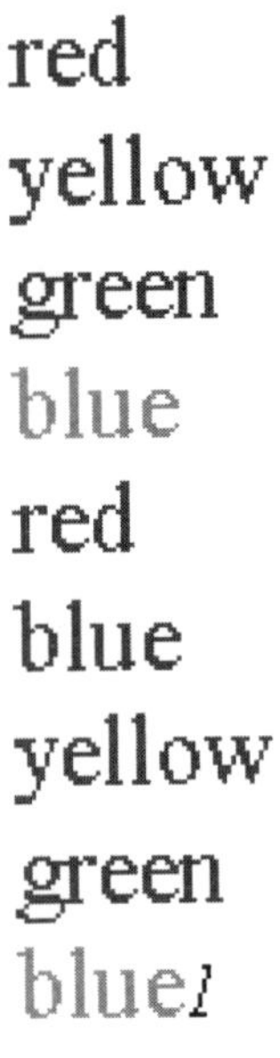

red

yellow

green

blue

red

blue

yellow

green

blue*l*

FIGURE 5.1: Color Test

If you're like most people, your first impulse was to read "red, yellow, green...," rather than the colors that the words are printed in – 'blue, green, red...' Noise has just interfered with your perception. When you look at one of the words, you see both its *color* and its *meaning*. If those two pieces of evidence are in conflict, you have to make a choice. Because experience has taught you that the meaning of a word is more important than the color of the word, interference occurs when you try to pay attention *only* to the ink color. The interference effect suggests you're not always in complete control of what you pay attention to. Noise interferes.

All physical processes exhibit some degree of noisy, or unpredictable, behavior. I've learned to selectively filter out noise, paying less attention to the predictable and more attention to the unpredictable. This focus on what really requires my immediate attention allows me to function in a very chaotic world.

5.2   Noise in Systems Development Projects

Systems development projects used to have much less noise. One of the first applications I ever built was an order entry system for Sears Roebuck & Company. Sears was automating the existing order entry process to improve efficiency. Since it wasn't reinventing the process, all I had to do was inspect what was already being done manually. I used assembler language to code the target application, which became one program in a job stream that ran daily on IBM System 360 computers. The IBM hardware, MVT operating system, assembler, and job control had been around for two years when I first started using them. When I had questions, I could turn to anyone in the department for answers. IBM manuals describing how the technologies worked were everywhere. There was very little noise in this systems development project. Almost everything was known and understood; I was the only unpredictable thing since I was a junior programmer.

During the 1980's and 1990's, systems started to be used for competitive advantage. Systems implemented wholly new processes or caused existing processes to be discerned in new ways (for instance, Internet banking). One technology followed another in rapid succession, many replacing their predecessors before they were thoroughly understood. For example, although many client server systems were deployed, the version control problems of sustaining multiple applications and dll's on multiple platforms and operating system releases were never mastered. Instead, the industry shifted to the thin-client, n-tier model, simplifying one problem while introducing a whole new set of challenges. I was recently at a board of directors meeting of a systems product company. One board member lamented, "Whatever happened to technology plateaus?"

Noise in systems development is a function of the three vectors of requirements, technology and people. If the product requirements are well known and the engineers know exactly how to build the requirements into a product using the selected technology, there is very little noise or unpredictability. The work proceeds linearly, in a straight line, with no false starts, little rework, and few mistakes. Noise increases as requirements are less understood and agreed upon. Noise increases as the ability to employ the selected technology is more uncertain. Development projects that build new processes on new technologies are very noisy and unpredictable.

The rollout of products based on new technology and functionality has accelerated. Certainty and reliability have been traded for competitive advantage. If too much time is spent thinking through requirements, competition gets to the market first. Products are both built into new technologies, and new technologies are used to build products! Building software for handheld operating systems that synchronize with object databases across wireless networks introduces enough new development and implementation platforms to make a sane person stagger.

For example, in the mid-1990's X-ray, CT Scan, and MRI pictures began to be generated in digital format rather than film. Healthcare institutions envisioned serving up these images on demand to radiologists as part of a workflow system. By applying Internet and Web technology, worldwide teams of radiologists could collaborate in real time. If the healthcare software company that I was working with could build systems to provide this functionality first, it would gain a significant competitive advantage.

One requirement was to serve up the digital image from a RAID 1 disk archive to the radiologist's workstation. This seemed pretty straight forward, and I expected a relatively predictable set of work for the team. As the team dug into the work, a whole raft of unexpected complications occurred. The radiologist's display could be either a high-resolution workstation or a regular computer monitor. The available bandwidth might be very high, or only 56kb. The radiologist needed to be able to rotate and zoom the images, and compare different images in a sequence so buffering might be required. A type of compression could be used to transmit images, but only if the degree of loss was within acceptable limits, such limits not having been yet formally defined. The FDA hadn't yet decided whether the display of these images was a medical device; if it were, a whole new set of testing and implementation requirements applied.

The development team was coping with new technologies, changing requirements, and a variety of implementation alternatives. It had to decide how to meld the technology and requirements into a demonstrable product in six months. Every time it dug into a piece of technology, new complications and difficulties arose. Every time it tried to finalize a require-

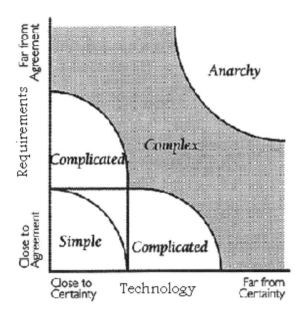

FIGURE 5.2: Project complexity. (From: <u>Strategic Management and Organisational Dynamics The Challenge of Complexity</u>—3rd Edition by Ralph D. Stacey, <u>Financial Times</u>, Harlow, England)

ment, new alternatives would be proposed. Both the requirements and the technology were unpredictable and so noisy that the team had trouble settling down and focusing on any one solution. Changing technology and requirements were making it hard for the team to focus and proceed.

Figure 5.2, Project complexity, is a graph that can be used to determine the noise level in any systems development project. On the y-axis, I plot the degree of uncertainty that exists about the project requirements. If project requirements are thoroughly understood, then noise will probably be low. If the requirements are only partially understood or are still emergent, then the noise level is likely to be high. On the x-axis, I plot the likelihood that the selected technologies will be able to help accomplish the project's goals. This is known as "technology certainty." If all of the technology is familiar and can be reliably implemented to achieve project goals, then the noise level is low. If the technology is emerging and has not been fully tested, the noise is high. For example, mainframe, batch system development is associated with simple, low noise projects. N-tier, web-deployed wireless technologies are associated with complicated or complex, high noise projects.

I haven't included the third vector, people, into the equation. When people are factored in, nothing is simple. The complexity of individuals and individuals working in teams raises the noise level for all projects. By factoring in people, I automatically increase a project's complexity category by one level. For instance, a project with certain technology and agreed upon functionality is now categorized as complicated rather than simple because of the people vector.

A project's noise category indicates what approach should be employed for managing the project and building the system. There are two approaches in process control theory to control and manage processes. The first model is called the **defined** process control model. When processes are simple with unobtrusive noise, I can write a definition of how they work and use this definition to repeat the processes over and over, each time generating the same results. These are called **defined processes**. Management and control is exercised by defining the processes so well that everything is known and predictable.

Management and control arise from the predictability of defined processes. Since the processes are defined, they can be grouped together and be expected to continue to operate predictably and repeatably. In such clusters of processes, the defined process control model can be used for modeling and controlling such simple systems as traffic lights, or such involved but defined systems as manufacturing pharmaceuticals. **Almost no systems development project is so simple, has so little noise, for the defined process control model to be appropriate by itself.**

If the process cannot be described in enough detail to be repeated, if there is so much complexity that any attempt to model the process results in different outcomes, the process is called a **complex process**. If I operate a complex process two times in a row, the results are more likely to be different than the same. The activities in the process are so noisy that their output cannot be predicted with an adequate degree of reliability. **Empirical** process control models are used to manage and control complex processes. Management and control is exercised through frequent inspection and adaptive response.

5.3   Why Current System Development Methodologies Don't Work

Most current system development methodologies claim that they can be used for a wide range of projects and system development efforts. The defined control and management model is employed by these methodologies. These methodologies contain a knowledge base of development processes and techniques. Every process and technique in the knowledge base is defined as though it were simple and repeatable. The knowledge base is threaded together by dependencies into defined project templates. Each template can be applied to a specific type of project, such as interface development, online development, and web development using object-oriented techniques. Since the processes and the relationships between them are defined, the companies purveying the methodologies claim that the templates can be used repeatedly for that type of project.

For the defined control mechanisms to work, these methodologies must define each process with enough accuracy that the resultant noise does not interfere with its repeatability, or the predictability of the outcome. I can watch engineers define a class numerous times and write down a definition of what I saw happening. This process definition is only useful if it can be repeated over and over to generate solid class descriptions. If my observations are general or loose because many variations are employed to derive a class, the process definition is useless. The process definition will be so weakly defined that, when it is employed, it does not generate repeatable results. When an activity is so complex or complicated that a different definition is required each time it is executed, the activity cannot be abstracted into a process definition.

All current systems development methodologies are based on partial and weak definitions of development activities. Methodologies often contain thousands of process definitions. I've evaluated process definitions in many major commercial methodologies. After lengthy inspection and analysis, I couldn't find a single process that was defined in enough detail to ensure repeatable outputs. For example, a process from one methodology described the resources to complete the process: 3.5 designers will complete a process within 16 hours if there are 4 classes. Classes to what level of functionality, with what interfaces, defined and built with what tools? What level of designers are these, with what skills in OO, and how do they feel that day? Without this level of definition, the process simply is not repeatable or predictable.

If I observe a class of activities that are simple and of relatively low noise, I can abstract them into a model that defines their behavior. This model defines the process operation in enough detail that I can then use it to guide and control future similar activities. Because I know what is going to happen, I can create a detailed description of it. Because noise is low, the project details can be used repeatedly with minimal disruption. The outcome of the activity is predictable.

Newton's laws are such an abstraction. Numerous experiments were run to measure the relationships between physical objects and movement. Relationships were detected and turned into formulae, or laws. Mathematically, a corollary to Newton's second law of motion can be expressed by the following formula: $a = F/m$ where a = acceleration, F = force, and m = mass. This formula is a defined process model that describes the relationships between acceleration and mass when a force is applied. This defined model has been abstracted from many observations, and is now described as a law. Since the definition is repeatable, control is exercised through applying the definition faithfully. The noise in the relationships between acceleration, force, and mass is not intrusive and can usually be ignored. For most cases, this formula can be used to calculate acceptably accurate results for any of the variables.

For a systems development process description to be defined adequately to be used in a defined process control methodology, it would have to take into account at least the following:

A detailed, complete description of all inputs, including their content, precision, and media.

An equally detailed, complete description of all outputs.

A description of the processes necessary to complete the transformation from inputs to outputs, with reference to the specific tools and techniques used.

A detailed description of the skills, training, and capabilities of the people who would perform this transformation.

A description of what a "work hour" constitutes.

Let's consider what might be meant by the term "work hour." Is this an hour of work from a well-trained, well-educated, well-mentored, fully conscious, no personal problems, working in the morning after a cup of coffee engineer? Or is it an hour of work from someone else? The consistent application of the term "work hour" requires consistent productivity from each worker during every hour.

The control process for defined processes is the pert chart. For a pert chart to work, work hours must be consistently estimated and measured. Otherwise, every process has noise and the cumulative noise and inaccuracy sinks the whole project plan.

Discrepancies, incompleteness, and slippage accumulate as the project based on a network of interdependent, partially defined processes proceeds. As one task is completed and the results of the task are used to commence the next task, whatever noise occurred during the first task is carried on to the second task, which in turn generates its own noise. The first task is the "90% complete" project. 90% of the work estimated in the task is done, but only 30% of the product is done. The situation gets worse in the second task, and in other tasks down the line.

The process below could be from any commercial systems development methodology:

"*Optimize the Logical DataBase*. *Evaluate entity attributes, volume information, and security requirements to determine where record types should be split or combined. Prepare an entity to record/segment/table type cross-reference, distinguishing between existing databases which are to be shared and new databases which are to be created. When an entity is mapped to more than one record, include an attribute to field mapping.*"

I know from experience that, given the same inputs, no two people will produce the same outputs from this process. Even the same person won't generate the same outputs two times in a row. Why? The process definition is too loose, too vague. The vagueness is of necessity. If I watch and describe four thousand and seventeen people try to optimize a logical database, I will wind up with four thousand and seventeen different descriptions. The only way that I can abstract the descriptions into a model, or process description, like that above is to drop detail. Unfortunately, the detail that is dropped is the detail that is required for repeatability. The looseness and lack of detail in the above process abstraction is easily seen when I try to employ it to optimize my particular data model. The following areas (as a minimum) are too loosely defined for repeatability:

How do I evaluate the entity attributes?

What are the properties of the entity attributes?

Are the entity attributes part of a model? On what sort of tool?

How do I open the file?

What are the rules for splitting or combining?

How is a project supposed to be constructed from a methodology that relies on the defined process control model? A project manager starts a project by selecting and customizing the appropriate project template. The template consists of those processes appropriate for the type of work that is planned. He or she then estimates the work and assigns the tasks to team members. The resultant project plan shows all the work to be done, who is to do each piece of work, what the dependencies are, and the process instructions for converting the inputs to the outputs. Figure 5.3, Pert chart, shows a pert chart that is the product of such efforts.

Having a project plan like this gives the project manager a reassuring sense of being in control. He or she feels that they understand the work that is required to successfully complete the project. Everyone will do what the methodology and project plan says, and the project will be successfully completed. However, the task details on which the plan is based are incomplete because the underlying processes are complex and noisy. Because the definitions are incomplete, the dependencies are inaccurate. These estimates render the assignments and estimates useless.

A Pert chart is constructed using dependencies. When one or more tasks complete, dependent tasks can be started. The degree of noise in each systems development process makes it very hard to define "complete." The boundaries between the various assigned tasks start to become increasingly noisy until the project plan itself is chaotic. For a defined process to work, the noise that occurs each time a task is executed has to be within acceptable bounds; otherwise the operation of dependent processes is adversely affected. In a large network of dependent processes, the amount of noise rises exponentially as it is perpetrated throughout the network.

I single out pert charts as a significant problem. Pert charts are useful to think through and model a sequence of activities. They are disastrous when used to control a complex project. Pert chart-based project control

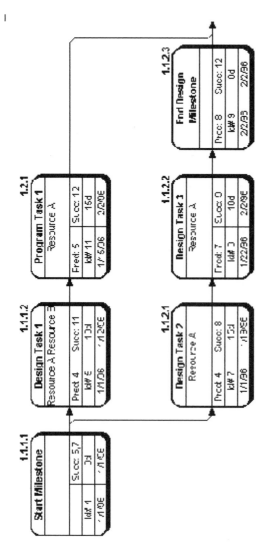

FIGURE 5.3: Pert chart

has led to systems development schizophrenia. Management thinks the pert chart models work in complex projects. It asks for progress reports based on the pert chart model. But the real work has very little to do with the pert chart. The work doesn't follow the pert chart. The work goes its own way, rapidly evolving after the first task to adapt to the complex problems at hand.

Developing complex software feels like running an obstacle course. Agility, flexibility and adaptability are required to succeed. Imagine a real obstacle course located at an Army training center. A team is asked to navigate the obstacle course as quickly as possible using a defined process. To prepare them, management has provided them with:

A map. The map isn't of this obstacle course, since no one has navigated it before. The map is of obstacle courses that others have run in the past.

A book containing descriptions of the various obstacles that have been found in other courses. Detailed instructions about how to approach, study, and navigate each obstacle course are provided.

A list of team assignments and expected progress. Management has painstakingly combined the map and book into what the team might find on this obstacle course. It has made team assignments. The assignments give team members specific duties at each obstacle. Each assignment tells them exactly what to do and allocates a fixed amount of time to complete it.

The team starts the obstacle course. Each member carries the map, the book, and the list of assignments. They study them as they go forward, doing exactly what the assignments say. The map is only a general and not an accurate description of the course, so reaching the first obstacle takes the team more time than was assigned. When it reaches the first obstacle, the obstacle only has vague similarities to the description in the book. Team members try to complete their individual assignments, but they are so inappropriate that several team members sustain injuries. The team has to devise an entirely new approach to get through the obstacle. Then each member has to fill out a time reporting form, including justification of why their the assignment took more time than expected to go over the obstacle!

Guilt entered the field of systems development when managers started using defined process control models to control and manage complex development projects. Managers lost control of the projects and were unable to predict the results of projects. The heavyweight methodologies provided management with plans that included time and cost estimates. The project manager used these estimates to contract functionality, time, quality, and costs with the customer. When the customer found that something they expected was not included, that quality was low, that dates slipped, they were furious. They had trusted the project manager's plans and estimates, but the project manager didn't deliver.

The project manager's management licensed the heavyweight methodology from a reputable vendor. The vendor told the project manager to follow the instructions in the methodology to plan and get reliable, predictable results. The methodology was well known, so it must work! But it didn't work!! The manager thinks,

"I did what the methodology told me to do. The developers must not have done what the methodology told them to do. Maybe they didn't report their progress accurately. Maybe they didn't follow the methodology's directions. They had failed to successfully complete well-described processes that a methodology vendor had told me would lead to predictable results. Those developers are to blame!!"

Guilt arose, and with guilt came apathy. Workers who do their best, but consistently fail to live up to their own expectations, eventually stop trying to do their best. It never seems to be good enough or appreciated.

The traditional, defined software development process is broken. Assuming that most projects have a high degree of predictability, it doesn't adequately detect the noise within complex projects or facilitate empirical responses to assess and correctly respond to the noise. Since the noise is unnoticed and ignored, the results are unpredictable. This incorrect formulation has led to innumerable cancelled projects, many wasted efforts to "get it right", and an overall failure to successfully manage software development. More significantly, many marketplace opportunities have been missed and vast sums of capital have been wasted. Unnecessary human suffering and stress have been borne.

5.4   Why Scrum Works

I said earlier that Scrum was simple and straightforward. There are no complicated process descriptions and there are no abstractions. Scrum starts with the tenet that very few activities in system development projects are identical and will generate identical output. Scrum expects every process to be unexpected.

When activities are so complicated and complex that they can't be defined in advance and aren't repeatable, they require the **empirical** process control model. Scrum employs the empirical process control model. Scrum regularly inspects activities to see what is occurring and empirically adapts activities to produce desired and predictable outcomes.

Chemical companies have advanced polymer plants that require empirical controls. Some chemical processes haven't been defined well enough for the plant to operate safely and repeatably using a defined process control model. Noise has rendered statistical controls ineffective. Frequent inspections and verification are required to successfully produce a batch. As chemical processes become better understood and the technology improves, the plants become more automated. However, assuming predictability too soon is the recipe for an industrial catastrophe.

The heart of Scrum is assessing the condition of activities and empirically determining what to do next. This determination arises from the experience, training, and common sense. Once a process is started, it is frequently inspected, assessed, and adjusted. The people inspecting the process expect the unexpected, monitor for it, and adapt as needed.

Empirical process control models are elegantly simple. They employ feedback mechanisms to monitor and adapt to the unexpected, providing regularity and predictability. The actors in a Scrum team empirically devise and execute the best processes possible based on their skills, experience, and the situation in which they find themselves. Figure 5.4, Empirical Management Model, depicts the empirical process control feedback loop used by Scrum.

"I" is input, or the requirements, technology - the team that will build a product increment from the requirements and technology.

"Process" is a thirty day iteration called a Sprint.

"C" is the control unit that monitors Scrum progress at Daily Scrum meetings and at the end of each Sprint.

"O" is the incremental product built during each iteration. [Peitgen][1]

During a Sprint, a team empirically determines how to build a product increment (Output) given the requirements and the technology available to them (Input). The team draws on its collective skills to accomplish its common goals. Teammates advise and assist each other, and together the team hunts down whatever resources it might need. The team is left alone to self-organize and forge a product from the requirements and the technology that it has been given.

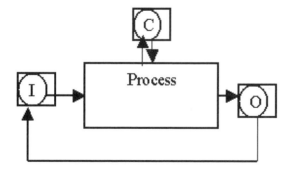

FIGURE 5.4: Empirical Management Model

---

[1] New development projects build the first increment from scratch.

The Scrum process controls complex activities. Ongoing inspections provide the information necessary to empirically determine what to do next. Control, or "C", is implemented through daily status meetings, Daily Scrums. During the Daily Scrums, management and the team inspect and measure the process to see if the progress and results are acceptable. If they are in fact acceptable, nothing happens until the next inspection. If they are not acceptable, there is still time to restore the process to acceptable performance levels.

At the end of each Sprint, there is another control. This control is called the Sprint Review. Sprint output is inspected. What the team has actually built is evaluated. Management, customers and the team inspect the product, reviewing an actual demonstration of working, executable product increment. People have less trouble making decisions when they can see their options right in front of them, so the product is demonstrated on a computer. Management, customers, and the team then decide what to do next; they adapt to what they have seen. The team may be given more training, the team may be recomposed, or more tools may be brought in. Anything that affects the ability of the team to build the next product increment can be changed.

Some of my customers have assigned process engineers to Scrum projects. They wanted to leverage the project experience by recording, abstracting, and formalizing the work. They intended to revert to the defined process control model and pert charts once they figured out what Scrum was about. The process engineers watched, interviewed, and recorded the work. When they went to add the work definitions to the organization's methodology, each project had to become a new, unique template. Every new project either addressed a new business domain or utilized a new set of technology. These customers concluded that the activities recorded were so complex that they couldn't be defined or abstracted. Each project was unique. Scrum is a harness on complex processes, a constraint on complexity.

As an alternative, these customers turned to knowledge management solutions to build a repository of organizational experience about building systems. They put the processes from their licensed defined methodologies in the knowledge base. They added their unique processes for version control, builds, testing, password management, requisitioning material, and other processes used to run a systems development project. The knowledge repository became the institutional expert, used when the team needed to know how to do something. The knowledge repository was not used to plan and drive work; instead, it was used as a reference for how to do work. The knowledge repository evolved as new knowledge was captured and new technologies were brought in.

There is nothing wrong with such abstracted process knowledge as long as it is recognized as incomplete and only appropriate for guidance. It cannot be expected to produce repeatability. Patterns represent just such knowledge, providing a framework within which to address problems [ScrumPattern]. Solid engineering teams draw on patterns, techniques, and specific technology knowledge to solve problems. Scrum teaches teams to rely on their wits, training, teammates, and fellow engineers.

5.5   Case Studies

In the following examples, the empirical process control model was implemented because the underlying activity could not be defined adequately enough to be repeatable. The underlying activity was complex.

The first example shows what happens when I think I can pick my daughter up from college without checking things out. She calls me on her cell phone when she's ready and tells me where to come. The process flow used to be: (1) receive call for a ride, (2) drive to location, and (3) pick up daughter. The reception on her cell phone isn't always great. There have been times when I thought that I heard her say to pick her up at her dorm, but she really said to pick her up someplace else. As a result of the noise in this communication, I drive to the wrong place. I've put in empirical controls to try to reduce the noise. This process is now: (1) receive call for a ride, (2) try to get her to repeat location if noise occurs, (3) ask wife and other daughter if this sounds like the right place to go, (4) drive there, (5) wait for a short time to see if she shows up, (6) if she doesn't show up, call home to see if she's called, (7) go to where she really is, and (8) pick her up. Since the process is noisy, I've had to add frequent monitoring and empirically adapt to the observations. Because the cell phone technology is uncertain and the location requirements change unpredictably, employing the empirical model gives me the level of inspection and control that ensures I arrive at the right place most of the time.

The second example happened when Scrum was implemented at Individual, Inc., in order to help the company develop another product, Corporate NewsPage (CNP). Individual, Inc. published customized news at customer sites through CNP. The product development team was under pressure to turn out a new release, but the team was busy porting the prior release from the base Sun platform to HP and IBM platforms. Both HP and IBM had released new operating systems, and the team had been caught unprepared. The technology they were using had changed, and the complexity of their project had skyrocketed. Suddenly they had to change operating systems, in addition to developing additional functionality for the new release.

Because the team was using Scrum, an empirical process, it stopped and reevaluated their priorities. Rather than doing as it had always done, the team asked whether its ordinary practices made sense under these circumstances. A little investigation showed that sales had not yet sold any sites that would use the IBM port, and had sold only one HP installation. By taking a step back from its work and evaluating the situation, the team was able to skip the ports and move on to tackle the new release. Was this just a case of using common sense? Yes, but that is the core of empirical processes.

CHAPTER 6

Why Does Scrum Work?

Software development is an activity that creates new products. Therefore it is more akin to new product development than to the manufacturing models that it has been forced to fit in the last 20 years. This new world-view represents a Kuhnian paradigm shift for software development because new product development processes require a new set of practices rooted in self-organization and knowledge creation to cope with the inherent activities of research and creativity involved in creating something new.　　—

6.1 Understanding Scrum

A few years ago, I started a project at a telecom company. During the first week I explained Scrum. After the brief, one-hour explanation that described the basic Scrum practices one of the members of the team asked me:

"If all we are doing in a Scrum meeting is to report what we did within the last day, report new issues, and state what we are going to be doing in the next day, why don't we write a database program on the web that captures this information. That way we won't miss any time at the Scrum meetings."

It seemed to others like a reasonable request. If these Scrum meetings were only capturing this information, why should we meet every day at the same time and talk? People could write their own statuses at any time. They could see what other people were doing if they wanted. Leave issues for management to resolve.

It was tempting to replace the meetings with the software; however, some things, like human interactions, should not be automated, so my answer to that request was:

"Scrum meetings do much more for a team than just capturing information. They don't only make everyone capture what they did, but it makes everyone say it in front of everybody else. That way everyone listens to what others are doing and they can offer to help them later. They don't only make everyone say what the issues are, but it makes everyone say it face to face to their management. This forces everyone to have courage and to be honest, and gives everyone a tool to put pressure on management about resolving issues. It also makes everyone promise in front of everyone else what you will be working on next, so it puts everyone's credibility and trust to the test. Scrum is about deep social interactions that build trust among team members."

Clearly, I knew something they didn't and it made a difference in the decision of changing or not changing Scrum. This is precisely the difference between knowing how to apply Scrum and knowing why it works. In most cases it is sufficient to know how it works, but knowing *why* it works is especially helpful when one proposes to either change some of the Scrum practices, or to incorporate other practices like XP practices.

I have found that the following related views are very useful to understand why Scrum works:

The new product development view of Scrum

The risk management and predictability view of Scrum

The Kuhnian view of Scrum

Knowledge Creation view of Scrum

The Complexity Science view of Scrum

Anthropological view of Scrum

The System Dynamics view of Scrum

The Psychological view of Scrum

The Football metaphor

These views are important to realize that while Scrum practices may look simple and unsophisticated on the surface, the dynamics they control and create have profound implications. My intent is not to provide a comprehensive and exhaustive explanation of the concepts involved – that would take several volumes with thousands of references. Instead, I want to provide a simple explanation of these concepts so that, you, the reader of this book, can build useful mental models of Scrum.

These views are related and they build the argument for this book: software development is like new product development not like manufacturing. This difference is revolutionary, and it leads to a completely new way of thinking about what software is and how to build it.

6.2   The New Product Development View of Scrum

Traditional software development methods are in a crisis because they cannot control software development despite their elaborate process models. But this crisis can be explained in terms of the incorrect assumptions that are made about software and software development by traditional methods.

First and foremost, the assumption that software is manufactured and that it therefore should follow similar processes to manufacturing is incorrect.

Manufacturing is about assembling the same model of something such as a radio, an automobile, or a plane over and over again. But software is about creating something new because - even if reusable parts are used - the configuration or arrangement of them will be new. For example, consider what happens when one uses a library or a component in an application. The component is parameterized and more often than not, some of its functionality is overridden.

This is a fundamental assumption that has haunted the software industry for the last 20 years or so, ever since Watts Humphrey prodded us to use a manufacturing model in software through the CMM (The capability maturity model). Humphrey borrowed the maturity model from MMM (Manufacturing maturity model) that Crosby exposed in his landmark book "Quality is Free"[Crosby], and that has left us with a history or 20 years of software development that has tried to emulate manufacturing process models.

In manufacturing, it makes perfect sense to demand "repeatable and defined" processes that assemble an identical model in an assembly line. But software has different demands: it is different for every arrangement.

Therefore, software development better fits the model of new product development. But creating something new requires research, creativity and learning. These activities are based on different assumptions and require a completely different way to estimate, plan, track, and manage than those techniques used in the manufacturing of products.

For starters, research and creativity activities are much less predictable. They may have bounds, like creating a design of a new VCR model, but they have many more options than manufacturing an instance of a given model.

Because software requirements for an application are never specified identically or even completely, software development always involves research. And because every application is different, their designs, by necessity, are always new. They can be similar and use patterns like MVC (model-view-controller), PAC (presentation-abstraction-control), or a Pipes and Filters architecture, but when they get down to a specific implementation, the business objects, the business rules, and the transactions and services required are different.

Nonaka and Takeuchi, in their famous Harvard Business Review article [Takeuchi and Nonaka], show how innovative companies create new products. In their analysis of ten of the most competitive and innovative companies on the planet they found that they require:

Built-in instability. Team members are given the freedom to do research and creativity but at the same time they are expected to produce up-to high standards.

Self-organizing project teams. A project team takes on a self-organizing character as it is driven to a state of zero information, where prior knowledge does not apply. Ambiguity and fluctuation abound in this state. Left to stew, the process begins to create its own dynamic order and the team starts to create its own agenda, taking risks, and creating new concepts.

Overlapping development phases. In an environment where some of the requirements are discovered while simultaneously something is created with the information at hand, it is imperative that the phases of discovery, invention, and testing overlap to drive the creation of a new product to completion through self-consistency. Most problems in new product development arise when the phases of the project are separated. Empirically, this overlap in phases enhances shared responsibility and cooperation, stimulates involvement and commitment, sharpens a problem-solving focus, encourages initiative taking, develops diversified skills, and heightens sensitivity toward market conditions.

Multi-learning. Teams must stay in close touch with outside sources of information so that they can respond quickly to changes in the environment. This learning manifests itself along two dimensions: 1) Across multiple levels (individual, group, and organizations), and 2) across multiple functions.

Subtle control. Although teams are largely on their own because they need this freedom to be creative and effective, management must establish some controls to prevent instability, ambiguity and tension from turning into uncontrolled chaos. These controls are:

Selecting team members and constantly balancing the team.

Creating an open work environment.

Encouraging constant communication with the customer.

Establishing an evaluation and reward system based on group performance.

Managing the differences in rhythm throughout the development phases.

Tolerating and anticipating mistakes.

Encouraging dependent teams to also become self-organizing.

Transfer of learning. Seeding new teams with team members of previous teams.

All of these are fundamentals of new product development; since Scrum adopts this paradigm, they are also fundamental to the correct implementation of Scrum.

6.3   The Risk Management and Predictability View of Scrum

> **Scrum advocates a new paradigm for software development that requires self-organization, while simultaneously providing risk-reducing practices to tame this new kind of organization.**
>
> —

Another useful way to look at Scrum is as a *risk reduction system*. This is a particularly useful way to look at Scrum, especially from the management perspective. In my experience risk and uncertainty have always been there in software development, but the advantage of Scrum is its ability to recognize them and to provide practices to tame them. Where do risk and uncertainty come from in software development?

The section above outlines a new way of doing software development that is based on the assumption that software is more like new product development. This assumption implies that there is a great deal of research and creativity that requires self-organization, learning, and overlapping development phases. However, the nature of these activities is arguably less predictable and involves more risk and uncertainty. As a consequence, Scrum provides new ways of estimating, planning, tracking and managing that cut through these risks and uncertainties.

Risk of not pleasing the customer. Scrum copes with the risk of not pleasing the customer by allowing the customer to see the product on a constant basis. Whenever possible, Scrum prefers to have a customer on-site but it mandates that the customer sees working software at least every Sprint. This validates the efforts of the team in providing the functionality promised at the Sprint Review Meeting and reprioritizing other functionality to be worked on at the Sprint Planning Meeting.

Risk of not completing all functionality. Scrum copes with the risk of not delivering all the functionality in a release by developing functionality in a prioritized way through Sprints. This ensures that all the high priority functionality will be delivered and that only lower priority functionality is missed.

Risk of poor estimating and planning. Scrum manages this risk through the Daily Scrums by always providing small estimates that are tracked within a Daily Scrum cycle, and through the Sprint cycle that has an invariant set of Product Backlog assigned to it. Within a Daily Scrum cycle, Scrum tolerates the risk that activities within this window may not be completed, but it provides management control to avoid errors greater than this cycle. Within the Sprint cycle, Scrum tolerates the fact that not all goals of the Sprint may be completed, but it adjusts its goals through the Sprint Review and the Sprint Planning Meeting.

Risk of not resolving issues promptly. Scrum puts the burden of proof on management by requiring daily active management. In Scrum, the role of management is bi-directional, in that management also reports to the staff how it is resolving issues through the Daily Scrums.

Risk of not being able to complete the development cycle. Scrum ensures that there aren't any major problems with the development cycle by delivering working software every Sprint. If there are any issues with engineering practices such as configuration management, regression testing, system testing or release management, Scrum irons out all the details by forcing a working release. In some cases, these issues actually impede the complete delivery of a Sprint, but the advantage is that the team is forced to confront the issues and solve them.

Risk of taking too much work and changing expectations. Scrum prevents the risk of changing the expectations of the customer and the team by disallowing any changes to the Product Backlog associated with a Sprint. That way the team feels that their goal is respected and the customer has clear expectations.

6.4   The Kuhnian View of Scrum

> Scrum represents a paradigm shift in software development. Scrum breaks the tradition of old paradigms and metaphors because it is based on the paradigm, practices and metaphors of new product development; therefore, it provides practices that support research, creativity, learning and knowledge creation; activities that in turn require a self-organizing structure.   —

Thomas Kuhn, one of the great philosophers of science, argues that scientific, and therefore technological revolutions come in cycles of "regular science", "crises" and "revolutionary paradigm shifts"[Kuhn]. His argument is based on the piecemeal refinement and higher demands for accuracy that each new theory brings.

At first, a theory better explains an event in the world, but then, as more details are calculated with it, it breaks because it can't account for some events or predicts results that are different from observed values. Eventually, as more and more "defects" are found with an existing theory, these defects give rise to a crisis that is only resolved by a new theory that better explains and accounts for the observed phenomena. Software development does not escape this historical evolution.

Software development saw a paradigm shift in the late 80s, when it was assumed that software behaved and could be controlled like a manufacturing product. This brought many good things. For example, all the tasks that took place in software development were defined, as exemplified by the CMM's KPAs (key process areas).

However, this paradigm has also put software development in a crisis. It is nearly impossible to develop software in short periods of time, with high quality and with a low budget using the "defined and repeatable" process approach. And as I have explained in the section above "The new product development view of Scrum", Scrum makes a radically different assumption about software development. This underlying assumption is so different that it is our estimation and hope that it will trigger a paradigm shift.

As of now, Scrum represents a competing worldview when compared to the many other styles of software development or business organization, but one that, given its success and simplicity, will convince the world of its superiority in the long term.

6.5 Knowledge Creation View of Scrum

I have proposed above that software development is the result of creating new products, and that by necessity it requires research and creativity. However, the commonality among research and creativity is knowledge creation.

The fact that we gather requirements for an application strongly indicates that they are in tacit form, and as we make design decisions we acquire knowledge that we eventually capture in the code or in an executable model. From this perspective, software is nothing else than *codified and explicit knowledge*.

Explicit knowledge means knowledge transmittable in a systematic language. For example, in software development, code, and documents, UML (Unified Modeling Language) models and graphics are explicit knowledge. Explicit knowledge is in sharp contrast with *tacit knowledge,* which is based on experience and typically reflected in our intuitions and reactions but not externalized. In software development we often find people with special abilities and knowledge that is not externalized. Good examples of this are software users, domain experts, and experienced programmers.

From the perspective of knowledge creation, Scrum has the effect of promoting the creation of knowledge [Takeuchi and Nonaka] through cycles of socialization, externalization, combination, and internalization of knowledge. See Figure 6.1, Knowledge conversion.

Socialization is direct conveyance of tacit knowledge through shared experience.

Externalization is the process of articulating tacit knowledge into explicit concepts.

Combination is a process of systematizing concepts into a knowledge system.

Internalization means embodying explicit knowledge in tacit, operational knowledge.

The daily Scrum meetings are a good example of this cycle. First, the tacit knowledge of a team member is socialized at a Scrum meeting. The externalization of this knowledge typically results in items in the Sprint Backlog, but it can be simply useful knowledge for other team members. Other team members can then combine this knowledge with more externalized or tacit knowledge and once again internalize it to make use of it during a day of work. The continuous application of this cycle through the Scrum practices throughout the organization results in the Knowledge

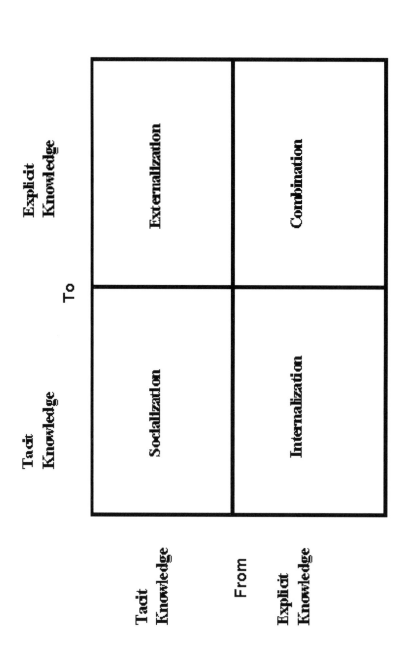

FIGURE 6.1: Knowledge Conversion. (From: Nonaka I., Takeuchi H., *The Knowledge Creating Company,* Oxford University Press, Oxford 1995.)

Spiral that spreads knowledge rapidly throughout the organization. See Figure 6.2, Knowledge spiral.

A Scrum team creates knowledge through these mechanisms:

Sharing tacit knowledge. Example: Developers exchanging ideas about requirements or design in a Scrum meeting or while working in pairs or triads with other developers.

Creating concepts. Example: The creation of design models like packages, classes, relationships and interactions.

Justifying concepts. Example: Developers validating requirements and designs.

Building an archetype. Example: Building a prototype.

Cross leveling of knowledge. Basically this starts the cycle all over again.

Though they are listed here sequentially, it should be clear that a developer is free to move between them adaptively.

6.6   The Complexity Science View of Scrum

I have proposed in the above sections that because Scrum assumes that software must be a new product requiring research and creativity, its organization must consist of self-organizing project teams and must have overlapping development phases. That means that the Scrum organization or processes cannot be statically defined or for that matter repeated. You can only hope to repeat the application of the Scrum practices but they will lead to different organizational or process arrangements every time.

However, to really understand the dynamics of self-organization, we must delve into Complexity Science.

6.6.1   Definitions

Complexity Science is the name commonly used to describe a set of interdisciplinary studies that describe self-organizing systems (SOS). These systems are so pervasive and are found in almost every science: Physics, Chemistry, Biology, Sociology, Political Science, and Anthropology. For example, an ant colony, the brain, the immune system, a Scrum team, and New York City are self-organizing systems. It is important to notice, however, that:

All human organization is self-organization.

Even in the case where some agents, like in military organizations, dictate the organization of some other agents, eventually the subordinate agents organize themselves into the mandated organization. Clearly, this kind-of self-organization is very inflexible. Compare that to the self-organization of a SWAT team. It still operates within some rules and bounds but their self-organization is much more flexible.

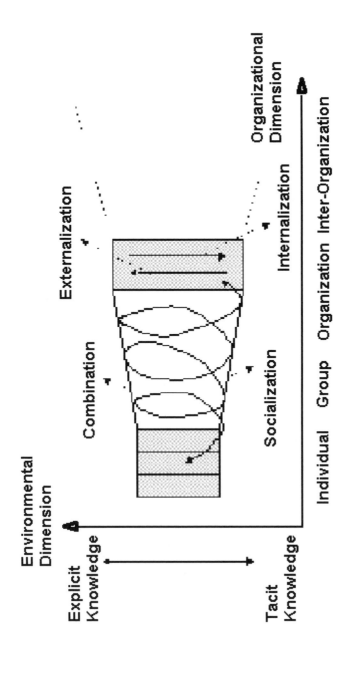

FIGURE 6.2: Knowledge Spiral. (From: Nonaka I., Takeuchi H., *The Knowledge Creating Company*, Oxford University Press, Oxford 1995.)

It is said that an organization is more *ordered* as the organization is better defined. For example, an assembly line in a factory is very well defined. It is said that an organization is more *chaotic* if it has a more dynamic configuration with less static patterns, for example, toddlers running around in a large room. It is said that an organization is at the edge of chaos if the organization lives in a state where there is order in chaos. Examples of this type of organization are SWAT teams, basketball teams, soccer teams and Scrum teams.

6.6.2 Features

Self-organizing systems share many features and Scrum has good examples of each of them [Holland98][Holland95]:

They are composed of **Agents**. Agents are independent actors that can act autonomously. For example, developers, the Scrum Master, and the Product Owner are agents.

They are **Open Systems**. They exchange energy, mass or information with their surroundings. For example, a Scrum team exchanges information with a customer and with other teams like the testing and production environment support teams.

They are **Dynamic**. Their state is constant flux. A Scrum team is constantly reorganizing on different time-scales: minute-by-minute on daily activities, daily at the Scrum meetings, and monthly at the Sprint planning meetings.

Flows. Flows mean exchange of mass, energy or information among agents. For example, in Scrum teams, there is constant information flow 1) among the developers during a typical development day, 2) among the developers and the Scrum Master at the Scrum meetings, and 3) between the customer and the Scrum team at planning meetings and on a daily basis.

They rely on **Dense Local Interactions.** The agents interact with each other according to rules and exchange information through flows *constantly and periodically*. For example, Scrum team members are constantly sharing information and knowledge through the day, and periodically at Scrum meetings, End of Sprint demonstrations and Sprint Planning meetings.

Emergence. Emergence is another way of saying that the whole is greater than the sum of the parts. Rules that are almost absurdly simple can generate coherent, emergent phenomena. For example, the rule about not changing the assignment of product backlog to a Sprint has deep repercussions. The customer can still add features but the Scrum team is undisturbed because its goal is respected, so its credibility is easier to maintain, as a result there is more trust from the client in the team. Therefore, this rule results in the emergence of a more stable customer-team relationship.

Building Blocks and Aggregation. Sometimes also called multi-scale effects. Building blocks are recurrent structures that are used as the parts of a Lego set. Aggregation is the ability to combine these building blocks. At each level of scale there are different building blocks that aggregate to form the building blocks of the next level of scale. Aggregations are typically based on recurring interactions that depend on pre-established flows. For example, a business organization can be seen as a collection of process teams and support teams. One of these support teams is the IT organization, which in turn is composed of application development teams, production environment support teams, testing teams, etc. The application development teams can in turn be made of one or more Scrum teams, which in turn are composed of individual developers.

Tagging. Tags are temporary labels on agents or artifacts that can be used for signaling and facilitating the creation of aggregates. For example, in a Scrum meeting, people are temporarily tagged as chickens and pigs. By definition people only involved in the development of the system like managers are chickens, and people committed to delivering the system, such as developers, are pigs. Another example of tagging is when a developer is tagged as an apprentice or a mentor (sometimes also called a coach or an architect).

Diversity and Specialization. Diversity states that there are many kinds of agents in a self-organizing system. Specialization in most cases is the root case of diversity. For example in a Scrum team, there are Product Owners, Scrum Masters and developers. Among developers there is also specialization and diversity. For example, a developer may specialize in: databases, Java, configuration management, requirements gathering, unit testing, etc.

Internal and Shared Models. Each agent in the system typically has its own internal models. In most cases, self-organizing systems also have shared models among some agents in the system. The internal models are typically affected by the flows during interactions among agents. For example, in a Scrum team, the Sprint Goal, the current Backlog, the requirements, and the architecture are shared models, with each of the developers having their own internal models.

Nonlinear Dynamics. Sometimes also dubbed non-linearity. Non-linear Dynamics means that the feedback loops in an agent colony obey non-linear rules. This is a characteristic of positive or negative feedback loops. For example, the combined effects of developers sharing knowledge among themselves, trusting each other, communicating often with a customer, and learning more about the technology they are working with have non-linear effects in their productivity over time. A team may double their productivity in their first 3 months working together. But it may double it again in the fourth month alone. In the best cases, this productivity can increase ten-fold (1000%) after a few months of working in a Scrum team.

6.6.3 Scrum Organization, Processes and Roles

A self-organizing system relies on the above features to function. However, one key characteristic of a self-organizing system is to be able to adapt. Because of this characteristic, self-organizing systems are similar to live systems. In fact, all living systems are self-organizing systems but not all self-organizing systems are live systems.

In that sense, a software development team is described as being more agile or more "alive" as its ability to adapt increases. Scrum rates very high in adaptability. Why? Throughout this book we have learned that Scrum doesn't use very many hierarchical controls of management, processes or even role definitions. The **organization** pecking order inside a Scrum team is really based on knowledge relationships: whoever knows more about a subject takes a higher pecking order in a discussion. The **development tasks** are reorganized dynamically, minute-by-minute in developers' collaborations, day-by-day in Scrum meetings, and Sprint-by-Sprint in Sprint planning meetings, so there aren't any static process definitions. Instead tasks, like organizations, are arranged dynamically using short feedback cycles. Finally, the **roles** of developers on a Scrum team also adapt in short time cycles. Where more traditional organizations call for the definition of static roles, Scrum developers can change hats dynamically, often passing as analysts, testers, coders, designers, architects and integrators in a single day. Simply said, everyone does everything that is in his or her power to deliver the system.

This type of organization doesn't fall into any traditional organizational structure or process structure. Instead, Scrum has a self-organizing structure close to edge of chaos. The dynamic structures are typically pairs or triads of developers that are working on a piece of the system. These pairs are formed for many different reasons: 1) mentor/apprentice relationships, 2) cross-functional relationships like domain expert/analyst/ developer teams, and 3) expert/expert team to achieve high levels of creativity and productivity. Scrum teams are therefore very dynamic and can be better understood as people (the adaptive agents) capable of dynamic behavior who develop software through dense local people-to-people and people-to-software interactions.

The extremely high ability to constantly reconfigure or adapt is driven in Scrum teams by the basic Scrum practices:

First and foremost, the **Scrum team values** allow diverse team members to share information, trust each other, collaborate in tasks, and truly commit to deliver the system. The Scrum team values define the interactions among team members and ensure that there are constant flows of information among them. These flows in turn build the shared models of the team. These values ensure that mentor/apprentice and cross-functional collaborations and interactions are successful.

Daily Scrum meetings. Each and every day, the team reflects where it is, what issues it has and where it is going, and adapts accordingly. Scrum meetings ensure that everyone knows what everyone else is doing, promoting opportunities for mentoring or collaboration.

Demo after Sprint. The Demo after the Sprint allows the team to give feedback to the customer on what the team accomplished, and for the customer to give feedback to the team. This allows the team to adapt according to the customer feedback and for the customer to adapt according to the work presented.

End of Sprint and **Sprint Planning** meetings. Every Sprint the team reflects on what it has accomplished at the Sprint in the End of Sprint meeting, and reconfigures in the Sprint Planning meeting to develop new functionality.

Adaptation and Natural Selection

It is interesting to see what researchers in Complexity Science say about organizations that live close to the edge of chaos [Kauffman93]:

There is an optimum of adaptability in systems that self-organize right at the edge of chaos.

Natural selection chooses configurations that are more apt to adapt.

Coevolving systems (ecosystems) whose members have tuned their structures to live close to the edge of chaos live longer.

Since Scrum teams live closer to the edge of chaos this means that:

Scrum teams are more adaptable than traditional teams that organize with defined organizations, defined processes and defined roles.

Scrum teams are able to survive longer i.e. stay in stable configurations for longer periods of time, because adaptability *selects* them to live longer.

Scrum teams coevolve better and longer with other teams that have similar structures. For example, if - in addition to the application development teams - the business organization uses Scrum and other adaptive techniques to organize itself, the whole eco-system will coevolve and live longer. This explains why Scrum works so well with business organizations that use adaptive methods, and with software teams that use agile methods like XP.

Scrum practices, though simple, indeed have deep implications for agility and adaptability.

6.7   Anthropological View of Scrum

The agents discussed above are humans, and therefore their interactions are best understood in the context of Anthropology[Harris97]. Basically, practicing Scrum changes the culture of an organization because Scrum comes with new values, beliefs, language, rules, roles, and practices. And some Scrum practices can also be seen as ceremonies and rites, like the Scrum meetings or the Sprint planning meetings.

For example, there is an immense culture building value in holding the Scrum meetings at the same place at the same time because this *ceremony* has the effect of bonding and jelling a group of individuals. Other examples are having the rule of "pigs and chickens", going around the room and taking the same places in the room every day, and collecting one dollar from people who are late.

However, changing cultures is one of the most difficult changes one can ever make. Here are some best practices that allow us to do it more effectively:

Support. Get the support from upper management. This will allow you to report success and correlate it to Scrum at the end of projects, and will allow Scrum to spread throughout the organization. This support is also important at the Sprint Planning Meetings, where the customer is heavily involved.

Language. Cultures create languages and languages create cultures, so introduce the Scrum vocabulary and enforce it.

Roles and Mentors. Seed your organization with mentors that already know the Scrum process. They typically are Scrum Masters but in some cases they can also be developers.

Values. Reinforce the Scrum values. For example, by providing weekly "brown bag" lunches where different topics are explored: patterns, refactoring, new technologies, etc.; you can reinforce the "sharing knowledge" value. Another example is keeping and publishing an honest Sprint Backlog, that promotes courage, honesty, and trust. Another example is introducing people that are in the habit of being "focused and committed" that can serve as role models.

Beliefs. Explain Scrum to the team members by holding presentations and publishing documents that show why Scrum is different.

Practices and Rules. Practice the Scrum practices and enforce all of its rules. Remember, every rule has a good reason to exist, and it results in emergent behavior.

6.8 The System Dynamics View of Scrum

In the section above where I discussed the Complexity Science view of Scrum, I said that flows and dense local interactions were needed among the developers of a software project. However, I said nothing about the efficiency of such flows and interactions. In this section I will expose some of the Scrum flow efficiency through the perspective of System Dynamics.

System Dynamics is the study of organizations by means of feedback loops. A little bit of history is in order. In the early 1980's there was a great interest in making business processes more efficient, in particular those that were concerned with managing inventories. Inventories cost money, so having "idle" money sitting somewhere is never a good idea. On the other hand, not having enough raw materials at any given time can effectively stop a production line. So having *minimal but sufficient* inventories is ideal.

To understand the conceptual solution above is not all that hard; however, to come up with practical solutions that actually implement this conceptual solution is much harder. Eventually luminaries like Eli Goldratt [Goldratt], figured out that smaller inventories could be maintained by using short feedback loops that moved smaller quantities into the inventory. Identical solutions came from MIT's Sloan business school as the solution of the famous "beer game": move smaller amounts in shorter periods of time.

But how does "inventory management" relate to software development? Well, any resource can be seen the same way including "developer's time", because whether companies use it appropriately or not, they have to pay either salaries or consulting fees. The virtues of Scrum from this perspective, are that Scrum provides very many feedback cycles at different levels of scale:

Measuring all resource inventory levels constantly and changing fast in small amounts how developers use their time.

Simply said, Scrum is the solution of the beer game applied to software development because Scrum makes it impossible for developer's time to go to waste or for issues to impede development. Here developer's time can be seen as "inventory" and issues impeding development can be seen as lack of inventory of another resource. For example, if a testing environment is not available, this can be seen as not having enough "testing environment inventory."

Software as well as business organization have been seen in this light before. For example, Jerry Weinberg, one of the greatest software gurus, bases most of his analysis in system dynamics archetypes [Weinberg]. Peter Senge, from MIT's Sloan school has also developed notation and techniques to document people interactions through system dynamics techniques [Senge].

6.9   The Psychological View of Scrum

I have said much about people interactions, but I haven't explained what happens to people working in a Scrum team from the inside out. Scrum has different effects on people. For most, belonging to a Scrum team gets them to be highly focused, effective, cooperative and committed over time. However, there are also the scant few that don't like Scrum, and that's because Scrum always tells the truth about everyone.

However, for the majority that do benefit from Scrum, their state of consciousness can be better explained by the concept of "flow". Mihaly Csikszentmihalyi from the University of Chicago defines "flow" as the state of an individual having the following characteristics:

They are working to accomplish clear goals. Both the Scrum Planning meetings, and the Daily Scrum meetings help define clear goals.

They get immediate feedback about their progress toward these goals. The daily Scrum meetings give this feedback.

They must use significant skill to achieve their goals. Scrum requires a balance of individuals with at least 50% of them to be experts, but Scrum also promotes fast learning, so skills transfer rapidly and effectively among the team members.

They are in control of the work and have it in their power to accomplish it. Scrum assigns work from the Product Backlog and creates a Sprint Backlog that controls the work at all times. Also, Scrum allows the elevation and resolution of issues through the daily Scrum meetings, removing any impediments from the way of the developers.

They can concentrate on the goals without being distracted. Scrum provides a comfort shell for developers where the Scrum Master acts as a firewall.

They become deeply involved in the work. Scrum drives individuals to focus, commit and excel.

They focus on the work and lose concern for themselves.

They experience an altered sense of time.

They consistently produce at high levels of accomplishment.

Scrum allows developers to concentrate most of their time in developing software, and by doing so developers enter "flow" state.

6.10   The Football Metaphor

This is a somewhat unrelated view of Scrum compared to the ones above and it is only provided here to explain Scrum's name. The first thing that people ask about Scrum is about the meaning of the word Scrum itself. Some think that it is an acronym; some think that it is an obscure word, but as said earlier in this book, Scrum comes from Rugby, and is a dense circle of people that typically is split by members of the Rugby teams that fight for possession of the ball:

One of the charms of Rugby Union game is the infinite variety of its possible tactics. Whatever tactics a team aims to adopt, the first essential is a strong and skillful pack of forwards capable of winning initial possession from the set pieces. For with the ball in its hands, a team is in a position to dictate tactics, which will make the best use of its own particular talents, at the same time probing for and exposing weaknesses in the opposing team. The ideal team has fast and clever half-backs and three-quarters who, with running, passing, and shrewd kicking, will make sure that the possession won by the forwards is employed to the maximum embarrassment of the opposing team.

The external perception of a Scrum meeting might look closer to a Scrum in Rugby, but from an information perspective, a Scrum meeting is closer to a football huddle: it is a short meeting to plan the next down. As such, we can draw the analogies in Table 1, Football metaphor.

Scrum Practice	Football Practice
Scrum meetings	Huddle
A day of work	a down
First and ten	a Sprint
Scoring (Touch down, field goal)	Delivery to production

TABLE 6.1: Football metaphor

Of course, this is just a metaphor, and all metaphors eventually break down, but it matches fairly close if we leave the analysis at the above level of abstraction.

C H A P T E R 7

Advanced Scrum Applications

Scrum works for all projects - projects of all sizes, projects that involve multiple applications reusing components; projects where extremely high quality is expected, and business projects.   —

7.1   Applying Scrum to Multiple Related Projects

In the previous chapters Scrum has been described in one-project applications. However, in large companies, many interrelated projects typically are developed at the same time with resources shared among these projects.

In these cases, the complexity of the environment is magnified by at least one level of magnitude, and it is ever more important to use Scrum to tame this complexity.

In this chapter I will discuss what it means to run Scrum for multiple concurrent projects, as well as some specific techniques that make this possible.

What do you need to know to make it work? The first thing you need to know about running multiple projects is that you should never start with multiple projects at once. In fact, you should fear the complexity of such an environment and all of its evils. Imagine this:

changes to many application requirements,

business changes – changes in management, strategy, marketing, operations and business processes,

complex system setups to support a large number of concurrent applications:

clusters of servers working together,

complex dependency relationships among shared components,

ripple effects for changed component interfaces,

complex people issues:

project managers demanding attention to issues relevant to their project,

the need to migrate programmers across different teams,

lack of overall system knowledge,

turnover.

You get the idea? It can get to be very complex. However, this is precisely how companies live in an environment that promotes reusability among many projects.

7.1.1 The First Application

The first application is developed using the techniques discussed in the rest of the book. However, you may want to pay close attention to how you package the different components for the first project if you know there is a chance they will be reused by other projects. However, don't forget that your primary concern in the first application is to deploy it to production. You can always refactor and repackage components for a higher level of reuse later – after the release to production. So don't get too hung up in trying to make everything reusable from scratch – it just doesn't work very well to foresee everything. However, do use every opportunity you can to set things up so that reuse will be easier – this should always be a secondary concern in your first application.

Here are some ideas that can help you get ready for reusability:

Partition the architecture into layers. An example layered architecture for an online system will typically look like this:

Workflows – units of work linked together,

Units of work – components that include the front ends and the basic mechanics for requesting services and rendering onto presentations,

Business Service layer – reusable strategies,

Transactions – that compose a service,

Business Object layer – including all of its forms: value, business and data access objects,

Architectural Services: logging, security, persistence, distribution, concurrency.

Partition every layer into smaller packages that can be reused by other applications.

Keep close control on the external interfaces of these packages once their designs start "freezing" – stop changing.

At this point, the management of the application is still done through a single person, just as described in other parts of this book that talk about the management of single projects. But what happens when a second application group wants to build a second application using some of the resources that the first application produced? This requires some change, as we will see in the next section, because now - instead of having one Scrum team - we have two and possibly three Scrum teams:

One team for each application and one team for the "shared resources".

7.1.2 Reusability

Very many developers and managers that work with new technologies touted as "reusable technologies" are accustomed to always working in the first release of an application. They tend to think that this is the most

interesting part of development. The contrary is true – the interesting part
of "reusability" starts to happen in the release of a second application and
beyond.

The assumption here is that the first application has either gone into
production or that it is very close to release to production. The key thing,
and this is a strong prerequisite to start a second application, is that:

Whatever are chosen as "reusable assets" need to be *stable*.

If this is not true, there will be many problems. The application group
that uses the shared components will complain that "things keep changing",
and that the shared components lack the technical excellence they were told
would be available for them. In some cases, and out of frustration, they
will give up on using a shared component and develop their own. This
might also create long-term problems based on lack of trust. On the other
hand, the development group that develops the components will complain
that they don't have the freedom to improve their components; they feel
"pushed into a corner". They may possibly argue they are being forced to
deliver something that wasn't intended for delivery.

My advice is simply: don't try to reuse anything that is not *stable*
enough.

Another important assumption is that the first Scrum team will continue to develop and support future releases of the first application.

Based on these two assumptions a second Scrum team is formed with
the idea to reuse some of the aforementioned assets developed by the first
team.

7.1.3   Initial Setup and the Shared Resources Scrum Team

The Scrum Masters of both teams get together, including some of the
upper management of both teams, and they agree to work sharing some
components.

At this point, the **Shared Resources** Scrum team is created. Sometimes this can be avoided if the shared resources are small, or if the number
of applications reusing the shared resources is one or two. However, if the
shared components are medium to large, and the first Scrum team is small
and/or has tight deadlines, a Shared Resources Scrum team dedicated to
support the shared resources must be created. The initial resources of this
team must include a mixture of some of the developers from the first application, and some new resources in order to prevent the complete depletion
of talent from the first team. Sometimes this team is labeled as the "Architecture Team" but I strongly prefer "Shared Resources" team because
it is more descriptive. But whatever name you decide, its responsibilities
are very clear:

To support and enhance the shared components satisfying
the requirements of multiple application teams.

The Shared Resources team might be just one person to begin with, and even a single person part-time. However, as the number of components and application groups supported increases, more resources will be needed to satisfy the development and support of the shared resources.

A key milestone of the initial process is to have the packages renamed and separated into a different package hierarchy. Depending on your development language and configuration management system, this means isolating separate packages into different projects so that they can be reused. This will cause the first application packages to change names, but typically these fixes are very easy to accomplish through a global search and replace utility.

From there on, the components isolated will be owned, supported and released by the Shared Resources team.

This initial setup can be done in conjunction with the development of the second application, but it is better to do it earlier rather than later. The danger is that if this setup is not done, the second application might just develop all of the components "all over again." Unfortunately this is often true, creating unnecessary expenses for companies.

The Shared Resources team also has the responsibility to coordinate and communicate changes to the shared resources. This might be difficult at times because the more applications that are dependent on shared resources, the more the "ripple" effect will be when changing the external interfaces of these components.

In general, start sharing components from the bottom layers of the architecture, such as the architectural services, and move through the layers until you reach the higher levels of reuse at the workflow level. In my experience, the different layers have different degrees of difficulty when shared:

The architectural services layer is easy to share – expect very little disagreement here.

The business object layer is difficult. There is typically some ambiguity and bias from applications to give special attention to abstractions that are more important for them. Resolve conflicts among the different application teams through hands-on meetings facilitated by an expert business object modeler.

The service layer is easy to reuse. It sits on top of the business object layers and typically uses the notion of "Strategies" [GOF]. The services are ***always*** taken from applications.

The "units of work" and workflow layers are easy. All units of work and workflows are ***always*** taken from applications.

Avoid the temptation of creating new business objects, services, "units of work", and workflows in the Shared Resource team. It is much better to abstract what is already built by another team and working. Similarly, create a new architectural service only when at least one application needs it. Don't ever create services that "in theory" will be used. This could be expensive and wasteful.

7.1.4 Developing the Second Application

Again, it is not required to do the initial setup described above before you start the development of a second application. However, it is strongly encouraged to be doing this at least simultaneously as the second application is started.

Developing the second application is essentially the same as developing the first application. The assumption that the second team with the internal shared components is the same as if they had bought these components off-the-shelf.

If the second application will also be contributing to the shared resources pool, use the same partitioning techniques that you used for the first application. When the intended shared components reach enough stability, then move them into a separate package and hand them off to the Shared Resource team. From then on, these components will be owned, supported and released by the Shared Resources team.

Just like in the first application, the second application's Scrum team has the primary responsibility of deploying their application. Their second priority is to think of reuse.

An important addition to the management practices is added at this point:

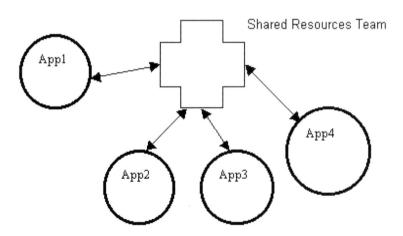

FIGURE 7.1: Multiple application environment.

It is a good idea to start meeting very often and regularly with the other Scrum Masters of the other applications and with the Scrum Masters of the support teams: Shared Resources, testing, and production support. These Scrum meetings are called "Scrum of Scrums", and I typically hold these meetings once or twice a week, and more often if needed.

One thing that is remarkable about Scrum is that it can in fact integrate very diverse teams like: 1) production support teams, 2) Scrum development teams, 3) XP development teams, 4) RUP development teams, 5) Mainframe development teams, 6) configuration management teams, and/or even 7) testing teams. In that regard, Scrum is unique in that it is able to provide a diverse number of teams an:

integrated and detailed management, estimating, planning and tracking process that can scale fairly well up to a whole business organization.

7.1.5   Developing More Applications

Essentially, repeat the steps described above in Section 7.1.2 "Developing the Second Application". Iteratively grow the architecture as you add more projects, each contributing with more and more shared components.

If you can run two teams sharing components, it is very likely that you can add more teams. But remember, if you plan to share components among very many different applications, you must setup a Shared Resources team.

7.1.6   Review of Specific Techniques

Let's review some of the techniques listed in this chapter:

Architecturally

Partition the architecture into layers

Partition every layer into components

Management techniques

Create a Shared Resources team

Hold frequent "Scrum of Scrums" meetings among the Scrum Masters

Reuse

Don't start sharing until components are stable

To begin reuse, package the components in a shared package and give the ownership to the Shared Resources team.

7.2   Applying Scrum to Larger Projects

Scrum works great for all project sizes but when applied to larger projects it requires some special considerations.

Large projects require careful thinking and planning when Scrum or any process is used. In this chapter I will provide some general guidance to tackle them. There is a strong similarity between managing a large project and managing multiple related projects. One consideration on why they are similar is reuse. In the case of multiple related applications, the reused components are the result of at least one application in production that now shares some of its resources with other applications. In the case of a large application, it is typical that multiple sub-teams work on the application simultaneously. Therefore, very similar rules apply.

7.2.1   The First Executable Prototype and First Branch of Development

First and foremost, don't try to get multiple units to do parallel development from day one. Parallel development, as said earlier, is difficult to accomplish, and while it apparently accelerates development, it can also bring many problems on its own.

Instead, first develop a minimal application that cuts through all the layers of the architecture using the techniques shown in this book, even if some of these layers are compromised. For example, you may not have a persistence service, or a transaction service, or a logging service ready; nevertheless, continue your development until at least one unit of work is ready. This minimal application may contain one or more entries from the product backlog and it is used to get the team warmed up. Even if this first release is not to be used in the real world, it is a good idea to jump all the necessary hoops as if the application will be released to production. This assumption helps resolve any issues with the development and release environments. Don't even try to do parallel development if the configuration management, testing, and release processes are not in place.

In small to medium applications it is easier to prioritize units of work according to their "business value" as said earlier. However, in large applications – especially if you want to do parallel development – the prioritization of the product backlog list has to also take into account the dependency among these units of work.

If at all possible choose a unit of work that has both high business value and uses a "root" domain object. By "root" domain object we mean a "fundamental anchor for your business and/or your application". In every business model there are a few objects or abstractions from which other objects or abstractions leaf. In a payroll system, for example, one cannot have employees without having persons first, and one cannot have payroll entries without employees. Person in this case is a root object because it leads to the definition of employees and employment that in turn lead to the definition of the branch. However, the person abstraction also leads to the definition of an indicative data branch that includes addresses, phones and email addresses; and the benefit plan branch, that in turn splits for different types of plans: 1) defined benefit (pensions), 2) defined contribution (401K), and 3) health and welfare (including medical, dental, and prescription benefits).

By partitioning a large application into several branches anchored into "root objects", large applications can be made identical to the "multiple related applications" practice described above.

7.2.2   Reusability

Eventually, as in the "multiple related projects" case, some abstractions will be candidates for reuse, and as I said earlier in the previous chapter:

Reusable assets need to be *stable*.

It is harder to predict reusability in general. It strongly depends on the application functionality and the domain model.

7.2.3   Initial Setup and the Shared Resources Scrum Team

It may take one or more branches in a large application to require a Shared Resources team. However, once a second branch is created the probability of reuse is very high if not for any other reason than for the reuse of architectural services: logging, persistence, security, printing, workflow.

Therefore, the creation of a minimal **Shared Resources** Scrum team is beneficial. As before the responsibilities of this team are:

To support and enhance the shared components satisfying the requirements of multiple sub-teams within a large application.

What happens when there are multiple applications and one or more are large applications? The rule then is to promote the release of shared components to the level that it makes more sense. If the components are only reused within a large application, then just promote them to the "large team shared resources team". However, if the components can be reused by more applications then promote the components to be released by the "Global Shared Resources Team."

7.2.4   Developing Through a Second Branch

The initial setup described above is a little bit more flexible in a large application; however, it is still strongly encouraged to let someone be the owner of the shared resources.

Because the branches have been decoupled, developing the second application is essentially the same as developing through the first branch. As the second branch is developed it may also contribute to the application's shared resources pool. Use the same partitioning techniques you used for the first branch. When the intended shared components reach enough stability, move them into a separate package and hand them off to the Shared Resources team. From then on, these components will be owned, supported and released by the Shared Resources team.

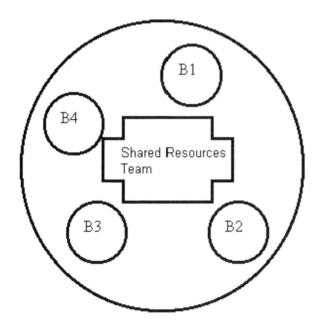

FIGURE 7.2: Large application with multiple branches B1, B2, etc.

Just like in the first branch, the Scrum team of the second branch's top priority is to deploy the application and their second priority is to think of reuse.

An important addition to the management practices is added at this point:

It is imperative to start meeting very often and regularly with the other Scrum Masters of the other branches as well as any support team Scrum Masters from the testing, integration, Shared Resources, and production support. These meetings are called "Scrum of Scrums", and they are held once or twice a week, and more often if needed.

7.2.5 Developing Through More Branches

Essentially, repeat the steps described above in Section 7.2.5 "Developing Through a Second Branch." Iteratively develop the application as you add more sub-projects. If you can run two sub-teams sharing components, it is very likely you can add more teams. But remember, if you plan to share components among many development branches within an application you must setup a Shared Resources team.

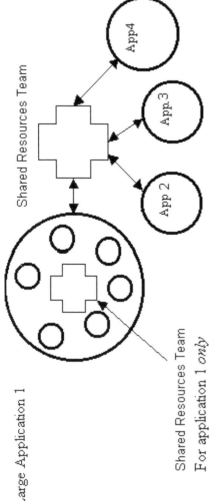

FIGURE 7.3: Large application in a multiple application environment

7.3 Case Study of Multiple-Related Projects: A Benefits Company

I'll now provide a case study of what took place at a benefits company over a period of nearly four years while the company launched its first e-commerce oriented web site and deployed a new family of web-based applications for its clients and internal users.

To summarize, in the end, the company developed 15 applications reusing many different components within the last year. However, it is not a story where everything went right from the beginning. Actually, almost quite the opposite happened. In retrospect, it is hard to imagine the outcome would be so bright after the first three years of web-development, because at that point the company had only one poorly developed web application in production. What happened in the last year that made the company successful?

The story started in late 1997, where the company's CIO directed the company towards e-commerce in order to offer prescription refills over the Internet. The first application deployment in late 1998 was successful but it was realized with a budget three times larger than planned and with a schedule twice as long as originally planned. Also, there were many technical concerns about the application.

However, the real problem was that five other business units were already lined up to develop web-based applications, with requirements to create up to 50 applications more within the next three years. But after the first web application, the IT department already had a bad reputation for taking a business unit's money and delivering late and over budget.

Frankly, the IT department at that point felt very scared. They had struggled to finish the first application, under the radar of all the top management in the company, and they weren't ready for more pressure. They did not feel they could develop that many applications in such a short time, especially since the budgets could not be enlarged. They felt pushed into a corner to deliver a *miracle*.

Parallel to the development of the first application, a so-called architecture group had been working on reusable architectural services components. It wasn't a coincidence that this group was created in early 1999, after the release of the first application. Its purpose was to create standard, reliable architectural services components so that other applications could be built over time – architectural services that in the first application released had a lot of problems. However, for political reasons, and in the name of "it is working, don't fix it", these services were not implemented in the first application until much later; actually, late 2000 as we will see later.

The application groups were told to wait to start development until the architecture team was done with the architectural services. But the architecture team was taking too long, so finally an application group agreed to co-develop the application while the architecture team finished all of the architectural services, which by then comprised a long and ambitious list.

The development of this second application started in mid 1999, but by late 1999, frustration started to show everywhere:

the application team members were complaining that the architectural services didn't work for them, and in some cases they either extended the services or just created their own.

the application team management was also getting frustrated and was blaming the architecture team management of being *careless and irresponsible*, because they allowed the interfaces of the architectural services to change often.

The architecture team, on the other hand, was frustrated to deliver what seemed *good architectural services*, but that the application team complained were either changing too fast, or simply not working correctly.

The highest point of frustration was reached probably in early 2000, when after failing many times to deliver on a scheduled date, the application team became both frustrated and fearful that the project would get canned and that the application team would be dismantled, or - in the worst case scenario - fired.

7.3.1   The Change in Direction

In May of 2000, however, my firm was contracted to help this situation. It was a desperate act of management to give it one last try. It was a "do or die" situation: either the effort would be successful within 3 months, or both the architecture team and the second application team would have to wait indefinitely. In the meantime, the company would stay with the legacy mainframe applications.

I recommended a short list of changes to be implemented:

Treat the architecture and the second application team as one team, and concentrate only on the delivery of that application.

Stop worrying about "reusable generic services" that may or may not be used, and concentrate only in what the second application needs.

Increase the feedback among all parties involved through the use of Scrum: application team members, architecture team members, production support team members and testing team members.

Stop worrying about documentation. Document the system after you go to production.

Find out a list of the minimal features that a production system will need and force both the application and the architecture team to work together on a daily basis to accomplish the work on that list.

The solution proposed was very radical and it caused many things to happen within the first month:

The official so-called "architect" of the system quit the project. Her primary reason was that she didn't have enough control over the architecture. However, with his departure, and without his explicit and draconian control, things started to move a lot faster.

The new "architect" allowed the architecture to be treated as if it were part of the application, meaning that everything in the architecture tasks was given priority in terms of the impact that it would have on the application schedule.

All documents other than the code, the user's guide, and the production support documents were stopped.

A list of essential features was created through a Product Backlog, and a Sprint Backlog was created for a Sprint.

The new architect and his new team were immediately assigned to work in pairs with the developers of the application.

Scrum meetings were held every morning at 9 am; this caused:

Team members to show up on time.

Team members to acknowledge their true status.

Team members to get familiar with what others were doing and the problems they were having. This caused the whole team to get an overall **sense of urgency.**

Management to resolve issues. During the first weeks it was noticeable that management wasn't involved in the project as much because they kept reporting – more than anyone else, the same status. By the end of the second week the most embarrassed team members were the production support manager and the testing manager who had not been able to establish the production and testing environments.

After only 1 month, a very imperfect release emerged. Everyone was excited. By working together the tension between the application team and the architecture team had decreased – they were in it together after all. Even some people dedicated to update the Rose diagrams in the architecture team had stopped documenting, and participated in the bug fixes. Actually, the Rose diagrams went untouched from there on, because everyone was much more excited about actually releasing code to production.

However, the system was still not in production. After a quick demo to management, a new planning meeting took place to choose the next wave of Product Backlog and the remaining bug fixes in the previous Sprint Backlog. The second release (after only three weeks) in early August provided an implementation of most functionality. And the final Sprint – the one that delivered the system to production in early September, mostly solved bugs.

We had actually missed the "end of August" deadline imposed by management to cut-off the project by seven days but by now top management saw results and they were pleased.

7.3.2   The Second Application

Meanwhile, I organized the second team and a newly created third team to follow in the first team's footsteps:

Choose a minimal list of features and create Sprint Backlogs;

Work with the architecture team by "pairing" resources to resolve issues and develop features; and,

Take the attitude of "servicing" the application teams within the architecture team.

The second application was released in later October. And the third application was released in January of 2001.

7.3.3   More Applications

As of the summer of 2001, there are ten applications in production using the same technology, five more under development to be released before the end of the year, and from fifteen to twenty five more scheduled to be delivered over the next two years. The third application team got a company wide award for its performance. They developed a fairly large application, involving dozens of screens and CICS transactions in only five months, with at least three-quarters of their team being retrained mainframe developers. What a contrast from the first few years of development!

7.4   Case Study of Large Project: An Outsourcing Company

In the spring of 1994, I got involved in a large software development project to outsource benefit management operations. Its goal was to implement software for 1) defined benefit (DB) plans like pensions, 2) defined contribution (DC) plans like 401Ks, and 3) health and welfare (HW) plans. Its primary goal was to replace an IBM mainframe-based system implemented with on-line CICS, assembler, COBOL, VSAM and IMS.

Customer service representatives and clients would continue to be the primary users of the software. The new 3-tier system was to be developed using Power Builder and VRUs (voice response units) on the presentation tiers, C++ on the middle tier, and Sybase and the legacy data stores on the backend.

Apart from the old technologies used - which were seen as a dead-end for the company's technology strategy - the old system was perceived as being very expensive, because the implementation of every client required new code. The methodology for the implementation of a new client was basically: 1) copy the code of the client that best fits the description of the new client, and 2) tweak as needed for the customer ad infinitum. Instead, the new system proposed to only implement the *differences* found from the base system and whatever a new client needed. In theory it would save a great deal of money to the company. An existing client that was willing to be the guinea pig drove the first implementation of the system. The risk to this client was minimal since their benefits program was outsourced anyhow, and there was a backup plan to continue its outsourcing with the mainframe system should anything not work as expected.

It was a good business plan. However, something went wrong with the software implementation. The first release was planned for January 1st, 1995, but that didn't happen. These are some of the characteristics of the project:

It took a very long time to gather all of the requirements up-front.

It took a very long time for the architecture to be *defined* in paper by the so-called architects of the system. In the meantime there were 30 coders waiting for their designs.

It took a very long time to develop the ability to do configuration management, testing and release management.

There was little or no communication with the customer.

There were excessive layers of management.

Most everyone was demoralized, overworked and frustrated and no one really believed in the project plan anymore. In fact, it used to be the center of jokes and sarcastic comments.

The organization kept changing organizational structure: from subsystem driven, to phase driven, to tier driven, to client driven, going around in circles.

By the summer of 1995, almost 2 years after the project had been started there wasn't even a single piece of functionality that ran end-to-end for the first customer. Then a second customer was signed-up. You could see *fear* in the eyes of people, who asked themselves "If we can't finish with one customer, how do they (marketing) dare to sell another one?"

By now, the project had consumed 30 million dollars and at its peak had 80 staffers and 80 consultants working full-time. The company was facing the possibility of lawsuits and had already paid high fines for not delivering the system to the first client in the first year, and was facing more fines for the first client and the second client, if the system was not delivered by January 1st, 1996.

By August of 1995, there was an incredible amount of staff turnover. Almost everyone that had worked on the first client was bailing out of the sinking ship, and new resources were interviewed and hired almost daily. The only problem was that there was an estimated three-month learning curve for the system; basically, the new resources would be actually useless for the 1/1/1996 release.

Despite this situation, and desperate to save the company's division from going bankrupt, I and a few other managers and technical resources proposed in late August to write the application for the second client using a different strategy. We would select ten of the best people in the organization, hire ten new ones and create a "small team" environment. We were tired of failing using the "rules" of the organization but we still believed in ourselves. It was very evident that neither the stiff processes, nor expensive tools, nor the beautiful Gantt charts we had used so far would help us.

I gathered some of the existing techniques to manage small to medium size teams and we chose org patterns and the Scrum techniques to manage our project. Org patterns had been recently published in the proceedings of the first two pattern conferences and Jeff Sutherland had recently announced Scrum in the OTUG (object technology user's group) mailing list.

So in early September, equipped with our newly found friends, we had our first "Sprint Planning meeting." We chose to implement the "indicative data" section of the application that included beneficiaries, their addresses, phones and basic plan information. This functionality was what was promised to the client by January 1st, 1996. We created a backlog that broke this functionality in assignable chunks. However, one of the key differences of Scrum was that it allowed Backlog items other than functional requirements. This made a tremendous difference because we could see for once the "hidden tasks" that we had left out by blindly making our plans "use case driven." We chose to have only two Sprints of about two months each. We chose to implement only indicative data in the first Sprint, and to implement plan information in the second Sprint.

Even before we had our first Sprint planning session, we started meeting every morning at 10 am for 15 minutes to hold the Daily Scrum meetings. These meetings kept us focused on what we were doing and they kept constant score on what was being done. They also allowed us to manage and expand the Backlog according to our needs. Our Backlog was kept as an Excel spreadsheet that included:

what was required to be done,

what was the priority of the work,

who was responsible if the item had been assigned,

a rough estimate of how long would it take to complete,

an entry for who had created the Backlog entry.

At the Daily Scrums items were either removed from the Backlog, changed status, or were added. We soon found out it requires quite a bit of discipline to run the Scrum meetings and to keep track of the issues. I acted as Scrum Master and struggled to keep the list in synch.

Our first iteration was a booming success. For the first time in two years we had produced something that actually executed and everyone was very excited. Our second iteration delivered our application on time for release to production, but we struggled a lot for this delivery. However, this struggle showed us what Scrum was really capable of. Scrum integrated all of the management tasks into managing the Backlog, and that included backlog items for everyone in the team including testing, production support, release management, configuration management, and of course software development. This feature of Scrum was perhaps the most beneficial.

Nobody could believe it. We had done with about twenty people what couldn't be done with 200 in the previous two years. And remember that half of the twenty were new hires.

The following year, we put four more releases in production, and we had expanded the number of concurrent Scrum teams to three. One Scrum took care of the conversion, another one was still dedicated to indicative data, and a third one was dedicated to pension calculations.

Before the first release to production, this division of the company was considering losses. A year later, it was a profitable operation.

CHAPTER 8

Scrum And The Organization

Most organizations aren't optimized for productivity. Scrum helps them to optimize, freeing employees to do their best and removing impediments to productivity. —

8.1 Organizational Impact

Scrum can be used to re-engineer an organization so that it is more productive. Organizations are rarely optimized for productivity. As they grow and mature, inefficiencies accumulate. Just as fat slowly accumulates and clogs human arteries, slowing the flow of blood through the heart, inefficiencies accumulate and clog the organization's arteries, slowing everything down. An informal organization arises within the formal organization. The people who are said to "know how to get things done" are the people who know how this informal organization works. These people know how to function effectively within both organizations, and for this reason, most successful managers have a few people like this on their staff. However, this is an inefficient way to boost productivity. It makes more sense to solve the underlying problems.

Many people come to work and are faced with obstacles they have to surmount before they can start working. As they work, they spend much of their time removing additional obstacles. They try to get out of meetings, they try to get purchasing to hurry up and get some needed software, they have to meet with personnel to go over a new review policy, and they are called into a status meeting. Not only do all of these obstacles take time, they interrupt the ability of a team and its members to focus on work. People need to get their minds around a problem, discuss it, and come up with the best way to solve it. The opportunity to do so at work is pretty rare.

Scrum makes obstacle removal an objective. The Scrum Master is responsible for listening to obstacles and removing them. Scrum tries very hard to free people to be productive, to do their very best, by providing uninterrupted time when they can work.

Scrum offers organizations the opportunity to identify obstacles to productivity. At every Daily Scrum, impediments to work are identified and plans are made to remove them. These impediments rarely represent isolated incidences of inefficiency within the organization. Rather, they are usually part of a larger problem. Scrum is constructed so these impediments are highlighted, day after day, until they are resolved. This is called "bottom-up process re-engineering," because the impediments are actual problems hindering important development projects. This type of process re-engineering is based on actual need.

At the Daily Scrum, the team is asked if there are any impediments to performing its work. This question is not regularly asked in most development projects, and these projects accumulate impediments like a ship accumulates barnacles, until there are eventually so many impediments on the project that it is hard for the project to make any headway. The most formal impediment identification mechanism I'd heard of before Scrum was called the "project post mortem." At the post mortem, after the damage is already done, management met with the team to identify what could have been done differently. Too little, too late.

Once a team identifies an impediment, it expects the impediment to be removed. A team assumes that if someone is asking if there are impediments, he or she is going to do something about the impediments. If management doesn't remove the impediments quickly, Daily Scrums grow progressively more demoralizing. They eventually become embarrassing. If management does not remove impediments, it becomes clear that it cares so little about the project that it would rather accept productivity loss than help the team. If management cannot or will not remove the impediments that are reported, then it sometimes makes sense to recommended that the Sprint be cancelled.

One of the most important responsibilities of managers is making sure that productivity remains as high as possible. Scrum provides management with a daily glimpse at productivity levels and the factors that are affecting them. It gives them a sort of managerial cheat sheet: a list of ways in which management can increase productivity. What an opportunity! Here is a chance for management to both remove the impedances forever and to help the project succeed. Every time managers hear the word "impediments," they should think "opportunity."

8.2   Impediment Example 1

The organization had a number of projects underway that would together build the next release of an Internet news service. A senior engineer writing C++ needed a library from RogueWave Software and requisitioned it from purchasing. During the Daily Scrum, the Scrum Master noticed that she kept bringing this up as an impediment. The Scrum Master knew that if she called RogueWave, the library could be delivered the next day. For some reason, she had already waited four days, and during this time, a key piece of software wasn't being developed.

The Scrum Master did two things. First, the Scrum Master immediately removed the impediment by calling RogueWave and buying the software. The engineer was productive the next day. Then the Scrum Master went to purchasing to find out what the hold up had been. There was one person doing purchasing work, and this person was wrapped up with the quarterly financials. Purchasing was backed up, and the Scrum Master recommended that additional help be hired during this busy time period.

8.3   The Scrum Master as a Change Agent

Who is responsible for removing impediments? The answer is the entire organization. The Scrum Master takes charge of the impediments, assuming responsibility for working with everyone in the organization to remove them. But the whole organization has to be committed.

The Scrum Master runs the Daily Scrums, is in touch with all aspects of the project, and is responsible for ensuring that impediments are removed. The Scrum Master needs to have management's full support and engagement. Most importantly, the Scrum Master needs to have the authority to cause impediments to be removed. If management disagrees with actions that the Scrum Master takes, it should offer suggestions, provide guidance, and give coaching. But no matter what, management must support the Scrum Master. In the previous example, management supported the Scrum Master's decision to acquire the RogueWave software library and promptly reimbursed the Scrum Master for the out-of-pocket expenses.

Empowering the Scrum Master to remove impediments is a touchy subject. An impediment is something that is putting a damper on productivity. If an organization welcomes these opportunities and appreciates the efforts of the Scrum Master, Scrum is operating as it should and productivity increases. However, attempts to remove impediments do not always go over well. Sometimes organizations have accommodated impediments for so long that they are unwilling to remove them. For instance, the head of purchasing might react negatively when the Scrum Master tries to have a problem in purchasing fixed. In some companies, the Scrum Master in the above example would have been criticized for not going through purchasing and for not following standard procedures.

A friend of mine asked, "How would this work in a large centralized purchasing department where change was nonexistent due to implementation of SAP, for instance?" The Scrum Master could still expense the software to immediately resolve the impediment. Then the organization would have an example to test the effectiveness of the SAP implementation in purchasing. Was the new purchasing process reducing productivity? If so, how could it be improved?

Scrum causes change. Organizations that implement Scrum should expect to enjoy greater productivity and the ability to produce regular, competitive releases. However, they should also expect to incrementally reengineer themselves. Scrum offers a great opportunity for increasing an organization's productivity. However, the Scrum Master needs to know what authority he has to rapidly resolve impediments. If the answer is "not much," then maybe the organization in question isn't ready to implement Scrum. This may provide an opportunity to reflect on the organization's priorities and on the balance between organizational stability, flexibility, productivity, and competitiveness.

8.4   Impediment Example 2

Complex, n-tier software was being built for delivery of products across the Internet at a company. As new engineers were added to the team, personnel would notify purchasing, which would acquire equipment and software according to standards set by a vendor. However, the standards were over a year old, and developers were trying to develop using multiple windows on 15-inch monitors. The engineers accepted them because they thought 15-inch monitors were what management had selected. Management's attention was focused elsewhere, and no one in management was aware that there was a problem.

During the Daily Scrums, the Scrum Master often heard about engineers using two workstations at once: one for development, and another obsolete workstation for email and office applications. The engineers had "requisitioned" second workstations from departing employees. This was very inventive of them; they were using available resources to solve their problem. However, the use of multiple workstations inevitably led to overcrowding. When the Scrum Master investigated the situation and found its root cause, the Scrum Master immediately contacted the vendor so that the team would only receive large monitors. The Scrum Master then worked with management to bring the workstation standard up-to-date and to make it easier for engineers to modify the workstation standard when necessary.

8.5   Impediment Example 3

A team was readying a tunable laser subsystem for an important electronics show. Two senior engineers were in charge of engineering the subsystem. Other members with less optical physics experience were handling the programming, parts assembly, and board preparation. During the Daily Scrum, the senior engineers kept talking about how much difficulty they were having obtaining parts. The subsystem was absolutely cutting-edge technology, so they had to procure very advanced components from other manufacturers. Telephone tag was consuming most of their time, breaking their concentration, and delaying the arrival of critical components.

The Scrum Master equipped the senior engineers with cell phones and reassigned a junior engineer to take the lead in understanding and procuring components. The Scrum Master had to use an engineer because of the complexity of the procurement and the amount of engineering discussion that had to take place for procurement to be handled correctly. Whenever a question arose that he couldn't answer, the junior engineer would call the senior engineers on their cell phones, resolve the question, and continue the procurement process.

8.6   Keep Your Eyes Open

Daily Scrums make team dynamics more visible, and the team learns to use them to discuss gripes, or impediments. Management must listen not only to the explicitly stated impediments, but also to the general conversation prior to and after the Scrum. Impediments that the team has come to think of as "our company's way of doing business" are often discussed then. Listen closely and think about what you're hearing at these Daily Scrums. Patterns emerge from conversations, jokes, and ribbings that lead the astute observer to find hidden impediments that everyone takes for granted. Remove them and make the team more productive.

8.7   Impediment Example 4

During one project the Scrum Master noticed that the engineers kept getting up and going to other cubicles to discuss what they were doing. The organization had everyone except senior managers in cubicles and wasn't amenable to an open workspace environment. Since the team was formed dynamically, the cubicles weren't adjacent, and the engineers had to break their concentration to get up and walk over to someone else's cube, who very well might not be there. With the participation of systems administration (cabling and phone extension changes), the Scrum Master moved the team so everyone was adjacent to each other. Then the Scrum Master put chairs by the cubicle walls, so team members could see over the cubes to ask questions and discuss design issues. Suddenly, the team's work area looked like a prairie dog town, heads popping up as team members worked more effectively with each other.

The productivity from rearranging the cube assignments resulted from astute observation by the Scrum Master. Rather than accepting everything as a given, the Scrum Master was driven to do anything to make the team's life easier, to make them able to be more productive.

8.8   Impediment Example 5

Each team member reported at the Daily Scrum that they had no impediments. However, for the last day they had been working on peer reviews, and they would be continuing to work on them for the next two days. The organization had a semi-annual review process when everyone who has worked with an individual is required to complete a "Peer Review" form. These were fodder for the individual's manager in completing the review. Since everyone worked with most everyone else, each individual had to complete at least five, and sometimes more than ten, peer review forms.

Everyone on the team saw this as a normal part of working at that company. The Scrum Master saw it as an impediment. This hadn't been planned into the Sprint Backlog and it had nothing to do with completing the project. The Peer Review process was an organizational responsibility, rather than project imperative. And the team members were used to organizational responsibilities taking priority over their project responsibilities. The Scrum Master got the team back on their project work and requested that management defer the Peer Review process until after the Sprint.

8.9   Organizational Encroachment

I worked at Wang Laboratories during its golden years (1980-1984) and during the start of its calcification (1985). Wang was growing rapidly during this time, and people were being hired left and right. As Wang grew, a lot of support functions were delegated to newly created support organizations. Soon senior vice presidents, who had vice presidents, directors, and managers reporting to them, headed these support organizations, like personnel and purchasing. They spent their time researching and developing policies, procedures, forms, and protocols that were imposed on the rest of the organization. Everyone had to follow these, since otherwise they'd be bucking the Senior VP. It became easier to do the organizationally imposed work than to see what was reasonable. Work gave way to bureaucracy. Initiative gave way to stagnation. This, of course, isn't the full story of Wang's demise by any stretch of the imagination. But it certainly did cause a lot of productivity loss to my projects.

Scrum, through the impediment identification, provides a way for management to become vividly aware of this organizational encroachment on productivity. Everyone griped about Peer Review, but accepted it and kept going. However, as a result of it being highlighted during the Daily Scrum, management was primed to see the consequences and take action. The whole review process was rewritten by line management *with the support of personnel,* into something much more streamlined and appropriate.

8.10   Impediment Example 6

During the Daily Scrum, the Scrum Master noticed the team members were counting their change. When questioned, they disclosed that they were determining if they had enough change to buy coffee. They had chosen to work late to deepen some functionality, and they wanted coffee to keep sharp. However, there was only one coffee machine on the floor and it required $.85 in exact change. In desperation, the team members sometimes had to hunt down the janitors and borrow change from them!

The Scrum Master had never worked anywhere that didn't provide either inexpensive or free coffee to its developers, so the Scrum Master was baffled by this oversight. The Scrum Master figured he would remedy this immediately, because it was a no-brainer, a slam-dunk, something with impact and little effort. The Scrum Master called the facilities manager and told her that the team needed coffee, and what would she recommend? She indicated that the company had coffee previously, but everyone griped about it. She had gotten tired of their complaints, and now there was no free coffee. The Scrum Master was aghast, and protested that if the team wanted to take caffeine to stay awake and write alert code, the least the company could do was provide the caffeine for free. The facilities manager retorted that this was a family company and it didn't want to encourage indulgence in drugs that kept the engineers away from their families. Then she went ballistic and informed senior management that Scrum was undercutting company values!

Whew, that was a workout just to get coffee. Eventually, coffee worked its way back into the organization, but each time with reference to when the Scrum Master got his head handed to him over a cup of coffee.

8.11   Scrum and Mission Statements

Organizations have mission statements. For example, a provider of health-care information systems has the following mission statement:

"XXSYS uses information technology to maximize value in the delivery of healthcare — by improving the quality of patient service, enhancing medical outcomes, and reducing the cost of care."

Everything an organization does probably should be in support of this mission, or be explained, or the mission revised to accommodate exceptions. Anything that an organization values that impedes that mission should probably be stated. For instance, in the infamous case of the free coffee, that organization's mission statement would have to be modified as such:

"XXSYS uses information technology to maximize value in the delivery of healthcare — by improving the quality of patient service, enhancing medical outcomes, and reducing the cost of care, unless the employees need coffee."

CHAPTER 9

Scrum Values

> Scrum is based on a set of fundamental values. These values are the bedrock on which Scrum's practices rest. —

As I've described Scrum, I've also described some of the values, or qualities, that the people using Scrum display – commitment, focus, openness, respect, and courage. These values all emerge as people participate in Scrum. Scrum teams are asked to take initiative, to wrestle with complex requirements and technology. To do this, the team must learn to rely on itself. During a Sprint, no one external to the team tells the team what to do. The team has to figure it out on its own. It may have to go up blind alleys, to make compromises, or even fail. But the team and its members have to be forthright and resolute as they attempt to do their work and meet their commitments. This section demonstrates how Scrum values emerged at a startup medical products company, MedImp (an alias for a real company).

Medimp produces an innovative product that allows healthcare professionals to capture healthcare charges and view laboratory results on a handheld computer. Several healthcare institutions were successfully using its products. Servers that synchronized the information to the handheld computers with healthcare institution's legacy systems were supplied and managed by MedImp. Consequently, when the healthcare institution signed up for MedImp's products, MedImp would bring servers into the institution, interface them, and then monitor and control them from MedImp. MedImp was an application service provider (ASP) to the healthcare institution.

I was brought in during mid-2000 as MedImp's sales and implementations started to ramp up. MedImp needed to deliver servers to new accounts while improving the total product reliability, availability, and sustainability (RAS). MedImp had recently formed a Systems Engineering team to take on this work. Their job was to build an ASP system that could deliver adequate RAS to the customer. My job was to show them how to use Scrum to continue delivering systems to customers while they improved RAS.

9.1   Commitment

> Be willing to commit to a goal. Scrum provides people all the
> authority they need to meet their commitments.   —

Most of us have trouble standing up and saying that we'll commit
to something. We've learned from experience that it's often best not to.
Scrum has practices that support and encourage commitment. For instance, the team has the authority to decide how to do the work it's selected. The notion that a team of people will have absolute autonomy and
full authority to do its best is novel in most organizations. Most employees
are used to being told what to do and how to do it. At first, people are
distrustful and do not believe that management will let Scrum operate this
way. But once people start experiencing empowerment, they begin to have
faith in their leaders and even in themselves.

When I arrived at MedImp, the systems engineering team was trying
to improve the product's reliability, availability and sustainability (RAS).
Every time a system at a customer site crashed, the team struggled to get
it back up again. Since the systems were at remote locations, the team
wanted to be proactive. Its goal was to notice that a system was going
down before the customer called.

The team was firefighting existing problems while trying to improve
RAS within the existing ASP model and determine the proper long-term
solution. The team's first step had been to upgrade to dual-CPU Compaq
servers. Its second step was to review offerings from vendors of monitoring,
control, and backup/recovery solutions. When I arrived, it was in the
middle of assessing solutions from many vendors.

I instituted Daily Scrums and became the Scrum Master. I immediately saw a major obstacle to committing to adequate RAS. "Adequate"
hadn't been defined! The service contracts didn't specify the performance
or the availability of the MedImp offerings. Because there was no stated
goal, the customers and management expected adequate to be perfection,
the absence of any problems. The systems engineers didn't know if ade-
quacy entailed 99% reliability 24x7, or 90% only during the hours when
the customers were using the system. Since the team didn't know the RAS
target, it didn't know which vendor offerings were appropriate. I quickly
escalated this issue to management and determined that the team had
to support 99.9% availability per month only during the shifts when the
customers were using the product.

The second issue in determining the right ASP solution was price.
Some of the vendors offered solutions that were quite expensive, and would
raise the price per ASP system by over $30,000. No one knew if this was
acceptable or not, since no one had a pricing model to use for various size

institutions. Was a \$100,000 solution acceptable to a 50-user healthcare institution, or would a \$20,000 solution be more appropriate? The prior model had simply been "as inexpensive as possible." Management revised the pricing model, establishing a "high water mark" to support 50 users that was \$50,000 in capital costs. The team also had to take scalability into account. The RAS model had to scale with the pricing model. Users expected fees to decline with volume, so RAS costs had to similarly scale downwards.

The team now had the requirements and could commit. It needed to build an ASP solution that was 99% available during shifts when the system was being used and which had an installed cost of less than \$50,000. Its job was to design, test, and start implementing a solution that met these criteria. The team was able to quickly focus the vendors on these requirements. Many of the solutions were too expensive, some of the solutions provided inadequate RAS, and some vendors just didn't have Linux products.

9.2   Focus

> Do your job. Focus all of your efforts and skills on doing the work that you've committed to doing. Don't worry about anything else.
> —

Producing a valuable product increment out of somewhat vague requirements and unstable technology is hard work. It requires attention and focus. The problem needs to dominate our thoughts, to fill our mind; all of our time at work should be consumed by our attempts to solve the problem. Once we are focused, all of our time is spent looking for and trying solutions to bring order to the problem. People who are attracted to building systems and products like to fix problems. Scrum lets a team set up problems and provides them an environment in which it can focus. But old habits are hard to break, and most of us are used to accommodating distractions. There are so many things to do at work. We are fodder that other people use to fill their days, and we use other people as fodder to fill up our own days.

The systems engineering team at MedImp was under the gun. It had committed to meeting RAS and pricing targets with an ASP solution that it designed. In every engineering problem, there are four constraints: cost, time, quality, and functionality. RAS represented the quality constraint. Implementation schedules driven by sales represented the time constraint. Functionality was variable so long as RAS was met. The cost of engineering the solution was also somewhat flexible, although I learned that it was difficult to increase our engineering costs since engineers were impossible to find and the fees were astronomical during this time period, the latter half of the year 2000. Most available systems engineers were skilled in Sun/Solaris using Oracle, but MedImp's existing ASP model used Compaq/Linux and Oracle. MedImp tried to find engineers who had experience with Intel and Linux architectures, but they couldn't be found, experienced or not, full time or contracted. The team wasted a great deal of time interviewing people who professed to have, but actually didn't have, the needed skills.

The team wasn't focused on the problem. It was spending all of its time maintaining existing ASP implementations and interviewing people. During the Daily Scrums, I noticed increasing frustration. How was the team going to meet its commitments if it didn't have the people? While discussing this problem, several of the systems engineers bemoaned the fact that they weren't using Sun/Solaris solutions. Their backgrounds were in Sun/Solaris. More talent was available on the street with Sun/Solaris skills. Why couldn't the team use Sun/Solaris? Then it hit them! The team had the authority to figure out how to meet its commitments. If it could design an acceptable ASP model using Sun/Solaris, that was fine! The result was that the team shifted to a Sun/Solaris solution. By doing so, not only did it draw on existing strengths and skills, but also it was able to utilize engineering talent available from Sun resellers and distributors. MedImp was also able to find Sun/Solaris engineers that could be contracted. The team was able to increase engineering costs to meet quality and time requirements, even in a desperately tight job market.

There are so many other distractions at work. Email is a big one, particularly with the "cc" feature and with mailing lists. Employees arrive in the morning to find a full mailbox that needs to be tended. During the day, all sorts of interesting email arrives. Commercial conversation groups provide even further distraction; they provide sounding boards for ongoing arguments and discussions about everything from raising kids, to skateboarding, to building computer systems. The team found that it was best to start "filtering" its email, most importantly all "cc" emails. The founders of the company, who came from an academic setting, loved the intellectual dialogues that these emails promoted, and the team had felt that - to live up to company expectations - it had to participate. I gave them "permission" to skip the participation, and the amount of email dropped to an acceptable level.

One of the finest Scrum Masters I've ever worked with had a saying: "What's that got to do with code?" She applied this rule unfailingly at Daily Scrums, thereby helping teams learn to focus on the task at hand. With time, this type of focus becomes ingrained and team members naturally deflected distractions.

9.3   Openness

Scrum keeps everything about a project visible to everyone.   —

Scrum keeps everything open and visible. Openness is required for Scrum to work, and Scrum mechanisms help foster this openness. Product Backlog, for example, is visible to everyone. Daily Scrums keep visible what a team is working on. The results of a Sprint are visible during the Sprint Review meeting. And work trends and velocity are made visible by tracking remaining work across time. Scrum removes the ability to dissemble. Responsibilities are clear, authority is allocated, and everything is visible.

While the Scrum team was Sprinting, management requested some team members to investigate and pursue an IBM solution. I immediately detected this distraction in the Daily Scrum when someone complained, "We can't meet with EMC to look at its Sun compatible storage solution because there's an IBM meeting!" I told them to skip the IBM meeting. The team learned that it has the right and the authority to meet its Sprint commitments. How it meets these commitments is up to them.

One Scrum practice that counters interference is the rule that no one is allowed to add work to a Sprint once it is underway. Once the MedImp team was underway, and the ASP model problem was being solved within defined constraints, no one was allowed to add work to the team's backlog by changing the nature of the ASP model problem. I've found this type of distraction to be particularly true in start up organizations because so many options are being explored at once. If the team can't stay with its commitments, the product just won't get out the door. People and teams spend their time chasing one option after another, and not much of anything gets produced.

It is better to produce something than it is to pursue many alternatives, please everyone, and produce nothing. The IBM partnering alternative was very attractive (and eventually selected), but the team was Sprinting to mold a Sun/Solaris solution. As Scrum Master, I asked management to decide whether to cancel the Sprint or not, because the IBM work was outside of the Sprint's backlog. If management had selected to cancel the Sprint, we could have redefined another Sprint to include the IBM work, but then the team probably couldn't have committed to delivering much of an improvement to RAS. Management agreed to ask IBM to proceed on its own, and instructed the team to continue the Sprint.

9.4   Respect

> Individuals are shaped by their background and their experiences.
> It is important to respect the different people who comprise a
> team.   —

First, management staffs a team. These are usually the best people
who are available. Scrum then establishes an environment in which these
people can work together as a team. Every individual has his or her own
strengths and weaknesses, comes from a unique background, and is trained
and gains skills through a unique history of education and employment.
Mix these individuals into a team and it gains the strengths of team dynamics. You also can anticipate prejudice, resentments, petty squabbles,
and all of the other negative attributes of human relationships. Stir into
this mix the difficult technology and emerging requirements of today's software industry and problems will undoubtedly occur.

Dave was hired to be the Oracle systems administrator in the systems
engineering team at MedImp. The team had committed to a Sprint goal.
Dave had assumed that the Sun/Solaris implementation of Oracle would be
similar to the IBM implementations that he had administered at previous
jobs. Unfortunately, Dave found that the tricks he had learned for IBM
didn't work on Sun/Solaris. Dave had also never implemented a solution
on a fault-tolerant EMC I/O subsystem using RAID 5. Dave struggled to
keep up with the database administration work he had committed to, but
he fell further and further behind.

The other systems engineers started to feel that Dave was slowing
them down. They had to help him with his work so they could progress
with their work. As their work suffered, they began to resent him. Dave
felt this and started to come in to work later and later in the day, not
wanting to face what he perceived to be his inadequacies. But Dave was
quite adequate. Dave was faced with a mix of requirements and technology
that was beyond his skills to solve in the allotted time. His fellow team
members weren't happy about the possibility that the team might fail to
achieve its goals, and they had found in Dave a convenient, if undeserving,
scapegoat. We all have seen this kind of situation. It sometimes gets out
of hand, and inevitably ends when the team loses Dave.

People are not used to working in self-organizing teams. By "self-
organizing," I'm referring to the team's adjusting and adapting to meet its
commitments for a Sprint. Although management has selected the team
members, Scrum leaves the actual determination of who does what up to
the team. The team self-organizes not only at the beginning of a Sprint,
but continually as work progresses throughout the Sprint. Since it is the
team as a whole that commits to the Sprint goal, the team is going to

sink or swim together. There are no individual heroics, just team heroics. When a team member is weak, other team members have to pick up the slack. Nothing helps people do their best, despite their shortcomings, as much as group pressure and a team environment.

Since the team had settled on a Sun/Solaris solution, Dave was doing his best. But he was frustrated to find that his skills weren't readily portable to the Sun/Solaris platform. The team needed good database administration. Because Dave was unable to provide what the team needed, the team felt that Dave was letting it down.

Scrum is empirical. The team can always reduce functionality or increase costs (if the budget allows) to meet its goals. Dave's job wasn't getting done. What could we do? Dave hadn't experienced Scrum before and didn't know that he was empowered to figure out how to meet his commitments. I posed this question to Dave – what was he going to do to meet his commitments? After brainstorming with the whole team about his options, Dave exercised his authority and brought in an Oracle database administration consultant to help and train him. Luckily, he was able to quickly acquire the services of one such consultant from a Sun reseller. The point the team learned from this was not to focus on what couldn't be done, but instead to brainstorm about how it could meet its commitments. These individuals had committed as a team, and so they needed to work together as a team. There could be no individual failures, only team failures.

It is important to do your best, to remember everyone else is doing his or her best as well, and to help your teammates whenever you can. After several Sprints, teams learn each other's strengths and weaknesses, accept them, and learn how to accommodate them and compensate for them.

9.5   Courage

> Have the courage to commit, to act, to be open, and to expect respect.   —

Few people come from a work environment with Scrum values. Although empowerment is a trendy word, most organizations are still hierarchical and authoritarian. For a team to act differently requires courage. I am speaking of two kinds of courage: the courage to find out that the environment will support these values, and the courage to be willing to find out that relying on one's own judgment is acceptable – even laudable.

Courage in Scrum isn't a visible, tangible thing. It is not some kind of romantic heroism. Instead, it is having the guts, the determination, to do the best you can. It's the stubbornness not to give up, but to figure out how to meet commitments. This type of courage is gritty, not glorious. Dave's courage was the willingness to openly admit that he needed help and to ask the rest of the team to help him figure out what to do. The courage went a step further when he assumed the authority to do something about his needs. I saw Dave vacillate for several weeks. Sometimes I'd see Dave fuming and blaming himself for not being "good enough." I helped Dave stand back and understand that he had authority to figure out how to fulfill that responsibility. Dave figured out how to rely on his initiative and wits to devise solutions to his problems. Dave learned that the only person who could decide how to do his work was Dave himself.

Scrum isn't for everyone. But it is for those who need to wrestle working systems from the complexity of emerging requirements and unstable technology.

Bibliography

[Agile]   Fowler, M. and J. Highsmith, *The Agile Manifesto*, Software Development, **9**(8): 28-32, 2001.

[Crosby]   Crosby P., *Quality is Free: The Art of Making Quality Certain*, Mentor Books, 1992.

[DeGrace]   DeGrace P. and Stahl L. H., *Wicked Problems, Righteous Solutions: A Catalogue of Modern Software Engineering Paradigms*, Englewood Cliffs, N.J., Yourdon Press, 1990.

[Dennett]   Dennett, D. C., *Darwin's Dangerous Idea: Evolution and the Meanings of Life*, New York, Simon & Schuster, 1995.

[Fowler]   Fowler, M.,*Is Design Dead?*, Software Development **9**(4), 2001.

[Goldratt]   Goldratt E., *The Goal: A Process of Ongoing Improvement*, North River Press Inc., Great Barrington, MA, 1992.

[Harris97]   Harris M., *Culture, People and Nature*, Addison Wesley Longman, New York, 1997.

[Holland95]   Holland J., *Hidden Order: How Adaptation Builds Complexity*, Addison and Wesley, Reading, MA, 1995.

[Holland98]   Holland J., *Emergence: From Chaos To Order*, Addison and Wesley, Reading, MA, 1998.

[Kauffman93]   Kauffman S., *The Origins of Order: Self-Organization and Selection in Evolution*, Oxford University Press, Oxford, 1993.

[Kuhn]   Kuhn T., *The Structure of Scientific Revolutions*, The University of Chicago Press, Chicago 1970.

[Levy]   Levy, S., *Artificial life: The Quest For A New Creation*, New York, Pantheon Books, 1992.

[McConnell]   McConnell S., *Rapid Development*, Microsoft Press, 1996.

[Miller]   Miller G., *The Magical Number Seven, Plus or Minus Two*, Psychology Review, 1956.

[Peitgen]   Peitgen, Jurgens, and Saupe, *Chaos and Fractals, New Frontiers of Science*, Springer Verlag, 1992.

[ScrumPattern]   Beedle M., Devos M., Sharon Y., Schwaber K., Sutherland J., *Scrum: A Pattern Language for Hyperproductive Software Development*, Pattern Languages of Program Design, Harrison N., Foote B., Rohnert H. (editors), Addison-Wesley, 4: 637-651, 1999.

[Senge]   Senge P. M., *The Fifth Discipline: The Art and Practice Of The Learning Organization*, New York, Doubleday/Currency, 1990.

[Takeuchi and Nonaka] Takeuchi H. and Nonaka I., *The New New Product Development Game*, Harvard Business Review (January 1986), pp. 137-146, 1986.

[Takeuchi and Nonaka] Nonaka I., Takeuchi H., *The Knowledge Creating Company: How Japanese Companies Create the Dynamics of Innovation*, Oxford University Press, Oxford 1995.

[Tunde]   Ogunnaike Babatunde A. and Harmon Ray W., *Process Dynamics, Modeling and Control*, Oxford University Press, 1994.

[Wegner]   Wegner, P., *Why Interaction Is More Powerful Than Algorithms*, Communications of the ACM **40**(5): 80-91, 1997.

[Weinberg]   Weinberg, G., *Quality Software Management (all volumes 1-4)*, Dorset House, 1992-1997.

Index

Early Childhood Theories and Contemporary Issues

An Introduction

Mine Conkbayir and Christine Pascal

B L O O M S B U R Y

LONDON • NEW DELHI • NEW YORK • SYDNEY

Bloomsbury Academic

An imprint of Bloomsbury Publishing Plc

50 Bedford Square	1385 Broadway
London	New York
WC1B 3DP	NY 10018
UK	USA

www.bloomsbury.com

Bloomsbury is a registered trade mark of Bloomsbury Publishing Plc

First published 2014

British Library Cataloguing-in-Publication Data

A catalogue record for this book is available from the British Library.

ISBN: HB: 978-1-7809-3656-7
PB: 978-1-7809-3753-3
ePub: 978-1-7809-3734-2
ePDF: 978-1-7809-3594-2

Library of Congress Cataloging-in-Publication Data

A catalog record for this book is available from the Library of Congress.

Typeset by Fakenham Prepress Solutions, Fakenham, Norfolk NR21 8NN
Printed and bound in Great Britain

For Paul and Delilah

Contents

Foreword

This book brings theories alive and places them right at the heart of the setting. It can be difficult to make theories immediately accessible to busy staff but this book achieves this not least because of Mine Conkbayir's combined skill as a writer and experience as a nursery practitioner and tutor and Professor Christine Pascal's academic credibility. Together they see the importance of practitioners understanding the relevance of theories to better inform high quality practice. They acknowledge that theories are not truths that can apply to every situation but support the use of theories as a helpful way of guiding practitioners to act responsibly and enable learning to take place successfully. Mine is clear that what matters is for practitioners to be able to make informed decisions about how best to respond to the needs of children, their families and the communities in which we work.

Written eloquently with many ideas, questions and suggestions, *Early Childhood Theories and Contemporary Issues: An Introduction* illuminates the salient ideas of traditional theorists and more modern thinkers. The book takes into account the more challenging aspects of embedding learning in the workplace by ensuring questions are built into each chapter to further stimulate debate and dialogue as we work together to ensure practitioners become increasingly more reflective in their work.

As CEO of the London Early Years Foundation, I will be delighted to see this book in our nurseries for staff to use as the need takes them. It will also be on our library shelves as a reference book for those staff who are currently making deeper studies including completing their Early Years qualifications.

June O'Sullivan MBE, Chief Executive, London Early Years Foundation (LEYF).

Preface

Having a good grasp of early childhood theories and what these look like in practice can make a positive difference to how you understand babies and children and the ways in which they learn. This book provides early years practitioners with easy access to a wide range of theories – both traditional and more recent, which can helpfully address the dilemmas and issues faced by today's workforce. We have therefore used those theories that we think have a resonance today, as a platform to discuss three key contemporary issues that practitioners grapple with at present. These being:

- Practitioners' knowledge base concerning development from conception to three.
- Creating inclusive and enabling environments.
- The importance of parents and the home learning environment.

These contemporary issues were highlighted by the practitioners as being particularly challenging in terms of providing high quality provision for babies and the under-twos. A range of sub-issues were also identified by the practitioners which we have categorized under each of the three contemporary issues.

The final chapter (15) is where it all comes together, because putting your knowledge into action then acts as a catalyst for reflective practice – a vital characteristic of professionalism. The work of Donald Schön (1983: 68) on 'reflection in action' encompasses the importance of not only seeking new information but allowing oneself to modify existing beliefs and ways of behaving in light of this new information:

> The practitioner allows herself to experience surprise, puzzlement, or confusion in a situation which she finds uncertain or unique. She reflects on the phenomenon before her, and on the prior understandings which have been implicit in her behaviour. She carries out an experiment which serves to generate both a new understanding of the phenomenon and a change in the situation.

We each enter the realm of early years from vastly different cultural, religious and social backgrounds, and hence, bring with us different perspectives about how children should be looked after and educated, but few of us question why this should be. The result can be practice that is influenced (implicitly or explicitly), by a collection of beliefs that have rarely been reflected upon or challenged. The collection of theories in this book is aimed to get you thinking deeper about what you do to promote children's learning and development and why.

We cannot stress the importance of reflecting on your practice while reading this book, so that you can start thinking about the changes you want to make to your personal practice – and that of your team's. The chapter on action research will help you to achieve your desired changes in the setting. This is how new theories and ways of doing are created – by you, the practitioner being the catalyst for change. It is one thing to read and absorb information, but to create new knowledge takes courage and we hope that this book can help to instil that bit of courage needed to dare to do things differently in your setting. How many times have you thought 'I would do things differently if I could' – this book is the starting point you need, to help you to put your knowledge into action! As Lewin (1948: 202) rightly identified:

> Research that produces nothing but books will not suffice.

Why this book is needed

Our sector is still child development light (Nutbrown, 2012), with practitioners at different levels having a scant knowledge and understanding of the underpinning theories and how these inform practice. A book like this will prove critical in helping the current workforce (including students) to understand how some of these theories still have relevance by locating them in a contemporary context. We decided on this selection of theories having liaised with a diverse group of early years practitioners who all expressed similar opinions about their areas of concern.

We felt it important to include a balance of 'old and new' because these traditional theories still have something to say concerning current practice even though aspects will not be so relevant today. Our argument is that if you do not understand history, you cannot hope to understand the present, and we certainly cannot afford to have practitioners caring for children who do not understand the sheer importance of their role in promoting children's learning and development – especially when it can make all the difference to their outcomes in the long term (Marmot Review, 2010).

Structure of the book

This book comprises two broad sections. The first section (Chapters 1 – 11) consists of those theories forming the bedrock of early years provision, which many practitioners have hitherto been guided by and base their work upon. The second section

(Chapters 12 – 15) consists of theories that look to the future – these being findings from neuroscience and the reconceptualization of childhood. (We use the term reconceptualization in place of postmodernism, although the two are often used interchangeably.)

This book begins with an introduction to theory, with an explanation of how a theory develops in light of the social and economic conditions which exist at the time. Each chapter follows a similar format, which comprises of a discussion of the individual theory (or concept) and how you can apply this to the babies and children with whom you work. Practical tips are also provided on how you can test these ideas out for yourself in the early years setting, alongside questions for reflection which encourage you to think about the theories in relation to the work that you do. Early language consultants, family support workers, nursery managers, nursery officers and head teachers, have each provided case studies which serve to bring some pertinent early years issues to life, across the 15 chapters.

Each chapter concludes with two sets of questions which are designed to help you to reflect in line with some of the reconceptualists' thinking and to question aspects of the theories that you feel do not conform with your experience of working with children and their families.

You will also see an annotated bibliography at the end of each chapter which we strongly recommend you refer to, especially if you are particularly interested in undertaking some further reading for study purposes.

A synopsis of well-known theories of child development is provided along with an overview of what this would actually look like in the setting. Take for example, Jean Piaget's theory of object permanence and egocentrism – some practitioners grapple with such concepts let alone how to support very young children through these developmental stages. In this book readers have an accompanying guide showing how they can support children through these stages and extend their learning and development.

As mentioned, the burgeoning discipline of neuroscience and its implications for understanding children's behaviour more effectively is examined, with practical tips on how practitioners can organize the learning environment and activities to best support babies' and children's holistic development. The reconceptualization of childhood is explored, in order to offer a possible way forward in understanding how babies and children develop – and of the adult's role in facilitating this process. As part of this overview, aspects of traditional theories are challenged, while encouraging practitioners to reflect on the children with whom they work and their capabilities at different ages. The widely accepted notion of developmental norms is challenged with accompanying explanations. Practical tips are provided to help you interpret your observations of babies' and children's behaviour, in light of the more current theories of child development. We recommend that where possible, these activities are undertaken in groups, in order to generate debate and new ideas.

A glossary of terms is included at the end of the book to help familiarize you with any words that you might not be familiar with. In this book, we use the term 'early years' when exploring theories and issues in early years provision. We mean this to encompass both the care and education aspects of early years provision, as the two are inextricably linked and cannot occur effectively without the other being in place. We also use the term 'she' when referring to individuals of both genders.

The aim of this book is to provide a bridge between theory and practice. We hope that you will be enthused and enabled to reflect on your current practice in light of this understanding and use this reflection to innovate and make changes which help you better realize your goals and ambitions for your work with children and families.

 Throughout this book you will notice this icon in the margin. This icon represents keywords which can be found in the Glossary of Terms section on pages 189 to 193.

Acknowledgements

We would like to thank those practitioners, head teachers and Early Years consultants who have given their valuable time to contribute to this book. Their continual hard work in the care and education of children and support for their families is helping to make a much-needed difference to raising the aspirations and life chances of children.

We are grateful for the involvement of Richard Hunter, Andrea Anastasis and Michael Jones. Many thanks are also due to practitioners at the London Early Years Foundation (LEYF) for their reflections and input, especially Chief Executive, June O'Sullivan.

List of Tables and Figures

Tables

Figures

An Overview of Theory and Practice in the Early Years

1

This chapter provides an overview of the theories considered in this book and what each means in the contemporary context of the early years sector. There exists a wide range of traditional and current theories of **pedagogy** and child development that influence practice today. What is essential is that as a practitioner, you can interpret these theories and put them into practice in a way that is meaningful to the children in your setting.

Having a sound understanding of these theories and of what informs your thinking and practice, will put you in a good position to implement the spirit of them, as well as critique and challenge them as you think is appropriate. Alternatively you might want to use them to support further experimentation and innovation in your practice. One theory does not necessarily 'fit all'. It is about using the theory confidently and applying it to inform your practice within your local community and working environment.

What is a theory?

Before you read on, it is worthwhile starting with a firm knowledge of what a **theory** is. A good working definition that we like is provided by the Oxford English Dictionary (2001: 947). A theory is explained as:

> An idea or set of ideas that is intended to explain something.

To summarize then, a theory can be an idea that is repeatedly tested, in order to prove its validity (Gopnik, 2001; Bowlby, 1953; Freud, 1949). However, not all theories are tested out (Rousseau, 1762; Locke, 1693; Plato, 473BC). They can be philosophical or hypothetical. As a reflective practitioner, it is up to you to judge the relevance of the theories that you read about, in order to confidently interpret, compare and put them into practice. In the main, a theory is a useful tool to help you *think* about your practice.

So, a theory can be understood using three alternative approaches:

- as explanation for some phenomenon
- as explanation for a way of doing something (for example, theory of good teaching)
- as a tool for thinking.

Any of these approaches to theory can have **empirical evidence** to support it (for example, theory of attachment), or could be an untested hypothesis.

Where do theories come from?

All theories reflect the time and context in which they emerge. For example, they can be devised in response to government policies or as a response to the socio-economic events of the time. One example of this is Bowlby's theory of attachment (1953). His theory was devised and tested not long after the Second World War and emphasized the role of the female parent in having the most powerful influence on early emotional development. Much of the initial research came from his studies of children whose lives had been disrupted by the Second World War as well as children in residential institutions and in hospitals. For more information about his theory, read Chapter 6.

Theories are not 'truths' that you can apply to every situation or child with whom you work. They arise very often, from asking questions and observing patterns of behaviour. For example, theories such as Piaget's stages of cognitive development (1952) were based upon his observations of children, and interactions with them while they worked on exercises he set. He did this because he wanted to understand how children learn at different ages and stages. His primary method of doing so was by carrying out observations of his own three children.

However, aspects of some theories like Piaget's do not stand the test of time. This is because of challenges made to some of his ideas by Gardner (1985) and Donaldson (1984) to name but two, as well technological advancements that have enabled us to learn more about how the brain develops. Refer to Chapter 12 for more information.

Nevertheless, theories have immense practical value. When educators, therapists or policy makers make decisions that affect the lives of children and their families, a well-founded theory can guide them in responsible ways. As a practitioner, how you interpret theories and concepts concerning early years curricula, can make all the difference to the **quality** of care and education that you provide for the children in your setting.

How do I use theories in the nursery?

Early years provision is informed by theories and approaches to learning that have been devised by educational thinkers throughout the ages. The McMillan sisters, Piaget, Vygotsky and Bruner have had their ideas translated into practice in early years settings globally.

In order to put these theories into practice in your setting – and indeed, to challenge them by testing out your own theories, you need to have a firm understanding of child development as well as an understanding of the theories of pedagogy and child development. Table 1.1 (see over) summarizes key ideas for each theorist, the implications of these for practice and their usefulness in addressing some contemporary issues. This table can then serve as a quick reference for you, and further detail can be found in each chapter.

You will notice that the contemporary issues are in bold. This is because these issues are set out as main headings in the book, with their related sub-issues identified in Table 1.1.

In conclusion, being able to interpret these theories and using those elements which you think are most helpful in informing your practice will prove advantageous to your team and ultimately, the families you serve, in the following ways:

- You can use them in staff meetings to stimulate debate and dialogue.
- You can test out current practices against them to see if they sit with what is known.
- You can use them to identify areas of practice which might need improvement or development or further research.
- You can carry out action research to support your team in making those changes to your practice that can best enhance the learning and development of babies and children.
- You can use the theories to check out the validity of suggested policy changes or to prioritize where change might be needed or resisted.
- You can use them to ensure you and your team will be better positioned to act as catalysts for change in your setting.

These are some ideas concerning how to use some key theories and indeed to generate your own research. Theories are only useful if we can put the ideas into action and through this, give them meaning in our practice. Chapter 14 will give you guidance on how to use these theories in action research.

Table 1.1 Overview of theories and practice in the early years

Theorist	Contemporary issues	Practice implications
Jean-Jacques Rousseau	**Creating inclusive and enabling environments** • Socio-cultural learning **Importance of parents and the home learning environment** • The impact of positive early interactions	• Practitioners facilitating children's learning by knowing 'where they are at' developmentally • Planning the environment to enable successful learning encounters • Formatively assessing and observing children to promote all-round development
Friedrich Froebel	**Knowledge base concerning development from conception to three** • The role of very early experiences on development **Importance of parents and the home learning environment** • The impact of positive early interactions	• Planning for meaningful play experiences which promote holistic development • Importance of the outdoor environment • Close work with parents is key, as they provide the first and most consistent educational influence in their child's life • Providing a wide range of play resources that vary in texture, size and weight
Rachel and Margaret McMillan	**Creating inclusive and enabling environments** • Cultural participation **Importance of parents and the home learning environment** • Countering poverty and disadvantage	• Regular provision of outdoor play and experiences beyond the nursery to promote physical health • Provision of healthy meals and educating children and their parents about the importance of healthy eating

Theorist	Contemporary issues	Practice implications
Sigmund Freud	**Knowledge base concerning development from conception to three** • Socio-emotional learning • The role of very early experiences on development **Importance of parents and the home learning environment** • The centrality of emotional-social development • The impact of positive early interactions	• Supporting children to behave in socially acceptable ways • Providing plenty of play that encourages children to express their emotions, for example, the arts, imaginative play and music and movement • Sensitively helping children work through their emotional crises
John Bowlby	**Knowledge base concerning development from conception to three** • Socio-emotional learning • The role of very early experiences on development **Creating inclusive and enabling environments** • Behavioural and academic expectations **Importance of parents and the home learning environment** • The centrality of emotional-social development • The impact of positive early interactions • Countering poverty and socio-economic disadvantage	• Carrying out home visits to get to know the child and observe them in familiar surroundings • Supporting babies' emotions through sensitive interactions • Ensuring that an effective key person is in place, with essential information concerning the child, shared
Jean Piaget	**Knowledge base concerning development from conception to three** **Creating inclusive and enabling environments** **Importance of parents and the home learning environment**	• Identifying the range of schematic behaviours that children demonstrate in the setting • Supporting and extending children's schematic play – and supporting parents to do this, through daily experiences

Theorist	Contemporary issues	Practice implications
Lev Vygotsky	**Creating inclusive and enabling environments** ● Cultural participation ● Socio-cultural learning ● The role of a support network in promoting language development	● Observing children and supporting them to achieve competency when it is just beyond their capability, independent of help ● Providing a wide range of activities which utilize children's different cultural and linguistic backgrounds
Jerome Bruner	**Creating inclusive and enabling environments** ● Cultural participation ● Socio-cultural learning ● The role of a support network in promoting language development ● Behavioural and academic expectations	● Supporting the child by providing a 'scaffold' (for example, through demonstration, breaking down a task or explanation). It also involves knowing when to remove this scaffold ● Working with all parents to incorporate their children's cultural backgrounds and knowledge in the curriculum
Colwyn Trevarthen	**Knowledge base concerning development from conception to three** ● Socio-emotional learning ● The role of very early experiences on all-round development **Creating inclusive and enabling environments** ● Cultural participation ● Socio-cultural learning ● Behavioural and academic expectations ● The role of a support network in promoting language development **Importance of parents and the home learning environment** ● The centrality of emotional-social development ● The impact of positive early interactions	● Ensuring that staff are confident in engaging in respectful and meaningful interactions with all babies and children ● Raising the status of the voice of all children in your planning and work with families

Theorist	Contemporary issues	Practice implications
Urie Bronfenbrenner	**Knowledge base concerning development from conception to three** ● Socio-emotional learning **Creating inclusive and enabling environments** ● Socio-cultural learning **Importance of parents and the home learning environment** ● The impact of positive early interactions	● Reflecting on your setting's position within the community and building on these relationships, for the benefit of the children and the families with whom you work ● Taking the time to truly understand the contexts in which family stressors occur. This can help you to be effective helpers
The use of neuroscience in the early years	**Knowledge base concerning development from conception to three** ● Socio-emotional learning ● Qualifications of the workforce ● The role of very early experiences on development **Creating inclusive and enabling environments** ● Cultural participation ● Socio-cultural learning ● The role of a support network in promoting language development **Importance of parents and the home learning environment** ● The centrality of emotional-social development ● The impact of positive early interactions ● Countering poverty and socio-economic disadvantage	● Working closely with parents to support them in their role as primary carers and educators ● Having an effective key person system ● Showing sensitivity to babies' current interests and supporting them in their explorations ● Helping young children to build those emotional skills that are needed to help the child to deal with a range of difficult situations

Theorist	Contemporary issues	Practice implications
The reconceptualization of early years education	**Knowledge base concerning development from conception to three** ● Socio-emotional learning ● Qualifications of the workforce ● The role of very early experiences on all-round development **Creating inclusive and enabling environments** ● Cultural participation ● Socio-cultural learning ● Behavioural and academic expectations **Importance of parents and the home learning environment** ● Countering poverty and socio-economic disadvantage	● Challenging universal truths concerning early childhood theory and the hierarchy of knowledge ● Daring to question the concept of quality in order to further improve your provision ● Redistributing power less hierarchically between practitioners, parents and children
Action research	**Knowledge base concerning development from conception to three** ● Socio-emotional learning ● Qualifications of the workforce ● The role of very early experiences on ● development **Creating inclusive and enabling environments** ● Cultural participation ● Socio-cultural learning ● The role of a support network in promoting language development **Importance of parents and the home learning environment** ● The centrality of emotional-social development ● The impact of positive early interactions ● Countering poverty and socio-economic disadvantage	● Critically looking at your provision and making changes which will best refine your practice ● Senior staff supporting team members to become catalysts for change

Jean-Jacques Rousseau (1712–78)

2

An introduction to Jean-Jacques Rousseau and his contribution to early child care and education

Rousseau was a philosopher and writer. Self-taught, he constructed theories concerning education that are still highly regarded today. Rousseau's beliefs with regard to his approach to education can be summed up perfectly in the above quotation. Rousseau argued that the momentum for learning was provided by the growth of the child (nature) and that what the educator needed to do was to facilitate opportunities for learning.

In this second chapter, some of the key ideas concerning Rousseau's **philosophy** of education will be examined in relation to current early years provision, followed by an examination of some key aspects of his ideology. This is in order to help you to reflect upon and make links to your practice as appropriate. Aspects that will be examined include the role of the adult, the role of the child as learner and the nature of knowledge.

Rousseau's life: Key events

Rousseau was born in Geneva, on 28 June 1712. His mother died a few days after childbirth and he was raised by his father during his early years. His father taught him to read and instilled in him an appreciation of the countryside – which is said to have inspired his belief in the power of the outdoor environment on children's natural curiosity in their world. His father gave him up to his relations who cared for him early on in his childhood. He was never formally schooled but was greatly influenced by his own reading of Plutarch's *Lives*. He found work as an apprentice to an engraver aged 12 but at the age of 16 he ran away after being badly treated. In 1745 he started courting a seamstress, with whom he had five children. However, Rousseau gave all five of his children to an orphanage, a decision he later came to regret. His reasons for giving up all five children included a lack of money to raise them and the belief that they would be better off in an institution as opposed to living with him (Wokler, 1996). Given that Rousseau was so passionate about how children should be cared for, raised and educated, his decision to give up his children is highly questionable.

Significant writings

In 1762 Rousseau published two great works:

- *The Social Contract*
- *Émile* (or, *On Education*)

In this book, we will provide a brief overview of *Émile* only, as the ideas discussed by Rousseau in this text are most transferable to your experiences in the early years setting today. Case studies and reflective questions are included to help bring his ideas alive for you in the current context.

Émile: Significant issues and links to current early years provision and thinking

If you're wondering how Rousseau's work is of relevance or use to you, read on. Many of his beliefs concerning childhood and how a child should be educated, can be found in his book, *Émile* – and surprisingly, even though it was written over 200 years ago, the issues remain the same. So, as you read, keep making connections to practice in your setting.

This seminal book continues to influence educational **epistemology** today, because of its contributions to developmental psychology. In this key text, Rousseau puts forward a range of powerful arguments concerning the role of education in childhood – each of which lends itself to current issues in the early years field. For example, he emphasized the need for individualized learning that is aligned to children's stage of development and interests, as well as adults carefully planning the environment in order to effectively control the learning that takes place. However, this latter point can be challenged in the current climate given that spontaneous learning and unplanned experiences are embraced.

The role of the adult in supporting the child's learning

Encouraging children to make sense of the world in their own way: To be active leaders of their own learning

Let us begin by exploring the role of the adult. Rousseau firmly believed that the adult's role was not to use rote learning to teach children but instead, encourage them to think about how to discover facts and knowledge for themselves:

> There is so much to be done that it is madness to try to make your child learned. It is not your business to teach him the various sciences, but to give him a taste for them and methods of learning them. That is surely a fundamental principle of all good education. (Rousseau, 1762. Cited in Darling, 1994: 33)

Encouraging children to seek out facts and consequently acquire knowledge for themselves is perhaps the greatest skill that adults can impart to them. This lends itself to instilling a sense of autonomy from the earliest stages of development, by encouraging children to make decisions about the experiences they wish to engage in and showing them how to do things for themselves.

Reflection in Action

1a In which ways do practitioners in your setting encourage the curiosity of babies and children?

1b Identify the ways in which this can be improved.

When early years practitioners have a good understanding of how learning takes place in babies and children, they are often more confident in encouraging the child to discover facts and knowledge for themselves. This approach will motivate the child to develop their own ideas and solve problems as they explore their world. In babies this strong curiosity and exploratory drive can be observed as they crawl or 'cruise' around their environment, constantly investigating different objects, textures and play resources. Practitioners can enhance these early investigations of children by providing a wide range of natural resources (for example, **treasure basket**s and **heuristic play** opportunities), and ensuring that the environment is stimulating and challenging, but uncluttered, safe and conducive to independent exploration and discovery.

Reflection in Action

1 Consider the layout of your indoor environment. How far and in what ways do you think it encourages babies' and children's independent exploration and discovery?

2 List the areas which you think could be improved. Share this with your team in your next team meeting.

The adult's role as facilitator

In line with Rousseau's beliefs, the role of the adult is mainly to facilitate learning through careful planning of the indoor and outdoor environment, and by engaging sensitively with the children during the experiences that are provided. This means offering a stimulating, open and exploratory indoor and outdoor environment, observing the children closely and engaging in genuine exchanges with them that help them to think about how the world works, and resisting the inclination to do things for them, which can create a 'learned helplessness' in some individuals.

Such approaches can consequently equip the child with transferable life skills which will always remain valid. In order to do this effectively, a sound knowledge of child development is clearly vital. While it is important that you have a clear picture of what a child should be able to do in terms of their all-round development, you should also be creative in your planning of learning experiences that are suited to each child's innate curiosity, their individual needs, abilities and talents. Some examples of effective planning are discussed in the next section 'Carrying out regular observations and assessments of babies and children'.

Careful control of the environment was advocated by Rousseau, in order to effectively facilitate the process of learning and development. He believed that children should only be exposed to experiences that are suitable for their age – not dissimilar to current practice. However, the key difference here is Rousseau's argument that the child should remain completely unaware of ideas which are beyond her grasp. Let's take the example of multiplication. Rousseau would suggest we wait until the child is older and 'ready' to totally understand, then they will be fully able to 'grasp' the whole concept. It is easy to learn our multiplication tables, because they are meaningful. However, play, games and sensitive adult interaction can lead children to a 'feeling' for a concept, and a real pleasure in understanding the concept fully when they are cognitively able. In early years and Key Stage 1 we can support children's growing awareness of the concept by of 'lots of', as in two 'lots of' three, and three 'lots of' three. It is the adult's use of language that is important here, and knowing the stage that the child is at, so that the idea makes sense. Ultimately, the adult should provide experiences and challenges in light of their knowledge of the child's learning style, personal limits and current ability.

Reflection in Action

1   Do you agree with Rousseau's belief that children should remain completely unaware of ideas which are beyond their grasp? Explain.
2   How do you support children to begin to engage with ideas and concepts that are challenging given their current abilities?

Carrying out regular observations and assessments of babies and children

Rousseau's approach to observation and **assessment** is in line with current practice which is not 'intrusive' in the child's daily business of exploration and learning, and is carried out on a formative (or on-going) basis. Below is just one example of how one nursery team uses their observations of children to inform their planning cycle.

Case Study

Within our nursery we have large white boards in each room. These are key to informing our planning cycle.

Staff observe the children throughout the day and write up the child's interests, with follow-on activities that will support and extend their interests in line with their all-round development. This leads us into planning focused activities which consist of having a small group of target children determined from information gathered from the white boards – they are always linked to the current **EYFS**.

Focused activities are observed and the information gathered is put into a 'next step' for individual target children. This is then fed back to the white boards and the cycle begins again. All observations of the children are placed in their individual Learning Journeys and monitored by their key person to ensure that we are meeting all areas of development for individual children. Parents are encouraged to read their child's Learning Journey regularly and to contribute to it.

Rousseau recognized that in order to support children to flourish, observing them during their play and assessing the information gathered was important, but that it was just as important not to create additional pressure for the child to 'perform' to a universal standard which would only serve to damage their self-esteem. He also emphasized the importance of monitoring and recording the child's progress, while being careful not to compare rates of development with other children. This is a real danger if practitioners become overly concerned with following developmental norms, to the detriment of allowing for individual differences among children:

Let there be no comparison with other children, no rivalry, no competition … Year by year I shall just note the progress he had made. I shall compare the results with those of the following year. (Rousseau, 1974: 175)

The photograph above is an example of one nursery team's approach to planning for babies.

Case Study

The Nursery Manager explains:

To begin the planning cycle, the **key person** first identifies the child's interests through observation, which are then written on the whiteboard. Once a week, the team meet in front of the whiteboard and discuss ideas and activities to support the child's interests. All ideas are written on the board which are then carried out, until the child's interests change. Some of these activities will be focused. During focused activities, the key person concentrates on the child's unique needs and their stage of development, with a view to extending the child's learning through careful planning for the child's next steps. Once the activities have been carried out, the initial idea gets ticked and so the cycle starts again.

Capturing spontaneous moments of discovery and curious exploration demonstrated by the child during their play and interactions provides a quick and easy way to identify what they currently enjoy and can do. Rousseau's recognition of the importance of tuning into the child's innate enthusiasm in particular areas of interest were ahead of his time:

What use shall we make of his disposition so that it may react in a way suited to his age? Let us direct his efforts and his knowledge, and use his zeal to increase them. (Rousseau, 1974: 256)

This remains just as significant today, and should provide the basis from which practitioners work with children. If you are to make children's time in the early years setting enjoyable and meaningful to them as individuals, their previous experiences, current interests and learning styles must be considered. This way, you can ensure that your provision is truly child-centred and attuned to children's current and ever-changing needs.

The child's role in her own learning

Learning through discovery

Rousseau placed great value on the child in her own learning. He emphasized the child's own innate curiosity and exploratory drive and suggested that the role of the adult was to shape an 'enabling environment' within which the child is motivated to explore and construct their own meanings and learning. He did not advocate too much planning, preferring to free the child to explore an experience or context in their own way and to 'discover' the potential in that environment for themselves.

Below is just one simple example of how children's innate enthusiasm and curiosity are nurtured by practitioners in one busy inner-city nursery:

Case Study

We were outside in the garden when we observed that a group of children aged between 3 to 4 years took an interest in the digging patch. They were all digging away with their spades and found a large amount of worms. We asked the children what they wanted to do with the worms and they said 'keep them!' So we took them inside in a container while the children talked about what they could do. Two staff members facilitated the discussion, and it was decided that the children would create a worm farm. They wanted one in each of the two rooms of the nursery so this is what we did. Having the worm farms meant that the children were able to investigate further into worms. This included talking about their features and what they ate, collecting books about them from the local library, drawing them, making models of them and what they most enjoyed doing – holding them!

> ### Reflect on This
> 1 How do you capture children's spontaneous moments of discovery?
> 2 Identify two ways in which you extend children's current interests:
>   a individually
>   b as a group

Learning in line with their current ability and interests

As part of his child-centred approach to education, Rousseau believed that children can only be taught effectively when they are ready, learning naturally through stages. Central to this was the idea that it was possible to preserve the 'original perfect nature' of the child, by setting up the learning environment in a way that is conducive to learning. As with effective practice today, this requires not only a sound knowledge of child development but also access to age appropriate resources and, more critically, an understanding of how to create the conditions that will enable the child to explore their world, and begin to make their own meanings about how this world works.

Rousseau and Piaget are similar in their view that children have to pass through each stage of development in sequence before they can go on to subsequent stages. Linked to this idea is Rousseau's belief that every child has an impulse toward activity and that development is a direct result of activity. This links to Piaget's sensory-motor stage of cognitive development (the first stage of cognitive development) where the infant primarily learns through movement and their physical explorations of the world. Both theorists believe that children learn through active exploration of their environment and that children should not be introduced to concepts that are beyond their age and stage of development.

It is important to note that development does not happen only as a result of **maturation** – there is a complex interplay between nature and nurture. i.e. the environment and the child's experiences also shape development. Rousseau's recognition of this has helped educators in their understanding of child development and good quality early years provision. The take-away message here is that although most children follow a similar developmental pattern and learn in ways that are similar to others, there are also ways in which they differ greatly. It is the adult's role to tune into these differences and plan accordingly, with a special emphasis on creating an environment that is shaped to support the child's self-directed learning journey.

His view places great value on childhood and all the learning experiences it can offer. This is evident in the current EYFS, which although interpreted differently across the UK, helps to ensure that children from different backgrounds and levels of ability can learn through **play**, while their welfare and all-round developmental needs are promoted by knowledgeable and reflective practitioners.

In conclusion, the advice for practitioners is clear – that babies' and children's knowledge is primarily experience driven, and contextualized by the society and culture of the time. This in turn requires continuous reflection on one's own guiding beliefs and practice, so as to ensure experiences provided are meaningful to individual children and in line with their current ability and interests.

Criticisms of Rousseau's ideas

Rousseau is best known for his ideas concerning children's education which were mainly expressed through his novel, *Émile*. In this, Rousseau provides a detailed examination of how children should be educated. While most of his suggestions are common to practitioners today such as observing and assessing children's development and encouraging their 'free' exploration of the environment, he has been criticized for certain elements of his theory.

First, the fact he did not test out his theories concerning how children should be educated needs to be considered. This is because most educational theories have been tested out with children – be it through observations of how they learn, setting tasks for them to solve or, seeking to understand their thought processes by speaking with them directly. Rousseau's ideas instead, arose from his values that were influenced by the Enlightenment. He therefore wrote about what he considered the perfect way in which to educate a child, based on these ideals. Yet, he did not practise as he preached. One critique of Rousseau and his work gives a stark account of his highly contradictory choices and lifestyle which inevitably led others to question the **reliability** of his theories. Cress (1987: 8) asserts that:

> His life contradicts, point for point, his lofty measures. The temptation is therefore great to take his work as smokescreen behind which Rousseau the apostle of independence could sponge off the rich, and Rousseau the advocate of family intimacy could hand his children over to an orphanage.

Rousseau's perspective on how to best educate a child has also come under scrutiny. This is mainly due to his emphasis on manipulating the child's environment, resources and experiences in order to best impart knowledge that the adult wants them to acquire and nothing else. It can be argued that such an autocratic and overbearing approach to education is actually an underhand way for the adult to maintain control and power over children, as opposed to allowing the freedom to choose which activities they partake in and how to express themselves. Consequently, Rousseau's ideas have been criticized in relation to diminishing children's creativity as they have no choice in the process of learning. Gray (2012) suggests that:

> Creativity is nurtured by freedom and stifled by the continuous monitoring, evaluation, adult-direction, and pressure to conform that restrict children's lives

today. In the real world few questions have one right answer, few problems have one right solution; that's why creativity is crucial to success in the real world. (Gray, 2009. Personal written communication)

Also, Rousseau's ideas concerning the optimal education were articulated through a fictitious account of a child who is solely educated on a one-to-one basis. However, the reality of working with children in today's society couldn't be any more different. Practitioners in busy early years settings have to work under conditions that may not be conducive to providing much individualized care. Factors such as ratios, time, documentation and available resources all exert additional pressure on staff, as well as having the responsibility of monitoring and supporting the development of a large number of key children. The multitude of issues and experience that children and their families bring all contribute to making it a challenging yet highly rewarding profession, which can make all the difference to children's ability to thrive both in the short and long term. This is all the more urgent for children living in poverty whose greatest chance of overcoming a life of disadvantage is through early intervention and effective early years provision (Marmot Review, 2012; Allen, 2011).

In this chapter we have tried to provide a balanced overview of Rousseau's ideas pertaining to education. Inevitably, some elements will resonate with you, while others will leave you questioning their relevance to educating young children in today's hi-technology, pluralistic society. Nonetheless, some of his ideas remain directly applicable to the planning of effective early years environments and these are identified below.

Rousseau in Practice

- Encouraging free play in the setting.
- Making outdoor play an integral part of the curriculum with a range of outdoor learning opportunities provided daily.
- Nurturing children's spontaneity during play experiences and interactions with other children and adults.
- Using observations to capture the babies' and children's spontaneous moments of discovery, and using the information to inform planning.
- Adults supporting child-centred play and learning.

Ideas into Action

Now that you have familiarized yourself with some of Rousseau's key ideas, make the links to practice in your setting by reflecting upon and answering the following questions:

1   Read the following quote by Rousseau:

> There is so much to be done that it is madness to try to make your child learned. It is not your business to teach him the various sciences, but to give him a taste for them and methods of learning them.

1a   List three ways in which this is relevant to early years practitioners today.

1b   What three methods can you adopt in the setting, to give children 'a taste for learning'?

2a   In line with Rousseau's belief that children's innate enthusiasm and curiosity must be nurtured, what do you and your team do as part of the daily planning, to promote these qualities in individual children?

2b   Do you think your provision in this area can be improved? If so, give two ways in which this can be achieved as a team.

Challenge the Theorists

1   Rousseau's educational theory in part, rested on teaching a child on an individual basis. How useful are his ideas to you as a practitioner working with children today?

2   Given that Rousseau never tested out his theories with children, how do you think they can have credibility in the care and education of children today?

Rousseau's Contemporary Legacy

Creating inclusive and enabling environments
- Socio-cultural learning

Importance of parents and the home learning environment
- The impact of positive early interactions

Links to other theorists
- Friedrich Froebel
- Johann Pestalozzi

Further Reading

Palmer, J. A. (2001) *Fifty Major Thinkers on Education: From Confucius to Dewy*. London and New York: Routledge.

> This book contains one chapter which discusses Rousseau's contributions to childhood development and education. It's comprehensive while being succinct. Suggested further reading is also included.

Rousseau, J. J. (1974) *Émile*. London: Dent and Sons Limited.

> Reading the original text is recommended for those of you studying at Foundation Degree level, or if you are particularly interested in gaining a deeper understanding about Rousseau's ideas concerning children's learning and development.

http://www.psychologytoday.com/blog/freedom-learn/200902/rousseau-s-errors-they-persist-today-in-educational-theory

> This blog by psychologist Peter Gray challenges some of the key tenets of Rousseau's ideas concerning childhood education. It makes for interesting reading, especially if you need to present a balanced argument concerning Rousseau's relevance to early childhood education.

Friedrich Froebel (1782–1852)

3

An introduction to Friedrich Froebel and his work in early child care and education

In this chapter, you will learn about the main elements of Friedrich Froebel's theory of education. As you read through this overview and attempt the questions towards the end of the chapter, you may well see the close connections between his ideas and early years education today.

Froebel, a German educator, was the first educational pioneer to introduce the idea of the *kindergarten* (or, garden for children) to early years. Life in a kindergarten was similar to life in a nursery today – save for all the technological advances we now have. Children were encouraged to explore their indoor and outdoor environment and to be active in their learning through a range of creative ways, most of which embraced nature. In Froebel's kindergartens play in the natural world and using predominantly natural materials was highly valued.

Before individuals like Froebel introduced their (then) radical ideas concerning early years education, life was very difficult for children. Children did not have rights and worked in the mines and factories from the age of 7 years. One of the reasons for this treatment was because children were viewed as 'miniature adults' that society needed to 'mould' into economically productive members of society as quickly as possible. Froebel's values helped to create a much-needed change in how children were viewed and treated – particularly concerning education. Although his views about the importance of play in supporting children's development are widely accepted today, this was almost unheard of in the nineteenth century, when play was not regarded as necessary by society and thus, not encouraged.

Listed on the following page are just a few of Froebel's contributions to the shaping of early years education:

Froebel's life: Key events

- 1816–30: Froebel opened the Universal German Educational Institute in Germany, where he carried out observations of children during their play. These observations informed his thoughts and ideas concerning play and the child's role in this.

- 1826: His seminal text *The Education of Man* is published. In this book, Froebel discusses his guiding principles of the child's role in play and learning, which is guided mainly by his deeply religious and spiritual beliefs.

- 1840: He opened the first kindergarten in Germany. Up until then, children aged under 7 years did not have an education system. This in turn meant that holistic development through play also went unacknowledged.

- 1851: A ban on all kindergartens was issued by the Prussian state (a militaristic kingdom within Germany). Some would question why the Prussian state would issue a ban on kindergartens – could it be due to feeling threatened by young children being encouraged to develop self-expression and free-thinking? Did it better serve the Prussian state to have young children 'trained' in one, uniform way with the ultimate goal being to raise useful and obedient members of society during that time?

- 1878: His book of rhymes and songs *Mother Play and Nursery Songs* (*Mutter und Koselieder*) is published.

The role of the adult in supporting the child's learning

Within Froebel's philosophy, there was an emphasis on partnership with parents – much like practice today. He viewed parents as the main educators of their children and that schools should welcome parents to get involved in their child's learning. Close work with parents was thus vital, in ensuring a consistent and positive influence in their child's life.

Parents were viewed by Froebel as being in a prime position to guide their child's learning and development from the beginning, advocating their perceptive input:

> It is not only conducive but necessary to the development and strengthening of the child's power and skill that parents should, without being too pedantic or too exacting, connect the child's actions with suitable language and behaviour. (Froebel, 2005: 79)

Although this may seem obvious in the current context, 200 years ago this was not mainstream thinking, given the lack of regard for children's well-being. Yet today, this emphasis on parents being their child's first and most enduring educators is also central in much of the legislation concerning the care and education of children. Just one example being the Every Child Matters Agenda (2003: 39), which states that:

> The bond between the child and their parents is the most critical influence on a child's life. Parenting has a strong impact on a child's educational development, behaviour, and mental health.

Partnership with parents not only requires practitioners to form and maintain effective working relationships with all parents but also requires the setting to be a part of the local community it serves.

The role of the practitioner is therefore critical, according to Froebel (1826) in planning and resourcing (indoor and outdoor) environments which support each child's developing autonomy and self-confidence. This cannot be effectively achieved without the on-going input from parents.

As part of the learning environment, activities and experiences need to be planned to promote feelings of wonder, joy, concentration and purpose for children, with practitioners facilitating the learning process through observing, participating in children's play (when deemed appropriate) and talking with the children to encourage them to reflect on their experience during their play/self-activity.

The child's role in her own learning

Froebel believed that children's motivation to learn about the world in which they live came from within (much like Piaget) – and that what they required to support them in their learning journeys was a good quality educational environment equipped with a wide range of resources that were suitable for their age and ability. He firmly believed in promoting children's self-activity – that is children following their own interests and using their imagination, creativity and intrinsic motivation to learn through their own explorations.

Reflection in Action

1 How do staff in your setting afford children the freedom to make their own choices?
2 How is the concept of responsibility taught alongside this? (This might include waiting their turn, how to work alongside their peers, treating resources with care and cleaning up after themselves.)

As part of this intrinsic motivation, Froebel emphasized the importance of the child having an '*inner connection*' with the objects she explores, which in turn would nurture her intellectual and emotional development. This concept of connectedness is thus a key aspect of the Froebelian approach to education, with resources and experiences provided to promote children's understanding of resources and ideas, and to build on this through their exploration. This in turn helped them to build on existing knowledge as they made new sense of resources provided.

Through his observations of children he concluded that children's play and self-activity were thus essential to holistic development – not least because his observations proved to him that humans are by nature creative beings and that this needs to be nurtured in order for the individual to grow to their fullest potential. Froebel's advice (2005: 88) to the practitioner is to:

> See and observe the child; he will teach you what to do. Quiet observation will make it easy to see how he follows spontaneously the road implied by the laws of human thought, proceeding from the visible to invisible and more abstract.

Froebel thus encouraged symbolic and imaginative play in his school because he believed that children show their highest levels of learning in their symbolic and imaginative play. This belief is similar to that of Lev Vygotsky. (See Chapter 8.)

Reflection in Action

1 In which ways do you and your team support children to make connections between different areas and experiences offered in the environment?
2 How might you further develop your practice in this area?

The great outdoors

Influenced by Pestalozzi and Rousseau, Froebel was a great believer in the role of the outdoor environment in promoting healthy development, particularly for children living in poverty and disadvantage. He introduced the concept of gardens for children, where they could participate in all aspects of growing seasonal produce – from harvesting to preparing. As educational tools, these gardens provided children with real world applications of mathematics, language and literacy to identifying the connections between food, health and the environment.

Regular opportunities for outdoor learning is no less important in the current context given the rise of childhood obesity, the preoccupation with computer games, isolation, increased vehicle traffic and negative parental attitudes towards outdoor play (due to fear) which all prevent children from reaping the benefits of exploring the wonders that the outdoor environment can offer. Children today are thus experiencing childhoods with minimal outdoor play, which leaves little room for developing important skills such as developing concentration, perseverance and coping with stressors. This makes the discussion of Froebel more important than ever. The research continually shows us that children who live in a stressful environment are therefore at greater risk of falling behind academically, and not developing effective communication or emotionally intelligent behaviour (*Living Conditions: The Influence on Young Children's Health*, 2012).

Björklid and Nordström (2007) focus on the benefits of access to public spaces and outdoor learning from a developmental perspective, explaining that children experience space differently from adults, which makes it critical for children to have a say in the decisions that shape their outdoor environments. They also stress the importance of promoting children's independent mobility, which continues to diminish due to a lack of access to outdoor opportunities. In recognition of the shift in lifestyles and the need to promote outdoor learning, the current early years framework for learning emphasizes the necessity of providing regular access to some sort of outdoor experience. This includes quality outdoor provision for children with disabilities, who can miss out on such valuable opportunities due to their parents not placing importance on outdoor learning or do not have the means to support their child to play outdoors. Section 3.57 of the Early Years Foundation Stage (2012: 24) states:

> The provider must ensure that, so far as is reasonable, the facilities, equipment and access to the premises are suitable for children with disabilities. Providers must provide access to an outdoor play area or, if that is not possible, ensure that outdoor activities are planned and taken on a daily basis.

Reflection in Action

1 How far does your setting adhere to this guideline? It might help to consider what helps and what hinders your provision in these respects.
2 Speak to your manager to find out more, if necessary.

The concept of forest schools, in both rural and urban areas, is a fairly recent interpretation of the enduring impact of Froebel's ideas. Incorporating a forest school approach can include visiting a woodland area once a week (it would need to occur on a regular basis in order to have any meaning for the children in terms of benefiting learning and development) and supporting children on their outdoor learning journeys. Outdoor learning like this helps to build children's emotional and social skills – partly through direct teaching during the experience, as well as the learning which occurs organically as part of the children's explorations. Related activities might include creating a story based on things seen in the woodland area, organizing a teddy bears' picnic, creating props to accompany story telling time, making collages with picture frames from twigs and leaves and for older children, learning more about natural resources such as wood as a sustainable resource.

There are advantages to using the urban environment, if visiting a woodland area is not a possibility. There's usually much more light in the town than in the forest and you are encouraging children to see their own surroundings from a different perspective rather than changing what they see every day for somewhere else. It's not going to replace the impact of the real woodland but, as an alternative, the sky's the limit.

What do you Think?

1 What might be some of the barriers to adopting a forest school approach to learning?
2 What could you do to bring the outdoors more centrally into practice in your setting?

One early years practitioner explains how they adopt an outdoors approach to learning as part of their setting's practice. The examples given have proved very successful with the children and are not too costly.

In our organization we provide a curriculum that is rooted in **emotional intelligence** and experiential learning – this applies to staff as well as the children. Innovative outdoor experiences are a key way in which we nurture young children's well-being, promote their problem-solving, resilience and ability to take risks. Tight budgets and small spaces do not deter our staff in planning for creative and imaginative outdoor provision – it spurs them on!

We've made a fire pit in our garden, we've built a den using branches and leaves as well as setting up an obstacle course using natural materials. We started off by talking about what we would expect to see in a wood and how to recreate it in our garden. This included encouraging the children to think about what they would do if they were in the middle of nowhere, to help them think beyond the practical realities that they encounter daily. We also formed links with the Royal Society for the Protection of Birds (RSPB) which has been very successful. During bird watch week the children built bird boxes and we all went looking for birds. We were surprised at how many we found by using the binoculars to get a good look!

Tips for outdoor learning in an urban setting

- Start by changing any obstructive mindsets.
- If possible, invest in affordable outdoor waterproof suits. This also solves the problem of parents getting upset about muddy clothes.
- Create opportunities for planting seeds, vegetables, fruits and herbs – children love to see how their produce grows and enjoy eating it. These activities also a great way to promote cross-curricular learning.
- Take photographs of the children engaging in a range of outdoor experiences – this provides a lovely way of capturing their learning as well as encouraging dialogue with the children.

- Make a book for parents that illustrates how children learn through outdoor play.

Froebel's *Gifts* and *Occupations*

In order to facilitate children's progression through the different developmental stages, Froebel invented *Gifts* (a range of natural resources designed to increase understanding of their properties) and *Occupations* (activities). The Gifts come in a wide range of sizes, shapes, textures and weights, designed to encourage the child's developing senses, skills and curiosity through play with them. They are designed to be given to the developing baby in sequence, with the lightest first, progressing to large wooden cubes and two-dimensional wooden shapes to be arranged on grids for the older child. As a result of their hands-on exploration with the Gifts and Occupations, the child builds their understanding from the material to the abstract, which in turn enhances their intellectual development as they come to understand concepts such as dimension, size and shape. As Froebel (2005: 288) explains:

> Each Gift should, in due time and in the widest sense, aid the child to make the external internal, the internal external, and to find the unity between the two.

The first Gift (for babies) is a set of lightweight balls of brightly coloured wool designed mainly to stimulate the senses of touch and sight. As the baby grows older, objects include wooden spheres, blocks and smaller shaped pieces, each designed to develop fine manipulative skills, hand-eye coordination and spatial awareness among many other skills. Froebel, after 1844, did however move away from the prescriptive use of his Gifts, as he saw how children used them so well without this in his observations of their creativity.

The Occupations are designed to further enhance children's play with the Gifts. Just some of the Occupations include painting, paper folding, wood carving, interlacing and threading. It's worth noting that although Froebel did not make the Occupations compulsory, he did devise a set of instructions for use which could be interpreted as prescribed. Although the Gifts and Occupations might not strictly be used as they were originally intended as part of the Froebelian approach, these tactile objects and investigative play are still widely recognizable across settings nationally and internationally.

Conversely, Froebel's emphasis on children exploring freely without being inhibited by prescribed activities that required fixed outcomes is also integral to early years practice today. Thus he introduced what is now called *free-flow play*.

Froebel's choice of natural (as opposed to synthetic) objects is in line with *heuristic play* and *treasure basket play*, which was pioneered by Goldschmied who was a Froebelian trained teacher. She too recommends the inclusion of natural objects over plastic toys for babies to explore. These two forms of investigative play are commonly used as part of quality early years practice for the under 3s today.

Reflection in Action

1 Consider your provision for heuristic play. Identify two strengths and two areas for improvement.
2 Children all develop at different rates. With regard to treasure basket play, do you think that staff consider the babies' individual stages of development when setting up the treasure baskets?

Inevitably, settings differ greatly in terms of their approach and resources to support heuristic play, what is important is that staff provide a wide range of contrasting objects in terms of size, shape, smell and texture for babies to explore. Goldschmied (1989: 11) says:

> Babies given safe, stimulating and supportive opportunities will use their senses to learn about objects they encounter. In doing so they will enter into a world of discovery, puzzlement, social encounter and communication ... As babies suck, grasp, touch and feel objects they rehearse behaviours which foster their earliest learning.

This approach can also be included as part of home learning – practitioners can encourage parents to use household objects and materials placed in wicker baskets for their babies to explore. It is not costly and is a great way of building concentration and supporting decision-making through independent play.

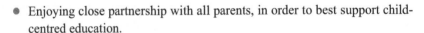

Froebel in Practice

- Enjoying close partnership with all parents, in order to best support child-centred education.
- Emphasizing outdoor play as an integral part of the **curriculum.**
- Providing a wide range of open-ended resources such as wooden blocks, recycled materials, water, sand and mark-making equipment.
- Using natural materials as far as possible.
- Creating a free-flow system of learning between the indoors and outdoors.
- Planning for play and particularly independent, child initiated play.

Ideas into Action

Now that you have familiarized yourself with some of Froebel's key ideas, make the links to practice in your setting by reflecting upon and answering the following questions:

1   What natural resources do you have in your setting, to support babies' and children's sensory development and emergent understanding of concepts such as weight, size, dimensions and different textures?
2   Froebel stressed the importance of partnership with parents. How is this promoted in your setting? (You also might want to identify any relevant policies and procedures.)
3   What do you think the similarities are between Froebel's and Goldschmied's approach to educating babies and young children?
4a Play and the outdoor environment were important in a Froebelian kindergarten. Do you think that provision for outdoor play is of good quality in your setting?
4b Devise a list of the strengths and areas for improvement.
5   In which ways do you think Froebel's educational philosophy influences early years provision today?

Challenge the Theorists

1 Given that Froebel's Gifts came with a comprehensive guide for their use, how valuable do you think they would be in encouraging spontaneous self-education through exploration?

2 Froebel was deeply religious and his theories concerning educational were hence influenced by his religious beliefs. How acceptable would his ideas be today, given the diverse make-up of children's religious backgrounds?

3 How do you strike a balance between adult-led and child-led learning experiences in your setting?

Froebel's Contemporary Legacy

Knowledge base concerning development from conception to three
● The role of very early experiences on development

Importance of parents and the home learning environment
● The impact of positive early interactions

Links to other theorists
● Elinor Goldschmied
● Jean-Jacques Rousseau
● Johann Pestalozzi

Further Reading

Bruce, T. (2012) *Early Childhood Practice: Froebel Today*. London: SAGE.

This book provides a practical perspective of Froebel's approach to early childhood education, with case studies, reflective questions and discussion concerning his relevance to current practice. This book is an effective resource for those unfamiliar with Froebel's key ideas, due its balance of theory and practical application.

Froebel, F. (2005) *The Education of Man*. New York: Dover Publications.

We would recommend this classic to those who are interested in Frobel's ideas and are interested in learning about his philosophy concerning early childhood education and the key principles of his theory. This original text also provides guidance on how to channel children's play in order to support the development of intellectual and social skills, which can be incorporated into practice today.

Rachel McMillan (1859–1917) and Margaret McMillan (1860–1931)

4

An introduction to the McMillan sisters and their work in early child care and education

This chapter examines the ground-breaking work of two sisters, Rachel and Margaret McMillan. They were born in New York after their mother had emigrated there from Scotland. Their youngest sister died of scarlet fever at birth, days after their father. Margaret was also affected by the fever which left her deaf until the age of 14 years. Following these events, they moved back to Scotland with their mother.

The sisters initially followed different paths in terms of their careers; Rachel was a health worker and a political campaigner whereas Margaret was a campaigner for nursery education and healthcare for young children. From their mid-twenties, they lived and worked together for the rest of their lives. Their involvement in the Christian Socialist movement provided the main vehicle through which they campaigned for the rights of the working classes. Christian Socialists have a radical commitment to responding to social issues that affect individuals' lives and their communities. They are driven by a strong sense of social justice, advocating for those who are unable to fight for their rights. Their work is achieved in various ways ranging from lobbying to having members in the Commons and Lords. It was this strong sense of social justice that inspired the sisters to advocate on behalf of families living in poverty, which in turn helped them to create major changes in legislation and early years provision in England.

The McMillan sisters are still highly regarded for their pioneering work in developing early years provision for children of poorer families in London, during the late 1800s and early 1900s. Although they both worked vigorously to support poor families, they did so in different ways, complementing each other's work. They crusaded against the key issues prevalent at this time, such as relentless family poverty, high unemployment among the working classes, poor personal hygiene and a lack of basic human rights for children. These issues remained a constant issue for the working classes who were caught in a cycle of deprivation.

Margaret McMillan played an important role in placing local issues on the political agenda by publishing articles in influential journals of the time. She used research findings and statistical data to illustrate the impact of poverty on poor families and the psychological effects of child labour. Her approach to alleviating the impact of these issues was robust and hands-on; she frequently visited slums and schools, giving lectures to families on basic child development and personal hygiene, showing them how to bathe and how to improve their general health.

Another key contribution of Margaret McMillan was her championing of the importance of teacher education for those who worked with young children. She established a teacher training college herself and promoted the need for trained and intellectually rigorous practitioners, who understood theory as well as practice. This view was highly contentious at that time and counter to the dominant view that any kind of 'nice motherly girl' would 'do' for the nursery. She spoke powerfully in many forums about the need for qualified staff and insisted that those with working with the poorest children should have a high level of skills as well as a caring and loving approach to the child.

There are lessons to be taken from the McMillans' radical approach to tackling society's ills that can be adopted to help improve the lives of poor families today. With poverty and its associated problems still on the rise, we can ill afford not to invest in children in their early years (Marmot Review 2010). Today, Sure Start Children's Centres exist nationally to provide health, education and social services for families. This is similar to what the McMillans pioneered at the turn of the last century for poorer, working-class families in order to improve health and educational outcomes.

Below is an outline of their long-lasting contribution to early years care and education:

Key events

- 1892: Margaret was responsible for establishing medical inspections in primary schools.
- 1903: Margaret McMillan became a member of the Froebel Society (which was set up to train teachers in Froebelian methods).
- 1906: Rachel worked very hard with politicians to campaign for school meals – her work proved critical in the passing of the School Meals Act in this year.
- 1908: Margaret and Rachel opened the first school clinic and a 'night

camp' for children living in slums. Here, they could wash and put on clean nightclothes.

- 1914: Margaret and Rachel pioneered the first open-air nursery for disadvantaged children in Deptford. Rachel focused on caring for their health, while Margaret focused on their education This nursery still exists today.

- 1917: Rachel McMillan dies.

- 1920: Margaret's book *Nursery Schools: A Practical Handbook* is published.

- 1925: Margaret's other key text *Childhood, Culture and Class in Britain* is published.

- 1930: Margaret McMillan established a college in Deptford to train teachers and nurses.

- 1931: Margaret McMillan dies.

The McMillans' approach to early years education

The impact of poverty on health

Central to the educational philosophy of the McMillan sisters was the importance of health. Like Robert Owen (1771–1858), they observed that deprived working and living conditions for the poor caused major, long-term health problems. Based on their work with families living in slums and their visits to schools, they showed that factors such as poor nutrition, a lack of hygiene, poor sanitation and living in damp conditions were detrimental to a child's health.

> The condition of poorer children was worse than anything that was described or painted. The utter neglect of infants, toddlers and older children, the blight of early labour, all combined to make race of undergrown and spoiled adolescents. (McMillan, M., 1925: 51)

As a consequence of living in poverty, the McMillan sisters firmly believed that children could not be expected to learn effectively, due to the associated chronic health issues. Hence, their inspirational open-air nursery (The Rachel McMillan Nursery and Children's Centre, which still exists today) combines aspects of health and education for children and their families. Here is an extract from a recent interview with the head teacher of the centre, in which she describes how the legacy of the McMillans' work continues to shape practice at the centre today:

Case Study

The philosophy of a holistic approach to children's learning by the McMillan sisters was innovative and ahead of its time. They understood that hungry, ill, tired children could not learn, thus limiting their life chances. Every Child Matters and the Children's Centre agenda echo the McMillans' efforts to combine services e.g. health and education in an attempt to close the gap. Poverty is relative, but, although living standards have risen since the McMillans' time, there are still poverty-stricken parts of our society who are not able to access the range of choices and opportunities that other, more wealthy, sectors of our society can. There is a huge range of evidence that shows that poverty creates an unequal society and limits children's life chances and choices. This is why high quality nurseries and Children's Centres, such as Rachel McMillan Nursery School and Children's Centre, are so important, they enable and empower communities and individuals to make changes to their lives, which improve their future choices and chances. We know that high quality early intervention, made in partnership with families, makes a huge difference to the lives of those families and their children.

Reflect on This

1 Is poverty an issue among some of the families in your setting?
2 What strategies do you have in place to help support families living in poverty?
3 Do you think that the intervention provided by your setting contributes to minimizing the impact of poverty for children and their families? Explain how.

Research studies have proved the McMillan sisters right; time and time again it has been demonstrated that quality early years provision can help to increase the life chances of children from disadvantaged backgrounds. As they had identified at the turn of the last century, early years intervention that includes integrated social, health and education services, is all the more important when children from the same community have starkly different opportunities, depending on their family's income, level of education and access to services (Penn, 2002).

Longitudinal studies such as the High/Scope Perry pre-school study (1962–7), the Head Start Project (1965) and the Effective Provision of Pre-school Education (EPPE) Project (2003) have shown that investment at this early age can reap rich rewards later on for the individual and the community.

Disadvantaged children benefit significantly from good quality pre-school experiences, especially where they are with a mixture of children from different social backgrounds. Outcomes are related to better intellectual and social/behavioural development for children. (The Effective Provision of Pre-school Education [EPPE] Project: Findings from Pre-School to end of Key Stage 1, 2004: 1)

Although poverty continues to impact negatively on educational and life outcomes, the work of the McMillan sisters cannot be underestimated in helping to alleviate its impact. Much of the initiatives, policies and legislation that exist today can be traced back to their crusading. Consider the vast array of health promotion campaigns that exist today; we see posters and advertisements telling us how to prevent cross-infection and the importance of getting enough exercise and eating a healthy, balanced diet in the fight against obesity.

Reflect on This

1 How do you stay informed of current health promotion campaigns?
2 Do you use this knowledge to help you plan health promotion activities in your setting? Provide a few examples.
3 What are some of the indicators of an effective health promotion activity? Provide at least three examples.

The role of play and outdoor learning in the curriculum

Within the daily routine at the Rachel McMillan Nursery, a play-based curriculum is provided, with children being given plenty of time and space to engage in purposeful activity to help promote their self-expression. Free-flow play which is child-centred is therefore at the heart of their curriculum; this is guided by the principle that:

> Children need time and space to engage in activities in depth and time to follow through, consolidate and reflect upon their own learning. (The Rachel McMillan Nursery and Children's Centre, 2012)

Being provided with opportunities to learn spontaneously, in their way and at their own pace, enables individual children to learn effectively through their first-hand experiences, but this too requires careful planning of the environment and resources therein, to ensure that children are actually reaping the benefits of their explorations – as opposed to being expected to learn without any structure in place whatsoever. In particular, the McMillan sisters promoted the importance of outdoor play, and she saw the outdoor world as another educator of the child, with play-based, sensory experiences being particularly important.

The Rachel McMillan Nursery and Children's Centre has at its core, **policies** and **procedures** that are still greatly influenced by its pioneers. Just one example of this is their 'Cold and Outdoor Policy' which highlights the importance of outdoor learning and the fact that colds cannot be caught by exposure to cold air. As obvious as this sounds, some parents do hold views that are contrary to those of the early years settings concerning outdoor play, so the more you know as an early years professional, the better equipped you will be when explaining the benefits of outdoor learning to parents of your setting. This is also highlighted in the Early Years

Foundation Stage (2012) which emphasizes the importance of providing outdoor play and learning experiences, especially for those whose only opportunity to play freely and safely outside is at nursery.

For this reason, the McMillans' educational philosophy is similar to Froebel's – who also placed great emphasis on the role of the outdoor environment in promoting a child's holistic development. The absence of outdoor spaces for children living in inner-city areas is thus compensated for in the McMillans' approach. For example, 'indoor' activities such as writing, reading and mark-making take place outdoors, with gross-motor equipment also provided, namely swings, slides and a playground area made from natural materials. From this, it is clear to see that the areas of Learning and Development in the EYFS can be promoted flexibly in such early years settings, which in turn fosters children's skills and confidence in all developmental areas which they might not have otherwise had the opportunity to extend.

Reflect on This

Consider your outdoor play environment. Identify the opportunities that are provided for all children to develop competence in their:

- Personal, social and emotional development (for example, self-management, collaboration and sociability)
- Physical development (for example, gross and fine motor skills)
- Communication and language (for example, speaking and listening)

Create a table as below, and insert your reflection on what aspects of your outdoor provision support the identified area of development and learning.

Aspect of your outdoor provision	Area of development and learning
	Personal, social and emotional development
	Physical development
	Communication and language

Opposite is a case study concerning how one inner-city nursery team encouraged parents to embrace the benefits of outdoor learning for their children's health and all-round development.

Case Study

We provide the parent/carers with a number of workshops throughout the year to promote outdoor learning – and not just confined to the nursery. We provide guidance concerning their children's lifestyles and how this affects their overall development. We ensure to take on board the parents'/carers' ideas and opinions to reinforce the fact that they are their child's first and most important educators, and to show them that their values and opinions count.

We also offer two 'stay and play' weeks within the year to allow parents to see and experience first-hand the activities that we provide for their children to support and extend their development and how they can adapt the activities to use at home and outdoors. All of our written resources are also available in the children's home language to further encourage their parents/carers to continue their learning at home.

The role of partnership with parents

Margaret McMillan emphasized the role of parents in their children's education, and hence stressed that schools needed to be places for families and for community development, not just for children. Family involvement was thus promoted in a range of ways, such as teaching parents about basic hygiene and nutrition as well as sharing information and knowledge about their children. Some of the health issues that Margaret McMillan worked to relieve – and documented in her book, *The Nursery School* (1919: 10) – are prevalent today.

> They arrive in the elementary schools at the age of five suffering from the results of rickets, bronchial catarrh and other ailments, and their brain-growth is hindered by the evil of their first years.

Interesting that rickets (a lack of vitamin D or calcium in a child's diet) is now back on the rise (**http://www.rcpch.ac.uk/news/rcpch-launches-vitamin-d-campaign**) due to lifestyle choices and parental concerns such as parents being too fearful to allow their children to play outdoors as well as the popularity of computer games. Here, Margaret McMillan also makes the prescient connection between poor quality early experiences leading to 'hindered' brain growth. Today, findings from neuroscience enable us to see just how such poor experiences affect brain development, from in-utero through to adulthood (Gopnik et al., 2001). The use of neuroscience in the early years is further examined in Chapter 12.

The sheer importance of building and maintaining an effective, two-way relationship with all parents in the setting cannot be taken for granted. With their collaboration and trust, children's needs can be met with greater ease along with a seamless continuation of learning that takes place at home and in the nursery. The Early Years Foundation Stage (2012: 1) states:

All settings should develop effective partnerships with parents in order to enhance the learning and development of the children with whom they work. Successful relationships become partnerships when there is two-way communication and parents and practitioners really listen to each other and value each other's views and support in achieving the best outcomes for each child.

Reflect on This

1   Does your policy on parental partnerships reflect the needs of your parents?
2   Do all staff members feel confident in working with families?
3   What strategies could your team implement to ensure that all staff are confident and competent in this area?

Concluding thoughts

In this chapter we have examined the integral role that the McMillan sisters played in shaping early years care and education as we know it today. Their tireless efforts at changing the way working-class families were viewed and treated led to much-needed changes in law and policy concerning children's rights and access to services for families living in poverty.

Although much of their work was driven by their religious and political beliefs, they nonetheless instigated much-needed changes concerning families living in poverty which are still in place today.

The McMillan sisters in Practice

- Lots of free-play and curriculum planning that enables all children to follow their interests.
- Encouraging children to play outside whenever possible – especially when it is raining, snowing or cold! A robust 'colds and outdoor play' policy is a useful tool to devise and implement.
- Regular healthy meals and naps during the daily routine, that meet children's individual needs.
- Close partnership with all parents to best nurture their child's learning and development.

Ideas into Action

1   Now that you have familiarized yourself with some of the McMillan sisters' contributions to early years provision, make the links to practice in your setting by reflecting upon and answering the following questions:

2   The Rachel McMillan Nursery and Children's Centre is still in existence today. In which ways is the pioneering work of the McMillan sisters relevant to the care and education of children today?

3   How is life different for children living in poverty today, compared to the 1900s?

3a Is outdoor learning sufficiently promoted in your setting? Discuss its strengths and weaknesses.

3b How would you encourage parents to embrace the benefits of outdoor learning for their child's health and all-round development?

Challenge the Theorists

1   Do you think that the McMillans' Christian Socialist values would be readily accepted in today's multicultural society? Explain the reasons behind your answer.

2   To what extent do you think the Sure Start initiative addresses the needs of families who live in disadvantaged areas? Identify its strengths and weaknesses.

3   Margaret and Rachel McMillan's political campaigning led to changes in legislation in the early 1900s. How easily do you think their proposals would be implemented today, given the pressures on the Welfare State?

The McMillan Sisters' Contemporary Legacy

Creating inclusive and enabling environments
● Cultural participation of children

Importance of parents and the home learning environment
● Countering poverty and disadvantage

Links to other theorists
● Jean-Jacques Rousseau
● Robert Owen
● Friedrich Froebel

Further Reading

Miller, L. and Pound, L. (2011) *Theories and Approaches to Learning in the Early Years.* London: SAGE.

> This book examines traditional and modern theories concerning learning and development. The sections on the McMillan sisters' key contributions to early childhood education and health are linked to current issues in early years provision. This is a useful resource which is easy to follow.

Steedman, C. (1990) *Childhood, Culture and Class in Britain. Margaret McMillan 1860–1931.* New Brunswick, NJ: Rutgers University Press.

> This biography provides a detailed account of Margaret McMillan's life and achievements in education, health and politics. It is a lengthy book, full of interesting issues that still have relevance to early years provision today. It is best used as a resource to dip in and out of.

Sigmund Freud (1856–1939)

5

An introduction to Sigmund Freud and his influence in early child care and education

This chapter examines the theories of the Austrian psychoanalyst, Sigmund Freud. While it cannot do justice to his expansive contribution to psychoanalysis, it does provide an overview of his ideas most pertinent to early years and child development. It will prove useful for you to consider his concepts in light of current psychoanalysis and findings from neuroscience, in order to understand how some of his ideas are still applicable today.

Freud was born in Austria, to Jewish parents. It is this part of his heritage that he most identified with and which he attributed his intellectual and professional success. He and his wife had five children; notably Anna Freud – also a successful psychoanalyst and psychologist who worked with her father. Her work mainly concerned child psychology with her theories developing from her work with children.

He remains the most influential figure in **psychoanalysis**, establishing the field of verbal **psychotherapy** (Storr, 2001). This is also known as the '*talking method*'. This method (whereby the patient reclines on a sofa while the analyst sits behind the patient, out of view so as not to distract them) is used globally today. His whole life was dedicated to the field of psychoanalysis, revising and reworking his theories throughout his long career. Freud is however, regarded as the most controversial figure in psychoanalysis, due to some of his assertions about human behaviour and its origins. These, along with criticisms and developments of his theories will be explored further on in the chapter.

While not directly related to the field of early years care and education, elements of his psychoanalytic theory can be applied to help us understand the reasons behind children's behaviour throughout their early development – his *theory of personality* (which is discussed in this Chapter) is one example of this. This understanding plays an important role in supporting early years practitioners to facilitate children's psychological and social development successfully.

Below is an outline of Freud's enduring contribution to psychoanalysis. Each concept will be discussed in relation to children's development and early years provision.

Freud's personality theory

The id, ego and super-ego

According to Freud, our mind consists of three interacting systems, these being the id, **ego** and super-ego; each of which operates at three different levels.

The **id** operates at the unconscious level of the mind, driven by **the pleasure principle** – that is, it seeks to obtain immediate gratification based on its needs and desires. Freud believed that infants do not realize that they exist separately from their mother/primary caregiver but that their identities are merged into one; this is evident from birth when we are all desire and need, lacking the ability to delay gratification. It is through the sensitive management of the parents/primary caregivers, that the child begins to understand what can and can't be done. i.e. whether the desire has to be deferred or realized. An example of this might be whether a child is allowed to have a new toy when he spots one in a shop window, or not.

The id's desires however, are negotiated by the ego and super-ego which operate at the conscious level of the mind and are driven by the reality principle. The ego strives to satisfy the id's desires in realistic and socially appropriate ways, as the infant develops understanding that they are not the only ones with needs and desires – and that getting these met can be delayed.

According to Freud, the **super-ego** comes into force at the age of five. The super-ego is the individual's sense of right and wrong. It works to suppress all unacceptable urges of the id and struggles to make the ego act upon idealistic values rather that upon realistic principles. It is little wonder that before this age, the child struggles with making the adjustment from having her needs met almost instantly as a baby, to having to understand that the world no longer operates around her and that she has to, instead, adhere to the social codes of society.

> ## Example in Action
>
> A child sees that her friend has a slice of chocolate cake; she has already eaten her share and wants another. She might cry or even try to take the slice of cake from her friend in order to satisfy her desire (id). The ego will weigh the costs and benefits of taking her friend's slice of cake before deciding to act upon the impulse to do so. The super-ego considers parental and societal values which might (or might not) be enough to stop the child from taking it.

Understanding the role of the id, ego and super-ego as part of a child's psychological and social development will enable you to provide meaningful experiences and activities that will encourage children's emergent self-discipline and ability to understand that they are not the only ones with needs and desires to be met. This is particularly significant in the nursery, where children often need to take turns, share and be patient.

The five stages of psychosexual development

Like Piaget, Freud believed that children pass through development in distinct stages and that each stage must be passed through in order to ensure healthy psychological growth. According to Freud, the five stages of psychosexual development are summarized in Table 5.1:

What is critical about each of the five stages is the adult's responses to the child's behaviour and the support they provide. This in turn will facilitate a smooth transition to the next stage. For example, a child in the anal stage of development will (according to Freud) be particularly interested in their bowel movements, as well as their potty training. This is a stressful time for the child and their parents while the child tries to gain control of their bladder and bowels and master physical, cognitive and language skills. Parents will thus need to be supported according to their individual needs, in order to help their child through this stage of their development.

Freud claimed that children display specific behaviours at certain stages of their psychological development. He named it psychosexual because within each of the stages, the libido (energy, force) fixates on different erogenous zones – for pleasure or potential frustration. So, if these stages were not passed through 'successfully', during adulthood these behaviours would become manifest as neuroses (also known as 'hang-ups' or fixations) in adulthood. Each stage is thus viewed as a conflict which must be resolved before the child can progress onto the next stage of development.

An example of this is the anal stage of development; a child who has started potty training too early or has been pressured by their parents during this stage, may well go on to develop an anally retentive personality in adulthood. This might manifest as obsessive cleanliness and an irrational fear of mess. An anally retentive personality is also likely to be fearful of authority.

Table 5.1 Freud's five stages of psycho-sexual development

Stage	Age range	Behaviour displayed	Resulting behaviour if stage is not passed through successfully
Oral	Birth–1 year	The mouth is the focus of pleasure. The child uses their mouth to explore and interact; this includes weaning and feeding as well as exploring objects.	If the child is denied the breast or is inhibited in their explorations, Freud claimed that oral fixations will occur in adulthood. Common examples include nail biting, smoking and thumb sucking.
Anal	1–3 years	The focus of stimulation is the anus, with the child gaining pleasure from the process of eliminating or retaining their faeces, as part of the process of potty training. This stage also brings with it conflict, as the child's desires clash with their parents' demands.	If potty training happens too early or is harsh, the child might become anally retentive in adulthood. This might look like obsessive cleanliness, respect for authority and hatred of mess.
Phallic	3–6 years	The genitals are the focus in this stage – children become aware of anatomical sex differences, resulting in feelings of attraction (to the opposite sexed parent), rivalry, jealousy and fear. Children want to possess the opposite sexed parent and to do away with the parent of the same sex. Freud called this the **Oedipus complex** (in boys) and the **Electra complex** (in girls).	Children overcome this conflict through a process of *identification* with the same sexed parent (imitating, adopting their values and taking on gender-specific roles). Adopting ideal values in turn enables the child's super-ego to develop at approximately five years old.
Latency	6–12 years	(Latency = hidden or dormant.) No further psychosexual development takes place during this stage. Freud believed that the child's libido is instead channelled into school work, hobbies and friendships (mainly of the same sex).	The libido interests are suppressed in this stage. What is important however is that the child develops self-confidence, social and communication skills.
Genital	12 years–adult	A time of sexual experimentation; this results in the individual settling down with a partner in their 20s.	Any unresolved conflicts or fixations resulting from previous stages might prevent such relationships, with sexual perversions occurring instead.

The role of play as therapy

The importance of play throughout childhood – and indeed adulthood, has long been acknowledged (Bruce, 2011; Broadhead et al., 2010; Moyles, 2010; O'Connor, 2000; Vygotsky, 1978). It provides relief from stress, it develops skills in sociability and allows the individual to work through fears and anxieties in a non-pressurized way. The process of play is more valuable than the production of an end product which in itself is highly valuable for children when trying to work through difficulties or master new skills.

Freud viewed play as a useful tool for children who suffered traumatic experiences, enabling them to act out feelings that would be otherwise too dangerous to express in social situations, viewing play as an escape from reality. Play therapy is still widely used on an international scale, providing individualized and group intervention for children who require emotional support to work through difficult feelings and experiences and to help them manage their relationships.

> The child at play creates a world of phantasy which he takes very seriously – that is which he invests with large amounts of emotion – while separating it from reality.
> (Freud, 2001: XVI in Storr, A (2001))

Although Freud viewed play as a separation from reality, he acknowledged its role in helping the child work through powerful emotions in a safe context. This in turn fosters the child's self-expression and intellectual freedom. Below is one example of how powerful play therapy was to a young child experiencing difficulty at home.

Case Study

Daisy (aged three years) was experiencing distress due to her mother and father fighting on a regular basis. They are separated but he visits Daisy a few times a week. As a result of the fighting, Daisy became withdrawn, anxious and found it difficult to play at nursery. As a result of her mother confiding in Daisy's key person, he took extra care in how he planned to meet Daisy's needs which he reviewed with her mother. Daisy's key person provided time and space for her to explore her feelings through free-play – usually at the sand tray, as she liked to play with the figures here. Daisy would tell her key person how the different figures felt and why. She always held on tightly to the seahorse, often explaining how 'she' couldn't sleep and that she was scared of being taken away. Her key person would spend much of the time listening to her and only talk if Daisy asked him a question, or to ask her about the needs of the 'characters' when she seemed to withdraw. Providing Daisy with this time to explore her feelings in a safe place, allowed her to feel calmer and less anxious and more relaxed.

Criticisms of Freud

Here, the contentious aspects of Freud's theories will be explored. Again, it is important to consider his ideas in relation to child development and how his ideas are relevant to your work with children.

His theory of the five stages of psychosexual development

The fact that Freud viewed children's psychological development primarily in sexual terms is a source of controversy (Bateman and Holmes, 1995; Crain, 1992). This is partly because this perspective reduces the emotional and social development of children to the physical, with other areas of a child's development growing from sexual development – not the other way around. Storr (2001: 136) highlights this in relation to attachment:

> With Freud, sex comes first, attachment afterwards. With John Bowlby, now established as the most important of the object-relations theorists, secure attachment comes first, sex afterwards.

As the research continues to prove, positive attachments (as discussed in Chapter 6) play a far more pivotal role in healthy psychological development, than how a child gains enjoyment from different parts of their body throughout their early development. What needs to be stressed is the undeniable significance of the early relationships and early experiences from birth, to help pave the way for developing a healthy and a positive sense of self (Oates, Karmiloff-Smith and Johnson, 2012; The National Scientific Council on the Developing Child, 2011). Such experiences and interactions will encourage the child to express themselves in ways that are not only comfortable to them but are also socially acceptable. Freud's psychosexual stages, however, focus on fixations on the different body parts (or erogenous areas) throughout childhood and do not encompass adulthood in any great detail.

   Erik Erikson, a student of Freud's, extended upon his psychosexual stages with his theory, **the psycho-social stages of development** (1950). Although also a stage theory, his was far more comprehensive, spanning across adulthood, as opposed to Freud's and Piaget's theories which only covered up to adolescence. Erikson's stages also emphasize the social and emotional aspects of human development as opposed to the sexual/physical aspects (as in Freud's theory). See Table 5.2 opposite:

Table 5.2 Erikson's five stages of psycho-social development

Age	Conflict
Infancy (0–1 year)	Basic trust versus mistrust
Early childhood (1–3 years)	Autonomy versus shame
Play age (3–6 years)	Initiative versus guilt
School age (6–12 years)	Industry versus inferiority
Adolescence (12–19 years)	Identity versus confusion
Early adulthood (20–25 years)	Intimacy versus isolation
Adulthood (26–64 years)	Generativity versus stagnation
Old age (65–death)	Integrity versus despair

Erikson emphasized the importance of each of the eight stages as a challenge that the individual must overcome, and how they do so will determine how each successive stage is dealt with. While this does not mean that progression throughout the life stages will not occur if the individual doesn't manage this task adequately, it might indicate that the challenges of stages not successfully completed may reappear as problems in the future.

What do you Think?

1 Which of the two perspectives of psychological and emotional development do you find more applicable in the early years setting?
2 What is your reason for your answer?

Freud also claimed that the first five years of life are vital in forming our personalities as adults (1920). How Freud was so confident about this assertion can also be questioned, given that this has never been proven. While it is true that our experiences of our parents (positive or negative) may shape our emotions in adulthood (Gopnik, 2009; Fonagy, 2001), findings from **neuroscience** now tell us that the brain's **plasticity** enables the individual to modify their responses to relationships and experiences. As Gopnik et al. (2001: 4) explain:

> Neither babies nor adults have some set of fixed, reflexive ways of learning, set down by evolution … the flexibility of the human cognitive system allows the individual to 'rewire' as it is greeted with successive forms of stimulation and experience.

The quality of those early experiences literally sculpt the brain's landscape, with neurons (brain cells) making connections in response to the experiences. The neural pathways built will thus be dictated by those experiences, be it positively or negatively.

The following case study provides an example of a child experiencing poor parenting and subsequent poor care in foster homes and the impact this had on his behaviour.

Read the case study and answer the questions that follow:

Case Study

Jimmy is eight years old. He was separated from his mother from two years old and placed in four different foster homes. When he arrived at his recent (and final) foster home, he was very withdrawn and couldn't socialize, not having had the opportunity to form any positive attachments. He would stay in his bedroom, switching off the light and staying under his bed where he felt safe and alone. He enjoyed playing computer games but couldn't stand to be around people – including his two younger siblings who were also with him. He didn't know how to receive or show affection; whenever his present carer tried to get close he would self-destruct because this served as a barrier which prevented him from being rejected again.

One and a half years later, Jimmy has slowly grown to trust his new family and is able to express his feelings, and give and show love. He finally feels a sense of belonging. He did however, suffer from panic attacks when parted from his carer, demonstrating rebellious behaviour. He said he 'was angry that she left him for a short time even though he knew she was coming back'.

Jimmy enjoys his new family life and now understands what it means to be loved unconditionally without fear or abuse. He takes part in regular family discussions concerning his feelings and how to manage them; he is making rapid progress academically and emotionally.

This positive change in Jimmy's life has been made possible due to being welcomed as a part of the family, with the respect, love and sensitivity that he deserves. This took a long time to achieve, with joined-up care and effective communication between carers, teachers and practitioners, with each being in tune with the child's complex emotional needs in order to meet them.

What do you Think?

1 What factors made it difficult for Jimmy to form attachments?
2 What short- and long-term support would you provide for a child who has suffered early separation and trauma?
3 How can such support contribute towards changing the child's pattern of behaviour?

The denial of sexual abuse

In this section, Freud's denial of the presence of sexual abuse will be briefly discussed. We must stress that this is by no means a detailed account and for further information, you should refer to the bibliography.

The subject of child sexual abuse is highly emotive and continues to pose painful and difficult feelings today. We do each however, have a responsibility to familiarize ourselves with issues concerning the safeguarding of children – this includes learning from the present and past.

In his early career Freud worked with many female patients who were referred to him, displaying symptoms of psychological ill-health such as partial paralysis, hallucinations and nervousness – referred to as *hysteria*.

He stated that some of his female patients' mental ill-health was a result of childhood sexual abuse in his paper *The Aetiology of Hysteria* (1896), but having been warned by the psychoanalytical community that this would be detrimental to his reputation and career as a psychoanalyst (Masson, 1984), he consequently stated that he had made a mistake in believing his patients and instead attributed their claims to fantasy. Messler and Frawley (1994: 16) highlight this in their discussion of adult survivors of childhood sexual abuse:

> The oedipal complex insisted that childhood sexual abuse was fantasy material driven by unconscious childhood sexual wishes; it protected parents at the expense of the patient's reality.

Masson (1984: 29) asserts that Freud's rejection of the existence of child sexual abuse was convenient for psychoanalysts and families in nineteenth-century Vienna, as it served to protect the interests of the privileged:

> It was a comforting view for society, for Freud's interpretation that the sexual violence that so affected the lives of his women patients was nothing but fantasy – posed no threat to the existing social order. Therapists could thus remain on the side of the successful and the powerful, rather than of the miserable victims of family violence.

Sexual abuse continues to be denied today and the reasons are manifold. What is vital is your awareness and understanding of these reasons so that you can play your part in recognizing the symptoms that some children might display and provide sensitive support in line with your setting's policies and procedures.

Reflection in Action

1a Explore your setting's guidelines for identifying and reporting child sexual abuse. How far do you think these are adequately acted upon?

1b How might you make staff more aware and confident in their practice concerning the identification and reporting of child sexual abuse?

Freud viewed female development from a male perspective

Ultimately, Freud focused far too narrowly on the five psychosexual stages of development which consequently left minimal room (if any) for social and cultural considerations concerning development. This is particularly evident in the second stage which he labelled the 'phallic stage'. As part of this stage Freud asserted that girls are actually mutilated and have to learn to live with the fact that they do not have a penis – believing that they suffered from penis envy. This of course was not the case and was never 'tested' or proved by Freud. For this reason, his theory was discredited by many researchers from different disciplines ranging from feminists to **psychologists** and fellow psychoanalysts of the time. Karen Horney (1926) for example, held opposing views to Freud, refuting his belief that women suffer from penis envy. She instead believed that the real issue was that girls and women had minimal power in European society in the 1800s, thus experiencing **status envy** – a concept that is not unfamiliar to many individuals living in Western society today but for different reasons. The issue is not so much an imbalance of power but one of greed, seeking happiness through financial and material wealth.

Concluding thoughts

This chapter has provided a brief overview of just some of Freud's contributions to psychoanalysis and child development. When we consider children's development, we look at it through a range of disciplines – and Freud's psychoanalytical perspective is just one interpretation. Your personal recollections of childhood and experience as an early years practitioner may well lead you to conclusions that contradict some of Freud's findings, and the fact that his errors have led subsequent theorists to take his ideas and develop them, enables more reliable theories to be developed. What matters, is that you have sufficient knowledge of these different perspectives in order to make informed conclusions when theorizing about children's behaviour and development.

Freud in Practice

- Sensitively helping children work through their emotional crises – this will require team meetings in order to ensure that staff are clear about what these might be so that strategies selected are suitable for children's individual personalities.

- Provide for plenty of play that encourages children to express their emotions, for example, the arts, imaginative play, music and movement.
- Supporting children to behave in socially acceptable ways.
- Working closely with parents to support their child through toilet training.

Ideas into Action

Now that you have familiarized yourself with some of Freud's key ideas, make the links to practice in your setting by reflecting upon and answering the following questions:

1 How can Freud's psychoanalytical perspective of child development inform your work as an early years practitioner?
2 Reflecting on Freud's concept of *personality development*, what advice could you give to the parent in the scenario below, to help her daughter develop the ability to delay getting her needs met?

   A parent approaches you for advice concerning her three-year-old child. The child often snatches the toys and other belongings of her sibling, not understanding that she cannot snatch but has to ask to play with these. This is causing stress in the family as the child cannot understand that she is upsetting her sibling and only focuses on what she wants.

3 Explain the similarity between Freud's oral stage and Piaget's sensory-motor stage.

Challenge the Theorists

1 Freud viewed development from a male perspective. Briefly discuss two problems with this, in trying to explain children's behaviour.
2 How far do you think our emotional-sexual relationships are pre-determined by our early relationships with our mother and father?
3 Given that Freud's theory is based upon case studies of adults, how can we be certain that their behaviour is caused specifically by a childhood experience?

Freud's Contemporary Legacy

Knowledge base concerning development from conception to three
- Socio-emotional learning
- The role of very early experiences on development

Importance of parents and the home learning environment
- The centrality of emotional-social development
- The impact of positive early interactions

Links to other theorists
- John Bowlby
- Jean Piaget
- Erik Erikson

Further Reading

Masson, J. M. (1984) *The Assault on Truth: Freud's Suppression of the Seduction Theory*. New York: Farrar, Straus and Giroux.

> This book claims, with evidence from the archive of Freud, that he rejected his initial theory that hysteria was caused by sexual abuse in order to protect his reputation. It is thought-provoking and challenging, causing the reader to reassess their views on Freud's Seduction Theory.

Mooney, C. G. (2000) *Theories of Childhood: An Introduction to Dewey, Montessori, Erikson, Piaget and Vygotsky*. St Paul, MN: Red Leaf Press.

> This book provides a clear and concise guide to some of the key theorists and how their ideas helped to shape views concerning child development and early childhood care and education. This is a good book to use as a quick reference or as a starting point for further reading and reflection.

John Bowlby (1907–90)

6

An introduction to John Bowlby and his contribution to early child care and education

This chapter examines the work of John Bowlby, the most famous of attachment theorists. His enormous contribution to the field of child care is still prevalent today and provides the foundation on which recent research studies into **attachment** continue to be carried out. The importance of attachment theory will be explored in terms of day care provision, with a discussion concerning optimum environments that foster the emotional well-being of babies and toddlers during non-parental day care. The questions towards the end of the chapter will help you to make connections to your provision for children and their families.

John Bowlby specialized in psychoanalysis and psychiatry, working as a psychiatrist in the army during the 1940s. He spent from 1948 to 1972 working at the Tavistock Institute (in London) as Director of the Department for Children and Parents and latterly, as a senior research fellow and teacher. It is however, for his work as consultant in mental health to the World Health Organization (WHO) that he is renowned. His seminal text *Child Care and the Growth of Love* evolved out of his report (1951) to the WHO.

Following is an overview of some of his key ideas. Although his research was carried out over 50 years ago, his conclusions remain just as pertinent today. While reading, consider the children and families with whom you work, as well as the support put in place to support positive attachment in families.

Attachment

This chapter begins with a description of the term attachment, with a discussion of the importance of forming attachments for a child's emotional well-being. This is followed by an examination of some of the key tenets of Bowlby's theory of attachment. Each one is highlighted under a separate sub-heading for clarity. While reading, it will be useful for you to bear in mind the cultural, religious and personal beliefs that will guide individual parents and families as well as yourself. These beliefs may well differ from Bowlby's assertions – whatever these beliefs may be, they must not jeopardize the child's well-being or happiness.

Attachment can be defined as the emotional **bond** between a mother (or other significant adult) and her baby. According to Bowlby, this attachment or bond needs to be made within the first three years of life – and especially during the first nine months of life, in order to provide the child with a positive 'blueprint' for forming future relationships. This is echoed more recently by the eminent child psychologist Oliver James (2007: 158) who states that:

> The period between six months and three years of age in humans is a Sensitive one for developing Secure attachments, and the pattern a child will have at 18 months can be predicted with accuracy by measuring his mother's pattern before he was born.

Infants who have a secure attachment with their mother are more likely to be confident, happy and generally more secure due to having their essential needs (for food, love and stimulation) met. However, where this attachment is disrupted or fails to take place, it can have disastrous effects for the infant in terms of their emotional well-being in the short and long term. Studies repeatedly show that they are likely to cry more frequently and generally be more unsettled in their temperament (Oates, Karmiloff-Smith and Johnson, 2012). They are also more likely to form insecure attachments during adulthood (Batmanghelidjh, 2011; Shea, 2010; Bowlby, 1953). As part of his attachment theory, Bowlby emphasized the importance of **monotropy**. This will be examined below.

Bowlby's concept of monotropy

While reading this paragraph, make your own judgements about this concept. Do you agree or disagree? What are your reasons?

Monotropy is the belief that the child has an innate need to form a bond with their mother/primary attachment figure. While Bowlby does not rule out a bond being formed with other significant adults, he placed great importance on there being one primary bond (usually with the mother), from which the child can enjoy unconditional love and responsive care. If this bond is not present or is interrupted, it can have long-lasting negative effects for the child's all-round development and ability to form meaningful attachments with others. Babies thus seem to be hard-wired to draw their mother's attention through behaviours such as smiling, crying and breast-feeding, each of which play a part in keeping the mother in close proximity.

What do you Think?

1 Where a child does not enjoy the security of a strong maternal relationship, what protective factors need to be present in their life, to help minimize the adverse impact of this?
2 What might be the long-term benefits of this for the child?

Mary Ainsworth (1971) who worked with Bowlby, built upon his theory of attachment in a number of ways. For example:

- She suggested that children have multiple attachments (as opposed to Bowlby's concept of monotropy)

- She devised the **'strange situation'** test to identify the different attachment behaviours of children.

Each idea will now be discussed in turn.

Children can form multiple attachments

Although Ainsworth did not dispute the significance of attachment, she did not believe that the primary attachment had to be the mother and instead proposed that children can form multiple attachments – be it with siblings, the father or other adults who provided reliable loving care. This is consistent with current attachment theory (Bowlby 2007; Schore, 2007) which emphasizes the importance of quality care that strengthens the attachment and in turn, gives the child a sense of security.

What do you Think?

Do you agree with Ainsworth? Briefly explain your reasons.

The 'strange situation'

Ainsworth also devised the well-known *'strange situation'* test (1971) to identify the specific attachment behaviours that children exhibit. Her test was a simple but effective way of identifying children's attachment types to their mothers. The 'strange situation' is summarized below:

1 The parent and the infant are alone in a room, as the child plays with some toys

2 The stranger joins parent and infant

3 The parent leaves the infant and stranger alone

4 The parent returns and stranger leaves

5 The parent leaves and the infant is left completely alone

6 The stranger returns

7 The parent returns and the stranger leaves

The child's attachment behaviour is observed and measured under the following four categories:

1 Separation anxiety: the unease the infant shows when left by the caregiver

2 The infant's willingness to explore

3 Stranger anxiety: the infant's response to the presence of a stranger

4 Reunion behaviour: the way the caregiver is greeted on return

Table 6.1 (below) outlines the behaviours that children most commonly displayed in the '*strange situation*'. The most common behaviour observed was the securely attached – which indicates a positive relationship between mother and child, one in which the child enjoys a steady and predictable pattern of love and care.

Consider the types of attachment behaviours that you observe in your practice. You might be able to identify them from the following descriptions.

Table 6.1   Types of attachment behaviour

Attachment type	Behaviour demonstrated by the child
Anxious/avoidant	The child might not be distressed when their mother leaves and might turn away when she returns.
Securely attached	The child might get upset when their mother leaves but is easily comforted when she returns.
Anxious/resistant	The child might initially be very clingy and distressed when the mother first leaves. Upon the mother's return the child might simultaneously resist contact and interaction while reaching up to be held and crying.

As early years practitioners, it's important that you are familiar with these attachment behaviours so that you can identify any potential concerns regarding the child's responses to her mother/primary attachment figure. Clearly, this in isolation might not mean anything but can be useful as part of a wider investigation into the child's welfare. Sir Richard Bowlby (2007) discusses the relevance of the 'strange situation' test in identifying the different attachment types in children. This identification can in turn, be used to gather the necessary support for the child (and where appropriate, their family).

By itself insecure attachment is very difficult to identify unless the Strange Situation Procedure is employed. Insecure attachment is found in approximately 40% of toddlers in the UK and USA, and is acknowledged as a risk factor that often contributes to the mental health problems of children and adults. (Bowlby, 2007. Personal written communication)

So, although the opportunity for a monotropic attachment is accepted as the desired norm for a child, it might not be realistic for all parents to provide this. For example, mothers who are substance abusers or suffer from depression, or who are overwhelmed by their social circumstances brought about by poverty or social disadvantage will not be able to consistently provide the love and care that an infant requires, due to being too consumed by their own needs or by their social situation over which they have very little control. Different child-rearing practices that do not conform to this concept can actually prove effective, such as raising children in a kibbutz (collective community) where the caring of children is done among many caregivers throughout the child's life (Fox, 1977). The decline in extended family networks also means that the child is more likely to be placed into day care provision.

In conclusion, what matters most is the quality of care provided for the child – be it with the mother, substitute carer or as part of early years provision. It is thus useful to bear in mind how Bowlby's research has helped to change professionals' attitudes to the importance of children's attachments and your personal role in fostering babies' and children's self-confidence and self-esteem.

Day care and attachment

The potential effects of day care on forming positive attachments will now be examined. *While reading, reflect on the quality of care provided in your setting – consider the factors that enable and inhibit babies and children in forming positive attachments.*

Babies need sufficient attention and time from their mother/primary attachment figure in order to develop as secure a primary attachment as possible before starting any form of non-parental day care. This is supported in the United Kingdom with statutory paid maternity leave for the first nine months. A child who has benefited from a **safe base** (Bowlby, 1988) with unconditional love, sensitive physical care and attention, can then go on to build emotionally healthy relationships with other significant adults.

Building positive attachments will prove all the more significant when a baby starts day care, as they will be among a larger group of babies and young children, with less time spent in one-to-one situations with one adult. This is one of the many reasons why the suitability of day care for children aged under 2 years is still debated. In larger groups, with different practitioners responsible for children's care and development, it is all too easy for individual needs to be overlooked and cues to be missed. This is especially true of provision where there is a high staff turnover, which prevents children from building relationships with key figures. Some studies show the adverse effects of poor quality day care on children's cognitive, social and emotional development (Bowlby, 2007; National Scientific Council on the Developing Child, 2005; Sylva et al., 2004).

Reflection in Action

How do you ensure that your key person approach promotes a sense of security and belonging in individual babies and children?

Debate and research studies continue to permeate attachment theory and provision for day care due to there being no definitive answer as to what is best for the child. This of course depends on factors at home as well as the quality of substitute care provided in early years settings. Bowlby's (1953) and Goldschmied's key person approach (1994) is just one way of ensuring that babies and young children benefit from a consistent and secure relationship with one practitioner. The key person provides continuity of care which can all too easily be missed in busy institutions such as nurseries and early years centres. As part of this approach, Goldschmied also emphasized the importance of nurturing parental partnerships which she referred to as triangular, consisting of the parent, child and the key person. She believed – as conscientious practitioners do today – that this relationship is stable and effective as long as each side is equally valued.

Children's need for unconditional love, attention and having their individual needs met respectfully and responsively within a secure environment cannot be underestimated. Whether it is residential or day care, babies and children need to be at the centre of the service – it is due to Bowlby's conclusions which led to much-needed changes in the care of children. All of which influence practice today:

- Children in day care nurseries and in residential care have a key person assigned to them – so that the child has one 'special' person responsible for their care in the setting.
- Parents/carers are encouraged to stay and settle their children in nurseries during the transition period.
- Parents are supported in maintaining their child's primary attachment bond to them.
- Parents/carers should stay overnight with their children when their children are in hospital, to help look after them.
- Babies are allowed to stay with their mothers after birth (as long as the baby is healthy).
- Parents are supported in looking after their newborn baby, to help the attachment process along.

Reflection in Action

1 Investigate your key person role and how far it supports all children's sense of security and belonging.
2 Make recommendations to your manager about how aspects might be improved.

In summary, although there is no definitive answer as to whether babies fare better attending nurseries, due to the vast differences in early years provision and family make-up, the implementation of a key person system, settling-in periods and all-round good quality substitute care serve to nurture infants' emotional well-being and social skills – especially where the care at home might be poor and inconsistent.

Maternal deprivation theory

Bowlby's theory of monotropy led to the formulation of his maternal deprivation theory. This section explores Bowlby's concerns regarding the impact of maternal deprivation on the child. These concerns are just as pertinent to attachment theory and early years provision at present. Maternal deprivation as formulated by Bowlby is categorized as partial deprivation or complete deprivation (1953). Partial deprivation can be present even if a child lives with her mother but she is unable to give her the loving care that she needs. This deprivation doesn't necessarily lead to detrimental effects if there is a trusted substitute caregiver to step into the breach. Complete deprivation on the other hand refers to the substitute care given in hospitals or nurseries where there is no 'one' person providing consistent, personalized care. Examples of maternal deprivation include mothers failing to form an attachment, substance abuse and the general inability to provide consistent love and care, each of which can have irreversible adverse effects on the child's emotional and mental health. This is outlined by Bowlby (1953: 39):

> Prolonged breaks in the mother-child relationship during the first three years of life leave a characteristic impression on the child's personality. They fail to develop loving ties with other children or with adults and consequently have no friendships worth the name.

Based on his many child and adolescent interviews, Bowlby reached some alarming conclusions. The result of these individuals having suffered maternal deprivation meant that behaviours such as delinquency, reduced intelligence, increased aggression, depression and affectionless psychopathy (the inability to show affection or concern for others) were commonplace. His paper, *Forty-Four Juvenile Thieves: Their Characters and Home Lives* (1944), which includes statistical tests as well as detailed case histories, highlights the tragic outcomes of maternal deprivation on children and young adults. Unfortunately, the associated problems for children and young adults that poor attachments bring are still prevalent today. One report by the charity Kids Company highlights this in no uncertain terms:

> If mothers and fathers are neglectful due to their struggle with their own survival, then their child is deprived of a buffer of a good attachment against violence and antisocial behaviours. (Kids Company, 2011: 3)

In light of this, early years practitioners cannot afford to dismiss the sheer importance of primary attachments on present and future emotional well-being, and must therefore invest in building positive relationships with the parents/primary attachment figures with whom they work, so as to provide a 'buffer' against the gaps present in some children's attachments.

Criticisms of Bowlby's attachment theory

While reading this section, reflect on the changes in family make-up, types of early years provision and the current political climate. Each of these factors is now very different compared to when Bowlby was making recommendations based on his research findings.

He emphasized the role of the mother only in attachment

Bowlby's report to the WHO, *Maternal Care and Mental Health* (1951), has been open to much criticism for its emphasis of the role of the mother as the primary attachment figure. This is mainly due to the political and economic climate at the time, which called for women to return to their role as housewife while their husbands returned to work after the Second World War. His research findings therefore proved convenient for the government's campaign to get women to give up the jobs that they had to take during the war, while their husbands fought.

His identified attachment behaviours are not exclusive to mothers

In his highly regarded book, *Maternal Deprivation Reassessed* (1972), Michael Rutter argued (against John Bowlby) that it was the norm for children to form multiple attachments rather than a selective attachment with just one person. In 1978 he showed that children display the same attachment behaviours as identified by Bowlby, to siblings, fathers and extended family members – not just the mother figure. More recent research studies have also contradicted Bowlby's findings

(Melhuish, 1991; Schaffer, 1977) which concluded that the quality of attachment and its impact on the child's emotional well-being was more important than having an attachment. While this makes sense, Bowlby's contribution to our understanding of the fundamental impact of disturbed attachments, maternal deprivation and poor care-giving on children's psychological and emotional development cannot be underestimated. His extensive studies and conclusions have paved the way for all subsequent attachment theories – which continues to change, due to the rapidly evolving make-up of societies and due to technological advances which now enable us to actually see the impact of specific attachments on the child's developing brain (Schore, 2007; Gopnik, 1999).

There were methodological flaws in his research studies

Although Bowlby's research findings have proved invaluable, the way in which he carried out his studies has been the subject of much criticism. For example, a lot of his work was carried out with young offenders, yet his findings were applied to the general population. He also drew upon retrospective data – that is, information gathered from interviews with young offenders and young adults concerning their childhood and past experiences. Retrospective data can be very unreliable due to accounts being inaccurate and subjective, and it is very difficult to isolate one factor such as maternal deprivation as the 'cause' of the behaviour in older children.

he said but that is not true, today.

Concluding thoughts

In conclusion, we cannot afford to downplay Bowlby's legacy concerning the sheer importance of attachment and its impact on emotional and mental well-being – both in the short and long term. The key is to view any theory critically and challenge any aspects that you feel do not conform to your experience with children. However, his work provided the springboard from which future theorists and scientists investigated the impact of day care, institutional care and foster care on brain development. More recently, the work of neuroscientists continues to show, with evidence, the direct effect on the developing brain when babies and children are deprived of loving relationships and experience poor quality day care. This may be one of the defining elements in a child's future life chances (Allen, 2011).

Bowlby in Practice

- Having an effective key person system in place.
- The need to support young children's early attachments positively.
- Practitioners supporting parents and primary carers to build a secure attachment – particularly when conditions in the home (or in the parent) make this difficult.
- Practitioners working with parents to enable a smooth **transition** from home to nursery.
- The link between early attachment and later social and emotional well-being.

Ideas into Action

Now that you have familiarized yourself with some of Bowlby's contributions to child development theory, make the links to practice in your setting by reflecting upon and answering the following questions:

1 What do you think are the positive and negative aspects of day care, on babies' and children's emotional and social development?
2 In which ways is Bowlby's influence evident in practice at your setting?
3 How are parental partnerships *promoted* and *evaluated* in your setting?
4 Identify the factors that make an effective:
   - Key person system
   - Key person relationship

Challenge the Theorists

1 Do you think that there exist other, more significant factors that shape a baby's/child's attachments? Identify these.
2 How relevant is the concept of monotropy given today's climate (consider the changes in family make-up, women working longer hours and returning to work after having a baby).

Explain the reasons behind your answer.

3 Read the quote below. Do you agree or disagree? Explain the reason for your answer.

According to Bowlby (1951):

> If the attachment figure is broken or disrupted during the critical two year period the child will suffer irreversible long-term consequences of this maternal deprivation. This risk continues until the age of 5.

Bowlby's Contemporary Legacy

Knowledge base concerning development from conception to three
- Socio-emotional learning
- The role of very early experiences on development

Creating inclusive and enabling environments
- Behavioural and academic expectations

Importance of parents and the home learning environment
- The centrality of emotional-social development
- The impact of positive early interactions
- Countering poverty and socio-economic disadvantage

Links to other theorists
- Allan Schore (findings from neuroscience pertaining to attachment)
- Colwyn Trevarthen
- Elinor Goldschmied
- Sir Richard Bowlby
- Erik Erikson

Further Reading

Bowlby, J. (1953) *Child Care and the Growth of Love*. London: Penguin.

> We highly recommend anyone with an interest in attachment to read this seminal text, which is based on a report prepared by John Bowlby for the World Health Organization. It clearly outlines the impact of maternal deprivation on infant mental health, alongside a range of supporting research evidence.

Gerhardt, S. (2004) *Why Love Matters*. London and New York: Routledge.

> Psychologist Sue Gerhardt provides a compelling account of why forming early attachments and positive early experiences are crucial in the shaping of all-round development. She supports her argument with references to current findings from neuroscience, which prove how these early experiences set down the neurobiological patterns in the brain.

Gopnik, A. (2009) *The Philosophical Baby*. New York: Farrar, Straus and Giroux.

> This is an absorbing and interesting book which examines the origins of the mind in relation to secure attachments. The chapter 'Babies and the Meaning of Life' is particularly insightful, with a range of links to ancient theories and current scientific understanding.

Jean Piaget (1896–1980)

7

An introduction to Jean Piaget and his influence in early child care and education

Jean Piaget is probably the best-known cognitive theorist concerning child development. He is also, however, the most challenged (Bjorklund, 2000; Donaldson, 1978). The reasons for this will be explored later in the chapter. Piaget originally worked as a biologist, studying molluscs (examples include mussels, clams, snails and slugs) in the early 1920s. Strange as the connection may seem, his studies of these animals in their different environments were the catalyst for his interest in studying children's cognitive development and how they learnt and adapted to their environments. He was particularly interested in the reasons children gave for their wrong answers on the questions that required logical thinking. His extensive studies of children (many of which were carried out on his own three children) contributed to his theories of how children learn from birth.

Piaget's key theories of cognitive development will now be outlined; as you read through them, **think critically:** *do you disagree with any aspects of his theories? Why is this? How far, and in what ways, do you think they add to your own understanding about the learning and development of young children?*

His approach is known as **constructivism**; this means that he believed children learn by doing – actively constructing their own knowledge as a result of their explorations, and building this knowledge upon previous understandings. This contrasts with **socio-constructivism** (Bruner, 1983; Vygotsky, 1978), the belief that children learn by constructing knowledge with other children and adults around them. The socio-constructivist theory places more emphasis on the social aspect of learning, whereas Piaget focused on the child learning individually.

Piaget's theories of cognitive development

The four stages of cognitive development

Central to Piaget's theory of how children learn are his four stages of cognitive development. Based on his studies of children, Piaget proposed that all children pass through four stages of cognitive development from birth, sequentially – this means that the child must successfully pass through each stage in order to pass onto the following stages and that no stage can be missed out. Piaget concentrated on the universal stages of cognitive development and biological maturation, and it is argued that he failed to adequately consider the effect that the social setting and **culture** may have on a child's cognitive development (Vygotsky's socio-constructivist theory of learning does however take these factors into consideration).

An important limitation to Piaget's ideas is their lack of recognition of the process of learning and development, which means his ideas may not fully account for the individual differences that result from the quality of relationships and interactions that the child has, or how the environment shapes the child's experiences and ability to learn and develop healthily. He did however show that children are highly competent thinkers, although they think *differently* to adults – contrary to the notion that they are simply incompetent thinkers in comparison. Piagetian-based educational programmes are guided by his firm belief that children are naturally curious and intrinsically motivated to learn about their world, with the role of practitioners being mainly facilitative. This means that the adult's role is to encourage children's independent explorations, providing them with appropriate prompts that help them to learn through the process of trial and error, as well as setting up the environment with resources and equipment (including labelling of resources) which enable children to be active in their learning.

The implications of these ideas for early years education have resulted in the development of curricular frameworks that are based upon play, discovery and active learning – which are seen as far more effective vehicles for learning for children as opposed to them being passive recipients of a curriculum. In recognition of Piaget's emphasis on children as constructors of their own learning, the revised EYFS contains detailed guidance for practitioners on how best to support all babies' and children's active learning, while taking into account those children who have special educational needs or English as an additional language.

Carefully read Table 7.1 opposite – as you do so, it will be useful to think of the children with whom you work.

Table 7.1 Piaget's four stages of cognitive development

Stage of cognitive development	Characterized by
Sensori-motor **(Birth–2 years)**	• Recognizing self as agent of action and begins to act intentionally: e.g. pulls a string to set mobile in motion or shakes a rattle to make a noise. • Achieving **object permanence** between 8–12 months: realizes that things continue to exist even when they are no longer present (or hidden from sight).
Pre-operational **(2–7 years)**	• Learning to use symbols such as language, number and pictures to represent aspects of their world. Pretend play develops as part of this. • Thinking is **egocentric** – has difficulty in taking the viewpoint of others. • Classifying objects by a single feature: e.g. groups together all the red blocks regardless of shape or all the square blocks regardless of colour.
Concrete operational **(7–11 years)**	• Thinking logically about objects and events, based on their own past experiences. • Achieving **conservation of number** (age 6), **mass** (age 7) and **weight** (age 9). This means that the child understands that quantities such as number, mass and weight remain the same, even when their appearance changes. • Classifying objects according to several of their features and ordering them in series along a single dimension such as size.
Formal operational **(11 years and up)**	• Thinking in **abstract** terms. This means they do not rely on concrete objects to solve problems as they can now solve them in their mind. • Concern with the hypothetical, the future, and ideological problems.

What do you Think?

What are the implications for staff in their relationships and roles when settling babies, given that they achieve object permanence between 8–12 months (i.e. they realize that things continue to exist even when they are no longer present or hidden from sight)? How does this knowledge impact on the way staff might better support young babies during transition points in caregivers?

Schemas

Piaget's concept of **schemas** is a key way of understanding how children acquire and extend their knowledge of how the world works. A schema can be defined as a pattern of behaviour which the child displays while attempting to understand a new piece of information, based on their experience of it. As the child has more experiences, this new information is used to modify or add to previously existing schemas. Athey (1990: 7) describes schematic behaviour as occurring 'when children are actively involved in learning and they are developing the mental structures that help them to think and move on'.

There exist approximately 12 types of schematic behaviour, each of which you have probably observed among the children in your setting. Table 7.2 shows examples of schematic behaviour.

Table 7.2 Types of schematic behaviour

Schematic behaviour	Examples from children's play
Trajectory	Throwing and kicking toys and soft toys, jumping on and off things and dropping toys onto the floor.
Enveloping	Wrapping up or covering toys and soft toys with tape and covering themselves and dolls in fabrics. The process of wrapping is important to a child in this schema.
Enclosure	Climbing into large cardboard boxes, building enclosures with blocks and filling and emptying a wide range of containers.
Rotation	Enjoying being swung around, rolling down surfaces, playing with wheeled toys and watching a spinning washing machine.
Positioning	This is similar to the orientation schema. Children show preference in how their toys are stored and how they play with them – for example, lining up toy vehicles or toys of a particular colour.
Connection	Connecting and disconnecting construction toy pieces as well as joining train tracks.
Orientation	This includes up, down, above and under and sideways. Children love to hang from climbing frames, lie down under tables and paint using brushstrokes in different directions.
Transporting	Carrying objects and toys from area to another. This can be in container, a wheeled toy or in their hands.
Transforming	Changing the appearance of substances, for example – adding water to dry sand and adding colouring to cornflour or sand.

Reflection in Action

1 Observe a child and look for patterns in their behaviour.
2 Do you recognize any of Piaget's schemas in these patterns of behaviour?

Schematic behaviour is present in babies and goes on until adulthood. A child might have a schema about a type of animal, such as a dog. If the child's sole experience has been with small dogs, she might believe that all dogs are small. Suppose then that the child encounters a very large dog. The child will eventually take in this new information, modifying the previously existing schema to include this new information.

Example in Action

The enveloping schema

Janie is ten months old and is currently interested in wrapping herself up in materials and playing games like peek-a-boo. At the moment, she loves to hide objects and toys in baskets and cover them with various-sized pieces of material. Upon observing Janie's interest in enveloping things (including herself!) her key person set up the indoor and outdoor environments with tents and tunnels, along with a range of containers containing natural objects and fabrics for Janie to explore. These containers proved very popular with Janie, as she loves to sit beside the containers with her key person, who often helps her to 'wrap' the objects and unwrap them again.

Key concepts used by Piaget

Assimilation – The process of taking in new information into our previously existing schemas is known as assimilation. The process is somewhat subjective, because we tend to modify experience or information somewhat to fit in with our pre-existing beliefs. In the example above, seeing a dog and labelling it 'dog' is an example of assimilating the animal into the child's dog schema.

Accommodation – Another part of adaptation involves changing or altering our existing schemas in light of new information, a process known as accommodation. Accommodation involves altering existing schemas, or ideas, as a result of new information or new experiences. New schemas may also be developed during this process.

Equilibrium and disequilibrium – Piaget believed that when knowledge can be easily assimilated, the child is in a state of equilibrium (balance); however, when their existing knowledge needs to be accommodated (changed), the child enters a states of disequilibrium (imbalance). This unsteady state continues until the child can modify her existing cognitive structures, to take in the new information.

What do you Think?

1 Give one example of a child going through the process of assimilation, accommodation, equilibrium and disequilibrium, as they try to grasp a new concept.
2 How could you support a child in their quest to grasp new concepts?

Criticisms of Piaget's theories

Although the legacy of Piaget's theories remains, aspects of them are widely criticized. Below is a brief outline; for further information you need to refer to the bibliography provided.

Relevance of tasks he set for children

Some of the tasks that Piaget set for children may have been too unfamiliar for the children, thereby causing them to fail. Several studies have shown Piaget underestimated the abilities of children because his tests were sometimes confusing or difficult to understand (Hughes, 1975). A well-known example of this is his '*three mountains*' task. During this task children (aged between 6 and 7 years old) were asked to look at three mountains on a table. Each of them was a different size and colour, with something different on top of each one; a cross, a house or snow. When asked what each child could see from where they were sitting, they all pointed out what they could see only. However, what needs to be considered is that the task itself could have led to the children not succeeding in the task. Factors such as monotony of the task, not being given clear instructions on how to complete the task and using objects that were culturally unfamiliar to the children, all prevented them from achieving as well as they could have.

He believed that children are egocentric and cannot decentre until the age of seven

Based on his child studies (1951) Piaget concluded that children below the age of seven could not decentre – that is, take on the viewpoint of others and that they are unable to infer what another person can see, think or feel. Subsequently however, researchers who carried out similar tasks but simplified them (Hughes, 1975; Elkind, 1967) found that children can actually decentre at a younger age.

What do you Think?

1 Have you observed children (aged under seven years) in your setting demonstrate the ability to take on board the feelings and thoughts of other children?
2 Describe one activity you would carry out with young children to help foster their ability to empathize with others.

Many of his child studies were carried out on his own three children

The majority of his extensive child studies were carried out on his own three children – thereby meaning that his findings were culturally biased, because his sample consisted of middle-class European children. This raises the larger question of bias which is an issue for all of Piaget's empirical work – Piaget carried out most of his studies alone on a select sample of children, which meant that he could not have gained a comprehensive understanding of children's cognitive abilities.

He believed that each stage of development had to be reached in order for the child to progress to subsequent stages

Unlike other child development theorists (such as Jerome Bruner and Lev Vygotsky), Piaget believed that children have to pass through distinct stages as part of their cognitive development. This does not acknowledge that the child may move in and out of stages as their developing understanding matures or as they tackle new circumstances and experiences. This in turn meant that he also did not consider the factors that might contribute to shaping the child's ability at a given time. For example, cultural differences among families around the world determine the amount of play and types of play resources available to the child, which consequently would impact upon results obtained from child studies. Other factors such as differences among children in the same age group and how clearly tasks were presented to them also contribute to how well they can carry out instructions.

Piaget's studies and neuroscience – the connection

Piaget was the first psychologist to make a systematic study of cognitive development based on his studies of children (he only observed children). While his simple but inventive tests revealed different cognitive abilities among children, findings from neuroscience now enable us to further explore his theories. For example, studies concerning neuron development and performance show evidence that correlates with Piaget's four stages of cognitive development – which is testament to some of Piaget's child studies and conclusions that were drawn over 60 years ago. Although Piaget could not have predicted that his theories would be supported by such technological advances, his work has provided a foundation from which subsequent investigations have taken place. Findings from neuroscience have thus enabled aspects of Piaget's cognitive development theories to be confirmed as correct, as well as challenged.

One example of this is his assertion that children did not develop moral reasoning or the ability to decentre until seven years old. Eminent American professor of psychology and researcher in cognitive development, Alison Gopnik explains one flaw in Piaget's assessment of young children's ability to decentre:

> Piaget thought that children didn't have genuine moral knowledge because he thought they couldn't take the perspective of others, infer intentions and follow abstract rules. Modern science shows this just isn't true. From the time they are born children are empathic. (Gopnik, 2009: 202)

What do you Think?

1 Have you observed children (aged under seven years) in your setting demonstrate the ability to take on board the feelings and thoughts of other children?
2 Describe one activity you would carry out with young children to help foster their ability to empathize with others.

Conversely, findings from neuroscience continue to show us that quality early experiences can actually speed up brain development (Howard-Jones, 2009; Case, Kurland and Goldberg, 1982), which means that the impact of special educational needs and differences concerning ability and capacity to understand at different ages and stages can now be considered when explaining children's cognitive development. Having this knowledge of the general pattern of development a child should pass through helps the early years practitioner when attempting to identify any deviations from this and to put the necessary support mechanisms in place for the child.

Concluding thoughts

To conclude, Piaget's vast contribution to our understanding of child development cannot be dismissed. It is due to his tireless work that we understand how children process new information from birth, and how learning and development progress. Early years provision for care and education is thus shaped by such awareness, with practitioners planning environments that are rich and varied for children to explore for themselves and in which they can actively construct their own knowledge (schemas). His work showed clearly that babies and young children are very able constructors of meaning and, hence, of learning from their own experiences. He also demonstrated that the process of learning cannot be separated from the child's lived experiences – especially in the earlier stages of development when learning is primarily hands-on and experience-driven. These ideas continue to profoundly shape our thinking and actions as educators in early years settings today.

Piaget in Practice

- Supporting children's learning through action and experimentation in their environment.
- Allowing children plenty of time to play and explore independently.
- Planning for learning that is in line with their cognitive abilities.
- Carrying out regular observations and assessments of children interacting and problem solving, to improve understanding of children's intellectual development.
- Focusing on the process of young children's thinking – not just the end product (this means paying attention to the many different steps it takes a child to reach an answer).
- All practitioners being able to identify babies' and children's different schematic behaviours and how to extend their learning in line with these.

Ideas into Action

Now that you have familiarized yourself with some of Piaget's most significant contributions to child development theory, make the links to practice in your setting by reflecting upon and answering the following questions:

1   Consider the babies in your setting; how can you promote object permanence among babies aged eight months old?
2   What experiences and activities could you plan to support children's progress in the pre-operational stage of cognitive development?
3a Refer to the table outlining the four stages of cognitive development. Do the behaviours 'match' the ages and stages of children in your setting?
3b Some children do not show behaviour typical of the stage of cognitive development for their age group, while others surpass expectations. Consider the children in your setting. What factors do you think contribute to these differences?
4   Revisit the process of schematic behaviour (outlined in Table 7.2). Give an example of this. To help you answer, consider the process that children go through when trying to learn new things in your setting.

Challenge the Theorists

1 Piaget was a constructivist; identify some of the positive and negative aspects of this theory in action, in an early years setting.

2 Research tells us the importance of positive early childhood experiences in promoting brain development. How does this complement the constructivist theory of learning?

3 Identify the grounds on which Piaget's theories can be challenged in today's society.

Piaget's Contemporary Legacy

Knowledge base concerning development from conception to three years
- The role of very early experiences on development

Creating inclusive and enabling environments
- Behavioural and academic expectations

Importance of parents and the home learning environment
- The impact of positive early interactions

Links to other theorists
- John Dewey
- Lev Vygotsky
- Jerome Bruner
- Sigmund Freud

Further Reading

Athey, C. (1990) *Extending Thought in Young Children*. London: Paul Chapman Publishing.

This book provides in-depth information concerning children's schemas and how practitioners can facilitate children's understanding of their world through their schemas.

Donaldson, M. (1984) *Children's Minds*. London: Fontana Press.

This classic text examines children's thought processes, while challenging certain features of Piaget's theory of intellectual development in light of more recent evidence. It is easily accessible and highly informative.

Piaget, J. (1972) *The Psychology of the Child*. New York: Basic Books.

This seminal text provides an in-depth look at children's intellectual development, including the logical inconsistencies that are inherent in this.

Lev Vygotsky (1896–1934)

8

An introduction to Lev Vygotsky and his work in early child care and education

This chapter explores the valuable contributions of the psychologist, Lev Vygotsky to early childhood education. Influenced by the work of Freud and Piaget, he created his own theories surrounding human psychology and the nature of learning (Kozulin, 1986). His ideas most pertinent to understanding how young children learn will be discussed with a range of suggestions as to how you can create a learning environment which best fosters individual children's learning and development in your setting. Case studies and observations are provided to help contextualize his theories.

Vygotsky was born in Belarus (a landlocked country in Eastern Europe, bordered by Russia, Poland and Lithuania). Born in the same year as Piaget (1896), Vygotsky studied medicine and law at university, beginning his career as a teacher before becoming a psychologist in 1924. He was a prolific writer, producing many articles, essays and books on subjects concerning child development, education and cognition of children – including children with physical and mental disabilities.

Although he died young – aged just 37 years, the work that Vygotsky produced continues to greatly influence early years education today. However, due to the political situation in the Soviet Union at the time, when most scientific and cultural freedoms were suppressed, much of Vygotsky's work was banned. His theories were often perceived as disloyal to the Communist Party under Stalin. Views that were not approved by the state were not tolerated under Stalinism and were brutally oppressed. Despite this state oppression, Vygotsky's ideas were kept alive by a group of his colleagues in exile (Luria, Leontiev, Bozhovich) and his work eventually came to the notice of the West in the 1960s, having been translated from Russian.

Jerome Bruner, an American psychologist (discussed in greater detail in Chapter 9) was greatly influenced by Vygotsky's theories concerning language development and the impact of the social environment on learning. He, too, came to the conclusion that the child learnt most effectively by using the **tools** (i.e. language, thought, ways of behaving, books and methods of problem solving) that are available to them in their particular cultural environment. Bruner is also credited for being instrumental in disseminating Vygotsky's ideas to the West back in the 1960s (Sheehy, 2004). The most significant of Vygotsky's contributions to early childhood education will now be discussed in turn.

Vygotsky on thought and language

Vygotsky was deeply interested in the relationship between thought and language as key elements of a child's cognitive development. Perhaps one of his best-known books was written on this subject, entitled *Thought and Language* (1978). He believed that while the two functions are independent of each other, they nevertheless support one another in the process of cognitive development.

Given his belief that relationships always have a cultural context, it is inevitable that the child's thoughts, too, will be culturally constructed. The social constructivist perspective of learning which he created is deemed particularly relevant to the development of young children because of its emphasis on children constructing their understanding of the world through interactions with other children and adults, using language to make sense of their environment and their place within it. Vygotsky (1985: 80) states that:

> Culture is the product of social life and human social activity. That is why just by raising the question of cultural development of behaviour we are directly introducing the social plane of development. Everything that is cultural is social.

Case Study

Thought and language in action
A five-year-old child is sitting at her dolls' house acting out a recent family holiday to Cornwall, reflecting on some of the things that she had done. She uses the new vocabulary that she had learnt (such as 'seaside', 'suitcase', 'surfing' and 'seagulls') while acting out the toys having to pack their suitcases to leave early in the morning – as she had done on her journey, and playing on the beach once she, her parents and siblings had unpacked their suitcases.

To summarize then:

- The cultural context in this brief case study is the family and their experience of the holiday.

- The child's thoughts were given an outlet in this play opportunity, in which the child gave a running commentary of some of her experiences on her holiday at the seaside. This is in line with Vygotsky's *overt inner speech three–five* years stage of language development. (See the description and diagram below.)

- The experience and the language triggered the opportunity to articulate her thoughts and practise her recently acquired vocabulary. In addition to practising vocabulary, what the language does is facilitate a working through of ideas and thinking about how society and relationships work, and making connections which are then processed cognitively and added and linked to other concepts, i.e. language allows and facilitates higher order thinking and the development of more complex concepts and hypotheses.

The sequence of language development, according to Vygotsky

Vygotsky's ideas concerning language development from birth up to late childhood (7 years plus) will now be outlined in this funnel-like diagram. It depicts the flow of language from birth, with typical behaviours that are demonstrated in each of the three stages.

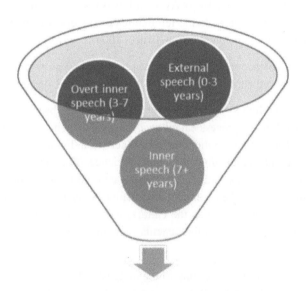

The development of language and thought

As the diagram shows, Vygotsky believed that children:

- Develop language first, as *external speech* – through social interactions with those around them. This starts from birth, with responses being made to the outside world (such as vocalizing in response to affection and responding to questions).

- *Overt inner speech* or monologue (the ability to talk to oneself) appears from approximately three years old, whereby the child can give a running commentary concerning tasks that she is engaged in. For example, a child playing with a doll trying to dress her might say out loud 'I've put your dress on, now I need to put your coat and shoes on'.

- The final phase of language development involves the child from approximately seven years, using *internal speech* (thinking silently to herself) to reflect on recent events or to plan.

Given that thought is *in part*, shaped by the child's first communication with those around them, it is inevitable that the culture too will be adopted as the two are inextricably linked. An example of this could be a primary carer speaking to their child in both Turkish and English, which would result in the child thinking and speaking in both languages. No language can exist outside of the symbolic order (i.e. the spoken and written word as well as pictorial signs), which consequently means that the child cannot make meaning outside of their relationships with those around them. The relationship between language and thought and how the two interact developmentally is thus central to the socio-constructivist perspective of learning. It is interesting to note that Piaget later agreed with Vygotsky concerning outer speech and inner thought, but because Vygotsky's work was not read in the West they could never meet. Piaget regretted that, and felt that his own work was more in tune with Vygotsky's than he was given credit for (Bruce, 2006).

> Human learning presupposes a specific social nature and a process by which children grow into the intellectual life of those around them. (Vygotsky, 1978: 88)

Here, Vygotsky highlights the fact that children actually absorb the culture that they are immersed in – a process called *enculturation*. The nursery experience is a good example of how enculturation can take place, as individual children learn the culture of other children and adults through experience, observation and instruction. Practitioners thus need to be aware of the various cultural norms among the children and their families so that they can support learning by enabling children to utilize their own cultural tools as well as the cultural tools of others. Cole, Hakkarainen and Bredikyte (2010: 3) explain the benefits to a child's cognitive processes when this happens:

> Very important is the sheer exposure to the material to be learned that is afforded by different cultural practices. It is a routine finding in research across many content domains that when children are asked to learn or solve problems based upon materials with which they are familiar, they learn more rapidly.

For Vygotsky, language has a key role in learning and development; by acquiring language, a child has the means to think in new ways and gains a new cognitive tool for making sense of the world. Of course, 'the world' as the child knows it is historically and culturally transmitted to them by their parents and immediate family, so language is constructed within this cultural/social context. This **primary socialization** paves the way for the child to socialize with other children and adults, be it in a nursery or other setting. Here, the child uses language to solve problems, to communicate their thoughts and to help (or obtain help from) other children and adults in their social environment.

Development of Vygotsky's concept of language before thought

Trying to answer the question '*What comes first, thought or language?*' is similar to asking the question, '*What came first, the chicken or the egg?*' Vygotsky firmly believed that language precedes thought, paving the way for thoughts to evolve as the child grows more competent in using language, which in turn helps the child to articulate their thoughts. An example of this is Vygotsky's *overt inner speech* (or monologue) stage of language development which occurs between three to seven years; language in this stage is used to help them process their thoughts, to plan and monitor their progress in tasks that they are engaged in – it is not language intended to be shared with another listener (Berk and Garvin, 1984).

A word of caution – while theorists such as Vygotsky and Piaget identified specific ages for particular behaviours, do not worry about trying to apply these too rigidly to the children with whom you work. Development is a highly individual process and is dependent upon a range of factors which makes it very unlikely that all children will follow the same age-specific pattern of development.

It can be argued that thought actually precedes language – after all, a baby sees and mentally processes everything in his environment long before he can name them verbally. It is however, through our received culture's language that we can then go on to label everything and articulate our thoughts once we are able to use language.

One study conducted by Hespos and Spelke (2004), on Korean and British babies aged five months old concluded that they demonstrated knowledge of objects and their positions in a 'non-linguistic context' when predicting the motions of these objects. This study showed that babies can in fact show evidence of their thinking through their actions (that is, think before they speak). For further information concerning this study, visit the following website: **www.yale.edu/minddevlab/papers/nature-children-think.pdf**.

Socio-constructivist theory of learning

Like Piaget, Vygotsky believed that children constructed their own knowledge through interaction with their environment. However, unlike Piaget, Vygotsky emphasized the role of the social context of learning. For this reason, Vygotsky is regarded as a socio-constructivist. The socio-constructivist theory of learning states that children learn through interacting with others, as they imitate each other, demonstrate how to get things done and how to behave in social situations.

A core element of interacting with each other in any social situation requires the use of language – Vygotsky used the term *cultural tools* to describe key characteristics that define how humans interact and make meaning. Exchanging the *cultural tool* of language is an integral element of socio-constructivist theory of learning, and it is this cultural element of Vygotsky's theory that differentiated him from Piaget.

Cultural tools as defined by Vygotsky exist in two forms; physical tools (a computer or a book for example) and psychological tools (such as language and thought). What sets human beings apart from any other species is our ability to communicate through language and it is this which forms the foundation of cultural tools. As keen symbol users, we draw upon books, maps, pictures, music and signs to communicate thoughts, feelings, ideas and information and with each other; each of which contribute to developing the child's curiosity and knowledge about the world. Vygotsky (1978: xxx) wrote:

> In the instrumental act, humans master themselves from the outside – through psychological tools.

In any given early years setting, the children are likely to come from diverse backgrounds and will therefore enjoy a rich exchange of cultural tools that are significant to their family. This can include books, rhymes, songs, events, festivals and ways of behaving. Such rich and varied exchanges, in turn, result in the child's intellectual development being enhanced with skills such as problem solving and imagination improving as they explore different resources and ways of communicating that are new to them. Vygotsky's concept of the **Zone of Proximal Development** (ZPD) is just one way in which adults support children to problem solve and achieve independence during learning experiences. The ZPD is discussed in greater detail below.

The Zone of Proximal Development (ZPD)

In the nursery, you are constantly observing children, noting what they can do and what they are trying to achieve with the support of adults or their friends during play.

The ZPD refers to the range of development a child goes through, from what they can achieve independently – at the lower end of the ZPD, to what they can achieve with the guidance of a more capable peer or adult – at the higher end of the ZPD.

For example, a child who cannot quite master tying their own shoe laces is in the **Zone of Actual Development** (ZAD). If her friend then demonstrates how to do this, guiding her through the process and thereby enabling her to achieve it, this is referred to as the Zone of Proximal Development (ZPD). In his influential text, *Mind in Society*, Vygotsky (1978: 33) explains the ZPD:

> It is the distance between the actual developmental level as determined by independent problem solving and the level of potential development as determined through problem solving under adult guidance or in colloboaration with more capable peers.

From this explanation, we can conclude that the ZPD is a prospective view of development as it emphasizes the *potential* for development through learning – as opposed to a *retrospective* view which emphasizes the child's abilities, *independent* of any assistance. So, the child's ability is determined by what they can achieve in collaboration with an adult or more competent peer – not by what they can achieve alone. That is not to say that working independently does not demonstrate a child's ability. The zone of actual development is what the child alone is doing and what the ZPD reveals powerfully is the child's emerging capabilities – which are important for the practitioner to consider in terms of positioning their input as an educator.

Vygotsky provided some good examples of this which are revealed when the child is playing and doing things which they might not yet be confident in doing alone, for example pouring juice, bathing a baby or collaborating with their peers as they engage in role play. Vygotsky (1934: 116) captures this beautifully in his well-known statement:

> In play, a child is always above his average age, above his daily behaviour; in play, it is as though he were a head taller than himself.

Vygotsky's concept of the ZPD is advocated as good practice with children, as it requires the practitioner (or another adult or capable peer) to observe and identify their abilities and develop strategies to help them move on to a higher level of understanding.

Jerome Bruner's concept of **scaffolding** (1983) works in a similar way, whereby the adult assists the child in their quest for competence and gradually withdraws the support when they can achieve the task independently. Both perspectives highlight the importance of the child co-constructing knowledge during meaningful interactions with an adult (or more capable peer) as they talk through different solutions to problems encountered in their play and how to overcome these – as opposed to the child being the *recipient* of knowledge from the adult. The concept of *sustained shared thinking* (*Effective Provision of Pre-School Education*, 1992) is similar to this, as the child and adult experience the learning journey together, using a process of trial and error to solve problems and engaging in meaningful interactions. Hohmann and Weikart (1995: 15) describe sustained shared thinking as:

> Active learning and learning in which the child, by acting with people, ideas and events constructs new understandings.

Below is an example of the ZPD in action:

> A 3 year old child (Lori) is sitting at a computer, beside two more children. She sees that they are playing the game 'Making Monsters'. She too, clicks the start button and begins to play. In order to complete the game, she needs to choose the correct number of eyes, arms, hands and legs, and colour these in. As this is Lori's second time playing this game, her key person (having watched her enter the computer area) sits beside her. Although she knows the correct number of limbs and where to place them, she has difficulty in controlling the mouse so her key person demonstrates this a few times in between encouraging her to have a go. Lori observes her key person as she repeats with words and actions, how to move the mouse. After a few attempts, she achieves this on her own. Her key person gives her verbal clues to help her type her name, which she does, before printing the document. Her key person praises her and tells her that she can go over to the creative area to put her picture up on the wall as part of a display on monsters and other scary characters from the children's favourite books, rhymes and games.

As this case study shows, children benefit from observing a more able peer or adult undertaking an unfamiliar task first, so that they can build understanding and the self-confidence that is needed to achieve. The computers were available to use on a daily basis with staff observing and facilitating the children's play. Repetition was also a key feature of the adult/child interactions which helped to consolidate understanding. It is also important to note that unlike Piaget, Vygotsky believed that learning leads development – whereas Piaget believed that development leads learning (1962). The ZPD embodies this belief and is exemplified in the following statement:

> What children can do with the assistance of others might be in some sense even more indicative of their mental development than what they can do alone. (1978: 85)

With this in mind, creating an effective climate for learning in which children and adults learn from one another does not happen by chance; careful observation and planning in line with the children's interests, abilities and needs is vital. This way, practitioners can create the optimum conditions for supporting each child in their individual ZPD – through meaningful participation in authentic and reciprocal learning experiences.

The ZPD is also useful when assessing individual children as it enables the practitioner to gain much more evidence of the child's current capabilities when the child is in the ZPD and so operating at the edge of their capabilities, rather than when they are in the ZAD (Zone of Actual Development). Unfortunately most tests and task assessments require a child to display independent capacity and this can often result in some children's capacities being underestimated and others being overestimated when using these forms of assessment. Practitioner observation of a child in their play, and within their normal daily life, when they are more likely to be operating in the ZPD can give a far more accurate indication of their developmental capacity.

The image below illustrates the range in the child's ability, within the ZPD.

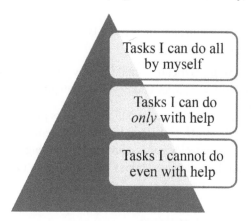

Tasks I can do all by myself

Tasks I can do *only* with help

Tasks I cannot do even with help

The ZPD and recent developments

Today, findings from neuroscience offer great insight into the positive impact of quality early experiences on the building of neural pathways and hence brain development, particularly during the first three years of life (Collaborative Frameworks for Neuroscience and Education, 2006; Shore, 2000). So, when practitioners have underpinning knowledge of how the brain is affected by experiences and interactions from birth, they can be best positioned to facilitate children's intellectual development and learning with the support of parents and primary carers, when providing a nurturing learning and care environment (Hohmann and Weikart, 1995).

The recent work of Bert Van Oers, a Professor of the cultural-historical theory of education, who works in The Netherlands, echoes the beliefs of Vygotsky concerning the impact of the social environment on learning and development. Like Vygotsky, he too identified that culture affects development, with the tools used by early years practitioners (or other significant adults) in their interactions with the child dictating the outcomes for the child. Van Oers et al. (2008: 7) postulate that:

> Learning is indeed transformed during cultural history in accordance with the prevailing psychological, epistemological and scientific points of view, in accordance with pedagogical, sociological and cultural views on the child and its position in the world.

It is therefore worth noting that how the practitioner (or other significant adult) interacts with the child will directly be influenced by their personal beliefs, their view of children and their worth in society. In light of this, the practitioner (or other significant adult) needs to reflect honestly about their values and their origins in order to ensure they are not treating children who are different, unequally. The current Early Years Foundation Stage (2012: 7) has a resounding resemblance to the Vygotskian method as it too, focuses on the child interacting with his environment and others through a play-based framework for learning:

- **Playing and exploring** – children investigate and experience things and 'have a go'.
- **Active learning** – children concentrate and keep on trying if they encounter difficulties, and enjoy achievements.
- **Creating and thinking critically** – children have and develop their own ideas, make links between ideas, and develop strategies for doing things.

Barbara Rogoff's concept of guided participation (1990) is just one development of Vygotsky's ZPD. Similarly, it advocates learning in a social context but extends upon the ZPD, with its emphasis on incidental and unplanned learning, as well as a mutual learning experience with the child and adult(s) benefiting from the interaction.

Vygotsky in Practice

- Carrying out regular observations in order to identify each child's ZPD and providing sensitive support during their play.
- Joint problem solving between practitioners and children during play.
- Giving children plenty of opportunities to engage in symbolic play.
- Providing tasks that are familiar but just beyond what they already know.
- Practitioners being mindful of possible cultural mismatch (the mental tools of home culture not matching up with the mental tools required at nursery).
- Planning and implementing activities that acknowledge and utilize children's different cultural and linguistic backgrounds.
- Working closely with all parents to support a continuous learning journey between home and nursery.
- Assessing children when they are in social contexts and engaging in collaborative play-based activity where they are likely to be performing at the edge of their capacity and so displaying their true developmental level.

Ideas into Action

Now that you have familiarized yourself with some of Vygotsky's contributions to early childhood education, make the links to practice in your setting by reflecting upon and answering the following:

1 Identify three play opportunities for a small group of children aged between three and five years, to develop their language and ability to reflect on recent events.
2 What changes can you make to provision in your setting, to ensure that the different cultural tools (for example language, ways of behaving and items from home) that the children have are acknowledged by all practitioners?
3 Read Vygotsky's statement below. Do you agree with Vygotsky? Explain the reason(s) behind your answer.

> What children can do with the assistance of others might be in some sense even more indicative of their mental development than what they can do alone. (1978: 85)

Challenge the Theorists

1 Vygotsky did not consider gender as part of his theory of the ZPD. Do you think that the practitioner can use the ZPD in the same way for boys and girls? Provide a brief explanation for your answer.

2 It can be argued that the concept of the ZPD is impractical due to the emphasis on one-on-one instruction in the learning process. What do you think? Support your answer.

3 Vygotsky believed that language preceded thought. What do you think? Explain the reason for your answer.

4 How far and in what ways do you think Piaget and Vygotsky were complementary in their thinking and how far were they in conflict?

Vygotsky's Contemporary Legacy

Creating inclusive and enabling environments
- Cultural participation
- Socio-cultural learning
- The role of a support network in promoting language development

Links to other theorists
- Barbara Rogoff
- Urie Bronfenbrenner
- Jerome Bruner
- Jean Piaget

Further Reading

Nutbrown, C. Clough, P. and Selbie, P. (2008) *Early Childhood Education. History, Philosophy and Experience*. London: SAGE.

> This book takes a creative approach to its examination of some of the foundation theories concerning childhood, learning and development. The imagined conversations between the theorists and the authors help to bring their ideas into the present, thus demonstrating their relevance today.

Sheehy, N. (2004) *Fifty Key Thinkers in Psychology*. London and New York: Routledge.

> The chapter examining Vygotsky's contributions to psychology and learning is comprehensive and easy to follow. This is a good book to use to start your study off or when you need to access accurate information quickly.

Vygotsky, L. S. (1978) *Thought and Language*. Cambridge: MIT Press.

> This is a key text of Vygotsky's and we would recommend reading it in order to familiarize yourselves with his concepts. It contains an introductory biography outlining the salient aspects of Vygotsky's short life, followed by seven chapters which examine his different theories. The chapter concerning Piaget's theory of children's thought and speech is revealing and enables the reader to compare and contrast the two theorists' ideas with ease.

Jerome Bruner (1915–)

9

An introduction to Jerome Bruner and his influence in early child care and education

Jerome Bruner is an American psychologist whose long and prolific career continues today as Research Professor of Psychology and Senior Research Fellow in Law at New York University. He is regarded as one of the pioneers of cognitive psychology for his many and varied research studies in the United States concerning the relevance of education, the impact of the cultural environment and social class on education and how children learn. Bruner's work is not however confined to America – he has also carried out the formative study on Under-5s in preschools in Oxford in the 1980s and more recently, he undertook an exploration of the Reggio Emilia project in Northern Italy.

Bruner's research concerning language and cognitive development and educational psychology during the 1950s and 1960s still has resonance in learning environments around the world at present (Rowe and Wertsch, 2002). Although some of his research was conducted in the United States, the issues that concerned him and led him to undertake the studies (which included racism, class and poverty and their impact on cognitive ability and educational outcomes) are just as relevant and still need to be resolved in the United Kingdom today. His major contribution to education was developing a theory of learning and teaching and the socio-cultural location of that process and also the role of practitioners as 'scaffolders' of this learning rather than 'transmitters of learning'.

Discussing some of his work concerning social class and the role of education, Bruner (1971: xii) had drawn the hard-hitting conclusion that:

> The education system was in effect our way of maintaining a class system
> – a group at the bottom. It crippled the capacity of children in the lowest

socioeconomic quarter of the population to participate at full power in society, and did so early and effectively.

Bruner was concerned with equality of opportunity and his work was to ensure early years was seen as pivotal in combating inequality. Today, we have the findings from the longitudinal study, the Effective Provision of Pre-school Education (EPPE) Project (2004), which, as part of its conclusions, outlines those factors that enable children from disadvantaged backgrounds to achieve and those which do not. Issues surrounding equality of opportunity within early years provision and how to achieve this are thus still central to planning and provision across settings today.

Bruner's major work, however, came out of his study of Vygotskian theory and was focused more on cognition and how learning processes work. He built on Vygotsky's work by providing an effective explanation of how learning is constructed and how children revisit the same cognitive schema but spirally, i.e. it's a little more sophisticated in their understanding each time they revisit as they layer their learning. He also showed how interaction with the environment, objects and people powerfully support and extend learning processes and that all this occurs in a cultural context which reinforces or distances certain ways of thinking and acting. For this reason, Bruner's work focused more on how learning occurs in the child's world and understanding the factors that shaped learning.

As well as being a key figure in disseminating the ideas of Vygotsky to the West during the early 1960s, Bruner was greatly influenced by Vygotsky's ideas and he, too, focused on the social and cultural influences on learning and development (2010). This is in contrast to the perspective taken by Piaget, who did not place as much emphasis on the impact of cultural and social factors in the process of learning. All three theorists are however referred to as Cognitivists, due to their theorizing into children's mental processes and hence their cognitive development. Bruner wrote a seminal paper concerning the contributions of Piaget and Vygotsky which drew parallels and showed they were not in fact contradictory notions of learning and development. He showed that both Vygotsky and Piaget were concerned with the developmental notions of learning and understanding and that Piaget did see the social and cultural aspects, i.e. his persepective was not solely developmental, and Vygotsky too acknowledged the developmental aspect to learning so was not solely a social constructivist. It is thus, a difference of emphasis as opposed to contradictory notions of learning and development.

Bruner has also supervised and collaborated with a range of current influential researchers such as Colwyn Trevarthen, Professor Kathy Sylva (one of the principal researchers involved in the EPPE Project), Alison Gopnik and Andrew Meltzoff (refer to Chapter 12 for information concerning their current work into early personality and brain development). Some of Bruner's most pertinent contributions to the field of education and child development will now be explored in turn. *It will be useful to consider practice in your setting while reading about his ideas concerning cognitive development and the education of young children.*

Spiral curriculum

Bruner devised the concept of the **spiral curriculum** in the 1960s. A core part of this concept is the belief that any given subject needs to be taught in line with what the child already knows and is able to do. From this point, the practitioner should plan learning experiences that the child can revisit in more depth in the future. Revisiting previous experiences results in the child consolidating their understanding as they continually return to basic ideas while new subjects and concepts are added over the course of a curriculum. When these are planned incrementally, the child has the opportunity to reflect on their learning, build on their knowledge and the ability to think creatively when encountering new learning experiences. Using the concept of a spiral curriculum therefore makes sense, especially in the early years where children learn most effectively through hands-on experiences and repetition of these experiences until they can fully understand the concepts being taught.

Achieving such individualized learning requires effective observation and assessment in order to ensure each child is enabled to take part in learning experiences that are not only matched to their current capabilities but are also just beyond their reach. This is similar to Vygotsky's concept of the zone of proximal development (ZPD) and is an essential part of child-centred practice.

Case Study

The spiral curriculum in practice

A small group of children became fascinated with fire engines having recently visited the local fire station. They engaged in the same play every day, which mainly took place in the small world area. The children continually pushed the trucks and fire engines around, making the siren sounds and creating fire scenarios for them to /'put out'.

The practitioner observed this over the week and following a planning meeting with her colleagues, extended the children's learning by planning a further trip to the fire station and organizing with the fire fighters to bring the fire engine to the nursery so that the children can have real hands-on experience and ask them any questions. Following the visit to the nursery, the practitioners further extended the fire engine theme by creating indoor and outdoor learning opportunities which entailed turning the home corner into a fire station and making a huge fire engine with props such as ropes and ladders in the garden. These resources enabled the children to carry out their role play along with the intervention of the practitioners who introduced new vocabulary to build on what the children had previously learned.

Reflection in Action

1 Consider the curriculum in your setting. In which ways do you think Bruner's spiral curriculum is evident in your planning and provision of learning experiences?
2 Can you provide a spiral curriculum without knowing or observing children?
3 How far can you intervene without interfering and hindering learning and development?
4 Consider the Case Study above. How can parents be involved to further build on their children's interests and knowledge?

Scaffolding

Bruner's concept of scaffolding is used to foster children's learning in curricula in early years settings and classrooms across the United Kingdom and America today (Copple and Bredekamp, 2009). Bruner provides a clear account of what scaffolding should look like in action:

> There is a vast amount of skilled activity required of a 'teacher' to get a learner to discover on his own – scaffolding the task in a way that assures that only those parts of the task within the child's reach are left unresolved, and knowing what elements of a solution the child will recognise though he cannot yet perform them.
> (Bruner, 1977: xiv)

Bruner (1996: xii) posits that:

> Any subject could be taught to any child at any age in some form that was honest.

This encapsulates the spiral curriculum of learning perfectly – the fact that concepts which can be considered as challenging (for example maths, physics and chemistry) can be taught to young children, as long as the practitioner provides learning experiences that are interesting and manageable. These learning experiences should also be continually reviewed as new concepts are introduced, to reinforce learning that has taken place and to instil a sense of self-confidence.

Following is an example of scaffolding taking place in a nursery. Read it carefully and reflect on the questions that follow.

Scaffolding is something that parents, teachers, support workers provide to children on a daily basis during interactions without giving it much thought; that is to say, it comes quite naturally. The purpose of this scaffolding is to allow the child to achieve higher levels of cognitive development by the adult:

1 motivating and encouraging the child;
2 giving models that can be imitated;
3 simplifying the task or idea;
4 highlighting errors or significant elements of the task.

In order for the process of scaffolding to be successful, the task needs to be made interesting and meaningful for the child. This in turn can result in the child fully engaging in the task and therefore benefiting from it. Bruner (1977: 80) identifies the useful elements of such a task:

> They must be based as much as possible upon the arousal of interest in what there is to be learned, and they must be kept broad and diverse in expression.

The scaffold provided by the adult is a temporary support structure around the child's attempts to understand new ideas and complete new tasks – once the child demonstrates ability independent of any adult intervention, the scaffold (support) should be removed.

Reflection in Action

1 Do practitioners always need to plan for scaffolding children's learning? Explain the reason for your answer.
2 Provide one example of how you have successfully provided a scaffold to promote a child's learning.

Language Acquisition Support System (LASS)

Bruner believes that children's mastery of language partly resides in the fact that they understand very early that interactions between themselves and others are intentional (Sheehy, 2004). This highlights the proactive role that Bruner assigns to children in their language development. This is in direct contrast to **Noam Chomsky's Language Acquisition Device (LAD)**, which proposes that language acquisition will inevitably take place in all individuals due to being born with an instinctive mental capacity and the necessary resources (brain, mouth, tongue, voice box and lungs) 'built in'. According to this perspective, language development thus requires minimal direct intervention from parents or teachers due to language being governed by these in-built factors. While Bruner fully acknowledges the role of the LAD, he stresses the importance of the child's social network (family, friends and teachers) in facilitating the child's development of language. These networks will lend themselves to meaningful interactions taking place which will enable the child to learn and use the rules and customs of the language. Contrary to Chomsky's nativist theory of language development, it is not inevitable that language will be learnt simply due to having the in-built mechanisms to do so. One tragic example of this is the case of 'Genie' (1957). This child was subjected to horrendous physical, mental and emotional abuse for the first 13 years of her life. Strapped to a potty chair and beaten daily, 'Genie' was isolated from all social interaction until adolescence. When she was 'saved' it was too late; she could not speak, could barely walk and lacked all social skills. She now lives in an adult foster care home. This is an extremely tragic example of what can go wrong when children are denied their basic human rights to love, shelter and stimulation.

Language use is indeed unique to humans; the human brain is designed in such a way that we are enabled to acquire and speak numerous languages (Pinker, 2000). However, language development cannot solely be attributed to being born with the necessary mechanisms (LAD). As Bruner identifies, it is also a result of the child being exposed to the right factors in the environment (such as age and stage appropriate play experiences for babies and children and meaningful interactions) which as a result, will make them capable of understanding language, and therefore learn it with ease (**LASS**).

> ## Reflection in Action
>
> Based on Bruner's LASS, list three factors that can promote a 3-year-old child's language development.

The three modes of representation

In his research on the cognitive development of children (1966), Jerome Bruner proposed **three modes of representation**. These modes explain how a child stores and processes information at different ages. Like Piaget (1953), Bruner acknowledged that young children use different types of thinking (or representation) at different ages, and that the latter modes depend on the earlier modes. The key difference in their theories is that Piaget proposed that children develop sequentially through the different stages of cognitive development, whereas Bruner's is not a stage theory as he does not stipulate fixed ages by which a behaviour should occur.

Below is a brief description of the three modes of representation. *While reading, reflect on the children you know and how they behave. Can you identify any similarities?*

> ## Enactive representation (action-based) 0–1 year
>
> Babies store information based on their hands-on experiences of physical objects, learning through their movement and actions. Knowledge is thus stored as 'motor memory'. Of course, it is not only babies who learn effectively through hands-on manipulation of objects but some adults also.

Iconic representation (image-based) 1–6 years

During this mode the child is still 'restricted' to dealing with concrete experiences and tangible objects. Information concerning objects in the environment is stored and categorized as images in the mind, which the child cannot think beyond. i.e. they are still unable to think in abstract terms.

Symbolic representation (language-based) 7 years onwards

The child is now able to think in abstract terms, no longer depending on the images used in the iconic mode. This is due to language having more of an influence on thinking. This means that information can now be stored as symbols (language and numbers).

It is through his notion of the spiral curriculum that Bruner argues even the more complex concepts such as mathematical and scientific ideas can be presented to children at almost any age, provided they are educated in an appropriate mode of representation. Remember, although symbolic representation is the final mode of representation, it does not replace the earlier modes, i.e. hands-on experience and visual resources are still highly necessary as part of a rich and varied learning experience.

Reflection in Action

Consider the concept of the changing of states of matter (solids, liquids and gases). How would you teach this in line with each of the three modes of representation?

Use the table below to note down your ideas.

Mode of representation	Appropriate learning experience	Reason for your choice
Enactive		
Iconic		
Symbolic		

Developments of Bruner's theories

More recently Bruner has come to be critical of some of his past work concerning children's cognitive development and the 'cognitive revolution', explaining that he focused too narrowly on the individual child and the internal factors that drove learning (1996). His more current work instead embraces the external (cultural, social and historical) factors that impact on learning. As a result of this change, Vygotsky's influence of Bruner's recent work has become more evident as a result, with the historical and social context of children taken into account. Understanding how culture (and the differences among children) impacts on the learning experiences is key to helping each child develop to their fullest potential. This is of course required in the Early Years Foundation Stage (EYFS, 2012). Practitioners thus have a responsibility to ensure positive attitudes to these differences so that a climate of mutual trust and respect is created in which every child knows that they can make positive contributions to society from the earliest age.

At a practical level, Bruner posits that as a result of cultural differences, children from different cultural backgrounds make sense of their experiences in different ways. For example, categorizations for communication (including sign language) will differ across cultures, and practitioners owe it to the families with whom they work, to familiarize themselves with these so that everyone is clear and can engage in a learning environment that is enabling and reciprocal in nature.

Bruner's influential book, *The Culture of Education* (1996), focuses on the cultural context of education, with arguments developed around schooling and education in general. In this book, Bruner uses the concept of 'mutual learning cultures' which takes into account the cultural, historical and social backgrounds of each individual child. In such classrooms or early years settings, teachers and early years practitioners create environments which enable all children to learn in a climate of trust, respect and reciprocity. He describes the mutual learning culture as one in which:

> There is mutual sharing of knowledge and ideas, mutual aid in mastering material, division of labour and exchange of roles, opportunity to reflect on the group's activities. (1996: xv)

Although this is considered the ideal, the constraints of achieving a mutual learning culture need to be taken into account; early years settings are very busy and lively environments with children differing greatly in terms of experience, ability, background, language, culture and emotional needs.

Careful observation, planning and monitoring of learning is therefore required to create a learning environment that not only embraces the different and contrasting cultural, historical and social backgrounds of all children but also uses these within experiences and interactions to maximize learning. Underpinning such good practice is the building and maintaining of positive relationships with all parents in order to instil a sense of trust and confidence that will enable the child's learning experiences to effortlessly flow between the early years setting and home.

Today, the Early Years Foundation Stage (EYFS, 2012) emphasizes the child's personal, social and emotional development as being at the core of their capacity to take part in learning experiences. Attributes such as self-confidence, self-awareness, managing feelings and behaviour and making relationships are thus highlighted in order to guide practitioners and parents in nurturing and developing these qualities and skills.

Bruner in Practice

- Having a robust observation and planning process that supports the notion of the spiral curriculum.

- Practitioners facilitating learning through effective scaffolding (i.e. through simplifying the task, motivating, encouraging and providing a model for the child to imitate).

- Using available resources and planning meetings to provide meaningful experiences that promote individual children's language development.

- Providing a wide range of activities and interactions to promote learning in each of the three modes of representation.

- Working with all parents and carers in order to understand and make the most of their children's cultural backgrounds and knowledge within the setting's planning and assessment process.

Ideas into Action

Now that you have familiarized yourself with some of Bruner's contributions to early childhood education, make the links to practice in your setting by reflecting upon and completing the following:

1 How could you and your nursery team ensure you offer progressively complex learning experiences to your children which build on from what they know and can do so in all areas of learning?

2 Create your own example of scaffolding learning during a play experience and explain how it supports cognitive development.

3 Compare Bruner's LASS with Chomsky's LAD. Which perspective do you agree with concerning children's development of language and why?

Challenge the Theorists

1 Read Bruner's statement below. Do you agree? Support your answer with relevant discussion and examples from your experience as a practitioner.

> Any subject could be taught to any child at any age in some form that was honest.

2 Bruner asserted that learning is contextually and culturally located rather than biologically driven. What do you think? (Consider the nature v. nurture debate to construct your argument.)

3 In which ways can Bruner's ideas about learning help practitioners to deal with **diversity** and difference in the early years setting?

Bruner's Contemporary Legacy

Creating inclusive and enabling environments
- Cultural participation
- Socio-cultural learning
- The role of a support network in promoting language development
- Behavioural and academic expectations

Links to other theorists
- Margaret Donaldson
- Lev Vygotsky
- Urie Bronfenbrenner
- Jean Piaget

Further Reading

Bruner, J. (1996) *The Culture of Education*. Cambridge, MA and London: Harvard University Press.

It is worthwhile reading this seminal text in order to fully understand Bruner's position concerning modern education and the central role that cultures play in forming and developing the mind. He sets out his thoughts and experiences in nine essays, which encourage the reader to reflect on the issues presented, both in terms of their professional experience and wider society.

Yelland, N. (2005) *Critical Issues in Early Childhood Education*. Maidenhead: Open University Press.

This book challenges a range of long-held beliefs that pervade early childhood education and the sections on Bruner serve to add vigour to the arguments presented. An excellent resource which contains complex ideas that are easily accessible.

Colwyn Trevarthen (1931–)

10

An introduction to Colwyn Trevarthen and his influence in early child care and education

Colwyn Trevarthen is Professor (Emeritus) of Child Psychology and Psychobiology in the Department of Psychology of the University of Edinburgh. Originating from New Zealand, he has worked with theorists such as Jerome Bruner as a Research Fellow at the Center for Cognitive Studies at Harvard University, where he began his research on infant communication. His work concerning the wide and varied areas of child development include infant **intersubjectivity** (the shared meaning which is created between an infant and adult in their interactions with each other), brain development, neuropsychology, the development of communication in young children, gestural and musical communication, the effects of disorders such as autism and maternal depression. He has also carried out studies concerning the impact of positive parental communication on emotional well-being and learning and parent-infant interaction. He often incorporates video footage of babies and mothers communicating in his speeches, which provides clear and powerful evidence in supporting his findings. Trevarthen's current research concerns the role of emotions and motives in education and psychological development from birth. As part of this, Trevarthen has conducted numerous studies on how the rhythms and emotions of children's play and fantasy, stories, songs and musical games support cultural learning (such as language development) in early childhood.

Due to his emphasis on the social, emotional and cultural context of learning and of cognitive development, Trevarthen's contributions to our understanding of child development places him close to the work of Jerome Bruner (whom Trevarthen refers to as 'the modern Comenius of educational reform'), Lev Vygotsky, and more recently, Daniel Walsh and Daniel Stern. All of these theorists complement each other's work to a lesser or greater extent. For example, Walsh (2007), Bruner (1986) and Vygotsky (1962) focus on the role of culture in learning and development, while Trevarthen (1998; 1978) and Stern (1998) are chiefly concerned with the role of interpersonal and emotional communication or inter subjectivity in infancy as preparation for learning shared meaning. They have both been key figures in the development of research employing microanalysis of videotape and film to study the affective regulations of mother–infant face-to-face interactions, by means of which they have traced development of intimate **protoconversation**s, games and the infant's sense of self and other. These themes of culture, communication in infancy and healthy psychological development are inextricably linked and it is useful for you to be familiar with them in order to be able to reflect on the role they play in fostering the all-round development of babies and children in your care.

The most pertinent of Trevarthen's theories relating to children's development will now be explored. While reading about his ideas, take time to reflect on your opinions of these in relation to your role in nurturing the confidence of babies and young children throughout your interactions with them.

Communicating with babies and toddlers

Supporting communication of infants is probably one aspect of your role that you do almost without thinking. After all, communicating with babies and children (be it through speaking, signing or body language) is a powerful means of learning. Given that a baby's need to be social is innate (Hobson, 2002; Donaldson, 1995) having shared their life with their mother for nine months in utero and listened to her voice for the last three months (Stern, 2000), they are born ready to communicate with their mother and soon with others in their world. It is now recognized that within hours, a baby is keen to engage in interactions and be social with those in their immediate environment. As Trevarthen and Reddy (2007: 9) bring to our attention:

> Face expressions, eye movements, vocalisations and hand gestures can become part of a mutually pleasing transaction, simply because they are made up in the communication and 'recognised'. This is proof of an innate capacity in a child for learning new meanings and for using them cooperatively, a 'nascent consciousness' for human meaning with human feelings of relatedness.

There are, however, important differences between families in terms of their culture, personal beliefs, and view of childhood itself which will all determine how much opportunity they afford to the child to take part in language (Pierce, 2000; Rogoff, Hammer and Weiss, 1999; Damast et al., 1996). So, when you consider that language or communication includes the infant's endeavours to communicate needs, feelings, and thoughts, the adult should be mindful of the fact the children with whom they work vary greatly when it comes to experience with language and consequently, their levels of self-belief, confidence and self-esteem. Vygotsky (1978), like Trevarthen, asserted that the role of the adult is crucial in supporting the child's language development. An adult who is sensitive and in tune with the individual child's cues will be best positioned to facilitate the development of language and thought. The role of dialogue between the adult and young child is thus paramount as this lends itself to creating an enriched environment in which the child can practise and master communicating their feelings and thoughts in a range of contexts.

Trevarthen's important work (1998) on pedagogy for 2-year-olds points to the critical importance of a pedagogy which centres around supporting and sustaining young children's attachments to those who are important in their world, including the family, peers and, of course, a key person in the nursery. It is through these close, affirmative relationships that the child develops a strong and positive sense of self with a confidence in their own individuality, dignity, self-belief and pride in their identity. It also celebrates and encourages the child's capacity to explore and make sense of their world with curiosity, openness and vitality. This relational and trans-formative pedagogy focuses on the child becoming a confident and capable learner within a connected, secure and enabling socio-emotional environment.

The role of activity and emotions in development

A child's emotional development is laid down from birth (Gopnik, 2009; Gerhardt 2004; Music, 2001). They very quickly understand whether they can trust those immediately around them or whether their world is an unsafe place, filled with uncertainty in terms of being able to enjoy loving and caring relationships that are consistent. This notion of 'trust or mistrust' is the first stage of Erik Erikson's theory of personality development (1950). Erikson asserts that from birth to one year, a baby will be able to distinguish whether they can trust their mother to love and care for them or not. This 'decision' will be based directly on the quality of relationship they have with their mother and how emotionally available she is. Self-identity and self-esteem develops or is shattered by inappropriate adult actions and interactions. Moving on from Erikson and Bowlby, healthy attachment develops through responsive interactions, which has big implications for curriculum planning and key aspects of learning and development.

Trevarthen, too, stresses the role of the primary caregiver in shaping the baby's emergent emotional and social development, especially in relation to nurturing their baby's attempts at understanding their world and their role in it and consequently, supporting them to learn about their culture through their interactions (Parker-Rees, 2007; Trevarthen, 1995).

His research findings reinforce the importance of respectful and nurturing relationships that encourage the baby to express their feelings of happiness, sadness, curiosity and humour (Trevarthen et al., 2002). Like Bronfenbrenner, he identifies that the child's personality or emotional development plays a role in shaping their environment, or others' responses to them. He asserts that:

> The child's emotional development is both a reflection of maternal care, and a factor in the making of new relationships. (Trevarthen et al., 2002: 27)

Unfortunately some children do not get to experience the 'safety net' of a secure attachment due to a wide range of factors such as abuse, parents being drug or alcohol dependent or being emotionally unavailable. This makes the role of practitioners all the more significant as they can play a part in compensating for the lack of security and love in the child's life through providing consistency of care, one-to-one attention and signposting parents to the relevant agencies that might be better positioned to intervene and support parents in caring for their child.

Discussing the implications for a child who has suffered abuse or neglect, Trevarthen explains that although the child may still be able to participate in some aspects of life, they will find it difficult to engage with others due to fear and mistrust. He therefore emphasizes the role of the arts as therapy which are designed to nurture the child's emotional well-being and sense of security, while promoting their communication. He identifies activities such as drama, music, dance or graphical story-making to help encourage the child to engage with others and express themselves in ways that are most comfortable to them (Trevarthen, 2008).

Reflection in Action

1 What types of practical support do you provide for parents who are not emotionally available to their children?
2 List some of the specific activities and experiences that you provide for babies and children who do not enjoy a secure attachment with their parents.
3 In which ways do you involve parents who are difficult to reach, in their child's care and education?

In order to provide quality care and education that meets the individual needs of all families, Trevarthen (2011: 173) explains that:

> Cultivation of 'childcare' and 'education' are both important for the well-being and development of a young child … Relations with parents and family must be kept alive when the child is in any institutional setting for care or for learning, and experiences at home should be related to and exchanged with those at nursery.

Given all the evidence, it comes as no surprise that the revised EYFS (2012) emphasizes the centrality of fostering a child's personal, social and emotional development. As part of this, skills and qualities such as helping children to develop a positive sense of self, self-respect and respect for others as well as building social skills and managing their own feelings are all strongly advocated as best practice. Having staff that are confident in nurturing every young child's emotional well-being will in turn support their emotional intelligence (Goleman, 1995) and their understanding of how to behave in social situations. The early years setting may well be the only place in which the child gets to practice their emergent social skills, it is therefore critical to ensure that your provision (particularly, the key person system) is designed to meet the unique and ever-changing needs of every young child.

What do you Think?

Consider the infant's emotional development. What are the implications for you, both at a personal and professional level? Give at least two factors for each.

Communicative musicality: The inventive rhythm of companionship

This concept refers to the unique features of the earliest interactions that occur between mother and child. Communicative musicality (Trevarthen and Malloch, 2002) also captures the tone, rhythm, pace and ultimately, the 'shared consciousness' between them during these interactions. This includes verbal and non-verbal communication. Trevarthen and Malloch (2002: 1) identify some of the main elements of communicative musicality as:

> Delicate expressions and sensitive responses passing between young infants and their mothers … rhythmic patterns of engagement that could be represented as musical or dance like.

Case Study

Yildiz is six months old. She is sat on her mother's lap, facing her, as her mother sings a song to her, alternating between Turkish and English, and tunefully counts the fingers on Yildiz's left hand in Turkish. Yildiz closely follows her mother's movements, squealing with laughter. Her mother imitates her laughter and then counts the fingers on her right hand, again in a soft Turkish tone. Yildiz kicks her legs out excitedly and makes the sound 'hahahaha!' Her mother again imitates her and proceeds to count her own fingers in Turkish and then English. She is speaking slowly, as she looks at Yildiz, smiling throughout. Yildiz grabs her mother's right hand, cooing and smiling. Her mother mirrors her actions and does the same.

Communicative musicality exists around the world (Kuhl, 1997; Masataka, 1993; Papousek, 1992), with language and gestures being used to communicate warmth, humour and feelings of happiness. So, although it is moulded by culture, characteristics such as intonation, pitch and rhythm are the same globally (Kuhl et al., 1997). The mother (or other primary caregiver) will often sing or communicate in tones and rhythms that are typical of their language, hence making communicative musicality a culture-bound activity. Take, for example, the power of music to relax and soothe a child, or a lullaby sung in the child's home language, to help ease them off to sleep.

Music and songs are, of course, key ways of helping the young child to familiarize themselves with their daily routine – singing about tasks such as putting on clothes, brushing hair and washing hair are all made fun by making up action rhymes to help build the child's understanding of not only what to expect in the routine (thereby promoting their ability to predict) but also their confidence in undertaking some of these tasks for themselves. Trevarthen (1999) has shown that developments in the first year show how shared participation in vocal games can encourage the young child's ability to imitate speech and gestures as well as build their understanding of conventional uses of actions and objects. The early years setting thus provides a highly suitable environment in which babies and young children can practise such skills.

How is communicative musicality important to early years care and education?

Consider the relationship between the mother (or other primary caregiver) and child, and the feelings of trust, respect and mutual enjoyment that such a relationship brings. Communicative musicality would not be possible if these factors were not present in the relationship, as the baby would not feel secure or confident enough to engage in this type of two-way interaction. This has implications for you as practitioners in the early years setting because you need to be attuned to babies' and children's cues in order to respond to them appropriately. This is partly achieved through engaging in warm and responsive interactions which promote their self-confidence and a positive sense of self.

Infants under one year, who have no language, communicate powerfully and constructively with **receptive** adults (Trevarthen et al., 2008). Note that Trevarthen identifies the importance of the adult being 'receptive'. Babies are highly intuitive beings and will very quickly understand whether an adult is someone that they can feel comfortable enough to engage with, or whether they have no interest. This will inevitably impact on the relationship between the adult and baby. Having a keen interest in all babies and children – as opposed to being concerned with exerting power over them – is critical, as this will enable you to build a trusting relationship in which the young child can expect to engage in experiences that can be initiated and ended by them in a non-pressurized way.

Working closely with all parents will also enable you to find out as much information as is necessary to help you tailor your provision for each family as much as possible. For example, learning and using key words in the child's home language, creating 'calm time' before and after lunch and having 'group time' between a key person and their key children, can all facilitate communicative musicality.

Reflection in Action

1 Do you think that the interactions between staff and children in your setting contain communicative musicality?
2 What factors do you think enable and prevent such interactions from taking place in your setting? Give two examples for each.
3 How can the key person system be used to promote communicative musicality in your setting?

To summarize, communicative musicality is just one of the indicators of a warm and trusting relationship between the mother (or other primary caregiver) and child. Through these interactions, the baby practises their social skills as they are afforded the time, space and patience to engage in meaningful exchange with the primary caregiver. It is worth noting that communicative musicality can be achieved easily during the daily routine – be it during a nappy change, during singing or just before the baby's nap time.

How maternal depression is hard for a child too

A child's happiness may well be the determining factor in her ability to live a fulfilled life both in the short and long term. The road to achieving this begins from conception, where the foetus experiences the effects of her mother's lifestyle and mood via the placenta – this organ produces hormones that help the baby to grow and develop, as well as providing nutrients and oxygen to keep the foetus alive. Conversely, if the mother suffers from depression, is alcohol or drug dependent, lives in constant stress (due to factors such as poverty, domestic violence or not having a support network), her unborn child will also suffer.

Having a baby is a life-changing event and it should be a joyful time, but for some mothers this is sadly not the case, with one in ten mothers suffering from depression (4Children, 2011). Mothers suffering from depression are often withdrawn, less attentive to their baby's needs, unable to show love consistently, lack patience during care-giving tasks and often get angry at the slightest 'provocation'. Discipline strategies are also inappropriate and often harsh (Field, 1992; Cohn et al., 1986). All of these factors preclude the possibility of a warm and secure relationship being built. Maternal depression is thus the cause of multiple psychological issues that can manifest very early on in infancy, with devastating results for the developing child. Cummings and Kouros (2009: 1) outline some of these:

> Maternal depression is demonstrated to contribute to multiple early child developmental problems, including impaired cognitive, social and academic functioning. Children of depressed mothers are at least two to three times more

likely to develop adjustment problems, including mood disorders. In infancy, children of depressed mothers are more fussy, less responsive to facial and vocal expressions, more inactive and have elevated stress hormones compared to infants of non-depressed mothers.

It stands to reason that even from their earliest days, babies born to depressed mothers show less response to facial and verbal expressions – these babies do not have a positive role model from whom they can learn how to express their feelings of happiness, sadness, or excitement. When these all-important initial affective experiences are missing, babies quickly develop atypical emotional behaviour (Murray et al., 1999) which can be very difficult to reverse.

Babies are highly intelligent and are born to be social (Trevarthen, 2012). From birth, they respond to other humans and seek to be in close proximity to their mother or primary caregiver. Studies which repeatedly show that babies are able to process and imitate expressions (Trevarthen, 2012; Meltzoff and Moore, 1977) are testament to the fact that babies need to experience love, warmth and affection from their mother (or primary caregiver) in order to thrive. When these all-important factors are missing from the baby's life, they very quickly come to realize that their world is not a happy place in which they can expect to be nurtured and have their basic needs met. The devastating effect of this is that babies will learn to self-soothe (i.e. thumb sucking, rocking, pulling their hair) to cope with distress and lack of affection. They might also appear to withdraw from their mother – not seeking cuddles or interaction. This is not because they do not want it, but because they know that their needs will go unmet.

Read the case study below and respond to the questions that follow.

Case Study

Imagine that you have recently become a key person to Jack, who is 9 months old. During your first meeting with his mother, she tells you that she suffered with postnatal depression and that she still gets depressed. She is on medication which she says 'helps a bit' but that she still struggles when it comes to getting on with Jack.

She mentions that they don't really play together and that she finds it difficult to show affection. During her one-hour stay at the nursery, you observe that Jack didn't attempt to play with his mother and did not respond when she kissed him goodbye.

Over the next few days you observe that he does not show any emotion. He also doesn't seem interested in exploring the environment, but with one-to-one encouragement, he does a little.

What do you Think?

1 What is the role of the early years practitioner in supporting a baby who is displaying signs of depression?
2 What practical support can the setting provide to help cultivate the relationship between Jack and his mother?
3 In which ways might Jack's all-round development be affected if he and his mother are not supported at the earliest opportunity?

Babies are highly sensitive and need to be helped to regulate their emotions and learn how to express their feelings in an atmosphere of respect and love. The first relationship(s) is thus vital in laying the foundations for healthy emotional development, which the baby can then take forward and use in other relationships with family members, early years practitioners and other babies and children. Trevarthen (2012: 7) identifies these protective factors as well as some of the consequences for the baby when these are not in place:

> A healthy mind builds proud memories in loving company with specially trusted family and friends, making a good, self-confident story. Loneliness, shame, depression and sadness are the emotions that identify loss of this collective story-making, which can be called 'socionoesis'. (Frank and Trevarthen, 2011; Trevarthen and Reddy, 2007)

Trevarthen (2012) believes that the 'distress felt in one (i.e. the mother) causes distress in the other' (i.e. her baby). Consequently, this disorganizes the relationship, leaving the baby confused and unsettled, while the mother struggles to meet her own, as well as her baby's needs. Ideally, babies suffering from the impact of maternal depression need to be supported as early as possible in order to ameliorate against any long-term damage to their growing emotional, intellectual, language and social development. This intervention and on-going support can be provided by the midwife, health visitor or family therapist – who is trained to provide on-going support to the mother and baby in a confidential space. Family therapists can be particularly helpful to a mother who is suffering from depression and is struggling to connect with and get along with her baby.

As an early years practitioner, your role is centred on ensuring the well-being and safety of those babies and children entrusted in your care. This means knowing your setting's policies concerning safeguarding and partnership with parents, and in this context, knowing the signs of depression so that you are in a position to identify and support (and refer) if necessary. The few hours that a child spends in the nursery on a regular basis can do much to help alleviate the effects of living with depression – provided that staff are well versed in attachment theories and can support babies and children in managing their emotions during difficult times. The concept of **containment** (Shuttleworth, 1989) is applicable here. Containment refers to a mother's ability to understand her baby's state of mind and feelings, and support her through difficult feelings (such as sadness, anger, frustration or fear) by identifying with her and talking her through her feelings as you hold her. This is all the more important to do with babies as they will be overwhelmed by such strong feelings and because they are pre-verbal, they will need sensitive support to help them work through these emotions. In the nursery, you are the baby's container, this means being attuned to them and picking up on their cues. This means knowing why they might be extra clingy (i.e. if they are unwell, tired, upset or experiencing a transition) and allowing them to stay close to you and play beside you.

Trevarthen in Practice

- Supporting all parents in nurturing their child's ability to learn at home and in the early years setting.
- Ensuring that practitioners are confident in engaging in respectful and meaningful interactions with all babies and children entrusted in their care.
- Undertaking regular observations of babies and children and using findings to inform your practice (which Trevarthen believes is the key to understanding the individual child).
- Raising the status of the voice of all children in your planning and work with families.
- Music therapy for children who have autism, or have suffered abuse or neglect.

Ideas into Action

Now that you have familiarized yourself with some of Trevarthen's contributions to early childhood communication, make the links to practice in your setting by reflecting upon and completing the following:

1   Note down your understanding of communicative musicality.
2a   Discuss one example of how you have communicated with a baby in this style.
2b   How do you think this interaction supported the baby's emotional well-being?
3   Identify two vocal games that you play with babies, to encourage their ability to imitate speech and build their understanding of conventional uses of actions.
4   How do you help babies to regulate their emotions?

Challenge the Theorists

1 Given that the first relationship is critical in laying the foundations for healthy emotional development, is 'all lost' for babies and children who do not experience this essential relationship?

2 How far is the emotional security and well-being of the adult practitioner critical in their relationship to the child?

3 How might Trevarthen's ideas work with children who have communicative disorders or delay?

4 How far do you think Trevarthen's ideas about adult–child relationships work in different cultures?

Trevarthen's Contemporary Legacy

Knowledge base concerning development from conception to three
- Socio-emotional learning
- The role of very early experiences on all-round development

Creating inclusive and enabling environments
- Cultural participation
- Socio-cultural learning
- Behavioural and academic expectations
- The role of a support network in promoting language development

Importance of parents and the home learning environment
- The centrality of emotional-social development
- The impact of positive early interactions

Links to other theorists
- John Bowlby
- Erik Erikson
- Margaret Donaldson
- Jerome Bruner
- Daniel Stern

Further Reading

Trevarthen, C. and Malloch, S. (2002) 'Musicality and music before three: Human vitality and invention shared with pride'. *Zero to Three*, September 2002, Vol. 23, No 1: 10–18.

This paper provides fantastic insight into the role of interactions, play and those first pivotal relationships with mothers, caregivers and practitioners, in shaping a baby's emotional well-being and all-round development. Fascinating issues such as personality development before birth, the transmission of culture through shared meaning-making and brain development are all discussed with research evidence woven to illustrate the persuasive points made.

Trevarthen, C., Rodrigues, H., Bjørkvold, J. R., Laurent Danon-Boileau, L. and Göran Krantz, G. (2008) 'Valuing Creative Art in Childhood'. Edited version published in *Children in Europe*, Issue 14: 6–9.

This paper examines the important role that art (making music, poetry, painting, movement and rhymes) play in nurturing young children's emergent emotional, intellectual and language development. The authors also explore autism in children and how this affects the ability to be creative. Four creative educators also contribute to this paper, discussing their experiences and beliefs concerning the importance of art for children's life and learning. These real-life accounts help to contextualize the issue of art in childhood, which, as a result, encourages the reader to reflect on how they support babies' and children's creativity through collaborative experiences and how they can build on this.

Urie Bronfenbrenner (1917–2005)

11

An introduction to Urie Bronfenbrenner and his influence in early child care and education

Urie Bronfenbrenner was a renowned Russian psychologist. He was also highly regarded for his work on the Head Start programme in America, which he co-founded for disadvantaged pre-school children. This programme successfully supported over 20 million disadvantaged children in America, to achieve better developmental outcomes than they might have done without the early intervention provided by the programme.

His major contribution to early years is his ecological theory (which is discussed in detail below). It is due to Bronfenbrenner's extensive ecological theory that we understand so much about the multifaceted nature of child development and all of the factors that affect it. He did, however, continuously revise this theory over the years. This in turn helped to consolidate and extend his ideas concerning children's development and the wide-ranging factors that affect it over time.

This chapter will outline this major contribution, with examples of it in action as well as questions for you to respond to.

Ecological theory

Bronfenbrenner's ecological theory (1979) is known as a 'systems theory' – one which proposes that development cannot be explained by a single factor but instead, by a complex system of relationships, over the course of time. At the core if his ecological theory is the belief that not only does the environment impact on the child's development but that the child also impacts on her environment. Below is just one version of his ecological theory. His idea is represented as a set of concentric circles, each one consisting of different individuals, organizations and services which the child interacts with – directly and indirectly.

There are five broad systems that impact on a child's development, these being:

- The microsystem
- The mesosystem
- The exosystem
- The macrosystem
- The chronosystem

Each of these systems will now be described in turn, with questions included to help consolidate your understanding of each system in relation to children's development.

The microsystem

This is perhaps the most important in terms of the child's early life. The microsystem consists of those activities and individuals who exert an immediate influence on the child's life. This includes parents, family members, community playgroups, nursery, school, teachers, friends and healthcare professionals. The microsystem also concerns the relationships between people in a given setting and the impact of these on the developing child. For example, the relationship between staff in an early years setting and how effectively they communicate with each other, can impact on individual children's development. If information is not communicated clearly and efficiently, this may result in the child's needs being unmet, dietary requirements may not be adhered to, informative 'handovers' may not be able to take place due to gaps in the information and parents may consequently feel a sense of mistrust and insecurity.

It is worthwhile noting here that how a child acts or responds to these people in the microsystem will affect how they treat her in return. Furthermore, a child's personality or temperament will also dictate how others will treat her. Where children have learning difficulties or additional needs, practitioners must make every effort not to label that child and make assumptions, as this will only lead to the child receiving unequal treatment and missing out on meaningful interactions.

Given that the microsystem exerts an immediate influence on the child, the concept of a learning community is relevant here. This community consists of those adults mainly concerned with the child's welfare (parents, other family members and practitioners) and concerns their respective learning journeys with the child. Listening to one another, sharing and reflecting on experiences and using this knowledge to inform future interactions is thus a crucial component of a learning community. Differences in individuals' cultural backgrounds will also impact upon the child's development due to contrasting values, methods of communicating and problem solving. Settings such as nurseries and schools therefore have a responsibility to encourage the participation of all children and families, while promoting one another's understanding of the similarities and differences between them.

Reflection in Action

1 List some of the primary responsibilities of a family.
2 What intervention might some families need most, in order to carry out their role? Give examples.
3 How can an individual practitioner support families to best fulfil their roles?
4 How can a community best support families?

One early years provider, the London Early Years Foundation (LEYF) uses a similar concept to Bronfenbrenner's ecological model, in order to demonstrate how they place the child at the core of their services (see diagram below).

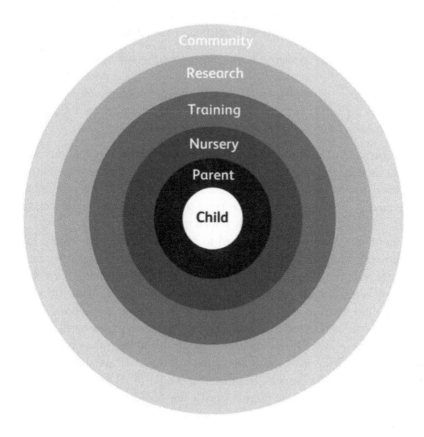

As with Bronfenbrenner's model, this highlights those factors that affect child development – some affecting the child directly, others indirectly. For example, although the training and research undertaken by practitioners do not impact the child directly, by building the knowledge, skills and understanding of practitioners, they can continually build on the care and education that they provide for all families. As a result, practitioners will be better equipped to help parents in nurturing their children's all-round development. This model reinforced the point originally made by Bronfenbrenner – that child development is powerfully shaped by networks and norms of reciprocity within a child's family, nursery or school, peer groups and the larger community. Thus, each of these aspects affects the child's opportunities both in the short and long term.

The mesosystem

This next level is concerned with how the different elements of the microsystem work together, for the welfare of the child. This can include the partnership between a child's parents and their key person in an early years setting, or the communication between a family's GP and the child's teacher. Bronfenbrenner et al. (1996: 20) describe the role of the mesosystem in relation to human development:

> In order to develop – intellectually, emotionally, socially, and morally – a human being, whether child or adult, requires the same thing: active participation in progressively more complex, reciprocal interaction with persons, objects, and symbols in the individual's immediate environment. To be effective, the interaction must occur on a fairly regular basis over extended periods of time.

The mesosystem clearly needs to be one which exerts a positive and enabling influence on the developing child, in order for her to have the best possible start in life. This is all the more important where families experience on-going difficulty such as poverty, domestic violence, substance abuse, if they have a child with special educational needs or if they are newly settled into a country.

Partnerships thus need to be created to facilitate parents with regard to their specific needs. This means providing resources that will best support parents who are, in one way or another, struggling to meet their children's needs for stable and loving care in a safe environment. Any support needs to be provided sensitively, with time and effort taken to build trusting relationships. Where this is not done, some families may feel threatened by authorities and health care professionals and further isolate themselves. Clearly, we cannot afford for this to happen as it will result in children not receiving the support that could help make all the difference to their development – and life chances. Bronfenbrenner's (1973: 1) identification of some of the societal challenges that parents faced a few decades ago could just as easily be applied today:

> In today's world parents find themselves at the mercy of a society which imposes pressures and priorities that allow neither time nor place for meaningful activities

and relations between children and adults, which downgrade the role of parents and the functions of parenthood, and which prevent the parent from doing things he wants to do as a guide, friend, and companion to his children.

Some problems are particular to living in poverty and living in deprived areas. These being urban decay, overcrowding, antisocial behaviour, gangs, lack of facilities for youths and children, poor lighting on estates and local councils failing to address such long-term problems. Accounts of gang attacks and murder are all too common in deprived areas, and combined with the aforementioned factors, can result in the demoralization of families, with diminished outcomes for families.

The problems faced by families as identified by Bronfenbrenner many years ago, could have been written about today. As in his ecological theory, he places the child at the centre of the model.

> In the planning and designing of new communities, housing projects, and urban renewal, the planners both public and private, need to give explicit consideration to the kind of world that is being created for the children who will be growing up in these settings. Particular attention should be given to the opportunities which the environment presents or precludes for involvement of children with persons both older and younger than themselves. (Bronfenbrenner, 1973: 2)

More recently, Bronfenbrenner (1996; 1979) outlined protective factors such as high quality health and social services, good child care and safe neighbourhoods as helping to mitigate the impact of poverty. As clear as it might seem, these are not easy to deliver when funding and high staff turnover are issues for local authorities and families struggle to access the support, due to being isolated or having English as an additional language, with no friends or relatives to help.

The case study below provides a clear example of how one Family Support Worker, working in a deprived part of London, supported one family to ensure that the baby's development was not impeded by her home situation, and as a result of the intervention is making good progress.

Case Study

I met A during outreach at a local well-baby clinic. I introduced myself and informed her about the service (Family Support, stay and play sessions and health care) at the local Children's Centre. A became upset and informed me that she would need Family Support. A's baby was three months old when I started working with them and was overweight.

I identified the following needs:

- Mobility difficulties – two hip replacements (which were not successful) due to a congenital disorder
- Depression/very tearful/low mood
- Isolation
- Low income

- Single parent
- Poor relationship with relatives, who do not help her.

My reasons for making this referral were manifold. I identified that the mother was not able to appropriately stimulate her baby. Due to her congenital disorder, the mother was not able to do any type of floor-based activities and was not able to access the stay and play activities at the nearby children's centre.

Her baby was rather large and on the 91st centile and her mother was finding it very difficult to carry her due to the pain in her hips. I observed on numerous occasions that the baby was sat in her buggy in front of the television.

When I broached the subject of nursery, the child's mother was very adamant that she did not want her baby to attend nursery. Her reasons were that she did not trust anyone and felt that her baby would be harmed. I informed the mother that the nursery would be the best environment at this point in time as her baby would meet all her milestones with qualified staff to support the both of them. After weeks of convincing and an invitation to visit the nursery, I organized a joint home visit with a social worker who reiterated the same thing; she finally agreed. I applied to the Early Years Priority Referral (EYPR) to secure a place at the nursery for her baby, and her baby will be starting at the beginning of this year. Children's Social Care will be providing transport to and from nursery for mother and child. I completed an eCAF with consent from the parent and contacted her health visitor to inform her that I will be working with A. I then referred the parent to adult social care. They provided a walk-in shower for her and a carer has been put in place to assist her with the domestic and personal care of her and her baby. I applied to two charities for a cot and wardrobe. This was successful and both have been delivered to the family.

As well as liaising with her health visitor I also worked with our multi-agency staff which includes a child psychologist, dietician, other Family Support Workers, health visitors, midwives, Family Health Advisors and the speech and language therapist. The charities I coordinated with included Save the Children, the Cripplegate Foundation charity for the household items and HomeStart Befriending Agency.

I am still supporting them, as the mother needs a lot of support and encouragement concerning her baby's transition from home to nursery. I am pleased to say that the baby is now 6 months old and progressing very well, as is her mother.

With Bronfenbrenner's mesosystem in mind, it becomes clear that universal services (including maternity, child health, social care, education and family welfare services) must first, truly understand the family's situation and the nature of any potential risk factors. This will enable relevant professionals to utilize resources that will best facilitate the improvement of individual families' lives. Where possible, when preventative care can be achieved, the impact of adverse living conditions on a child's learning and development can be significantly reduced. It is also important to bear in mind, as illustrated by the mother's reluctance for her baby to attend nursery due to her suspicion of officialdom, that use of professionals 'parachuted' in to support parents reflects a deficit model of parenting, focusing on what parents cannot do or are not doing. An alternative approach would be to use a community generative approach, focusing on what parents are doing to enhance their child's welfare, and building on this. This latter approach avoids blame being placed on parents for not accepting support offered (the so-called hard-to-reach parents) when that decision could be seen as perfectly rational when viewed from the parent's perspective – agreeing to send your child to nursery is likely to result in surveillance of the child and parenting skills, itself likely to lead to further criticism of parenting.

Recent public health guidance published by the National Institute for Health and Clinical Excellence (NICE, 2012) makes recommendations across the health, social and education services that are required in order to best support the emotional and social well-being of vulnerable children aged under 5 years. The guidance acknowledges that the disadvantage experienced by children in their early years can have a lifelong, negative effect on their health and well-being. This is further supported by Shonkoff and Garner (2012) who showed how early experiences and environmental influences affect lifelong health, not just educational achievement. This disconcerting message makes it all the more clear just how critical the role of each individual is in the safeguarding and promotion of children's well-being. However, recent reports into the health, social and education services (Munro, 2011; Allen, 2011; Field, 2010; Tickell, 2010) have found that these are generally poorly coordinated and integrated – both at a local and strategic level. Although quality of provision differs from region to region, every effort must be made by all local authorities to ensure excellent practice that is standardized across the nation. This can be achieved by sharing good practice between local authorities.

The exosystem

This third level consists of those people and institutions that the child doesn't interact with directly, but still affect the child's well-being. The structures in this level interact with structures in the child's microsystem to exert a positive or negative influence on the child's overall development. The structures in the exosystem include extended family networks, parents' work setting and policies, community resources and the mass media.

One example of the exosystem in practice can be a parent being made redundant. Although the child clearly has no direct contact with the work setting, the impact of the redundancy will be direct – available finances will be significantly reduced and parents will as a result be stressed and/or depressed, which, if it inhibits the parents' emotional presence, will inevitably affect the child's emotional well-being as well as all other areas of their development. Conversely, working long hours can also negatively impact on a young child's well-being as they will be away from their primary carer for extended periods, having to adapt to a daily routine and have their needs for physical care, stimulation and affection met by adults with whom they will have to build a relationship. If the bond their parents is weak, the young child will have an even harder time trying to build new relationships. Bronfenbrenner identifies the demands of work as being in direct conflict with the needs of a developing child due to the family's needs taking second place to those of work setting. He asserts that:

> With more and more parents working full time, there has been a decline in the involvement of parents as active participants in and mentors of activities with children and youth. There is growing conflict between the demands of work and family. (Bronfenbrenner, 1996: 26)

Reflection in Action

1   Social change can be seen to have created a range of adverse living circumstances such as chronic stress, over-stimulation, hectic lifestyles, family breakdown and reduced parental participation in children's care.
2a. Consider the dynamic between the key settings in which children live: home, nursery/school and the cultural community.
2b. How are the relationships between the home, cultural community and your setting actively encouraged and nurtured by your team? Give examples.
3   Note which of these in your opinion is the weakest. How could your setting improve this relationship?

Where parents do not have the support of family members to help in providing continuity of care in the long term, the effects of being apart from primary carers may be felt by parents and children all the more. Seldon (2009) however identifies some possible answers to the problem, such as communities getting together to form needed groups and activities, recreation facilities being provided for children and youths. His emphasis is on activities organized by the community – not councils, in order to encourage a sense of unity and ownership among families on a wider scale. This finds support in a report carried out by the Calouste Gulbenkian Foundation (2011) which shows that communities can be strengthened when people of different ages are encouraged to interact and get involved in their local neighbourhood.

Bronfenbrenner's inclusion of the mass media in the exosystem is highly appropriate today, given how ubiquitous it is. Bronfenbrenner's belief that the mass media exerts a negative influence on development is similarly accurate. When we consider how the rapid technological advances have completely changed how we can work, shop, interact and make friends, as well as computer games, television, advertisements and films, it is little wonder that he expresses concern. The ever-present problem posed by exposure to inappropriate content in computer games and the mass advertising that is a core feature of such games are all threats to a positive world view and healthy development. All this connected with excessive individualism (fuelled by the mass media), continuing isolation among families and less time spent with family – or other adults who can provide long-term care and positive role modelling, affect the child's sense of trust, their self-perception and their perception of others.

> The teen-age and adult models widely watched by children and youth on the media (TV, films, video games, CDs, and the internet) continue to emphasize commercialism, sexuality, substance abuse, and violence. The end result is a lack of positive adult models for internalizing standards of behaviour and longer-term goals of achievement, and thereby an increasing number of autonomous peer groups bereft of adult guidance. (Bronfenbrenner, 1996: 27)

Such damaging influences are furthermore compounded when the adults that are in the child's life struggle or fail to meet their needs for a stable and loving life.

Read the case study below and answer the questions. While reading, be mindful of Bronfenbrenner's ecological theory and how all the 'levels' are exerting an influence.

Case Study

Jenny, a three-year-old girl, starts at your nursery, attending three days a week. She is finding it difficult to settle in and make friends, often hitting and shouting at the other children. When staff have tried to intervene, she shouts at them too and she has bitten her key person. Jenny does not seem to enjoy most of the activities in the nursery, often opting to move from one play area to another, without interacting.

She is the youngest of three siblings, with their mother having sole responsibility for the children. Their father is in and out of prison which is just one reason for Jenny's mother's depression. Living on an estate which is notorious for gang attacks and drug abuse are also contributory factors. The mother is on prescribed medication which results in her feeling desensitized to the point of being detached from her children.

Reflect on This

1 What in your opinion is the most pressing issue presented here?
2 Which resources/agencies might you draw upon to support you?
3 Given that the connections between these agencies can often inhibit intervention that is mutually supportive, how can partnerships be improved to ensure better developmental outcomes for children?

The macrosystem

This comprises the outermost level of the ecological model and includes government resources, laws, cultural values and customs. It can be viewed as the most important element of the model as it is a society's values which will dictate how a country is governed. For example, if a government fervently believes in marriage, they are more likely to allocate resources to this group (such as the Married Couple's Allowance in the United Kingdom) and penalize those who do not conform to their beliefs. Governmental attitudes will always be a source of contention for its people due to conflicting beliefs and hence, the distribution of funding and resources that some will benefit from, while others do not.

The cultural values of a society thus permeate across all levels of the ecological model, affecting work conditions, policies and the very relationships that directly affect babies and children in their microsystem as they affect parents' ability to function. Where living conditions are overly demanding and resources are scant, this makes parents' roles all the more challenging and as a result, the child's microsystem is likewise affected.

What also needs to be considered is that Bronfenbrenner's ecological model will also differ greatly from country to country. For example, the priorities of a wealthy nation will be in contrast to those of a developing country. Policies in wealthy nations tend to focus on investment in competing in a global economy, whereas policies in developing countries focus more on treating infectious diseases (which in wealthier countries are curable, but due to poor sanitation are fatal in poorer countries). Shonkoff (2012) offers an interesting solution to the enduring conflict between what are deemed as priorities:

> When funds earmarked for child survival compete with potential investments in early childhood development, science suggests that the reduction of significant adversity could advance progress toward both objectives. (Shonkoff, 2012: 2)

What do you Think?

1 Re-read the quote above and answer these questions:
2 In which ways do you think reducing the impact of adversity can help to improve child development?
3 What outcomes will each of your suggestions have, for the child and family?

To conclude, effective functioning of child-rearing processes in the family and other settings requires national policies (for example, the Head Start programme) and practices that provide the necessary time, space, stability, recognition of belief systems and customs that support child-rearing activities. This means on behalf of parents, caregivers, other professionals, as well as relatives, friends, neighbours, communities, and the major economic, social, and political institutions of that society.

The chronosystem

This aspect of Bronfenbrenner's model refers to the passage of time that affects the child's environments. It is not a 'level' of the model as such but more about the transitions a child makes over time during the life course. This may be internally, such as physiological changes within the child caused by growing older, or externally, such as the impact of war. Transitions in a child's life, such as divorce, also exist in the chronosystem. Initial feelings may inevitably be very challenging for a child to deal with, but with the passing of time and with the right support, the intensity of feelings may well subside.

The ecological model and recent developments

Bronfenbrenner's theory is undoubtedly very comprehensive and useful in enabling us to understand the power of different environments and relationships between children and their carers – and the wider community. It has, however, been criticized for focusing too narrowly on the context (i.e. the impact of environments and relationships), at the expense of considering two other crucial factors that help to explain child development (Bronfenbrenner, 1989). These being:

- The role of the individual in their own development
- Genetics

His later work thus focused on the role of nature as well as nurture on child development. It is therefore best used like all other theories explaining child development – in addition to each other, not as the sole method of trying to explain it. Consider child development like a big puzzle, with all the different theories piecing together to help you complete the full picture.

Bronfenbrenner in Practice

- Nurture your partnerships with all parents – this way, you will be better positioned to support them and together, promote their children's development.
- Take time to truly understand the contexts in which family stressors occur. This can help you to be effective helpers.
- Early intervention is key – act on any concerns as swiftly as possible, so as to minimize the impact of adversity and maximize the support available.
- Reflect on your setting's position within the community – as a team, devise an action plan that will guide you in building these relationships, for the benefit of the children and their families with whom you work.
- Think about how the individual child and her temperament and personality

influences her environment and those within it. What can be done to support or mediate this further?

● In what areas of Bronfenbrenner's ecological model is your setting actively making a contribution to the child's world? What impact does this activity have for the child?

Ideas into Action

Now that you have familiarized yourself with some of Bronfenbrenner's contributions to early years development and care, make the links to practice in your setting by reflecting upon and completing the following:

1   Identify three key implications of Bronfenbrenner's theory for your practice.
2a   Consider the effect of the microsystem in relation to your role. Identify two areas of strength in your practice.
2b   Now identify two areas for improvement and explain how you will achieve this.
3a   Consider the effect of the mesosystem in relation to your role. Identify two areas of strength in your practice.
3b   Now identify two areas for improvement and explain how you will achieve this.

Challenge the Theorists

1   How far do you think Bronfenbrenner lost sight of the child's own agency in his exploration of how their outer world shapes their experiences?

2   How might this affect adult perceptions of children?

3   How far do you think he acknowledged the emotional world of children in his ideas?

Bronfenbrenner's Contemporary Legacy

Knowledge base concerning development from conception to three
● Socio-emotional learning

Creating inclusive and enabling environments
● Socio-cultural learning

Importance of parents and the home learning environment
● The impact of positive early interactions

Links to other theorists
● Colwyn Trevarthen
● Jerome Bruner
● Lev Vygotsky

Further Reading

Bronfenbrenner, U. (1979) *The Ecology of Human Development: Experiments by Nature and Design*. Cambridge, MA: The President and Fellows of Harvard College.

> This is perhaps the most famous of Bronfenbrenner's books. Here, he details the relationship between the developing child and the five systems that make up his ecological theory. Chapters 7 and 8 which focus on the role of children's institutions, day care and pre-school as contexts for human development are highly pertinent to those working with and for children. The strength of this book resides in how Bronfenbrenner manages to provide a clear and engaging account of how children are affected by their different environments.

Pound, L. (2009) *How Children Learn 3: Contemporary Thinking and Theorists*. London: Practical Pre-School Books, 9–11.

> The pages identified above provide a good overview of Bronfenbrenner's contributions to child development theory, which makes this book a useful study aid. This is a text designed as a basic introduction to his ideas and to go deeper you need to read more widely about his ideas.

Bridging the Gap: Understanding the Use of Neuroscience in the Early Years

12

An introduction to neuroscience and its influence in early child care and education

This chapter focuses on the field of neuroscience and its implications for provision in early years settings. In this chapter a range of researchers in the field will be referred to, as opposed to just one. This is to acknowledge the cumulative role the extensive investigations carried out by these individuals have played in building current understanding about brain development. A brief glossary of commonly used terms is included, in order to make the chapter easier to grasp, followed by a range of topical discussions with case studies and points for reflection. The chapter contains discussion in favour of, and opposed to, the contribution of neuroscience and its use in early years provision, in order to provide a balanced and coherent perspective.

Listed below are the sub-headings included in this chapter, to help make it easier for you to navigate through all of the information, in a way that's easiest for you.

- What is neuroscience?
- Know your terminology
- What you need to know: The importance of development from conception to three years
- Did you know? Facts about the growing brain
- Building the social brain
- Neuroscience and early emotional development
- Getting the balance right
- Criticisms of neuroscience
- From theory to practice: What students have told us
- Concluding thoughts

What is neuroscience?

Neuroscience is the study of the brain and the central nervous system. Researchers in this field use equipment such as scanners, computers and dyes to find out how the brain develops and functions – both in healthy brains and those which are affected by psychiatric and neurological disorders.

Know your terminology

As with any subject, it's always advisable to be conversant with the terms commonly used. As a professional (or training) practitioner, it is your responsibility to keep abreast of developments in early years as well as to be 'fluent' in the language used by professionals across a range of associated disciplines. Neuroscience is just one of these. Understanding and using subject-specific language will help to consolidate your knowledge and build confidence in the parents, carers and other professionals with whom you work.

Just a few of the commonly used terms concerning neuroscience that are in this chapter – and many related books and articles, are as follows. So, make the effort to remember them and use them as part of related study or professional dialogue.

- **Neurons** – Brain cells which carry messages through an electrochemical process. Neurons work together to help us make sense of what's going on around us, to help us plan what we're going to do and – everything else.
- **Synapse** – The wiring/networks between neurons.
- **Synaptic pruning** – A process which eliminates weaker synaptic connections, while stronger connections are kept and strengthened. Experience determines which connections will be strengthened and which will be pruned.
- **Synaptogenesis** – The formation of synapses between neurons.
- **Synaptogenocide** – The loss of/'dying' of synapses between neurons.
- **Windows of opportunity** (sometimes called sensitive periods) – The idea that the young child's brain is open to experience of a particular kind at certain points in development. For example, the belief that learning a language is easier during childhood, rather than during adulthood.

Each neuron is specifically designed to bring information to the cell body and take information away from the cell body. Neurons have specialized extensions called dendrites and axons.

- Dendrites bring information to the cell body.
- Axons take information away from the cell body (these long wires connect one neuron to another neuron's dendrites).

The connections that neurons make are called synapses. Children who don't have opportunities to play or are rarely cuddled have underdeveloped brains. These children have the same number of brain cells, but fewer synaptic connections between them. (This will be discussed in detail later.)

What you need to know: The importance of development from conception to three years

The plethora of books, articles and reports concerning early brain development generally expound the importance of building a healthy brain from birth. Yet it is far more useful to start from conception. This is because the foetal brain is almost entirely dependent on a range of factors while growing in utero.

Professionals in the field now refer to this crucial developmental phase as **the first 1,000 days** – the time from the start of pregnancy to a child's second birthday. This is due to research consistently showing the impact of children's early experiences on their adult emotional and mental health as well as their educational and employment opportunities (Barker, 1995).

The first 1,000 days are not only crucial for the baby but for the mother also. Parenthood is a time of great upheaval and change, which can lead to feelings of intense anxiety, uncertainty and in some women, depression. These issues may exist alongside existing issues such as lifestyle habits that are highly detrimental to the well-being of the baby.

The lifestyle habits or choices of a pregnant woman therefore have a huge impact on her baby's brain development (and of course, their all-round development). For example, when a parent chooses to breastfeed, the benefits for her baby include protection from infections and diseases while helping to build a strong physical and emotional bond between mother and baby. Conversely, smoking, drinking heavily or taking recreational drugs can have irreversible effects which can be too late to 'repair' at birth. Heavy drug abuse during pregnancy can lead to the baby being born addicted to drugs, experiencing withdrawal symptoms. Different drugs will have different effects; the stronger the drug, the worse it will be. Consider the use of marijuana – when a pregnant woman gets 'stoned', the baby is also under the influence of the drug – all at a time when the developing foetus is trying to grow neurons and other crucial elements of the brain.

Other effects of substance abuse on the foetus include:

- Low birth weight
- Early delivery
- Miscarriage
- Hindered development

- **Foetal Alcohol Syndrome (FAS).** This refers to a range of mental and physical defects that develop in a foetus, as a result of high levels of alcohol consumption during pregnancy
- Defects of the face and body
- Intellectual disability
- Heart problems
- Death

Below, is a **vignette** concerning a young child living with the consequences of his mother's substance abuse. Read it and answer the questions that follow.

> You have recently become key person to a child (Jack) who is aged three years and six months old. His mother is a single parent. She finally left her boyfriend after years of being together in an 'on and off' relationship.
>
> Jack's mother has no extended family and sometimes struggles to get by with her son – financially and emotionally. They live on the 16th floor of a tower block in the city. Although she has some friends, she is often too depressed to see them. She has mentioned domestic violence and using drugs and alcohol to 'take the edge off life'. However, she has not yet elaborated as she gets too upset when she has tried to explain.
>
> During her pregnancy she did not stop drinking alcohol, which resulted in Jack having FAS. He has very poor coordination and must be closely supervised during all activities. He also wears a helmet for most of the time as he frequently has accidents due to his poor spatial awareness and weak eyesight. Jack has learning difficulties that are exacerbated by a short attention span and hyperactivity.
>
> He has been at the nursery for six weeks but is finding it difficult to make friends and engage in activities.

Reflect on This

1 As his key person, explain the types of support you can put in place for:
   a Jack;
   b His mother.
2 How can your suggestions foster Jack's emotional well-being and his ability to learn?
3 Why is this particularly important in the early years of a child's life?
4 What might happen if Jack and his mother do not receive adequate, on-going support?

The message therefore needs to be reframed to include that critical time before birth, so that prospective parents and anyone who works with children and families can at least be armed with knowledge of how to best support healthy brain development

– from conception. The positive thing is that good quality provision can mediate a lot of this because children are resilient with the right support.

Did you know? Facts about the growing brain

You might be surprised to know that the human brain contains roughly 100 billion neurons – most of which are formed during the first five months after conception. That said, the process of brain development is far from complete at this point. Despite this great number of neurons present at birth, the brain requires a great deal of help to continue developing healthily. The brain can be described as being **activity-dependent** – the fact that the brain partly depends on external stimulation in order to develop. This can be through play, communicating with others and enjoying warm and responsive relationships. Synaptogenesis (the forming of networks between neurons) is highly prolific during this time, occurring directly as a result of stimuli that the baby is exposed to in their environment. Hence, the early years of a child's life are arguably the most important period in terms of growth, learning and development. The significance of this is highlighted by Riley (2007: 3) who states that:

> Immediately after birth, bombarded by stimulation of all the senses, the synapses begin to form prolifically. The most important phase of experience-dependent synaptogenesis is thought to be from birth to three years.

Quality of experiences is key – not least because, while exposure to vast and varied experiences may well lead to a larger quantity of neuronal connections being formed, those that are unused will 'die off' (synaptogenocide). Researchers such as Goldman-Racik (1987) and later, Katz and Schatz (1997: 120), found that:

> Early brain development involves a large overproduction of synaptic connections; some of these connections will become redundant and are subsequently pruned away.

This indicates that *over*exposing a child to learning experiences in the hope that they will become more intelligent is not necessary but that the quality of daily experiences and interactions with adults and other children is what really matters. Making time for cuddles, sharing stories, talking, singing and playing with your baby (or child) are enormously beneficial to the developing brain, as they help to positively stimulate the growth of neurons which will support the child throughout their life.

This message was further reinforced for us while watching the film *The Angel's Share* (Ken Loach, 2012). This film depicts the life of a young man living in Glasgow, who was born into a life of drugs, poverty and crime, perpetuating the cycle himself as he grew older. Cut to a scene in hospital where his girlfriend who has just given birth shows him their baby for the first time and tells him in no uncertain terms:

The midwife says only half his brain is formed ... and the other half depends on what we do over the next few years ... Robbie we have to do good for him and if you won't help I will have to do this on my own.

Listening to the first part of that speech, we were so disheartened – but by the time the girl had finished, we were full of hope for this young couple who aimed to do everything in their power to give their new baby the best possible start in life.

What do you Think?

Draw a table like the one below and write down as many positive and negative factors that affect the developing brain from conception, into early childhood.

Positive factors affecting early brain growth	Negative factors affecting early brain growth

Building the social brain

Blakemore (2009) and Gerhardt (2004) highlight the significance of social and emotional experiences a baby has between six and 18 months. It is thought that during this time social intelligence is at its most sensitive, with neuronal networks forming and strengthening in response to the experiences that the baby is exposed to. These networks (or patterns) can be used to organize experience and make interactions with others more predictable.

High quality early years provision can make all the difference in promoting the social skills of babies and young children. This will be especially valuable where babies and young children are deprived of warm, reciprocal relationships in the home, which provide the 'blueprint' for them in terms of norms of behaviour and expectations. Trevarthen's research findings (2012) concerning the impact of maternal depression on an infant's growing emotional, intellectual, language and social development, is just one example of why this issue is critical.

Providing a flexible routine which includes responsive interactions with babies and children can help to foster a sense of security and well-being while helping them to develop independence. Opposite are just two examples of how this is achieved.

Case Study

Lunch time
Becky is feeding George, an eight-month-old baby. After a few spoonfuls, he grabs the spoon from Becky's hand and attempts to feed himself. She observes him as he enjoys waving the spoon and grabbing the food on it. After a few attempts at feeding himself, Becky gives him another spoon to play with instead of taking the spoon from him, as she could see that he was really trying and was happy. She gets another spoon and continues to feed him in between his attempts, while praising his efforts at feeding himself.

Case Study

Conflict resolution among children
Harry is in the book corner with two of her key children (Alfie and Jack, both aged two years old). They are looking at different tactile books but at one point, Alfie looks at the book Jack is reading (a pop-up book on dinosaurs) and takes it from him. Jack tries to take it back and both boys start to cry. Harry steps in to help the boys. 'Alfie, I know that you're upset because you like that book and want to read it, but it's not nice to grab it from him. How about we all read it together? I'll hold the book, Jack can turn the pages and you can roar like the dinosaurs!' Both boys nod yes and cuddle in to Harry. They all sit down on the rug and read the story.

Both experiences demonstrate how responsive and sensitive intervention from the practitioner supports babies and children in their quest for independence and self-control.

By supporting the diverse needs of children, practitioners can promote their understanding of time, patience, communicating their needs and thoughts as well as how to be a member of a group. Practitioners therefore need to show sensitivity to children's current interests and support them in their explorations, in order to best promote development of the brain.

Reflection in Action

1 List four different types of learning experiences that you have carried out, which have successfully promoted the social skills of children aged between 9 and 18 months old.
2 How can you tell that these learning experiences had a positive impact on these young children?

Neuroscience and early emotional development

Most of us in the early years field appreciate the impact of unhappiness or stress on a child's ability to take advantage of learning opportunities. Now, findings from neuro-science confirm what we know (Gopnik et al., 1999). When a child feels unhappy or does not feel secure and comfortable in the setting, she cannot be expected to take full advantage of what is on offer, as feelings of stress and sadness will inhibit the urge to explore and interact with others – thereby inhibiting the process of learning and development of necessary life skills. This finds support in Goleman (1996: 196) who explains that:

> The first three or four years of life are a period where the toddler's brain evolves in complexity at a greater rate than it will ever grow again ... During this time severe stress can impair the brain's learning centres and so be damaging to the intellect.

 Stress is a known inhibitor to learning due to a chemical released in times of stress. This chemical is **cortisol**. (When cortisol levels are too high, this can destroy brain cells and weaken connection, resulting in a reduced capacity to learn.) Goleman emphasizes the importance of early experiences as the brain grows most rapidly during the early years, which places responsibility on the practitioner to provide optimum conditions for care and learning to take place. Following a key person system makes this easier, as staff can better meet the needs of individual children in partnership with parents. This is all the more important because it is only expected that young children will experience separation anxiety and feelings of uncertainty as their home routine is disrupted. Children may also experience stress when adapting to a new routine and building relationships with unfamiliar adults, who are to become their main caregivers throughout the day, for up to five days a week. Building genuine and caring relationships with babies and children will prove invaluable in reassuring them and instilling a sense of security.

Goleman's views on this are supported by Gerhardt (2004: 190) who draws our attention to the importance of quality interactions which nurture the infant's emotional well-being, both in the present and the future:

> What really matters is whether the caregiver meets the temperamental inclinations with the kind of response the baby needs to establish the foundation for later emotional and social discipline.

Children who are frequently exposed to stressful experiences or whose needs for attachment and affection are unmet continually experience a rise in cortisol levels that remain raised and are consequently 'set' even higher in instances of emotional difficulty. Again, this places responsibility on early years practitioners to provide consistency in their approach as well as being emotionally present for the child. This is all the more necessary given that cortisol inhibits 'feel good' hormones from being produced during stress, which means that children need the support of sensitive adults who are tuned in and able to help regulate their emotions.

Getting the balance right

Conversely, key persons need to balance the meeting of children's emotional needs and over-protecting them. This is particularly important in helping the child to develop coping strategies in times of heightened anxiety. A certain amount of cortisol is actually beneficial to the child in terms of being able to cope during times of upset, as it triggers the 'fight or flight' response in the child during demanding situations (Belsky et al., 1998). This is particularly significant concerning children in day care, where there are often a large number of children who will inevitably experience feelings of frustration and anger at certain times, and will hence need to develop their own coping strategies during times of heightened stress.

Gopnik et al. (2004) discuss the importance of stimulating experiences and healthy attachments in affecting the formation of connections between the neurons, and consequent brain growth. These experiences cause the brain to organize and reorganize and, when this growth reaches its peak during the first year, the brain cells make new connections and terminate those that are not required. The connection between various cells depends on how the young child is treated by primary caregivers.

Reflection in Action

Consider your setting's planning and provision of experiences which are aimed to promote:

● Personal, Social and Emotional Development
● Understanding the World

1 Do you think that provision is effective for babies aged 18 months and under?
2 What do you think needs to be improved? Explain your reasons.
3 How does your key person system provide security and consistency for babies and young children?
4 In which ways does it promote independence? Provide two practical examples.

To conclude, it is evident that the practitioner's role is pivotal in supporting the healthy development of the brain and in nurturing the building of emotional skills that are appropriate in helping the child to deal with a range of different situations (Trevarthen, 2012; Dowling, 2005). This also means allowing them to express the range of emotions that are part of the human experience (such as anger, fear, happiness and empathy) in a climate of trust and understanding in order to best facilitate brain development and emotional well-being. Findings from neuroscience should, therefore, also be used to support the planning of provision.

Criticisms of neuroscience

Too much 'hype'

As with most disciplines, neuroscience is not without its critiques. Dr John Bruer, founder of the McDonnell-Pew Program in Cognitive Neuroscience, is dubious about what he sees as the over-enthusiasm surrounding neuroscience. He identifies the potential it has to exploit anxious parents and practitioners through government policymakers manipulating conclusions from studies to suit the requirements of their particular position concerning birth to 3s (2002). As well as noting the reticence of the educational research community, he says:

> Serious scientists, committed to applying research to improve child development, would likely be perplexed by such ill-founded recommendations and frustrated by the public's acceptance of them ... At best, brain-based education is no more than a folk-theory about the brain and learning. (Bruer, 2002: 132)

It is important to note here that the scepticism may well be due to the fact that conclusions from brain science are not yet being used to their fullest potential in terms of informing curricula and practice. Instead they are being used as part of advertising campaigns (advertisements for juice drinks and bread fortified with essential fatty acids to improve concentration) and patented schemes such as Brain Gym. Such campaigns and products have the power to sway public opinion, and can often be misleading in their presentation – instead of being presented in a manner which is concise in its facts, and without the surrounding 'hype'. It is therefore important that although Bruer's view is acknowledged, practitioners do not dismiss the potential advantages of incorporating findings from neuroscience in early years education (Johnson and Mareschal 2001; Shonkoff and Philipps 2000), and instead seek to make the necessary connection between the two fields, so that findings can be used to improve current provision. This view is also espoused by Meade (2001: 118) who highlights some of the potential advantages of neuroscience in early years care and education:

> Neuroimaging technologies, such as PET scans (Positron Emission Tomography) not only have allowed neuroscientists to study brain activity, but have also led to new or revised perspectives about early childhood development.

Critical periods

The concept of critical periods has come under scrutiny for a number of reasons and it is worthwhile for practitioners to be familiar with arguments that are for and against, in order to make reasoned judgements about its advantages and disadvantages. For example, critical periods do not apply to all areas of learning and it is therefore important that early years professionals and policymakers take this into consideration when devising learning programmes and delivering advice for parents/ primary carers that are based upon critical periods. For example, language acquisition can occur during adulthood as well as childhood – therefore rendering the notion of critical periods and related learning interventions somewhat erroneous. It is for this reason that Bruer refutes the concept of critical periods:

> The brain's plasticity allows lifelong learning – vocabulary growth and IQ measures are linked to experience, exposure to new words and ideas. Humans can thus benefit from such exposure at any time of life. (Bruer, 1999: 119)

Thus, the concept of *sensitive periods* or *windows of opportunity* are now more widely accepted because, as is outlined by Johnson (2002) and Bruer (1999), all is not lost if a child is not exposed to specific stimuli before the age of three years. The case of the Romanian orphans is also indicative of this, in which babies and children who lost their parents in the war were raised in extremely poor care and were seriously neglected in terms of their basic needs and needs for stimulation and affection. This resulted in global developmental delay and difficulties in forming relationships with other adults and children. However, later studies of some of the children who were raised in care but then adopted, actually found that they did manage to acquire skills in communication, problem solving and in forming relationships, but the process took longer than was usually expected of children of a similar age (Young Brains report, 2007).

One of the main findings from the Young Brains report (2007) highlights the link between plasticity and learning:

> Key messages from the research are that young brains are exceptionally plastic so they are shaped by experience and the plasticity allows for catching up if development and learning are hampered in any way. (David, Goouch, Powell and Abbot, 2003: 127)

In conclusion, it is apparent that although there are periods during which learning can occur more easily for the child, it certainly does not mean that this will stop after three years. Current emphasis needs to shift from 'birth to three' to encompass the period before birth and after three years.

From theory to practice: What students have told us

Having taught child care and education for the past ten years, a trend became apparent: too much emphasis on traditional theories of child development that have not allowed for more current ideas concerning learning and development in the early years. This means that many practitioners are not yet able to utilize findings that are directly relevant to the work that they do on a daily basis.

This was confirmed for us during a small-scale research study that was conducted concerning neuroscience and its use in the early years. During a semi-structured interview one of the responses from a nursery manager on the Foundation Degree in Early Childhood Studies was:

> Come to think of it, you're not trained to think that way. You're trained to think cognitive development which is one part of it, but the actual biology of the brain and how that develops – the physiology of the brain – we do not get any of that input. That's left to the medical professionals, nurses' training.

This was a typical view expressed by all participants, who all demonstrated in-depth knowledge concerning child development and of the more traditional theories such as Piaget, Vygotsky and Bruner. All participants however, were unable to discuss in any depth findings from neuroscience to support them. They all had a scant understanding of brain development but did not know of any researchers or theorists in this field from which they could ground their responses.

Although a snapshot, this **small-scale study** indicates the need to incorporate neuroscience and its applications to teaching on child care courses – including foundation degrees. This way, practitioners at all levels can put the theory into practice. Some courses of study do cover neuroscience but until this is done across all programmes it will be inconsistent, resulting in mixed messages about its relevance to early years care and education.

Concluding thoughts

Neuroscience can have a positive impact upon helping practitioners to understand how children's brains develop and their significant contribution in this process. Recommendations to enable this to happen include attending training on neuroscience for early years practitioners nationwide in order for staff to become familiarized with it and to overcome any misconceptions. Although the training may be of benefit to staff, unless it is delivered by professionals who have a thorough knowledge of the subject area, it may still be over-simplified and thus of limited use if not applied practically.

Another way of ensuring change at a local and national level would be to incorporate relevant neuroscientific findings into early years policy and practice throughout settings in England. Clearly, this will take a long time and require close monitoring of implementation by designated practitioners in settings nationwide. To enable this to take place the ideas and views of practitioners and managers should be ascertained regularly, as well as sharing good practice across settings that is informed by neuroscience, thus demonstrating how neuroscience can be applied practically. This will serve to unite neuroscience and the early years.

We hope that we have presented a balanced argument concerning the potential use of findings from neuroscience in early years practice.

Neuroscience in Practice

- Earlier intervention with parents (and where relevant, signposting prenatal support).
- Earlier intervention to children with disadvantaged home environments and/ or poor family relationships.
- Close links with health colleagues.
- Adopting a key person approach.
- Ensuring that babies enjoy consistent and affectionate relationships with staff.
- Focus on socio-emotional relationships and climate in a setting.

Ideas into Action

Now that you have familiarized yourself with some of the uses and influences of neuroscience to early years development and care, make the links to practice in your setting by reflecting upon and completing the following:

1 In what ways can the evidence from neuroscience be used to inform and shape your provision and relationships with children and families?
2 How far and in what ways do you think neuroscience is an early childhood discipline?
3 Identify three aspects of your practice which neuroscience can help with and three aspects of your practice which do not benefit from this knowledge.

Challenge the Theorists

1 How far do you feel neuroscience has moved early childhood education (ECE) towards a medicalized and pathologized model of early development?
2 How far do you feel a child's temperament and personality shape environmental influences?
3 How far and in what ways can neurological research add value to the ECE existing evidence base?
4 Do you think this research is overvalued in the sector and why?

The Contemporary Legacy of Neuroscience in the Early Years

Knowledge base concerning development from conception to three
- Socio-emotional learning
- Qualifications of the workforce
- The role of very early experiences on development

Creating inclusive and enabling environments
- Cultural participation
- Socio-cultural learning
- The role of a support network in promoting language development

Importance of parents and the home learning environment
- The centrality of emotional-social development
- The impact of positive early interactions
- Countering poverty and socio-economic disadvantage

Links to other theorists
- Colwyn Trevarthen
- Daniel Goleman
- Urie Bronfenbrenner
- Jerome Bruner
- Jean Piaget
- Elinor Goldschmied
- John Bowlby
- Lev Vygotsky
- The McMillan sisters

Further Reading

David, T., Goouch, K., Powell, S. and Abbott, L. (2003) *Young Brains. Research Report Number 444*. London: Department for Education and Skills.

> This research report consists of a review of literature concerning brain development which includes for example, discussion of the nature versus nurture debate, the importance of the first 1,000 days, as well as an insightful section on the practical implications of brain research for early years practitioners. This paper is not too lengthy and is packed full of useful information. A wide range of references that can be followed up makes this an excellent study resource.

Dowling, J. E. (2004) *The Great Brain Debate. Nature or Nurture?* Princeton, NJ and Oxford: Princeton University Press.

> This book contains three parts – parts one and two cover the developing brain and the adult brain, while part three provides an examination of the aging brain. The in-depth discussions concerning brain plasticity, the role of nature

and nurture as well as learning languages are each grounded in the latest brain research, and are easy to follow. This is a good book to dip in and out of, depending on your area of interest or need.

Gopnik, A., Meltzoff, A. and Kuhl, P. (1999) *How Babies Think*. London: Phoenix.

This book contains seven chapters, each focusing on different topics such as what newborn babies know, how babies and children learn about people, what scientists have learned about children's brains, and possibilities for the future – not just for early years practice but for today's children. The authors write in a highly engaging style which brings the complex issue of neuroscience to life.

What Next? Reconceptualizing Early Years Education

13

Reconceptualizing early education: An introduction to critical approaches

In this chapter we will seek to reframe current understanding of child development theories and commonly held beliefs about early childhood education. This will be achieved by including discussions that challenge widely held beliefs alongside a range of reflective questions for you to respond to. As the title indicates, the focus is on reconceptualizing what we know and understand about early years education – that is, to examine alternative perspectives of child development theories. We hope this will enable you to reflect on what you already know but also be prepared to critique this knowledge and understanding and consider alternative meanings and realities within your practice.

Alternative perspectives and those which challenge universal 'truths' about anything (in this case early years education) are commonly referred to as **postmodern**. However, this term has been superseded by the term *reconceptualizing*. We feel that this term is more helpful as it is more user-friendly, links to the development of our thinking about practice more clearly and is more conducive to encouraging you to challenge those widely held beliefs concerning the education of young children.

Ideas and opinions concerning how children should be raised and educated are complex and there is not one definitive response that 'ticks all the boxes'. This is due, in part, to the following factors:

- Personal experience
- Culture
- Societal expectations and norms
- Government initiatives and priorities

- Social changes
- Peer and media culture
- Relationships and interactions
- Increasing diversity in our societies and communities

Practitioners' frames of reference and their knowledge of theories of child development are important in early years professional practice; if practitioners are to provide quality early years care and learning experiences, they need to be informed of, and keep abreast of, developments in theoretical understanding and its applications in recent research. This requires practitioners to actively seek new ways of knowing and understanding children's behaviour that is more aligned to the children's experiences and diverse backgrounds (Dahlberg, Moss and Pence, 1999). Such reassessment of knowledge can result in practitioners having the ability to refer to a wider range of current research and theoretical findings and hence support children and their families more responsively. For example, by keeping abreast of current factors affecting the development and well-being of young children in a globalizing and modernizing world, the practitioner can adjust their interactions and actions according to the child's own reality and experiences.

Reconceptualizing early years, or looking at it from a postmodern perspective, can be quite daunting for some practitioners, as it sometimes requires 'unlearning' years of learning. That said, with experience comes confidence and an ability to question those widely accepted bodies of knowledge which provide 'truths' about child development and childhood itself. This does not mean that everything is up for grabs, but standing still in our thinking is a bad thing – we need to innovate in our thinking and practice in order to progress – we are not talking revolution but evolution, where some old ideas die and new ideas take over and this is progress.

So, stepping out of your comfort zone of the known and entering the unknown – trying out new ways of thinking, relating, experiencing and understanding the world – is a very important aspect of your personal, professional development. Brew (2001: 7) puts this succinctly:

> In order to learn we need to develop the capacity to unlearn. This does not happen through a process of gentle accumulation of knowledge or of understanding; it may involve the crumbling of dearly held views.

Problematizing (challenging) and *deconstructing* (breaking theories down) in this way can actually lead you to developing your own theories based on studies that you might undertake with babies and children in your setting. After all, knowledge does not rest in one place, nor with experts; it's more about looking where knowledge is created and how.

A range of statements will now follow which will form the sub-headings for discussion. While reading, keep an open mind and do not be afraid to challenge your own long-held beliefs. These statements (or issues) were selected as they are commonly made as part of the **reconceptualization** of early years.

Suppose there is no one definition of quality and that it depends on perspective, location and context?

In this section the concept of quality will be examined and deconstructed. Different definitions of quality will be explored in order to draw out the similarities and differences between them, as diverging opinions do exist. Alongside this discussion the benefits to practitioners of rethinking their views concerning what constitutes quality in light of considering these alternative perspectives are also included.

In an attempt to define quality, Andersson (1990) argues that quality consists of the daily elements of the nursery routine that are not given much thought, even though these elements may be carefully planned into the daily routine. Andersson (1990: 38) states that:

> Quality is an underlying dimension of the daily work in all early childhood services ... Quality is what is under the surface, the persistent daily work done by the staff which can be hard to fully recognise.

The nature of quality is, however, transient as it is affected by factors that are specific to one context at any one time. For example, the needs of children and their families in one setting will differ from another. This is due to a wide range of factors including socio-economic status, language, learning difficulties (child or parent) as well as resources available in the setting that meet the needs of children both individually and collectively.

What do you Think?

1 How would you define quality? Make a note of your answer.
2 Have a conversation with your manager (or another colleague). Ask them what aspects of provision in your setting they think constitute quality early years education and care.
3 Have the same conversation with a parent/primary carer. How do their answers differ?
4 Do their responses make you think differently about the definition of quality?

Guidance documents and policies (national and local) are thus enforced to set a minimum standard regarding expectations of quality across settings that are designed to meet the diverse needs of children and their families. However, strictly adhering to guidance and policies concerning quality can pose a problem for early years practitioners, including management. This is partly due to the fact they are subject to revisions which, although sometimes necessary, can inhibit practice being consolidated due to a lack of time to embed and amend practice as teams feel fit.

Too many changes can thus cause inconsistency in provision as managers can feel under pressure to impose changes to keep in line with 'best' practice requirements, which can destabilize staff and, in turn, their opinions of what they think 'quality' provision should look like. This is recognized by Woodhead (2006: 76) who explains that:

> Treating quality criteria as being relative rather than fixed, negotiated rather than prescribed, might be interpreted as undermining for managers, whose role is already difficult.

Quality, then, can only ever be subjective in its nature. Contentious issues such as the importance placed on childhood, the unique needs of families and the role of women in society each make it a concept that is difficult to define and achieve. It has also been argued that what constitutes quality is all too often defined through a monocultural lens (Cannella and Lincoln, 2004) – that is, to be defined by one leading culture which sets the benchmark for all other countries and cultures. A typical example of this is Western culture (Europe and the United States) being viewed as the 'ideal' and the leading example which all other cultures should look to for direction. If this is true – and reconceptualists fervently believe that this is the case (Venn, 2006; Lyotard, 1993; James and Prout, 1990), then achieving quality will be a continuous struggle for those 'other' cultures that do not conform to the norms set by Western society.

Cannella (2007: 21) offers an innovative way of taking the early years profession forward, in light of the many different perspectives and disciplines that continue to guide, and sometimes divide, practice:

> Reconceptualist work has fostered the recognition of the historical, political, and complex nature of the knowledge that we use and the contexts in which we find ourselves. I believe that the reconceptualists and developmentalists should join together to generate new discourses and to construct actions that actually challenge the power that has been created over children.

It is therefore useful if practitioners view quality as a relative concept that will mean different things to different stakeholders. What might be deemed as excellent for one setting could be deemed quite irrelevant to another (Woodhead, 2006). In light of this, practitioners must also keep up to speed with nationally defined quality benchmarks and criteria which provide clear guidance regarding how to achieve quality practice throughout the different areas of provision. Although such guidance on quality is usually generic, it still provides a basic benchmark that teams should aim for. Furthermore, practitioners need to have their own expectations of what high quality provision should look like, in order to strive to achieve excellent practice that is aligned to each family's needs.

When practitioners have a vision of what they think best practice is, they are equipped to challenge aspects of guidance that they feel is not relevant to practice in their setting, and also create their own benchmarks of quality against which they can evaluate their own performance.

Some nursery managers told us how they defined quality provision, how their view of quality aligns with legislative and guidance definitions of quality and whether they feel pressurized to conform to such definitions of quality. The three pie charts below summarize their responses, followed by a more detailed account of their feedback.

Question 1

In response to the question, 'What do you think is the most important element of quality?', the majority of nursery managers (34 per cent) said that having 'passionate staff' was the most important factor in achieving quality practice.

What do you think is the most important element of quality?

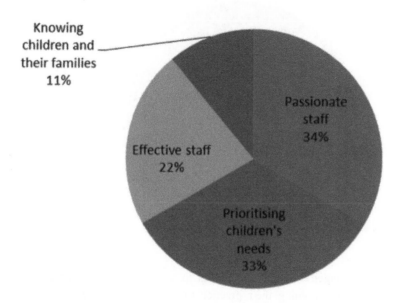

Some additional answers to this question concerned the practitioner's qualities in general. One manager's full answer to question 1 was:

> For me, quality in the nursery includes a variety of things, such as staff that are trained and enthusiastic (want to be working with children, happy and approachable). Staff should be able to articulate what they do and why. They also need to know their children and their families, and work with them to enable children to fulfil their potential. It's also about having evidence that measures and ensures quality, e.g. the **RAG** rating by the local, council, Ofsted, **ITERS**, **ECERS** and more importantly, parents' views of our provision.

Not surprisingly, all responses included reference to working with parents, providing age and stage appropriate resources and warm interactions – all of which provide the backbone of good quality care and education. It is thus apparent that all managers had a very similar view of what quality practice entails and how to achieve this.

Question 2

This question sought to elicit whether the managers felt that definitions of quality set down in legislative and guidance documents were in line with their own views of quality. Reassuringly, all respondents replied yes.

Legislative and guidance documents each have their own definition of quality provision.
Are these in line with your view of quality?

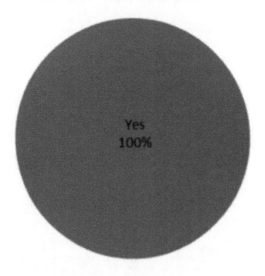

Conversely, each manager's answer enabled us to understand their approach to achieving quality while aligning their practice to legislative requirements. One manager told us:

> All of these documents need to be used with a level of creativity that suits children, staff and parents in the nursery, so that it doesn't become too prescriptive. That's why these are in line with my view of quality – for me it is a mix of legislation and guidance and being creative in meeting requirements, which staff need to be able to understand and unpick in order to provide what our families need the most.

Another manager painted the picture of the stark reality that teams have to cope with in order to meet quality standards. This is due to a range of factors that work to exert excessive pressure on teams who, in trying to achieve and maintain quality, struggle because expectations of providers are incompatible with their experiences.

> Legislative and guidance documents each have their own perspective of quality provision. This is great in essence but difficult in practice due to issues such

as ratios, the benefit cap and the two-year-old scheme. Each key person has a minimum of ten children, fifteen in some settings. Workload is high and key persons are not able to deliver the high quality to all children (time factor) as they will not be able to develop the special bond with their key children.

The factors identified by this manager are not uncommon in early years settings and the larger the setting, the more magnified the issues become. If teams are under-resourced it makes it that much harder to meet the needs of individual children. Providing an effective key person system was thus the most pressing issue in meeting quality requirements.

Question 3

This final question sought to elicit whether managers felt under pressure to conform to definitions of quality in legislative and guidance documents. The majority of managers (43 per cent) said yes, while 29 per cent said that it depends on certain issues, and 28 per cent said that they did not feel pressured to conform.

Do you feel under pressure to conform to definitions of quality in legislative and guidance documents?

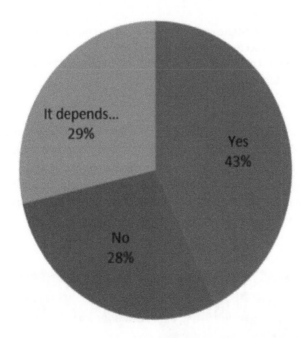

I do sometimes feel under pressure to conform but am lucky to have had good teachers who have taught me to look at things from different angles and perspectives. Our organisation is supportive of creativity and individuals are given scope to develop different approaches to meeting quality requirements as long as we can give a rationale to back our decisions.

Again, the need for creativity and freedom appears to be integral for managers in their quest for quality. When managers demonstrate the confidence to look at issues from a different perspective and dare to try different strategies to meet their objectives, the process and outcome can be very liberating and rewarding for them and their team. Leadership skills such as thinking and behaving creatively, having a problem-solving approach to difficulties and making failure a positive learning experience, each work to promote innovative practice. This, in turn, will equip teams to respond inventively and robustly to challenges in providing high quality care and education in today's diverse world.

Leigh (2009: 236) encourages senior staff and management to challenge convention so that teams do not become too constrained while trying to conform. He poses a set of questions that enables senior staff to think about how creativity can be fostered among their team. He asks:

> How much freedom does your team actually possess to try new ways of doing things? Are they so constrained by rules and conventions that there is little chance of anything more effective and productive emerging? How could you bend the rules and release the energy to invent?

Reflect on This

1   How do you demonstrate creative leadership to respond to the challenges and changes the sector faces?
2   What do you feel are the main constraints on creative leadership in the current climate?

To conclude, then, quality is something that everyone recognizes in one shape or form but for which no one can provide a universal definition. Achieving it thus requires practitioners to critically engage with the subject in order to draw their own conclusions based on their professional experience and the experiences of the children and families with whom they work. This makes the journey to achieving high quality provision that bit clearer and more attainable.

Suppose that children did not follow strict developmental patterns – what is the implication of that?

Related to the concept of quality is the issue of **developmentally appropriate practice (DAP)**. This American framework for best practice is grounded in research on child development and learning. A part of DAP is the assumption that the quality of practice can be determined by knowledge of child development. While this framework takes into account cultural and individual differences in children, it is largely based on Western societal norms of development and so may not be appropriate to apply for all children, causing us to underestimate the capabilities of some children and families.

Reconceptualists are critical of DAP because practitioners are guided by Western norms of development and therefore what is regarded as good quality is thus dictated by these norms. Given the diverse make-up of the children with whom practitioners work, these norms cannot be solely relied upon to inform practice as they are not actually based on children from different cultural and ethnic backgrounds. While these norms claim to take such individual differences into account, it is by no means the same as setting norms from cultures that stray from the Western perspective. Walsh (1997: 45) succinctly describes the role of culture in a child's development:

> Culture is both the context within which the child develops and the context into which the child develops. Development is best understood as the process of growing into a culture, in specific cultural and historical contexts.

What do you Think?

1 Which theory is Walsh's idea similar to?
2 What implications does it have for you and your team in the setting?

Children and families bring with them a wealth of experience that is often tied to their personal, cultural and religious backgrounds, and if practitioners are to better understand these and support the development of all children they need to consider more than one way of understanding children's behaviour, as opposed to relying predominantly on the developmental approach. Dahlberg, Moss and Pence (1999: 23) discuss the over-generalization that occurs when what is considered the 'norm' is adhered to:

> The developmental psychology we know is tied to a culture which produced it. In purveying what is advertised as a general, universalist model of development, developmental psychology is a vital ingredient in the globalisation of childhood.

Although a difficult feat to achieve, it is important to try not to subscribe to the grand knowledge base that is derived from this universalist perspective. Doing so serves to perpetuate the notion of a superior culture to the detriment of other non-Western cultures, which will in turn inhibit knowledge being produced and acted on from research that originates from 'other' cultures.

Adhering to frameworks for learning such as the EYFS (2012) requires practitioners to have a sound understanding of developmental norms and thus, to plan and implement activities as well as observe and make assessments based on their knowledge of child development. This should not mean that provision should entirely be based on ages and stages but all too commonly it is. This is partly due to the constant barrage of information concerning age and stage appropriateness of learning experiences, instead of redirecting the focus to developing new ways of understanding the unique child.

In today's fast-moving, super high-tech world, early years practitioners need to make the move away from such traditional concepts and dare to embrace alternative ways of understanding the child (for example, from a postmodern or post-colonial perspective). This can lead to a richer understanding of the child, one which acknowledges that children are powerful, intelligent and social – from birth.

Dahlberg, Moss and Pence (2009; 1999) posit that this is already happening, due to a fundamental change in thinking, which has resulted in a shift from interpreting the child from the concept of a found world, and instead, towards a concept of constructed worlds. This perspective places 'power' or agency in the hands of the child, who constructs knowledge and understanding of the world by interacting with it, exploring, investigating and drawing their own conclusions. When children and their families are afforded opportunities to construct their worlds in this way, it stands to reason that the concept of a 'found world' cannot and should not be used when examining child development and the theories therein.

In relation to this, Katz (2003) challenges the concept of what is deemed as developmentally appropriate and emphasizes the importance of questioning this. For example, 'how do educators know what children should be learning?' and 'how are children's "stages" of development determined?' In most cases unfortunately, the answer remains – through the Western lens. What is needed is a shift to viewing the child not from a developmentalist perspective but one that embraces the historical, cultural and social context of learning and development (Bruner, 1996).

In conclusion, it has been argued in this section that a more creative approach is needed when discussing individual children's development, which considers multiple perspectives of the factors affecting how a child develops. In today's multicultural society it is not enough, nor acceptable, to rely upon the traditional (i.e. Western) perspective of developmental norms. Children's ability to learn and thrive is dictated by a wide range of issues which vary greatly from one culture to another. The presence of war, quality of home experiences, learning difficulties that the child or their parents might have, access to education and healthcare as well as the child's individual temperament each influence a child's development and ability to thrive. Practitioners therefore need a robust understanding of these issues, and have the confidence to question norms. This way, expectations of children can be realistic, with learning experiences and support provided that are in line with their interests and needs – as opposed to being led by prescribed norms that have little meaning in practice.

Suppose parents had as much knowledge about parenting as the experts and could guide them as there is no right or wrong?

In this section we will discuss the issue of parenting in relation to power. We will explore where power lies when it comes to understanding parenting – or professionals would have us think it lies, and why this might be. We will also explore possible consequences if parents had as much knowledge about parenting as the experts. While reading, draw your own conclusions in relation to not only what you read but your experience of working with families and professionals that are in place to support them in the care and education of their children.

From the **post-structural perspective**, power does not reside with one body, nor is it absolute. It is viewed as more fluid, changing over time, depending on who it resides with. Conversely, power does not always have to be a negative force (Usher and Edwards, 1994). Foucault's ideas concerning power are also pertinent here. He believes that power continually shifts and no one can own it all the time because it is dynamic. According to Foucault (2009: 119):

> What makes power hold good, what makes it accepted, is simply the fact that it doesn't only weigh on us as a force that says no, but that it traverses and produces things, it induces pleasure, forms knowledge, produces discourse.

In light of the post-structural perspective of power, certain aspects of early years practice need to be reflected on and viewed differently. Take, for example, the issue of parental partnerships. Practitioners are constantly reminded of the need to build and maintain effective partnerships with parents, for the sake of their children. The EYFS (2012) and The Children Act (2004) reinforce the importance of sharing information with parents and liaising with them concerning their children's welfare, but to what extent can this be achieved in reality? Some parents are happy to get involved in their child's education and are confident in their role. Some, however, are not as confident – nor able to give their children the love and care that they deserve, while others are suspicious of the motivation of services which are seen as remote and judgemental. Where families put their child at risk and fail to meet their basic needs, it is difficult to distribute power equally between professionals and parents as they often have to make decisions on behalf of the child and their family to safeguard their well-being.

What do you Think?

1   Given that legislation and policies are devised by authorities, how can power be distributed evenly among parents and practitioners?
2   How can the partnership between parents and practitioners:
   ● encourage the sharing of power?
   ● inhibit the sharing of power?
3   What might be some of the issues in giving equal power to parents?

Parenting is as complex as it is diverse. We each have our guiding principles and opinions on how best to look after and educate children based upon our childhood experiences, cultural background and ability. For these reasons, when it comes to differentiating between what is right or wrong, there are clear occasions in which professionals must act and assert power in order to safeguard the well-being of children. This may seem difficult when there are contentious issues due to some religious and cultural practices which have led some parents and guardians to harm their children. However, experience of such cases show that early intervention carried out by practitioners who act rigorously and consistently is required.

The tragic child abuse cases over recent years in which a range of multi-disciplinary professionals failed to protect children provide further evidence of the importance of active and early intervention in such cases. Thus, when it comes to knowledge and power, practitioners need to be confident in exerting power in order to protect vulnerable children. This is easier said than done when some practitioners lack sufficient knowledge about certain religions and cultures and, consequently, do not feel confident enough to question or challenge aspects of their practice that are opposed to protecting and promoting the basic rights of children.

Generally, when parents are included in their child's education and are enabled to take an active role in this, the outcomes are better for all concerned (Desforges and Abouchaar, 2003). The various strategies that are employed by settings to encourage the sharing of knowledge and power between staff and parents are a far cry from some policies of the 1960s which prohibited parents from entering the school gates. Parents are now actively encouraged to share their opinions and be proactive in their child's life at nursery, with links to home learning promoted. It is also now acknowledged that because parents often see things from a practical angle, their input can be highly valuable in terms of influencing changes to policy and practice in early years settings.

Concluding thoughts

In conclusion, it is up to practitioners to think critically about how they can encourage parents to contribute to the running of the setting – be it sharing skills, taking on parent governor roles or even helping them to enrol on courses to become, for example, learning support or nursery assistants. Any team that claims to look to their parents as 'experts' needs to be mindful of the fact this includes some potentially challenging issues – for example, acknowledging their different and sometimes opposing (religious, cultural and personal) views and that ultimately, power does reside with legislators, policy makers and curricular frameworks, each of which exist to uphold the rights of the child to be safe, healthy and to play. Where teams can achieve this shift in power relationships through innovative practice, there is greater scope to include parents as authentic partners who can guide practitioners in the planning and delivery of services that take into account their expertise. This way, the different voices will culminate in a richer knowledge base in which knowledge is 'permitted' to be flexible, have multiple interpretations and be open to change.

Reconceptualizm in Practice

- Challenge universal givens and the hierarchy of knowledge.
- Accept that there are many truths and realities and all are valid.
- Reject the authoritarian concept of what knowledge is.
- Seek out the multiple perspectives of knowledge which exist.
- Redistribute power less hierarchically between practitioners, parents and children.

Ideas into Action

Now that you have familiarized yourself with some key ideas of reconceptualizm to early years development and care, make the links to practice in your setting by reflecting upon and completing the following:

1a Do you think there is an over-emphasis on developmental theory in early childhood education? Please explain your answer.

1b List the advantages and disadvantages of closely adhering to developmental theory as part of your practice.

2   How do you create space and time to listen to children's views?

3   What is the value of disrupting (or questioning) how quality is defined in early childhood education?

Challenge the Theorists

1 How do the dynamics of power and knowledge impact your partnership with parents?

2 In your opinion, what value does challenging long-held beliefs concerning early childhood education have in your daily work with children?

3 How are children, parents and staff actively encouraged to challenge stereotypes? (For example, stereotypes pertaining to culture, race, class, gender and learning difficulties.)

The Contemporary Legacy of Reconceptualizing Early Years Education

Knowledge base concerning development from conception to three

- Socio-emotional learning
- Qualifications of the workforce
- The role of very early experiences on all-round development

Creating inclusive and enabling environments

- Cultural participation
- Socio-cultural learning
- Behavioural and academic expectations

Importance of parents and the home learning environment

- Countering poverty and socio-economic disadvantage

Links to other theorists

- Gunilla Dahlberg
- Peter Moss
- Alan Pence
- Daniel Walsh
- Michel Foucault

Further Reading

Dahlberg, G., Moss, P. and Pence, A. (1999) *Beyond Quality in Early Childhood Education and Care*. London: Falmer Press.

> The authors take a reconceptualist position as they present a range of issues which they problematize. Key concepts are described, such as power, children's choices in their education and quality are deconstructed, which enable the reader to reflect on their personal views and perhaps even alter aspects of these in light of the authors' arguments against universal truths. They offer a sharp critique of centrally prescribed quality standards and suggest the whole concept of quality has become problematic and an unhelpful way to think about service delivery.

Yelland, N. (2005) *Critical Issues in Early Childhood Education*. Maidenhead: Open University Press.

This book takes a critical look at issues concerning child development and early childhood education, which encourage the reader to challenge long-held beliefs and traditions. The 15 chapters are written by different teachers, practitioners, professors and researchers, focusing on a range of pertinent issues, with questions for reflection. This book is an excellent introduction to the reconceptualization of early childhood.

Bringing the Theories Alive – How to Undertake Action Research in Your Setting

14

This penultimate chapter is all about **action research** and you – the reflective practitioner. Now that you have read about some of the more pertinent theories concerning child development and how they help to explain and support our thinking about some of the current issues in early years, this chapter will describe how to conduct a small piece of action research together with your team in the work setting. As you read, you will learn about action research (also known as practitioner research), how to carry out a small-scale study and some of the reasons why it might be useful to do so. We are aware of different methodological approaches to research but we have chosen to focus on action research as we believe this is often the most fruitful for practitioner researchers.

Why should I bother?

The ultimate goal of improving practice is to ensure that children and their families reap the benefits of a high quality service that meets their all-round needs. Given that families are so diverse and so many have complex needs, this makes it all the more necessary to engage in the process of on-going evaluation, change and improvement in order to ensure that this can and does happen. Kurt Lewin (1951: 169) succinctly captures the need to integrate theory and practice in this well-known statement:

> There is nothing so practical as a good theory.

Theory without practical application is of little use to anyone, and this is a lesson that many early years practitioners still need to embrace. During your experience of working with children and their families, you might well have had a 'hunch' or a hypothesis concerning certain aspects of provision in your setting. Although your hypothesis might be correct, unless you do something about it, you cannot hope to move your practice on. Elliot (1991: 69) highlights the link between practice and theories, stressing the interdependence of the two:

> Action research theories are not validated independently and then applied to practice. They are validated through practice.

The concept of **praxis** is therefore critical here. Praxis is the idea that theory and practice are inextricably linked and cannot be separated, with theory informing practice and practice informing the development of theories (Pascal and Bertram, 2012; McNiff et al., 1996). Early years practitioners therefore need to see themselves as *reflective practitioners* – capable of generating new knowledge based on their action research. Schön (1983: 68) encompasses the importance of not only generating new information but allowing oneself to modify existing beliefs and ways of behaving in light of this new information:

> The practitioner allows herself to experience surprise, puzzlement, or confusion in a situation which she finds uncertain or unique. She reflects on the phenomenon before her, and on the prior understandings which have been implicit in her behaviour. She carries out an experiment which serves to generate both a new understanding of the phenomenon and a change in the situation.

So the two main goals of action research are:

- To make improvements to practice in a setting
- To generate new knowledge or theories

Given that one of the main goals of action research is to produce change in a setting, embracing change is an issue that needs to be carefully considered by the practitioner researcher. But the initial change in attitudes and consequently practice, can be daunting, and resistance to change might be a barrier that you will have to overcome. Some possible reasons for this could be:

- Fear of the unknown – staff might not understand the proposed change or their role in bringing about the change.
- Some staff might feel that the identified issues and proposed changes are direct criticisms of their practice.
- They might feel insecure about contributing effectively to the process of change.
- They might feel exhausted at the rate of change in the setting, which can prevent consolidation of knowledge, with staff not being able to embed themselves in practice.

Your responsibility as a reflective practitioner ultimately, is to provide high quality provision that promotes the well-being and outcomes for all children. This is all the more crucial for children experiencing poverty and disadvantage, where effective early years education and care can help ameliorate the impact of disadvantage (Field Report, 2010). It can also provide useful evidence about the impact and outcomes of your practice, which helps in the accountability demand. Well-informed **reflective practice** is therefore extremely useful to all concerned. The message here, then, is that it's not enough to 'sit back' and observe change taking place; it is about creating a culture of reflection across your setting, for the benefit of the children, which includes encouraging the contributions of all staff. This can, in turn, instil a sense of ownership and responsibility among the team – not only in seeing the unfolding of the action research process through but in raising standards of provision. Action research is therefore a useful tool for increasing the professionalization of the early years workforce.

What is action research?

Action research can be described as a lived experience, due to the practitioner taking on the role of researcher, 'leading' the team on a joint journey of discovery. For this reason it is also described as a 'living inquiry' (Wicks et al., 2008). Kemmis and McTaggart (2005: 564) say action research:

> Involves learning about the real, material, concrete, and particular practices of particular people in particular places.

Action research is mainly a practical activity, involving the contribution of (for example) staff working together in a nursery, to make changes to their practice. From the action research process, new knowledge or theories are created. It doesn't seek to reproduce knowledge, and generally, findings and conclusions from one action research project in one setting cannot be **replicated** in another, although there may be some transferable learning. This is partly because action research usually evolves from a problem within a setting that is often small-scale and only affects those involved, thus solutions are specific to the participants only. McTaggart (1988) refers to action research as 'collective self-reflective enquiry' that participants undertake in order to improve the rationality of their own social and educational practices. The notion of collective self-reflective enquiry is a good working definition that grounds the concept of action research firmly in the realm of the practitioner.

Kurt Lewin (1946) was a seminal theorist who is most commonly known for putting action research into practice during the 1940s in the United States. He is also credited for coining the term action research. Lewin used action research as a tool to devise strategies to overcome problems in a social context, for example, the workplace – which is what it is used for in a range of diverse work settings today. Action research also draws upon the input of those involved, making it a collective process. His action research model is still used today to help guide professionals through their action research projects.

His model is shown below.

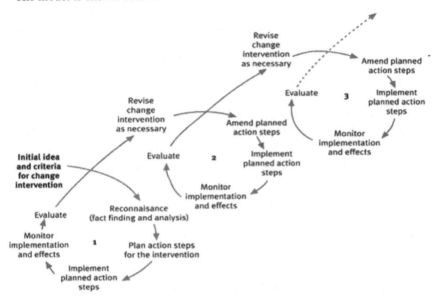

As you can see, the model proposes a spiral of three distinct steps. Each step is represented as a circle of **planning**, **action** and **reconnaissance (fact-finding)** about your results of the actions. The cycle can (and should) be repeated as many times as you deem necessary. Other key theorists in this field such as McNiff (1988) and Whitehead (1987) have extended on the concept of a spiral, proposing that instead, the action research process consists of spirals upon spirals. This is due to the original question often changing and leading to further questions, which results in other related issues being identified.

The basic action research spiral is described as follows:

1   The first step is to examine the idea carefully, using resources available. Further fact-finding about the situation is usually required. If this first step (or stage) of planning is successful, two items emerge: namely, an overall plan of how to reach the objective and secondly, a decision with regard to the first step of action. Usually this planning has also somewhat modified the original idea (Lewin, 1946).

2   The next step consists of a circle of planning, executing (carrying out your plan), and reconnaissance (fact-finding concerning your question) in order to evaluate the results of the second step, and prepare the rational basis for planning the third step, and for perhaps modifying again the overall plan.

3   This final step is a repetition of the first steps, which is carried out in light of any changes to your initial question and resulting modifications to your actions in the initial process. The above three steps can be repeated iteratively and several times until you achieve your goal.

Put another way, the whole cycle consists of *planning, doing* and *reviewing*. Once you have grasped the basic process of action research, you can begin to make it your plan. The start of your personal and professional journey into action research might begin with the question '*How do I improve my work?*'. You thus need to know the principles that influence your practice (so that you are clear about what you do and why you do it). This generally involves four aspects:

1 Imagining a solution
2 Implementing the solution
3 Evaluating the solution
4 Changing practice in light of the evaluation

A word of caution – what you think is a 'small' issue might be symptomatic of much wider ones. This will require you to be ready to adopt a robust style to solving the 'problems' that you initially identified in your setting. This is why the small problems may be symptoms of a larger and deeper values-based issue.

Some areas that you might instigate change in could be:

- How can I improve the quality of the key person system?
- How can we improve the setting's provision of educational experiences for babies?
- How can we improve the effectiveness of joint problem solving between practitioners and children during play?
- How can we improve the support system provided to promote children's language?
- How can we assess the suitability of resources for children with learning difficulties?
- How can we improve the status of the child's voice in our curriculum planning?
- How can we build on the setting's partnerships within the community?
- How can we build on our parent and staff relationships?

What do you Think?

1 Reflect upon an area of provision in your nursery that you think needs improving
2 Why do you think it needs improving?
3 What evidence have you gathered that supports your concern?
4 Could this issue be indicative of any underlying issues in the setting? Briefly explain.
5 What can you do to change this issue?
6 Make a note of what evidence you will need to gather as part of your investigation.
7 How could you ensure that your findings are accurate?
8 How can you modify practice in light of your findings?

Below is an account provided by a Deputy Nursery Manager who, upon noticing a recurrent problem in her setting, decided to act on it, as part of her action research project on a programme of study. Read it and answer the questions that follow.

Case Study

In my current setting, I had noticed that generally, our outdoor provision for play wasn't as good as it could be. The same equipment would be out in the outdoor area (i.e. balls, bikes and scooters). There was nothing that really encouraged children to try 'risky play'. Obviously practitioners are afraid to carry out risky activities because of the danger element and are afraid of their children being hurt. That said, I felt that these risky activities should be explored at a young age, because as with life at all ages, difficult situations need to be overcome and promoting the self-confidence to do so, starts at the earliest age. Also, the risk of danger is minimal as long as activities are initially risk-assessed and well supervised.

To show that there was an issue, I wrote observations of children at play, made note of plans for outdoor play, the equipment they played with and how staff interacted with the children. I also conducted several semi-structured interviews with practitioners, to find out their choice of 'risky activity' for children and the majority replied 'the climbing frame'. Those who said this also said that they wouldn't put it out frequently because they were scared of accidents.

I tried to promote 'risky play' in my setting by initially creating a presentation for my colleagues (and to my study group, who were also senior early years practitioners). As part of this I shared my results, which all staff found quite surprising as they 'didn't realize it was that bad'. I made my presentation very interactive and with the input of my team, we created an action plan for change. This took three months to carry out, as we had to make changes to our whole approach to 'risky' play'. This involved me asking our training department to deliver training, and appointing a practitioner to monitor progress of the change by gathering evidence which we then reviewed at different points of the process. I also designated different staff the responsibility for carrying out a range of risky activities with the children which worked really well.

The outcome was really positive. The whole team is now more confident in providing 'riskier' activities, they aren't as scared to try out new and exciting activities and they now look forward to such valuable experiences. The children have definitely benefited from it – they all want to have a go and feel so proud knowing that they've tried something new, or something that they used to be unsure about. The boys in particular took more risks at the beginning but then after a little while the girls joined in just the same as the boys. I didn't think I could get the whole team motivated but giving everyone a voice and supporting them to make the change, made it work for us.

What do you Think?

1 What do you think your role involves in the action research process?
2 How would you ensure that everyone contributes to the process of creating change?
3 What would you do to make sure that the change is maintained and monitored for effectiveness?

Adopting a qualitative approach immerses you (the researcher) in the 'thick of it', learning from fellow practitioners and seeking answers to problems collectively. Engaging in dialogue as you investigate with colleagues opens up a rich world, full of various interpretations, which you can then 'unpack' in order to build the bigger picture. Once you have a rough idea of what is going on, you can then start to use different methods to draw your conclusions and find ways to best modify practice.

How do I carry out a small-scale study?

As long as you have an idea of the issue you want to explore, or know that you want to change an aspect of your provision, action research need not be a difficult process. Below is an outline of the basic phases of action research offered by McNiff (2002), whatever the initial inquiry or question might be. This outline also works as your action plan for change:

- We review our current practice
- identify an aspect that we want to investigate
- imagine a way forward
- try it out
- take stock of what happens
- we modify what we are doing in the light of what we have found, and continue working in this new way (try another option if the new way of working is not right)
- monitor what we do
- review and evaluate the modified action
- and so the cycle continues.

Now that you have a clear idea of the steps to take as an action researcher, you also need to pay close attention to some related issues that you need to address all throughout your action research. For example, how will you show that you have considered the different ethical issues? What methods will you use to collect and interpret your data (or evidence)? What will inform your decision? How will you ensure that everyone including your colleagues is treated fairly during the process? How will you use the evidence that you gather? Who will you share your results with? These questions will now be answered in turn.

Choosing the best *methodology* (your rationale for selecting your data collection methods) for your action research is key. Your methodology will be influenced by your values which will underpin the entire action research process. Hughs (2001: 32) defines methodology as:

> What to investigate, how to investigate it, what to measure or assess and how to do so.

Undertaking action research involves the researcher adhering to an **interpretivist paradigm**. This paradigm (or perspective) assumes that there is no one version of the truth and that multiple versions of the truth exist among those involved in the research context. This means that knowledge gained from the interpretivist paradigm does not seek to make generalizations about the world, but instead to gain detailed insight into an issue that occurs in one context.

Thus, the researcher can immerse themselves in the process as they elicit and interpret the views of those involved in the process, and draw their conclusions using appropriate methods.

How do I collect my data?

There are two main methods used to gather data as part of the action research process. These are:

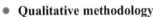
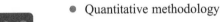

- Quantitative methodology
- **Qualitative methodology**

Due to this chapter focusing on action research, only the qualitative method will be explored, given that this method best lends itself to gathering detailed data about the improvement of practice within a professional setting.

Qualitative research is chiefly concerned with finding out the opinions and values of individuals in a specific context, which results in the researcher obtaining multiple interpretations of a situation. This approach, which looks into the quality of responses, draws upon semi-structured interviews, participant observations and case studies of those involved in the action research process. It is a sound idea to draw upon a range of methods to gather your evidence, in order to ensure that you not only capture the different perspectives of participants but also that your data produces similar answers. This is referred to as **triangulation** of methods. MacNaughton, Rolfe and Siraj-Blatchford (2004: 53) say that:

> Qualitative research is concerned with the quality of the data it produces, rather than just the quantity ... aiming to learn about it in terms of the people involved.

> ## What do you Think?
>
> 1 How might you ensure values about different approaches to raising young children are congruent in your setting?
> 2 What methods would you choose?
> 3 How will these methods help you to elicit the information you would require to move practice on?

Ethics

The issue of **ethics** in all research and action research is critical. Ethics, or rules of conduct as described by Reynolds (1979), refer to the ethical/moral considerations of a research study. MacNaughton, Rolfe and Blatchford (2004: 270) define ethics as:

> A consideration of the effects of the research on the rights and well-being of those who may be affected by the research.

The rationale underpinning action research is learning through practice – a learning journey that is open, honest and democratic. Adhering closely to an ethical code during your process will enable you to achieve personal and professional learning from which all stakeholders can benefit. The issue of power is therefore central to the process of action research and practitioner researchers have to be very careful about power and ethics. Action research can be a highly effective tool in enabling the workforce to gain recognition and credibility for its generation of new knowledge – but this needs to be achieved in a climate of trust, openness and democracy. Pascal and Bertram (2012: 9) say:

> We have to reflect more critically on how to more authentically realise the participatory practice we strive for. This requires courage, risk taking, and further innovation, alongside a more rigorous and critical engagement in the redistribution of power and the living out of ethics. This could give us the chance to achieve more open, inclusive, democratic research that has the capacity to answer the deeper questions we face in developing ECEC in the 21st century.

A few simple yet important ways to make sure your action research meets ethical standards are as follows.

Seeking consent from participants

Once you have explained the purpose of the action research and how your findings will be used, and that all information provided will be treated with the strictest confidentiality, you will need to obtain your colleagues' permission for their participation. (This can be done via a letter.)

Conversely, where individuals feel strongly opposed to participating, they have the right not to participate and need to be informed of this from the outset. This of course includes children and parents, as well as practitioners. This means that you will need to think carefully about how you request permission, taking special care with the young, the vulnerable and those who find expressing their views more difficult. It is important that all potential participants understand their rights in the research process.

Telling participants that they are free to opt out of the action research process at any point if they feel uneasy

You should inform participants at the start of the process, that they are free to leave at any point should they wish to do so. Your colleagues will want to support you in wanting to improve practice in your setting and most will want to 'get on board' but for one reason or another, some will not be able to commit to the whole journey (Robson, 1993). Reflecting on personal values and practice can prove too much for some individuals and a lack of time to commit may also be an issue for some, so it's important that you inform them they can opt out should they feel the need.

Acknowledging feelings arising from the process

If you are leading the process, you need to inform participants that they are free to express their feelings if they felt uncomfortable with any aspects of the procedure, which might include being recorded. If this is the case, you can use alternative methods such as a questionnaire which will still enable you to obtain the information you require. This will prove important in helping the participants feel comfortable during the process and in ensuring that the power is more equal between you (the action researcher) and participants. As long as your methods are specific, ethical and doable (Roberts-Holmes, 2005), straying from your initial plan a little will not affect the outcome of your action research. At the end of the process you should also thank the participants for their contributions as well as share your findings with them at the end of the process. From this you can begin your discussion of your action plan for change – in line with your initial research question.

Co-constructing ethics with participants

Co-constructing the ethics of your research with participants will encourage a sense of ownership on their part. Moreover, it will send the message that with rights come responsibilities which both parties must respect, in order to ensure that it is an equitable experience for all concerned. Once the ethics are co-constructed, it will make for a more productive and open partnership as the participants can exercise a degree of control over the process as well as being clear about the reasons for the research and how the findings will be utilized.

Objectivity versus subjectivity in action research

Action research is subjective. Due to its interpretivist nature, practitioners undertaking action research embrace intimacy or closeness to the subjects of study, not distance – i.e. we are attached not detached in the process. João and Júlia Formosinho's (2012) informative research findings concerning participatory research are worth looking at for further information if you are interested in learning more about the dynamics of power and democratic participation in research.

McNiff (2002: 4) explains that:

> Action research is very subjective as its methodology is defined by the individual researcher, so it is difficult to provide a philosophical framework to encompass all action research studies.

Think of yourself conducting a small piece of action research in your setting – not only would you be leading the project but you will also be immersed in the whole process. Typically this means selecting the best methods to obtain the information you need, interviewing your colleagues, interpreting their responses while trying to remain unbiased as well as drawing your conclusions and making useful recommendations. This makes the issue of subjectivity and trustworthiness all the more significant because as a practitioner researcher, it is a challenge to do all of these things while making sure that your research is rigorous and credible throughout.

What do you Think?

How might you ensure that your findings are trustworthy, even though the action research process is subjective in nature?

Pascal and Bertram (2012: 2) posit that the concept of praxis is no longer sufficient in itself and that practitioner researchers need to actively engage with the dynamics of ethics and power throughout the whole process in the creation of new theories that are authentic and trustworthy. They suggest:

> Praxis in itself is not enough, and to authentically realise a participatory paradigm in our work requires us to develop a worldview in which reflection

(phronesis) and action (praxis) done in conjunction with others, needs to be immersed within a much more astute awareness about power (politics) and a sharpened focus on values (ethics) in all of our thinking and actions. We see this mix of phronesis, praxis, ethics and power at the heart of what we increasingly recognise as a 'praxeological' worldview in modern early childhood research.

We gain rigour or trustworthiness by checking out our findings with other participants and making sure we have obtained various perspectives (which we achieve through triangulation of methods). Given that our judgements will always be influenced by personal experience, emotion or bias, checking your views against your colleagues involved in the action research and triangulating your findings will help ensure that your research includes these different voices. This in turn will create a more democratic process due to the multiple perspectives and understandings being elicited.

What do you Think?

1 Why might taking an objective position as an action researcher be problematic?

Who do I get on board?

Action research is always done *with* people – not *to* them. The process is thus participatory and should always be democratic, so as to encourage a whole team approach in the generation of new knowledge. It is carried out by you – the practitioner or anyone else in the setting who is familiar with the context and can put the results into practice. Colleagues, children and parents are often included in the action research process, depending on the nature of the inquiry and the evidence required. The following questions are designed to help you to think about some of the choices you would make as a researcher and participant when instigating change in your setting. Read them and respond as you find most appropriate.

What do you Think?

You are concerned about the quality of your setting's educational experiences for babies.

1a   Who would you involve in the action research?

1b   How will your choice of participants help you to collect the evidence that you need?

1c   How will you obtain informed consent from these babies?

2   What methods will you use to ensure these very young children's voices are listened to as part of the research process?

3   How will you ensure that practitioners do not feel attacked or unduly criticized by comments or findings made during research process?

As mentioned in the introduction, our aim is to help you to think deeper about what you do and why.

Using action research theories will support you and your colleagues to discover the underlying assumptions you have about your work and to advance your practice (Pascal and Bertram, 2010, personal written communication) by enabling you to adopt a fresh approach to existing practice. By drawing upon the viewpoints of all participants in the action research process, your findings will be strengthened due to the range of interpretations sought. This will ultimately serve to build the **validity** of the research.

As researcher and participant, you will also need to be psychologically and emotionally prepared to take the good with the bad. This might include knowing how to manage divergence in opinions, loss of motivation in the action research and receiving on-going feedback. This can at times, be uncomfortable to take on board, but is an inevitable aspect of change-oriented research. MacNaughton (2005: 294) says:

> At its core, action research is about activism and working towards emancipation and social justice, and as a methodology it requires much of both the participants and the researcher. It is change-oriented and anyone involved must be prepared to confront themselves and each other and be changed.

Take a look at the following action plan. It has been successfully used by a number of nursery teams in one organization, to help them start their action research, following a training session on what it is, how to carry out the process and how to devise a plan that would help them utilize findings.

This plan is easy to follow for those of you new to action research. You might want to explore if this kind of format would work in your setting.

Action Plan

Complete this Action Plan, based on one area of provision in your nursery that you think needs to be improved. You should share this completed Action Plan with your Manager and carry out the action research process in your nursery team in order to find a resolution to your identified issue.

Name:
Nursery:
Timeline for completion of action research process:

1 **What do you want to research?**
2 **Why?**
3 **What are you going to do?**
4 **How will you involve your team?**
5 **Is the research just for your nursery, or could it be wider?**
6 **What are your steps?**
7 **How will you know if it's worked?**
8 **Feedback to your team.**

Concluding thoughts

In conclusion, action research is a key element of the professionalization of the workforce. It provides the means through which you can instigate improvements to your provision and create new knowledge and theories in early childhood. The ideas that we have provided for you to try out in this chapter are designed to help you to get thinking reflectively about your practice and to start making changes. It is also part of the profession reclaiming the change process for yourselves and taking responsibility for informing yourselves and others about how to move the quality of practice forward. This will make practice improvement more powerful and effective for those involved and ensure development is owned and located by those whom it affects, including children and families.

Action research in Practice

- Taking a critical look at your existing provision.
- Questioning aspects of your practice, both individually and within your team.
- Speaking the language of action research with staff and children.
- Encouraging all staff to get into the habit of gathering evidence, to help inform change.
- Involving the children and parents in the process of change.
- Using your evidence to help make policy changes in your setting.

- Embedding critical reflective practice in the daily life of your setting.
- Providing opportunities for dialogue and the co-construction of practice with those who experience it at the front line.

Ideas into Action

1 Why should ethical considerations underpin research processes and outcomes?
2 Identify two ways in which you would ensure the trustworthiness and credibility of your research.

Challenge the Theorists

1 Given that action research is interpretative, can objective knowledge be created which is not biased in favour of the researcher?

2 How far does action research promote the professionalization of the workforce given that the results it produces cannot be generalized?

3 How realistic is it to expect practitioners to undertake action research, given the existing demands placed on them?

Action Research – its Contemporary Legacy

Knowledge base concerning development from conception to three
- Socio-emotional learning
- Qualifications of the workforce
- The role of very early experiences on development

Creating inclusive and enabling environments
- Cultural participation
- Socio-cultural learning
- The role of a support network in promoting language development

Importance of parents and the home learning environment
- The centrality of emotional-social development
- The impact of positive early interactions
- Countering poverty and socio-economic disadvantage

Links to other theorists
- Jean McNiff
- Jack Whitehead
- Patricia Lomax
- Glenda Mac Naughton
- Sharne Rolfe
- Donald Schön
- Chris Pascal and Tony Bertram
- Júlia and João Formosinho
- Paulo Freire

Further Reading

Bruce, T. (2006) *Early Childhood: A Guide for Students*. London: SAGE.

> Chapter 26 of this book is all about practitioner research. It contains a discussion on the nature and necessity of research, as well as guidance on how to carry out the different research tasks and the benefits of undertaking research. It is easy to read and the exercises serve as useful catalysts for ideas that you can put into action.

MacNaughton, G., Rolfe, S. A. and Siraj-Blatchford, I. (2004) *Doing Early Childhood Research. International Perspectives on Theory and Practice.* Maidenhead: McGraw Hill. Open University Press.

> This is an excellent book for those new to conducting research as well as those who are very experienced in the process, as it provides comprehensive and step-by-step guidance on how to carry out research (and action research). Part of this guidance includes a range of international case studies, which enable the reader to understand exactly what is required of the researcher and participants. Related key issues are also examined such as ethics, paradigm, design and review of literature. The glossary of terms is helpful in clarifying understanding of commonly used terms in early childhood research.

McNiff, J. and Whitehead, J. (2009) *Doing and Writing Action Research*. London: SAGE.

> This is an excellent and very readable book for those who require detailed guidance concerning how to write up their action research. Some space is given to the importance of undertaking action research and how to do this, but the principle aim of this book is to provide information concerning what the report needs to consist of and how to write a high quality report.

Back to the Future: Lessons from the Past into the Present

15

What this chapter is about

This final chapter provides an overall synthesis of each of the theories explored in the book in relation to a range of contemporary issues which are challenging the early years sector. Theories, unlike issues, tend to remain constant. However, sometimes they do get revised, with some of the more traditional or long-standing theories being challenged due to critique and advances in technology. For example, the fact that young children are now exposed to more interactive forms of entertainment means that they are displaying a different set of skills compared with three or four decades previously and this change affects theories of child development (Schore and Schore, 2007; Dowling, 2004). The issues faced by early years practitioners also shift as society progresses and populations change. For example, we see greater access to health and social care, more government initiatives to alleviate the effects of poverty, more state intervention in family life and increased expectations and guidance for parents to support their children's learning and development from birth.

Nevertheless, we believe long-standing theories can still have great relevance in today's world of practice. Given this dynamic context, for this discussion we have taken the main tenets of the theories past and present, and made a direct link between these and a set of issues that have been identified by practitioners as most pressing in their work today. We believe that it's critical to have a sense of the past in order to better understand the present; and given that some of the challenges facing parents and practitioners have a long legacy in early childhood practice, the strategies and resources that we can access today are often rooted in past experiences and thinking. In short, the theories included in this book have been selected and reflected upon simply because they have a resonance in today's world.

How the information can help you to enhance your professional skills

The information presented in this chapter is designed to help you to think critically – not just about the issues that you deal with in your setting today, but those impacting more widely in the sector. Consequently, we hope that this summary of the most pertinent theories, and their links to current issues, will equip you to ask further questions concerning aspects of your provision and also inspire you to carry out small-scale research projects in your setting with the aim to improve your practice. While reading, we suggest that you continually ask yourself, '*How are these theories helping me to think about issues differently?*' A combination of questions, case studies and suggestions for practice which relate to each issue, are included to exemplify the issues faced by practitioners.

The three contemporary issues will now be explored in turn, each of which contains related sub-issues. These are signposted under sub-headings, to make it easy and quick to find the information that might be of relevance to you. We hope that all the theories and ideas presented in the chapters on reconceptualization and action research will inform and underpin your critical stance as you reflect on each of the three contemporary issues in this final chapter. These ideas encourage you to question the assumptions, terminologies and values that are embedded in the issue as is positioned in the discussion below and to reflect upon what is emphasized and what is left out. We hope that this will also encourage you to raise your own further questions and to seek additional evidence through undertaking your own research and action in your workplace.

The three contemporary issues and their related sub-issues are as follows:

1 **Knowledge base concerning development from conception to three**
   - Socio-emotional learning
   - Qualifications of the workforce
   - The role of very early experiences on development

2 **Creating inclusive and enabling environments**
   - Cultural participation
   - Socio-cultural learning
   - The role of a support network in promoting language development
   - Behavioural and academic expectations

3 **Importance of parents and the home learning environment (HLE)**
   - The centrality of emotional-social development
   - The impact of positive early interactions
   - Countering poverty and socio-economic disadvantage

Contemporary issues facing the early years sector today

Knowledge base concerning development from conception to three

Socio-emotional learning

The period from conception to three years plays a critical role in determining the well-being and development of children, especially in the longer term. Personal, social and emotional development, physical development and communication literacy are therefore at the centre of the revised EYFS, forming the prime areas of learning. This shift to a more learning-oriented programme with lots of interaction, stimulation and action reinforces the sheer importance of this period – and in turn, the place of early years provision in providing high quality care and education.

The early years sector is currently benefiting from understanding more about the abilities of young babies from birth than ever before. This is due to advances in technology that enable us to actually see how experiences and emotions affect the brain's wiring during those first few critical years following birth. Renewed government interest in early years provision and its positive impact on child development (Truss, 2012; Department for Education and Skills, 2010) has also put early years provision in the public eye.

The importance of the first three years of a child's life cannot be overemphasized. It is during these early years that a child grows and develops most rapidly in terms of learning how to walk, talk, and form attachments. Between late pregnancy through to the second year the brain is in a critical period of accelerated growth (Teaching and Learning Research Programme, 2007); children thus need to receive the best possible start in life in order to help ensure they grow into confident individuals who are able to achieve their potential. This includes enjoying optimum care and education from both primary carers and early years practitioners.

Practitioners working with babies need to understand them and all that they attempt to communicate in order to meet their needs for love, stimulation and care. Furthermore, in order to understand how babies and children can form multiple attachments (Rutter, 1979; Ainsworth, 1971) and the conditions that are necessary to enable this, one would also need to be familiar with the original concept of attachment (Bowlby, 1953). This way, informed decisions about their emotional development can be made. It is, after all, the early experience of the baby that lays the foundations for a secure and happy childhood – and adulthood. O'Sullivan believes that:

> The early experience of the baby lays the foundations for a secure and happy childhood and optimistic adulthood. So be kinder to babies and the world will be a better place. (O'Sullivan, October 2012. Personal written communication)

Qualifications of the workforce

There is unequivocal evidence that the existing knowledge and skills of practitioners working with infants from birth to three needs to be of a level that enables them to meet the diverse needs of this age group. This means the competencies and skills of the current and future early years workforce needs to be significantly upgraded and enhanced, as currently England has an underqualified and undertrained workforce. There is a long-term Government strategy to reform and restructure wage and qualifications for early years practitioners and to upgrade the minimum entrance level into the profession. It is widely agreed (Nutbrown, 2012) that working with our youngest children requires an advanced level of skill and professionalism.

Practitioners who work with babies and young children are at the front line in terms of supporting parents by promoting well-being and development in partnership with them. This is all the more important where parents experience on-going difficulty and require support in providing a safe, nurturing environment for their children. Where practitioners are qualified and hold relevant experience, they can help make all the difference to children's outcomes – both in the present and their future. Nutbrown and Page (2008: 58) assert that:

> For 'teachers' we should now read 'practitioners' and/or 'educators' because everyone who works with young children needs to have a secure knowledge base from which they help young children to learn and also to make judgements about their developmental needs on a daily basis.

The argument for a well-trained workforce is clear when the outcome involves better educational achievement of all children that starts with an enriching early years experience. In recognition of this, the UK Government has committed, from 2013, to provide free early education for the most economically disadvantaged 20 per cent of two-year-olds. This opportunity makes it all the more important for practitioners to be adequately skilled and knowledgeable concerning their role when working with children from birth to three years, particularly those who are most vulnerable. Sue Gregory, the regulator's director of education (2012), also wants to see early years practitioners educated to a higher level, to ensure a minimum knowledge and skills set which babies and young children can benefit from. This would be a timely change given that early years workers, although undoubtedly doing vital, life-changing work, are low-paid and low-status and overwhelmingly women, and this reinforces the notion that actually the work is unimportant 'childcare' which itself seems to contradict the Government message that this work is vital – if it is so vital, why is it not properly recognized and rewarded?

The revised EYFS (2012) also emphasizes the need for a well-trained workforce, in order to ensure quality provision for all children from birth to five years, provided by staff who are passionate, knowledgeable and attuned to children's needs, temperament and current interests. Sufficient qualifications combined with regular and ongoing training can help ensure that all staff are competent and confident in meeting the care and development needs of the babies and young children in their setting.

To conclude, while research and consequent beliefs about learning and development from conception are progressing rapidly, it remains important for practitioners to be well-versed in the developing knowledge base about this in order to make professional judgements about factors affecting emotional development and what this looks like for children today. Concerning oneself with current information only, without reflection, makes for a narrow frame of reference with little scope for developing a deeper understanding that is influenced by a range of theoretical perspectives.

The role of very early experiences on development

The work of Piaget was central in mapping out the rapid and iterative developmental stages which help to guide early education and care practice to ensure it is suited to a child's capacity and capabilities. His work also challenged those who did not recognize the critical importance of the earliest developmental stages on longer-term maturational progress. However, given new knowledge and understandings it is now clear that we need to draw upon more than maturational or biological explanations of child development (Piaget, 1969) and embrace socio-cultural theories (Bruner, 1996; Bronfenbrenner, 1979; Vygotsky, 1978) and especially scientific theories into our professional practices. It is these that most enable us to understand the impact of the environment and external stimuli on a child's early development.

Research repeatedly tells us the fundamental importance of the earliest interactions and experiences a baby has and how these impact on emergent emotional and social development as well as the ability to learn and get on in school, later on in childhood (Teaching and Learning Research Programme, 2007; Shore, 2001; Walsh, 2000). Gopnik (2009) and Gerhardt (2004) highlight the influence of external stimuli in the wiring of the baby's brain and ability to become emotionally and socially competent. Wiring is concerned with the impact that the baby's early experiences and interactions (be it positive or negative) can have on the developing brain and how connections are made in response to these early experiences; the more connections that are formed, the more the young child is capable of understanding and doing (Gopnik et al., 2004). In addition, if the stimuli and interactions are not positive, the child might develop insecure attachments and be unable to cope with her own feelings as well as others', due to neuronal pathways being formed that, as a result, dictate the child's psychological patterns (Shore, 2001). These experiences cause the brain to organize and reorganize, and when this growth reaches its peak during the first year, the brain cells make new connections and terminate those that are not required. Early brain growth is extremely susceptible to adverse environmental factors such as nutritional deficits and **dysregulating** interpersonal emotional experiences, both of which negatively impact on infant mental health.

Suggestions for practice

- Ensure your team makes every effort to provide high quality experiences that nurture the emotional well-being and sociability of the under-3s.

- Take a stock-check of your play resources and environments for the under-3s. Check that they are designed to promote exploration, experimentation and manageable challenge.

- As a team, use part of your next planning meeting to discuss your provision for children with EAL and those who are from different cultural backgrounds.

- Discuss and record the strengths and areas that require improvement in regard to your provision for these children.

- Devise an action plan to help you make the changes that you identified. Allocate a 'project lead' to monitor implementation of the plan.

Creating inclusive and enabling environments

The following sections explore the impact of those experiences and environments which best support children's communication and developing capacity to interact positively and inclusively in their social world. Issues such as cultural participation, socio-cultural learning and the role of a support network in promoting language and interaction are each discussed, with relevant theories interwoven throughout each discussion. Case studies are included to help trigger ideas for making practice inclusive and enabling so that every child can benefit from and contribute to a diverse and meaningful learning experience. The behavioural and academic expectations that some children contend with are also discussed, with suggestions for practice.

The ability to communicate effectively is a lifelong skill that needs to be developed from birth. Usually, most children develop language without any difficulties at all. For some, however, communicating and developing language is not such an easy feat. Factors such as having English as an additional language (EAL), having a stammer, shyness, parental attitudes towards their children and the quality of the home learning environment all have a significant impact on acquiring and using language to communicate (Department for Education Research Report, 2010).

Cultural participation

A discussion concerning language development would not be complete without paying attention to the cultural participation of children. Culture includes the beliefs, customs and behaviours of any given group in society. It is also realized through ethnicity, language, socio-economic status, values, gender, disability and technologies used.

The need to include and promote the learning and well-being of all children in any given setting is highlighted in the EYFS (2012), which enforces the importance of providing anti-discriminatory practice and equality of opportunity to ensure that every child is included and supported. This means really getting to know individual families and their children from the outset and planning the curriculum and daily routine around their needs. Following one of the four main principles of the EYFS – that every child is a 'unique child' – is just one way of guaranteeing practice that maximizes the potential of every child, while taking into account differences in cultural background, home experience, ability and first language.

One Early Years Educator working in a Children's Centre in Harrow describes how they promote communication among children for whom English is an additional language. This case study provides practical examples of how cultural participation of all families is achieved.

Case Study

In our setting, 50 per cent of children have English as an additional language (EAL), with the main religious group being Muslim, followed by Hindu and Atheist families. EAL is our biggest issue, so we focus on providing more hands-on and experiential activities, with an emphasis on encouraging parents to keep their native language going at home. We work closely with all our parents, allocating an interpreter where necessary, so that we as a team are clear about each family's needs and how we can meet these. Having this regular dialogue helps us to know where each family is at, with regard to their beliefs, customs and preferred way of teaching their child.

In the setting, we speak both languages, using key words in the children's home language, as well as displaying key words around the room. Having staff who are fluent in some of the home languages spoken by families is a great bonus – both in terms of working with children and helping us to keep building on our good practice. We promote literacy in the same way as we do for our children whose first language is English, but with more use of picture books to encourage children to speak about what they see, without the pressure of having to read if they are not quite ready. This works really well as parents do the same with their children at home.

Michael Jones, an Early Language Consultant, believes that further research needs to be carried out, in order to build understanding of the factors affecting cultural language development. He says:

I think that someone needs to explore in-depth how differing beliefs and childrearing practices influence cultural language development (and that can include beliefs and 'culture' within a family); and particularly within the UK child day care and school context. Not all cultures and families believe in childhood as important as a separate stage of human development, nor in the importance of parents playing with and talking to children.

Gordon Wells in his ground-breaking Bristol Study found that in his samples of recorded conversations between children and their parents, most parents only really got in conversation with their children at home when the child took an interest in what the adult was doing. This produced some very interesting learning. Also the children came to see certain activities and objects in the home as being very important, because the parents spend a lot of time doing them (cooking, washing up, doing the laundry) or touching them (the TV remote, books, hair straighteners, big brother's train track).

That for me is a very interesting concept, because it's the opposite of what we do in early years where we promote talking about what the child is doing. Some of the parents I know just can't relate to our concept of playing and talking informally with their children: it's just not part of their background. But if we talk to them about involving children in daily chores and what adults are doing, they can readily relate to this, as it fits in more with their own experience as children and within the countries/communities they originated from.

The children are still getting interaction and conversation, and research shows that this can be very rich and rewarding for both parties, emotionally and linguistically. I'm very interested in this idea, as the REPEY study showed that in 'high quality settings' the adults and children were involved in conversations that had high interest for both adult and child. I imagine this was something like an adult sharing a book that she really likes with a child who has the same interest and may even have the same book at home.

I think the same happens with songs too. Where a family are very religious, and their main family gathering is going to church (as is the case with many of the West African families in Thurrock) then we talk about songs the families really like, as well as the type of dance music they play, and encouraging them to sing with their children. The children love this, and learn a lot from it. I think this can have a huge relevance for the family and really improves links with the setting. The practitioners and teachers need to be open to this too, which is not always the case.

Socio-cultural learning

There are many theories that exist which explore children's language development, and due to the length of this book, only a few that are most applicable will be discussed. Let us begin with Vygotsky's socio-cultural perspective of language acquisition (1978). He believed that children develop language as a result of their interactions. Language is thus viewed as serving two key functions – as a psychological tool and a cultural tool. Through their early interactions and collaborative learning experiences, children are enabled to use language both as a cultural tool and a psychological tool – organizing their thoughts, for reasoning, planning and reviewing. This more advanced use of language comprises Vygotsky's third and final phase of language development, inner speech (see Chapter 8). Vygotsky firmly believed that children achieve such higher cognitive skills through their social environment. This includes engaging in interactions with more knowledgeable others (MKOs) such as more capable peers and adults who act as a support throughout the child's ZPD.

While he believed that children learn most effectively through active participation, Vygotsky also believed that knowledge is socially constructed. This makes sense given that everything a child is exposed to and experiences can only ever be context-specific, dictated by the customs and values of any given culture.

The cultural values and customs suggest what is important to learn in different countries, cities, neighbourhoods and even estates. These values are determined and shaped by socio-economic status, political and religious beliefs and level of education. Practitioners therefore need to be mindful of the impact of these factors on different families and work with them in line with their unique situation.

Rousseau also believed that society itself is a construct that is formed in order to protect individuals (as well as to maintain civil order). Unlike Vygotsky who viewed it as a positive construct, Rousseau viewed it as a necessary evil. In his key text, *The Social Contract* (1968: 50), Rousseau makes his well-known statement 'man is born free, but everywhere he is in chains' to express his discontent concerning the role of individuals in society. Paradoxically however, in order to achieve equality for all, Rousseau believed that children should be educated in isolation with learning solely dictated by the teacher until the age of 12. This way, he thought that the child would be shielded from prejudice and social injustice until she is old and wise enough to make her own well-informed decisions. These dilemmas continue to challenge us in our practice.

What do you Think?

1 How far are we supporting the development of unique individuals and how far are we encouraging social solidarity and community cohesion?
2 How far do we want children to be independent and autonomous, and how far do we want them to work in collaboration with others?
3 What balance do you feel you have in relation to these questions in your setting?

The role of a support network in promoting language development

Similarly, Bruner (1983) viewed language as an accelerator to learning and cognition as children become more adept at interpreting the world around them. Language (a key tool in aiding a child's ability to learn) speeds up thinking skills as the child is able to identify and communicate all that they are finding out about by continuously building on this knowledge. Bruner's language acquisition support system (LASS) is a useful way of explaining children's language development (see Chapter 9). His theory proposes that children acquire language through a process of active engagement with others in their immediate environment – who act as a support in the child's efforts at communication as they talk together, making and sharing meanings about the world. Not only does this lead to a widened vocabulary but also higher thinking skills (Evangelou et al., 2009).

One study conducted by the Education, Audio-visual & Culture Executive Agency concluded with the clear message concerning the teaching of language in the early years:

> What seems essential for all approaches is a positive socio-emotional climate, with emotionally safe and stable relationships, with sensitive-responsive, non-intrusive teachers. There is no reason why an orientation on emerging school skills using authentic activities in which teachers participate, cannot go together with a positive socio-emotional climate. (2009: 32)

Suggestions for practice

- Consider the babies in your setting – make sure staff support babies' attempts at communication in a meaningful way.
- Reflect on the language used by adults in your setting – it must always be professional, and age/stage appropriate when interacting with all children.
- Review the play spaces that you provide (indoor and outdoor); these must support children's attempts at communication during the range of experiences they engage in (playing together, exploring, eating, dancing and making things).
- Create environments in which children are encouraged to support each other during interactions and play.
- Ensure your team understand any of the existing speech, language and communication needs among the children. This will support a whole team approach to helping individual children.

Behavioural and academic expectations

The fact that speech, language and communication needs (SLCN) manifest so differently in individual children can lead to their need being misinterpreted or missed altogether. For example, a child who has communication difficulties might display poor behaviour, find it hard to learn how to read, have difficulty in social-izing with other children and could as a result, end up isolating themselves. If left undiagnosed and untreated, such signs of SLCN can lead to the child suffering due to being misunderstood, labelled as a 'challenging child' and ultimately, missing out on invaluable support that could make all the difference to their ability to thrive at a personal and academic level.

Conversely, when children are supported in their efforts at interacting with other children and adults, the outcomes can be very positive. Providing extra time, practice and predictability in the daily routine will help to build confidence when interacting with others. Specific activities and games can also encourage children to listen, speak and learn how to take turns during conversations. Making up and telling stories, identifying, describing and naming games are just a few examples of how this can be achieved.

There is a plethora of research studies which explore the various speech and language difficulties experienced by children in their early years. The current emphasis on this may well be due to the sheer number of children presenting communication difficulties which require long-term intervention, as well as those research findings which tell us what happens when it's 'too late' (Marmot Review, 2010; Allen and Duncan Smith, 2008; Clark and Dugdale, 2008). This current emphasis exists in various contexts, including the Government's roll-out of free childcare provision for 2-year-olds living in disadvantaged circumstances, the review of the EYFS and early intervention strategies (Department for Education and Skills, 2010).

One in ten children has a communication difficulty in the United Kingdom which requires on-going speech and language therapy (ICAN 'Cost to the Nation' Report, 2006). Given that as many as half of all children start primary school with delayed speech and language skills (Department for Children, Schools and Families, Bercow Report, 2008), the situation is clearly critical. Where a child's needs go unmet, a range of long-term consequences may result. Behavioural difficulties, emotional and psychological difficulties, lower educational attainment, poorer employment prospects and in some cases, descent into criminality have all been reported (Department for Children, Schools and Families, Bercow Report, 2008; Clark and Dugdale, 2008).

Research findings carried out by The National Literacy Trust (Clark and Dugdale, 2008) enables us to 'fast-forward' to the future regarding some of those young children who do not get their essential needs for affection, stimulation and education met.

> Literacy problems in the prison population are often compounded by a wide range of factors, including child abuse and neglect, linguistic impoverishment in the childhood home, low verbal ability, uncorrected visual and hearing impairments in childhood, unskilled teaching in the junior school and mistaken conjecture about literacy practice, substance misuse, low non-verbal ability, childhood hyperactivity-impulsivity and inattention, impairments in empathy and social cognition, depression, and – often as a default and catch-all explanation – developmental dyslexia. (Rice and Brooks, 2004: 4)

Research indicates time and time again, the fundamental role of the early years in building strong foundations (Dale et al., 2003; Hart and Risley, 1995) concerning language and communication development. With the right support at the right time, children displaying communication difficulties can catch up (I CAN Talk Series – Issue 7 Speech, Language and Communication Needs and the Early Years 2009; Clark and Dugdale, 2008). Early identification and intervention are thus critical in supporting individual children who display SLCN from the earliest possible stage.

Ideally, in order to ameliorate the impact of speech, language and communication difficulties, multiple key approaches are required, such as better understanding of the different SLCN that exist – this includes practitioners and parents. Widely accessible information in the form of public health messages from conception also play a significant role so that new or first-time parents are aware of problem signs to look out for, as well as provision for health care and education adopting a wide range of strategies that are tailored to children's individual needs. This makes the role of community midwives, health visitors and GPs all the more important as they are best positioned to identify any cause for concern and work with the family directly. This way, parents can be supported from the outset to create as good an environment as they possibly can that helps meet the communication needs of their child. Below are just a few ways in which you can support children when they experience difficulties or conflict during their interactions.

Suggestions for practice

- Make the time to talk to children and encourage them to express themselves – for example, through music, dance, art or role play.
- Provide outdoor experiences – taking children into another space can help to create calm in stressful situations.
- Stimulate and distract children into a different activity.
- Identify and emphasize the positive.
- Try to situate yourself near to children's play without interfering.
- Try to avoid 'policing' children's play – this can inhibit children's attempts at conflict resolution.

Importance of parents and the home learning environment (HLE)

Parental engagement, and the home learning environment (HLE) that parents provide, are issues that are currently in the spotlight due to our knowledge of the impact that the HLE has on the child's learning and development – as well as on their aptitude for learning in later childhood. Recent research studies and reports consistently tell us the positive impact that a good quality HLE has on the child's all-round development and conversely, what a poor quality HLE can do to a child's ability to learn and thrive (Munro E. and Department for Education, 2011; Melhuish et al., 2008; Parents Early Years and Learning [PEAL], 2005).

There is no one definitive way to provide an effective HLE, but it should include some or all of the following elements on a regular basis: affectionate interactions, sharing books regularly, reciting nursery rhymes, playing games, providing a range of resources and activities that are appropriate to the child's age and stage of development, as well as trips outdoors, to local parks, art galleries, museums, theatres, libraries and play groups. What we are recommending here is parents being children's companions and enjoying everyday life together with lots of interaction and talk. All of these are associated with better developmental outcomes (Daycare Trust, 2010; Sylva et al., 2004).

The quality of the HLE provided by parents also differs depending on a range of factors, including:

- The type of attachment between mother and baby
- Emotional and mental well-being of the mother/primary carer(s)
- Level of education of the parents/primary carers
- Family income
- Resources available to the child
- Support available to the family

Reflection in Action

1 Is the HLE promoted in your setting?
2 In which ways is this achieved?
3 What positive changes has it made to the children's ability to learn? (Consider the ability to concentrate, engage in activities, take turns, listen and persevere.)
4 Has it made any differences to partnership with parents in your setting? Briefly note down how.

As an early years practitioner, it is also worth noting that the HLE provided by parents may not be a conscious decision, i.e. they might not have thought about its long-term implications on their child's ability to learn and their future educational outcomes. You are therefore in a good position to support parents in your setting to provide the best possible start for their children – without it being costly or time-consuming. Simple things such as suggesting reducing the amount of time that the television is on, can encourage more interactions between parents and children, as it has actually been proven to be a hindrance in children's effort at communication and hence, language acquisition and communication (Department for Education and Skills, 2010).

Freud powerfully and provocatively foregrounded the long-term and deep impact a child's relationship with their parents has on the development of emotional health and well-being, and the nature of their longer-term emotional attachments. Froebel, too, emphasized the need to work closely with parents and families in order to best promote children's learning and development. He placed particular emphasis on promoting educators' understanding of the mother's role in preparing her children for school. He wrote a range of books on this subject, some of which contained practical guidance for mothers on how to engage with their babies and children. His book *Mutter und Kose Lieder* (*Mother Songs*) is a more well-known example of this. It contained beautiful illustrations accompanying various action rhymes which were designed to be played between mother and child, in order to promote babies' and children's fine and gross motor skills, co-ordination and senses. Pictorial instructions were also provided to support understanding. Below is an extract of a rhyme entitled 'The Finger Piano' from the book:

> Children dear,
> The lovely music hear;
> Little fingers downward go;
> Hark! the answer, sweet and low:
> La! la! la!
>
> Thus the hand, so small a thing,
> Still may sweetest music bring.
> Fingers, you must move along,
> You may help to make the song.
> Up and down the fingers go,
> Waken, music, sweet and low! (Froebel, 1878: 62)

This lovely rhyme is not dissimilar to those sung by families and practitioners today, but what is markedly different is the fact that this was revolutionary at the time of his writing as families did not have much say in their child's education, especially the poor. Froebel however, embraced the role of parents and families as he acknowledged their importance in promoting their children's growth and development.

In line with current early years provision, Froebel also advocated children's need to play in order to learn. He believed that play provided the best vehicle for learning as children are enabled to use their own creativity and power, as opposed to having to (predominantly) engage in adult-directed tasks which thus do little to spark innate interest and curiosity.

Reflection in Action

1 How do staff in your setting help parents to support their baby's learning in the home?
2 How do you support the child's transition between home and the setting, making sure there is something familiar to the child that links these places in their world?

The centrality of emotional-social development

Both Freud and Bowlby's research studies showed the fundamental importance of secure attachments between mother and child. Both showed – in a range of settings and at different ages – the impact that disrupted attachments have on the young child both in the short and long term. Bowlby's work also indicated that maternal deprivation (where the child lives with her mother but she is unable to give the loving care and attention needed) has a negative long-term impact on the child's ability to form meaningful relationships with others, their resilience and self-confidence (Bowlby, 1988; 1953). Practitioners therefore play a key role in supporting all parents (or other primary caregivers) to understand how to provide a good quality, stable home environment that meets the child's needs for love, affection and stimulation. This can be through providing practical things to do together or by signposting to relevant services to best support parents in their role. Spending quality time together which is warm and nurturing, such as playing, singing, reading, listening to and responding sensitively to the infant's feelings, will make connections between the brain cells. These connections help children to manage their feelings and emotional situations – both in early childhood and later in life.

The impact of positive early interactions

Trevarthen's research findings (2002; 1999) concerning the significance of responsive interactions between babies, young children and parents, continually reinforces their roles in supporting healthy emotional and social development. He demonstrated that such relationships encourage the baby to form meaningful relationships with others and to express their thoughts, feelings and their emergent sense of humour (Trevarthen et al., 2002) in a climate of trust and security. In turn, this feeling of security lends itself to the young child being better equipped to learn and progress. Consider it from a personal perspective – we know too well how difficult it is to embrace new challenges and learn new concepts when we experience stress or do not feel at ease. This feeling is amplified all the more in young children, who need the support and guidance of trusted and capable adults.

Trevarthen also, however, identifies potential conflict concerning the building of responsive relationships between families and the influence of hyper-mobile environments where mobile phones, television and the internet all vie for the attention of family members in the modern home. Trevarthen (2011) thus recommends the input of 'institutions with experience in the practice of pedagogy' to support parents in creating the time and space for their children's efforts at being communicative and curious. He says:

> Relations with parents and family must be kept alive when the child is in any institutional setting for care or for learning, and experiences at home should be related to and exchanged with those at nursery or playgroup, or with a child minder. (Trevarthen, 2011: 10)

This is reinforced by just one of the research findings reported by Melhuish (2012) which shows that encouraging the active participation of parents in their child's all-round needs for stimulation – be it in or out of the home context – can make a long-lasting positive difference to their educational outcomes:

> Policies that encourage active parenting strategies (including for disadvantaged parents) can help to promote young children's cognitive development and educational achievement both early and later in development. (Melhuish, 2011: 4)

The message, then, is clear – the types of environment, and particularly the socio-emotional environment, created for children in their early years is crucial in providing a strong foundation that will start them off on the best trajectory, personally and academically.

Countering poverty and socio-economic disadvantage

Knowing how to reach disadvantaged parents is key to encouraging their participation in their children's life at nursery, as well as supporting them to be active in their role as primary caregivers. The McMillan sisters' work with the poor and excluded in London provides a strong model even today of the need to support families in a developmental and professional way. Families living in poverty or those who experience long-term stress, depression or live in other demanding circumstances may find it difficult to meet their children's needs for stimulation to support their development. You therefore need to be realistic about what parents can contribute to their child's education and how you can help them to maximize this, be it through appropriate learning experiences, the key person system, providing resources to read and use at home (in the child's home language) or by providing parents' courses on a range of subjects that they feel they would most benefit from. It is important to bear in mind the need for practitioners to be sensitive to parents' feelings about being labelled as 'failures' where support is offered, and therefore for practitioners to start from where the parents are, and build on the positive things they are doing in raising their children. It will also be useful for settings to continue to provide a balance between child-initiated and adult-initiated activity as a fluid and continuous process in all learning activity as best practice throughout the foundation stage phase.

Investment in the early years can make all the difference to a child's future educational attainment. It's therefore critical to provide all parents, especially those living in disadvantage, with individualized support that will maximize every child's opportunity to benefit from education (Henley, 2012; Desforges, 2003).

One head teacher of a primary school in North London gives a detailed account of the challenges he faces with regard to supporting and extending children's development in the school. This case study highlights the challenges posed in providing an education for disadvantaged families, as well as those who are not.

Case Study

As head of a school with a high deprivation indicator (+60 per cent Free School Meals entitlement, poor dental health, high levels of obesity, accommodation with multiple occupiers, low employment, < 50 per cent English as a First Language, low levels of home literacy/numeracy, high rates of benefit take up, high pupil mobility = +18 per cent), the challenge to provide an education that fits and suits all is immense. The low baselines that children enter into Early Years with, with regard to communication and knowledge and understanding of the world and their place in it means that children make slower initial progress against pupils from language-rich environments. Key parenting skills and expectations are often lacking so that children are found to be working in a month band significantly lower than peers whose demographic is not that described above e.g. 4-year-old nursery children with language and communication skill of 30–36 months.

This challenge is replicated in all the subsequent years until transition to secondary school (Year 7).

To counter the low baseline, staff with outstanding language and communication skills are required that model the learning required to make accelerated learning – it's not enough to have personnel, additional adults need to bring value. Therefore, highly trained practitioners are needed at all levels to provide models, emotional and learning support. These staff are generally in short supply and settings with high levels of need either keep their staff or there is employment mobility.

This issue has a bearing on staff structures as there needs to be budget allowances made to employ good staff or retain them. In settings with low staff turnovers, relationships are sustained between the child's setting and home and therefore greater sustained progress is likely to be made as professional trust and knowledge of the home is an important piece of the progress jigsaw.

Suggestions for practice

- Check your policies concerning parental partnerships – do they promote supporting the HLE?

- As a team, adopt a range of 'formal' approaches to interest and engage parents in their children's learning, such as providing workshops (informed by parents' needs), home visits, 'stay and play' and open days to encourage on-going dialogue.

- Encourage parents to carry out learning activities with their child that can be incorporated into domestic chores or which can involve other members of the family.

Concluding thoughts

We hope that you have found this final chapter useful in terms of helping you to reflect on some of the contemporary issues that are challenging the sector. We believe deeply in the capacity of practitioners to transform children's lives – we bear a huge responsibility towards these young children and their futures, but we also have the gift and privilege of knowing that we can make a real difference to their lives. Importantly, this means we need to think and act in the language of possibilities not impossibilities when it comes to supporting families and to know that there is always some small act we can do which matters and which might be the ripple from which a huge wave of change begins. Being reflective and understanding theories which help us to think harder about children's learning and living is an integral part of this. We hope this book is a contribution to that journey. As Sinclair (2006: 49) says:

> Investing in early years is as close as it gets to magic without being magic. Parenting support and enriched day care, preferably both together create children with better behaviour and attitudes who will arrive at school with a capacity to learn.

Glossary of Terms

Action research is mainly a practical activity, involving the contribution of (for example) staff working together in a nursery, to gather evidence to help them make more informed changes to their practice. It is usually led by a practitioner who takes on the role of researcher.

Activity-dependent refers to the fact that the brain partly depends on external stimulation in order to develop. This can be through play, communicating with others and engaging in activities that stimulate the senses.

Assessments are judgements made that are based on a collection of information, for example, observations.

Attachment can be defined as the emotional connection between a mother, father and/or other significant adult, and her baby.

Bond is a form of attachment behaviour that one person has towards another. (For example, the bond between a parent and child, between friends or other family members.)

Conservation (of mass, number or volume) is the ability to logically determine that a certain quantity will remain the same despite adjustment of the shape, perceived size or container.

Constructivism is a concept of learning that posits that children learn by doing – actively constructing their own knowledge as a result of their explorations. This perspective emphasizes that children initiate their learning, building on what they already know and understand.

Containment refers to the adult's ability to empathically respond to a baby's or child's feelings of distress and pain by holding the feelings of distress and pain in her mind and demonstrating understanding and affection.

Cortisol is a hormone that is released during times of stress. When cortisol levels are too high, this can destroy brain cells and weaken connection, resulting in a reduced capacity to learn.

Culture includes the beliefs, values, customs and behaviours of any given group in society. It is also realized through ethnicity, language, socio-economic status, values, gender, disability and technologies used.

Curriculum refers to the planned learning experiences in a setting, which can be informally or formally experienced. Learning goals attached to each learning experience are often a key aspect of a curriculum.

Developmentally appropriate practice (DAP) is an American framework for best practice. It is grounded in research on child development and learning. Within DAP lies the assumption that the quality and nature of practice is determined by a knowledge of child development.

Diversity refers to the understanding that everyone is unique and different. It also includes acknowledging individual differences concerning race, ethnicity, religious beliefs, gender, socio-economic status, political beliefs, age, physical abilities, or other beliefs.

Dysregulating (or emotional dysregulation) is an emotional response that is poorly modulated, and does not fall within the conventionally accepted range of emotional response. Emotional dysregulation can be associated with experience of early psychological trauma, chronic maltreatment or brain injury.

The Early Childhood Environment Rating Scale – Revised (ECERS-R) is a tool used for assessing the quality of provision for children aged 2½ to 5 years in early years settings.

Early Years Foundation Stage (EYFS) is the Statutory Framework that all early years providers must adhere to concerning the welfare and development of babies and children up to five years.

The ego is a Freudian concept which operates based on the reality principle, which strives to satisfy the **id**'s desires in realistic and socially appropriate ways.

Emotional intelligence refers to a person's ability to recognize, control and evaluate their own emotions and the emotions of others.

Empirical evidence refers to information that is acquired by carrying out systematic observations, assessments and experiments.

Epistemology is the study of knowledge and justified belief concerning the nature of knowledge.

Ethics refers to the steps taken by the researcher to ensure that their study is carried out with due consideration to participants and those affected by the study.

Foetal Alcohol Syndrome (FAS) refers to a range of mental and physical defects that develop in a foetus, as a result of high levels of alcohol consumption during pregnancy.

Heuristic play is exploratory play with a range of natural materials.

Hypotheses are predictions made about a situation that are based on limited evidence.

Id is the only component of personality that is present from birth. This aspect of personality which is entirely unconscious, seeks to obtain immediate gratification based on its needs and desires.

Infant Toddler Environment Rating Scale (The) – Revised (ITERS-R) is the tool used for assessing the quality of provision for children aged between 0 and 2½ years.

Interpretivists believe that we continually recreate our social world by frequently negotiating the meaning of our actions and circumstances and those of others. The interpretivist paradigm does not seek to make generalizations about the world, but to instead gain detailed insight into an issue that occurs in a specific context.

Intersubjectivity refers to the shared meaning which is created between an infant and an adult in their interactions with each other.

Key person refers to the special responsibility that designated practitioners have for a set amount of children. Responsibilities include showing a special interest in the child through close personal interaction, undertaking observations, maintaining records and sharing information with the parents.

Language acquisition device (LAD) concept proposes that language acquisition will inevitably take place in all individuals due to being born with an instinctive mental capacity and the necessary resources (brain, mouth, tongue, voice box and lungs) 'built in'.

Language acquisition support system (LASS) refers to the role of the child's social network (family, friends and teachers) in facilitating the child's development of language. These networks will lend themselves to meaningful interactions taking place which will enable the child to learn and use the rules and customs of the language.

Maturation is the process of becoming mature. It includes the development of the child's abilities and characteristics from birth – usually in an ordered sequence.

Monotropy is the belief that the child has an innate need to form a bond with their mother/primary attachment figure.

Neurons are brain cells which carry messages through an electrochemical process.

Neuroscience is the study of the brain and the central nervous system.

Objectivity in research refers to the extent which the researcher is unbiased. Training and selecting specific methods can be used in research to minimize researcher bias.

Object permanence is the realization that things continue to exist even when they are no longer present (or hidden from sight). It occurs in babies aged between 8 and 12 months.

Paradigm is a way of 'seeing' and interpreting the world. Each paradigm is a specific collection of beliefs about what constitutes knowledge, together with practice based on those beliefs.

Pedagogy refers to the practice of teaching, including the methods used by the teacher (or early years practitioner).

Philosophy can be described as the study of the fundamental nature of knowledge, values, reality, and existence.

Plasticity refers to the ability of the human brain to change as a result of one's experiences.

Play is the primary way in which babies and children learn about their world. It includes a wide range of experiences which are beneficial to all-round development. Children's play is often self-initiated and intrinsically motivated.

Pleasure principle (The) according to Freud's psychoanalytical theory, is the instinctive drive to seek pleasure and avoid pain. It is the driving force of the **id**, which seeks immediate gratification of all needs, wants, and urges.

Policy is a written course of action, which is intended to guide and determine practice.

Positivists attempt to predict andexplain their environment in terms of cause and effect relationships. The positivist paradigm posits that the only authentic knowledge is knowledge that is based on actual experience, and so scientific methods such as carrying out controlled and systematic observations and collecting data are adopted.

Postmodernism includes theories that reject the concept of universal 'truths' and dominant discourses concerning the nature of learning and development, and foregrounds the way power is used to control the discourse.

Post-structuralism theory posits that power does not reside with one body, nor is it absolute. It is viewed as more fluid, changing over time, depending on who it resides with.

Praxis is a continual and intertwined process of practice based on theories and vice versa.

Primary socialization refers to the way our attitudes, values and morals are shaped by our immediate family and friends.

Procedure is a way of performing that must be followed in line with a setting's guiding principles (or policy).

Protoconversation refers to the interaction between an adult (typically a mother) and baby which take place before the baby's onset of spoken language. It includes gestures, sounds and words to convey meaning.

Psychoanalysis (created by Sigmund Freud) refers to the range of therapies informed by the theory of psychoanalysis. It is designed to treat individuals with mental health disorders.

Psychologist is an expert or specialist in psychology.

Psychotherapy is treatment of mental disorders by psychological rather than medical means.

Qualitative approaches to research include more narrative methods of data gathering such as observations and semi-structured interviews. Qualitative approaches are mainly concerned with understanding the opinions and values of individuals in a specific context, which result in the researcher obtaining multiple interpretations of a situation.

Quality refers to all those characteristics of practice that enable children to fulfil their potential. This includes effective leadership, trained and enthusiastic staff, a safe and stimulating indoor and outdoor environment, providing anti-discriminatory practice and partnership with all parents.

Quantitative approaches to research include more statistical and experimental methods of data gathering such as gathering statistical data, social surveys and experiments within groups, whereby specific variables can be changed in order to validate findings. The focus of quantitative research is generally on 'hard' facts and numbers.

RAG rating is a performance measurement tool used by councils, organizations and teams that monitors how effectively tasks are being carried out. The RAG rating for individual performance measures is determined as:

Red if worse than target, and below an acceptable level

Amber if worse than target, but within an acceptable level

Green if on or better than target

Receptivity (or being **receptive**) means being open to another person's feelings and responding swiftly.

Reconceptualization is the deconstruction and re-thinking of issues in early childhood education, acknowledging that there are multiple realities and truths. Reconceptualists often challenge long-held beliefs in early years such as child-centred practice, developmentally appropriate practice and definitions of quality provision.

Reflective practice means thinking critically about your practice – the elements that have gone well and those that could be improved. As a result of your reflections, you make changes to your practice, in order to refine it.

Reliability refers to the stability, accuracy and consistency of a research study. Reliability is achieved through using appropriate methods to gather data.

Replication is the ability to carry out the same experiment, with different researchers in different settings.

Safe base is the term used to describe the feeling of security created by an adult who has a close relationship with a child (key person, parent or other adult). This adult supports the child in the task of balancing their need to feel safe and be in close proximity to the adult, with their need for free exploration.

Scaffolding is provided by the adult during activities or tasks, as a temporary support structure around the child's attempts to understand new ideas and complete new tasks. Once the child demonstrates ability independent of any adult intervention, the scaffold (support) can be removed.

Schema is as a pattern of behaviour or organizing framework which the child displays while attempting to understand a new piece of information, based on their experience of it. As the child has more experiences, this new information is used to modify or add to previously existing schemas.

Small-scale studies are research projects that are carried out with a small number of people over a short period of time.

Socio-constructivism is a concept of learning that suggests children learn by constructing knowledge with other children and adults around them. The socio-constructivist theory places emphasis on the social aspect of learning.

Spiral curriculum refers to the re-visiting of previous experiences over time which results in the child consolidating and deepening their understanding as they continually return to basic ideas while new subjects and concepts are added over the course of a curriculum.

Status envy (or status anxiety) is the collection of feelings such as jealousy, resentment and desire, as a result of aspiring to a better lifestyle. This might include earning more money, owning an expensive car, living in a lavish house. It also includes focusing on how one is perceived by others.

Subjectivity refers to the researcher's feelings, perspective or interpretations that influence their observations and conclusions of a study. One's interpretation of the world is influenced by societal and cultural powers.

Super-ego is the last component of personality to develop (according to Freud, the super-ego begins to emerge at around age 5). The super-ego provides guidelines for making judgements between what is morally right or wrong.

Synapse (plural = synapses) is the wiring/networks between neurons.

Synaptic pruning is a process which eliminates weaker synaptic connections, while stronger connections are kept and strengthened. Experience and emotion determine which connections will be strengthened and which will be pruned.

Synaptogenesis is the formation of synapses between neurons.

Synaptogenocide is the loss of/'dying' of synapses between neurons.

Theories are ideas or concepts that have usually been tested out, to explain a phenomenon. Not all theories are tested out.

three modes of representation (The) refers to how a child stores and processes information at different ages.

Tools as defined by Vygotsky exist in two forms: physical tools (a computer or a book for example) and psychological tools (such as language and thought).

Transition is a change in a child's life. Some examples include moving house, the birth of a sibling or graduating from nursery to infant school.

Treasure basket play is used with babies from the time that they can sit unaided. A treasure basket is a low-sided ridged basket that is filled with a range of natural objects such as paper, cardboard, wooden, leather and scented objects. Plastic objects are not acceptable.

Triangulation is the use of multiple research methods or the inclusion of information from a range of sources in a study that enable the researcher to obtain data which produce similar answers or ensure the trustworthiness of a finding. If these fail to do so, then the researcher might have to re-think the original question and/or methods used.

Validity is the process which a researcher undertakes to ensure their study investigates what it aims to. Research must be valid if its results are to be trustworthy and accurately interpreted.

Vignette is a brief account or story designed to evoke thoughts and feelings concerning its content.

Windows of opportunity (sometimes called sensitive periods) is the idea that the young child's brain is open to experience of a particular kind at certain points in development – for example, the belief that learning a language is easier during childhood, rather than during adulthood.

Zone of actual development refers to the child's abilities to achieve a goal (for example, assembling a model, threading beads or tying shoe laces) independent of any support.

Zone of proximal development (ZPD) refers to the range of development a child goes through, from what they can achieve independently – at the lower end of the ZPD, to what they can achieve with the guidance of a more capable peer or adult – at the higher end of the ZPD.

Bibliography

Books and articles

Addison, J. T. (1992) 'Urie Bronfenbrenner'. *Human Ecology*, 20(2): 16–20.

Allen, G. (2011) *Early Intervention: The Next Steps*. London: Crown Copyright.

Andersson, B. E. (1990) Cited in Abbot, L. and Rodger, R. (1994) *Quality Education in the Early Years*. Buckingham: Open University Press.

Athey, C. (1990) *Extending Thought in Young Children*. London: Paul Chapman Publishing.

Attenborough, R. (2000) *The Words of Gandhi*. Second Edition (Newmarket "Words Of" Series). New York: Newmarket Press.

Baker-Sennett, J. and Matusov, E. (1997) 'School "Performance". Improvisational Processes in Development and Education'. In Bereiter, C. (2002). *Education and Mind in the Knowledge Age*. Mahwah, NJ: Erlbaum.

Barker, D. (1995) *Nutrition in the Womb*. London: The Random House Group Limited.

Bateman, A. and Holmes, J. (1995) *An Introduction to Psychoanalysis: Contemporary Theory and Practice*. London: Routledge.

Berk, L. E. and Garvin, R. A. (1984) 'Development of private speech among low-income Appalachian children'. *Developmental Psychology*, 20, 2: 271–86.

Bernard van Leer Foundation (2012) 'Living Conditions: The Influence on Young Children's Health. *Early Childhood Matters*, Issue 118. The Hague: Bernard van Leer Foundation'.

Bertram, T. and Pascal, C. (2012) Editorial. *European Early Childhood Education Research Journal*, Volume 20, Issue 1, March 2012: 2–9.

Bishop, D., Price, T., Dale, P. and Plomin, R. (2003) 'Outcomes of early language delay: II. Etiology of transient and persistent language difficulties'. *Journal of Speech, Language, and Hearing Research*, 46: 561–75.

Björklid, P. and Nordström, M. (2007) 'Environmental child-friendliness. Collaboration and future research'. *Children, Youth and Environments*, 17(4): 388–401.

Bloom, P. (2000) *How Children Learn the Meanings of Words*. Cambridge, MA: MIT Press.

Bowlby, J. (1944) *Forty-Four Juvenile Thieves: Their Characters and Home Lives*. London: Baillière, Tindall and Cox.

—(1953) *Child Care and the Growth of Love*. Harmondsworth: Penguin.

—(1988) *A Secure Base: Clinical Applications of Attachment Theory*. London: Routledge.

Brew, A. (2001) *The Nature of Research: Inquiry in Academic Contexts*. London: Routledge Falmer.

Broadhead, P., Howard, J. and Wood, E. (2010) *Play and Learning in the Early Years*. London: SAGE.

Bronfenbrenner, U. (1973) *Two Worlds of Childhood: U.S. and U.S.S.R.* New York: Pocket Books.

—(1979) *The Ecology of Human Development: Experiments by Nature and Design.* Cambridge, MA: The President and Fellows of Harvard College.

—(1989) Ecological systems theory. In R. Vasta (ed.), *Annals of Child Development*, Vol. 6 pp. 187–249. Greenwich, CT: JAI Press.

Bronfenbrenner, U., McClelland, P., Wethington, E., Moen, P. and Ceci, S. J. (1996) *The State of Americans: This Generation and the Next.* New York: The Free Press.

Bronfenbrenner, U. and Morris, P. A. (1998) 'The Ecology of Developmental Processes'. In Damon, W. and Lerner, R. M. (eds), *Handbook of Child Psychology*, Vol. 1: Theoretical Models of Human Development, 5th edn, pp. 993–1023. New York: John Wiley and Sons, Incorporated.

Bruce, T. (2006) *Early Childhood: A Guide for Students.* London: SAGE.

—(2011) *Learning through Play: For Babies, Toddlers and Young Children.* London: Hodder Education.

—(2012) *Early Childhood Practice: Froebel Today.* London: SAGE.

Bruer, J. (2002) *Avoiding the Paediatrician's error: how Neuroscientists Can Help Educators (and themselves).* New York: Nature Publishing Group.

Bruner, J. (1971) *The Relevance of Education.* New York: The Norton Library.

—(1977) *The Process of Education.* Cambridge, MA: The President and Fellows of Harvard.

—(1986) *Actual Minds, Possible Worlds.* Cambridge, MA: Harvard University Press.

—(1996) *The Culture of Education.* Cambridge, MA, and London: Harvard University Press.

Calouste Gulbenkian Foundation (2011) *It's Our Community. Policy Paper.* UK Branch: Calouste Gulbenkian Foundation.

Cannella, S. (2007) Cited in Yelland, N. (2005) *Critical Issues in Early Childhood Education.* Maidenhead: Open University Press.

Cannella, G. S. and Lincoln, Y. (2004) 'Claiming a critical public social science: reconceptualising and redeploying research'. *Qualitative Inquiry*, 10(2): 298–309.

Case, R., Kurland, D. M. and Goldberg, J. (1982) 'Working memory capacity as long-term activation: An individual differences approach'. *Journal of Experimental Psychology: Learning, Memory and Cognition*, 19: 1101–14.

Clark, C. and Dugdale, G. (2008) *Literacy Changes Lives. The Role of Literacy in Offending Behaviour.* London: The National Literacy Trust.

Cohn, J. F., Matias, R. and Tronick, E. Z. (1986) 'Face-to-face Interactions, Spontaneous and Structured, in Mothers with Depressive Symptoms'. In Field, T. and Tronick, E. Z. (eds), *Maternal Depression and Child Development: New Directions for Child Development.* San Francisco: Jossey-Bass, pp. 31–46.

Cole M., Hakkarainen P. and Bredikyte, M. (2010) *Encyclopaedia on Early Childhood Development* 6. CEECD / SKC-ECD.

Copple, C. and Bredekamp, S. (2009) *Developmentally Appropriate Practice in Early Childhood Programmes: Serving Children from Birth Through Age 8* (3rd edn). Washington, DC: National Association of Young Children.

Crain, W. (1992) *Theories of Development: Concepts and Applications.* New Jersey: Prentice Hall.

Cress, D. A. (1987) *Jean-Jacques Rousseau. The Basic Political Writings.* Cambridge, MA: Hackett Publishing Company Incorporated.

Cummings, M. E. and Kouros, C. D. (2009) *Maternal Depression and its Relation to Children's Development and Adjustment.* Montreal, Quebec: Centre of Excellence for Early Childhood Development.

Dahlberg, G., Moss, P. and Pence, A. (1999) *Beyond Quality in Early Childhood Education and Care. Languages of evaluation.* London: Falmer Press.

Dale, P., Price, T., Bishop, D. and Plomin, R. (2003) 'Outcomes of early language delay: I. Predicting persistent and transient language difficulties at 3 and 4 years'. *Journal of Speech, Language, and Hearing Research*, 46: 544–60.

Damast, A. M., Tamis-LeMonda, C. S. and Bornstein, M. H. (1996) 'Mother–child play: sequential interactions and the relation between maternal beliefs and behaviours'. *Child Development*, 67(4): 1752–66.

Darling, J. (1994) *Child-Centred Education and its Critics*. London: Paul Chapman.

David, T., Goouch, K., Powell, S. and Abbott, L. (2003) *Young Brains*. Research Report Number 444. London: Department for Education and Skills.

Daycare Trust (2010) *Supporting Parents in Helping Their Children to Learn at Home: Some Tips for Childcare Providers*. London: Daycare Trust.

Department for Children, Schools and Families (2008) *The Bercow Report. A Review of Services for Children and Young People (0–19) with Speech, Language and Communication Needs*. Nottingham: Department for Children, Schools and Families Publications.

Department for Education (DfE), (2013) *More Great Childcare. Raising Quality and Giving Parents more Choice*. London: Department for Education.

Department for Education and Skills, (DfES) (2003) *Every Child Matters: Change for Children*. London: Department for Education and Skills.

—(2010) *The Benefits of High Quality Childcare: A Guide for Parents and Carers*. London: Department for Education and Skills.

—(2012) *The Early Years Foundation Stage: Statutory Framework for the Early Years Foundation Stage: Setting the Standards for Learning, Development and Care for Children from Birth to Five*. London: Department for Education and Skills.

Eliot, L. (1999) *Early Intelligence: How the Brain and Mind Develop in the First Five Years of Life*. London: Penguin.

Desforges, C. and Abouchaar, A. (2003) *The Impact of Parental Involvement, Parental Support and Family Education on Pupil Achievements and Adjustment: A Literature Review*. Research Report 433. London: Department for Education and Skills.

Donaldson, M. (1984) *Children's Minds*. London: Fontana.

—(1995) *Human Minds: An Exploration*. London: Allen Lane/Penguin Books.

Dowling, J. E. (2004) *The Great Brain Debate. Nature or Nurture?* Princeton, NJ, and Oxford: Princeton University Press.

Education, Audio-visual & Culture Executive Agency (2009) *Early Childhood Education and Care in Europe: Tackling Social and Cultural Inequalities*. Brussels: Eurydice.

Elkind, D. (1967) Egocentrism in adolescence. *Child Development*, 38: 1025–34.

Elliot, J. (1991) *Action Research for Educational Change*. Philadelphia: Open University Press.

Erikson, E. (1950) *Childhood and Society*. Albury: Imago Publishing Company.

Evangelou, M., Sylva, K., Kyriacou, M., Wild, M. and Glenny, G. (2009) *Early Years Learning and Development. Literature Review*. London: Department for Children, Schools and Families.

Field, F. (2010) *The Foundation Years: Preventing Poor Children becoming Poor Adults*. Report of the Independent Review on Poverty and Life Chances. London: Crown Copyright.

Field, T. (1992) 'Infants of depressed mothers'. *Development and Psychopathology*, 4: 49–66.

Fonagy, P. (2001) *Attachment Theory and Psychoanalysis*. New York: Other Press.

Formosinho, J. and Formosinho, O. (2012) 'Towards a social science of the social: the contribution of praxeological research'. *European Early Childhood Education Research Journal*, 20, No 4: 591–606.

Fox, N. A. (1977) 'Attachment of kibbutz infants to mother and metapelet'. *Child Development*, 48: 1228–39.

Frank, B. and Trevarthen, C. (2011) 'Intuitive meaning: Supporting Impulses for Interpersonal Life in the Sociosphere of Human Knowledge, Practice and Language'. In Foolen,, A., Lüdtke, U., Zlatev, J. and Racine, T. (eds), *Moving Ourselves, Moving Others: The Role of (E)Motion For Intersubjectivity, Consciousness and Language*. Amsterdam: Banjamins (in press).

Freud, S. (1949) *The Ego and the Id*. London: The Hogarth Press Ltd.

—(1990) *Beyond the Pleasure Principle*. New York: W. W. Norton and Company.

Froebel, F. (1878) *Mutter Und Kose Lieder*. Contributor: Susan E. Blow. New York: D. Appleton and Company.

—(2005) *The Education of Man*. New York: Dover Publications.

Gardner, H. (1985) *The Mind's New Science: A History of the Cognitive Revolution*. New York: Basic Books.

Gerhardt, S. (2004) *Why Love Matters*. London and New York: Routledge.

Give Me Strength. A Campaign from 4Children to Avert Family Crisis (2011) London: 4Children.

Goldschmied, E. (1989) 'Play and Learning in the First Year of Life'. In Williams, V. (ed.) *Babies in Day Care. An Examination of the Issues*. London: The Daycare Trust.

Goldschmied, E. and Jackson, S. (1994) *People Under Three. Young Children in Day Care*. London: Routledge.

Goleman, D. (1996) *Emotional Intelligence*. Cambridge, MA: Harvard University Press.

Gopnik, A. (2009) *The Philosophical Baby*. London: The Bodley Head.

Gopnik, A., Meltzoff, A. and Kuhl, P. (2001) *How Babies Think*. London: Phoenix.

Gregory, S. (2012) *Investing in Their Future: How do we Ensure our Children get the Good Quality Early Years Provision They Need if They and the Country are to succeed in the future?* The first Ofsted Annual Lecture on Early Years, 3 December 2012. London: Ofsted.

Hart, B. and Risley, T. (1995) *Meaningful Differences in the Everyday Experience of Young American Children*. Baltimore, MD: Paul H. Brookes Publishing.

Henley, D. (2012) *Cultural Education in England. An Independent Review by Darren Henley for the Department for Culture, Media and Sport and the Department for Education*. London: Department for Education.

Hespos, S. J. and Spelke, E. S. (2004) *Nature*, 430: 453–6.

Hobson, P. (2002) *The Cradle of Thought: Exploring the Origins of Thinking*. London: Macmillan.

Hohmann, M. and Weikart, D. P. (1995) *Educating Young Children*. Ypsilanti, MI: High/Scope Educational Research Foundation.

Horney, K. (1926) The flight from womanhood. *International Journal of Psychoanalysis*, 7: 324–9.

Hughes, M. (1975). *Egocentrism in Pre-school Children*. Unpublished doctoral dissertation. Edinburgh University.

Hughs, P. (2001) 'Paradigms, Methods and Knowledge'. In MacNaughton, G., Rolfe, S. A. and Siraj-Blatchford, I. (2004) *Doing Early Childhood Research. International Perspectives on Theory and Practice*. Maidenhead: McGraw Hill/Open University Press.

ICAN (2006) *I CAN Cost to the Nation of Children's Poor Communication Report*. Issue 2 London: I CAN.

James, A. and Prout, A. (1990) *Constructing and Reconstructing Childhood*. Basingstoke: Falmer Press.

James, O. (2007) *They F*** You Up*. London: Bloomsbury.

Johnson, M. H. and Mareschal, D. (2001) Cognitive and perceptual development during infancy. *Current Opinion in Neurobiology*, 11: 213–18.

Katz, L. C. and Schatz, C. J. (1997) Cited in David, T., Goouch, K., Powell, S. and Abbott, L. (2003) *Young Brains*. Research Report Number 444. London: Department for Education and Skills.

Kemmis, S. and McTaggart, R. (2005) 'Participatory Action Research: Communicative Action and the Public Sphere'. In Denzin, N. K. and Lincoln, Y. S. (eds), *The Sage Handbook of Qualitative Research*. 3rd edn. London: SAGE.

Kids Company (2011) *Waiting for Something Good*. London: Kids Company.

Leigh, A. (2009) *The Secrets of Success in Management*. London: Pearson. Prentice Hall Business.

Lewin, K. (1948) *Resolving Social Conflicts; Selected Papers on Group Dynamics*. New York: Harper and Row.

—(1951) *Field Theory in Social Science; Selected Theoretical Papers*. New York: Harper and Row.

Locke, J. (1964) *Some Thoughts Concerning Education*. London: Barron's Educational Series.

Lyotard, J.-F. (1993) *The Postmodern Explained*. Minneapolis: University of Minnesota Press.

MacNaughton, G. (2005) Cited in MacNaughton, G., Rolfe, S. A. and Siraj-Blatchford, I. (2010) *Doing Early Childhood Research. International Perspectives on Theory and Practice*. Maidenhead: McGraw Hill/Open University Press.

MacNaughton, G., Rolfe, S. A. and Siraj-Blatchford, I. (2004) *Doing Early Childhood Research. International Perspectives on Theory and Practice*. Maidenhead: McGraw Hill/Open University Press.

Marmot Review (2010) *Fair Society, Healthy Lives: A Strategic Review of Health Inequalities in England Post-2010*. London: Published by the Marmot Review.

Masson, J. M. (1984) *The Assault on Truth: Freud's Suppression of the Seduction Theory*. New York: Farrar, Straus and Giroux.

McMillan, M. (1919) *The Nursery School*. London and Toronto: J. M. Dent and Sons Ltd.

—(1925) *Childhood, Culture and Class in Britain*. London: Virago.

McNiff, J., Lomax, P. and Whitehead, J. (1996) *You and Your Action Research Project*. London: Routledge.

McNiff, J. and Whitehead, J. (2002) *Action Research for Professional Development. Concise Advice for New Action Researchers*. New Zealand: Teaching Development Unit.

—(2009) *Doing and Writing Action Research*. London: SAGE.

Meade, A. (2001) Cited in David, T., Goouch, K., Powell, S and Abbott, L. (2003) *Young Brains*. Research Report Number 444. London: Department for Education and Skills.

Melhuish, E. C. (2010) *Impact of the Home Learning Environment on Child Cognitive Development: Secondary Analysis of Data from Growing Up in Scotland*. www.scotland.gov.uk/socialresearch (web only publication).

—(2011) Pre-school matters. *Science*, 333: 299–300.

Melhuish, E. C., Sylva, K., Sammons, P., Siraj-Blatchford, I., Taggart, B. and Phan, M. (2008) 'Effects of the home learning environment and pre-school centre experience upon literacy and numeracy development in early primary school'. *Journal of Social Issues*, 64: 157–88.

Meltzoff, A. N. and Moore, M. K. (1977) 'Imitation of facial and manual gestures by human neonates'. *Science*, 198: 75–8.

Messler, D. J. and Frawley, M. G. (1994) *Treating The Adult Survivor Of Childhood Sexual Abuse: A Psychoanalytic Perspective*. New York: Basic Books.

Miller, L. and Pound, L. (2011) *Theories and Approaches to Learning in the Early Years*. London: SAGE.

Mooney, C. G. (2000) *Theories of Childhood: An Introduction to Dewey, Montessori, Erikson, Piaget and Vygotsky*. United States of America: Red Leaf Press.

Moyles, J. (2010) *The Excellence of Play*. Maidenhead: Open University Press.

Munro, E. and Department for Education (2011) *The Munro Review of Child Protection: Final Report – A Child-Centred System*. London: The Stationery Office.

Murray, L., Sinclair, D., Cooper, P., Ducournau, P. and Turner, P. (1999) 'The socio-emotional development of 5 year-old children of postnatally depressed mothers'. *Journal of Child Psychology and Psychiatry*, 40: 1259–78.

Music, A. (2001) *Ideas in Psychoanalysis: Affect and Emotion*. London: Icon Books Ltd.

Nutbrown, C. (2012) *Foundations for Quality. The Independent Review of Early Education and Childcare Qualifications. Final Report*. London: Department of Education.

—(2013) *Shaking the Foundations of Quality? Why 'Childcare' Policy Must Not Lead to Poor-Quality Early Education and Care*. Sheffield: University of Sheffield.

Nutbrown, C. Clough, P. and Selbie, P. (2008) *Early Childhood Education. History, Philosophy and Experience*. London: SAGE.

Nutbrown, C. and Page, J. (2008) *Working with Babies and Children*. London: SAGE Publications Ltd.

Oates, J., Karmiloff-Smith, A. and Johnson, M. H. (2012) *Early Childhood in Focus 7. Developing Brains*. Milton Keynes: The Open University.

Obholzer, K. (1982) *The Wolf Man Sixty Years Later*. Trans. Shaw, M. London: Routledge.

O'Connor, K. J. (2000) *The Play Therapy Primer*. New York: John Wiley and Sons.

O'Sullivan, J. (October, 2012) Personal written communication.

Oxford English Dictionary (2001). Oxford: Oxford University Press.

Parker-Rees, R. (2007) 'Liking to be liked: Imitation, familiarity and pedagogy in the first years of life'. *Early Years*, 27(1): 3–17.

Pascal, C. and Bertram, T. (2012) 'Praxis, ethics and power: developing praxeology as a participatory paradigm for early childhood research'. *European Early Childhood Education Research Journal*, 20, No 4: 477–92.

Penn, H. (2002) 'The World Bank's View of Early Childhood', in *Childhood*, 9, 118, http://chd.sagepub.com/cgi/content/abstract/9/1/118.

Piaget, J. (1951) *The Child's Conception of the World*. London: Routledge and Kegan Paul.

—(1952) *The Child's Conception of Number*. London: Routledge and Kegan Paul.

—(1972) *The Psychology of the Child*. New York: Basic Books.

Pinker, S. (2000) *The Language Instinct: How the Mind Creates Language*. New York: Perennial, an imprint of HarperCollins.

Plato. (2007) *The Republic*. London: Penguin.

Pound, L. (2009) *How Children Learn 3: Contemporary Thinking and Theorists*. London: Practical Pre-School Books.

Pugh, G. and Duffy, B. (2007) *Contemporary Issues in the Early Years*. London: SAGE.

Rice, M. and Brooks, G. (2004) *Developmental Dyslexia in Adults: A Research Review*. London: National Research and Development Centre.

Riley, J. (2007) *Learning in the Early Years*. London: SAGE.

Roberts-Holmes, G. (2005) *Doing Your Early Years Research Project*. London: Paul Chapman Publishing.

Robson, C. (1993) *Real World Research*. Oxford: Blackwell Publishing.

Rogoff, B., Hammer, C. S. and Weiss, A. L. (1999) Cited in Trevarthen, C., Barr, I., Dunlop, A.-I., Gjersoe, N., Marwick, H. and Stephen, C. (2002) *Review of Childcare and the Development of Children Aged 0–3: Research Evidence, and Implications for Out-of-Home Provision: Supporting a Young Child's Needs for Care and Affection, Shared Meaning and a Social Place*. Edinburgh: The Scottish Executive.

Rousseau, J. J. (1968) *The Social Contract*. London: Penguin Books.

—(1974) *Emile*. London: Dent and Sons Limited.

Rowe, S. M. and Wertsch, J. V. (2002) 'Vygotsky's Model of Cognitive Development'. In Goswami, U. (ed.) *Blackwell Handbook of Child Cognitive Development*. Malden, MA: Blackwell Publishers.

Rutter, M. (1979) *Maternal Deprivation: New Findings, New Concepts, New Approaches*, London: The Society for Research in Child Development Incorporated.

Schaffer, R. (1977) *Mothering*. Cambridge, MA: Harvard University Press.

Schön, D. (1983) *Educating the Reflective Practitioner*. San Francisco: Jossey-Bass.

Schore, J. R. and Schore, A. N. (2007) *Modern Attachment Theory: The Central Role of Affect Regulation in Development and Treatment*. Published online: 8 September 2007. Springer Science and Business Media, LLC 2007.

Seldon, A. (2009) *Trust. How We Lost It and How We Can Get it Back*. London: Biteback Publishing Limited.

Sheehy, N. (2004) *Fifty Key Thinkers in Psychology*. London and New York: Routledge.

Shonkoff, J. P. (2012) 'Leveraging the biology of adversity to address the roots of disparities in health and development'. *PNAS*, 1–5. Paper given at the Arthur M. Sackler Colloquium of the National Academy of Sciences, 'Biological Embedding of Early Social Adversity: From Fruit Flies to Kindergartners', held 9–10 December 2011 at the Arnold and Mabel Beckman Center of the National Academies of Sciences and Engineering in Irvine, CA.

Shonkoff, J. P. and Garner, A. S. (2012) Committee on Psychosocial Aspects of Child and Family Health; Committee on Early Childhood, Adoption, and Dependent Care; Section on Developmental and Behavioural Paediatrics. The lifelong effects of early childhood adversity and toxic stress. *Paediatrics*, 129: e232–e246.

Shonkoff, J. P. and Phillips, D. (2000) *From Neurons to Neighbourhoods: The Science of Early Childhood*. Washington, DC: National Academic Press.

Sinclair, A. (2006) '0–5 How small children make a big difference'. *The Work Foundation*, (3): 1.

Smith, L. (1995) 'Introduction to Piaget's Sociological Studies'. In Piaget, J. *Sociological Studies*, 1–22. London, New York: Routledge.

Steedman, C. (1990) *Childhood, Culture and Class in Britain: Margaret McMillan 1860–1931*. New Brunswick, NJ: Rutgers University Press.

Stern, D. N. (1998) *Diary of a Baby: What Your Child Sees, Feels and Experiences*. New York: BasicBooks.

—(2000) *The Interpersonal World of the Infant: A View from Psychoanalysis and Development Psychology*. (Paperback 2nd edn, with new introduction) New York: Basic Books.

Storr, A. (2001) *Freud: A Very Short Introduction*. Oxford: Oxford University Press.

Sylva, K., Melhuish, E., Sammons, P., Siraj-Blatchford, I. and Taggart, B. (2004) *The Effective Provision of Pre-school Education (EPPE) Project: Findings from the Pre-school Period*. London: Department for Education and Skills.

Teaching and Learning Research Programme (2007) *Neuroscience and Education: Issues and Opportunities. A Commentary by the Teaching and Learning Research Programme*. London: Institute of Education.

Trevarthen, C. (1995) 'The child's need to learn a culture'. *Children and Society*, 9(1): 5–19.

—(1998) 'The Concept and Foundations of Infant Intersubjectivity'. In Bråten, S. (ed.), *Intersubjective Communication and Emotion in Early Ontogeny* (pp. 15–46). Cambridge: Cambridge University Press.

—(1999) 'Musicality and the intrinsic motive pulse: evidence from human psychobiology and infant communication'. *Musicae Scientiae*, Special Issue 1999–2000. Liège: European Society for the Cognitive Sciences of Music (ESCOM).

—(2011) 'What young children give to their learning, making education work to sustain a community and its culture'. *European Early Childhood Education Research Journal*, Special Issue, "Birth to Three", Sylvie Rayna and Ferre Laevers (eds), 19(2): 173–93. London: Routledge.

Trevarthen, C., Barr, I., Dunlop, A.-I., Gjersoe, N., Marwick, H. and Stephen, C. (2002) *Review of Childcare and the Development of Children Aged 0–3: Research Evidence, and Implications for Out-of-Home Provision: Supporting a Young Child's Needs for Care and Affection, Shared Meaning and a Social Place*. Edinburgh: The Scottish Executive.

Trevarthen, C. and Malloch, S. (2002). 'Musicality and music before three: Human vitality and invention shared with pride'. *Zero to Three*, September 2002, Vol. 23, No 1: 10–18.

Trevarthen, C. and Reddy, V. (2007) Consciousness in infants. In Velman, M. and Schneider, S. (eds) *Companion to Consciousness*, pp. 41–57. Oxford: Blackwell.

Trevarthen, C., Rodrigues, H., Bjørkvold, J. R., Danon-Boileau, L. and Krantz, G. (2008) 'Valuing creative art in childhood'. Edited version published in *Children in Europe*, Issue 14: 6–9.

Truss, E. (2012) *Affordable Quality: New Approaches to Childcare*. London: Centre Forum.

Usher, R. and Edwards, R. (1994) *Postmodernism and Education: Different Voices, Different Worlds*. London: Routledge.

Van Oers, B., Wardekker, W., Elbers, E. and Van der Veer, R. (2008) *The Transformation of Learning: Advances in Cultural-Historical Activity Theory*. Cambridge: Cambridge University Press.

Venn, C. (2006) *The Postcolonial Challenge. Towards Alternative Worlds*. London: SAGE Publications Limited.

Vygotsky, L. S. (1926) *Pedagogical Psychology*. Moscow: CRC Press.

—(1962) *Thought and Language*. Cambridge, MA: MIT Press.

—(1978) *Mind in Society: The Development of Higher Psychological Processes*. Cambridge, MA: Harvard University Press.

—(1978) *Thought and Language*. Cambridge, MA, and London: The MIT Press.

Walsh, D. (1997) Cited in Yelland, N. (2005) *Critical Issues in Early Childhood Education*. Maidenhead: Open University Press.

—(2005) Cited in Yelland, N. (2005) *Critical Issues in Early Childhood Education*. Maidenhead: Open University Press.

Wertsch, J. V. (1985) *Vygotsky and the Social Formation of Mind*. Cambridge, MA: Harvard University Press.

Wicks, P., Reason, P. and Bradbury, H. (2008) 'Living Inquiry: Personal, Political and Philosophical Groundings for Action Research Practice'. In Reason, P. and Bradbury, H. (eds) *The Sage Handbook of Action Research: Participative Inquiry and Practice*. London: SAGE.

Wokler, R. (1996) *Rousseau*. Oxford: Oxford University Press.

Woodhead, M. (2006) *Changing Perspectives on Early Childhood: Theory, Research and Policy*. London: UNESCO.

Yelland, N. (2005) *Critical Issues in Early Childhood Education*. Maidenhead: Open University Press.

Websites

Bowlby, R. (April, 2007) Personal written communication.

http://socialbaby.blogspot.co.uk/2007/04/richard-bowlby-stress-in-daycare.html (accessed 10 August 2012).

http://socialbaby.blogspot.co.uk/2007/04/richard-bowlby-stress-in-daycare.html (accessed 14 November 2012).

http://www.child-encyclopedia.com/documents/Cummings-KourosANGxp.pdf (accessed 22 February 2013).

http://www.esrc.ac.uk/_images/Framework-for-Research-Ethics_tcm8-4586.pdf (accessed 12 August 2012).

http://foucaultqts.blogspot.co.uk/2009/07/memorable-quotes-from-truth-and-power.html (accessed 15 February 2013).

Gray, P. (February, 2009) Personal written communication.

http://www.psychologytoday.com/blog/freedom-learn/200902/rousseau-s-errors-they-persist-today-in-educational-theory (accessed 10 February 2013).

http://www.legislation.gov.uk/ukpga/2004/31/contents (accessed 17 December 2012).

National Scientific Council on the Developing Child (2005). *Excessive Stress Disrupts the Architecture of the Developing Brain: Working Paper 3.*
http://www.developingchild.net (accessed (20 September 2012).

http://www.ncb.org.uk/ecu/publications-and-resources/online-resources/information-gateway/working-with-parents-the-peal-project (accessed 22 October 2012).

Pascal, C. and Bertram, T. (February, 2010) Lecture presented at British Early Childhood Education Research Association (BECERA) Conference, February 2010, Birmingham, UK.

http://www.slideshare.net/CREC_APT/becera-praxeology-keynote-0213 (accessed 3 September 2012).

http://www.rcpch.ac.uk/news/rcpch-launches-vitamin-d-campaign (accessed 15 December 2012).

Vygotsky, L. S. (1933) *Play and its Role in the Mental Development of the Child.*
http://www.marxists.org/archive/vygotsky/works/1933/play.htm (accessed 3 February 2013).

Waniganayake, M., Cheeseman, S., Gioia, K., Harrison, L., Burgess, C. and Press, F. (2008) *Practice Potentials: Impact of Participation in Professional Development and Support on Quality Outcomes for Children in Childcare Centres.*
http://www.workforce.org.au/media/36200/factsheet_action-research_overview.pdf (accessed 22 January 2013).

www.yale.edu/minddevlab/papers/nature-children-think.pdf (accessed 25 January 2013).

Index

Tables page references are in italics.